A Theory of Virtual Agency for Western Art Music

MUSICAL MEANING AND INTERPRETATION
Robert S. Hatten, editor

ROBERT S. HATTEN

A Theory of Virtual Agency for Western Art Music

INDIANA UNIVERSITY PRESS

This book is a publication of

Indiana University Press
Office of Scholarly Publishing
Herman B Wells Library 350
1320 East 10th Street
Bloomington, Indiana 47405 USA

iupress.indiana.edu

Library of Congress Cataloging-in-Publication Data

Names: Hatten, Robert S., author.
Title: A theory of virtual agency for Western art music / Robert S. Hatten.
Description: Bloomington : Indiana University Press, 2018. | Series: Musical
  meaning and interpretation
Identifiers: LCCN 2018021852 (print) | LCCN 2018023643 (ebook) |
  ISBN 9780253037992 (e-book) | ISBN 9780253037978 (hardback) |
  ISBN 9780253037985 (pbk.)
Subjects: LCSH: Music—Philosophy and aesthetics. | Agent (Philosophy) |
  Act (Philosophy)
Classification: LCC ML3845 (ebook) | LCC ML3845 .H353 2018 (print) |
  DDC 781.1—dc23
LC record available at https://lccn.loc.gov/2018021852

1 2 3 4 5   23 22 21 20 19 18

To Eden, with love

Contents

Acknowledgments

I begin by thanking Mary Ellen Poole, director of the Butler School of Music, and Douglas Dempster, dean of the College of Fine Arts at the University of Texas, for their continuing support. A Walter and Gina Ducloux Fine Arts Faculty Fellowship funded my faculty leave during fall 2013; it enabled me to begin assembling my earlier work and further developing new ideas on musical agency for this book. I began trying out these ideas through papers at Indiana University and Northwestern in fall 2013, with students in a seminar on virtual agency at Texas in spring 2014, and through a weeklong series of lectures and classes on musical agency at the Kraków Academy of Music in April 2014 (the latter being one of five teaching residencies for which I offer special thanks to Professors Mieczysław Tomaszewski and Teresa Malecka and one of my assistants, Małgorzata Pawłowska, along with many other dear colleagues at that institution). I am also grateful for the feedback of countless students and faculty at those institutions and other venues where I gave keynotes or lectures on aspects of my theories of musical agency, including Eero Tarasti's International Congresses on Musical Signification, held at academic institutions in Kraków, Louvain-la-Neuve (Costantino Maeder and Mark Reybrouck), and Canterbury (Nicholas McKay); the Durham international conference on music and emotion (Michael Spitzer); the late Schubert conference at Maynooth, Ireland (Lorraine Byrne Bodley and Julian Horton); the Laboratory on Musical Rhetoric at the Boito Conservatory in Parma (Riccardo Ceni, Andrea Padova, and Carlo Lo Presti); the Steve Larson memorial conference at the University of Oregon (Jack Boss and Stephen Rodgers); and the graduate student conference at the University of Arizona (Gabriel Venegas and company), where I also co-directed a student workshop on Romantic form with Boyd Pomeroy. Javier Clavere kindly invited me to give lecture-demonstrations and a master class on the Mozart piano sonatas at Berea College, where he performed the entire cycle. I introduced refractive counterpoint in a special session on musical agency at the 2016 Society for Music Theory conference in Vancouver (Edward Klorman), applied my ideas to twentieth-century repertoire at a special session on analysis at the 2015 meeting of the International Musicological Society in New York (Elliott Antokoletz), and organized sessions with my students on musical agency at conferences of the Semiotic Society of America in Seattle, Pittsburgh, and Puebla, Mexico. I received helpful feedback during a Householder residency at Florida State University and during presentations of invited papers at the following conferences: a narrativity in music conference at Paris and Strasbourg (Márta Grabócz); the 2016 LangArts conference on gesture in Paris (Véronique Alexandre Journeau); several Beethoven Easter Festival

Symposia in Warsaw (with special thanks to Mme. Elżbieta Penderecka and Magdalena Chrenkoff); study days on Mozart at the University of Manchester and on performance at the National University of Ireland at Maynooth; and symposia on performance at Princeton and musical meaning at Southern Methodist University. I am further grateful for opportunities to lecture on virtual agency at the Royal Irish Academy of Music in Dublin, the Szymanowski Academy of Music in Katowice, and in the United States at the Eastman School of Music, the University of Michigan, Michigan State University, the University of California at Santa Barbara, Louisiana State University, and the University of Kentucky. Finally, I am deeply appreciative for the Marlene and Morton Meyerson Professorship (beginning in fall 2015) at the Butler School of Music, which supported my research and funded the superb engraving, by David Ferrell, of my musical examples.

Although I cannot begin to name all those who have helped me think through ideas that eventually found their way into this book, I give special thanks to Michael Klein and Michael Spitzer, who read the first complete draft of the manuscript in fall 2016 and offered valuable suggestions, and to David Lidov, Nina Penner, and John Turci-Escobar, who read and gave thoughtful feedback on individual chapters. I also thank two editors of earlier articles, portions of which appear here: Lorraine Byrne Bodley (on late Schubert) and Danuta Mirka (on topic theory).

I am grateful to all my students at Indiana and Texas for their enthusiasm in exploring virtual agency as a key to interpreting musical meaning. It has been a special delight to foster original applications and extensions of this approach in completed dissertations by Michelle Clater on agency in Requiem settings (Indiana), Ian Gerg on the virtual observing agent (Texas), an extensive DMA document on Medtner by Brad Emerson (Texas), recently completed dissertations by Eloise Boisjoli on sensibility in Haydn (Texas), Joel Mott on linearity and agency in Prokofiev's war symphonies (Texas), Trina Thompson on the rhetoric of suggestion in Debussy songs (Indiana), and a dissertation in progress by Bree Guerra on musical emotion and enactive theory (Texas).

I thank Janice Frisch, music editor at Indiana University Press, for her wisdom and guidance through the years. She and her production team have helped shepherd this book through its many phases, and I owe them a debt of gratitude not only for my manuscript but for others forthcoming in the Musical Meaning and Interpretation series.

Finally, where would I be without my lovely wife, Eden Davis? I thank her for her love, inspiration, and encouragement, which helped me through the difficult days. This book is dedicated to her.

A Theory of Virtual Agency for Western Art Music

Introduction

Situating Virtuality: Virtual and Fictional Agency

How might one theorize the phenomenon of virtual agency in music? In the first part of this introduction, I examine what we mean by the term "virtual," exploring definitions and usages across a range of contexts from everyday language to recent technology, and noting their implications for our understanding of agency. I then explore how various virtual worlds may hold fictional stories that, in some cases, may imply further levels of virtuality and fictionality. After this initial orientation and conceptual engagement, I introduce my perspective on virtual agency as crucial to the understanding of Western art music, situating my theoretical and historical presuppositions in the context of previous work in this area. The following prelude lays out the fundamental inferences of a multilevel theory of virtual agency, and subsequent chapters explore evidence for various inferences of virtual agency in music from the twelfth through the twentieth centuries.

Defining the Virtual

When we say we are virtually finished with a work, we generally mean that our project is almost done. But "virtually" adds a connotation that "almost" does not, even if in everyday usage the two adverbs may be used synonymously. Virtually suggests an impending reality that one can already envision, and it may even imply that our work could function adequately in its current unfinished state, if not as well as it would if it were completed. Thus, a virtual implies not only an actual but something that can imaginatively substitute for that actual with respect to some function. This concept of virtuality has much in common with Charles Sanders Peirce's basic definition: "A virtual X . . . is something, not an X, which has the efficiency (*virtus* [literally, strength]) of an X" (1902, 763).[1]

For my purposes, a virtual agent in music is not an actual agent, but its efficiency lies in its capacity to simulate the actions, emotions, and reactions of a human agent. More theoretically, the virtual addresses the gap between music's actual material or physical aspects as (organized) sound and those both irreducible and emergent semiotic inferences that enable us to hear music as having movement, agency, emotional expression, and even subjectivity. Thus, a virtual agent in music can never be actualized in any literal sense (as in "it's virtually/almost an actual agent; just give me time for a finishing touch"), but a virtual agent can be interpreted as functioning in important ways like an actual agent—for example, having a degree of independent action. A virtual agent can be further embodied with other humanlike characteristics. It can also be fictionalized as an actor in a dramatic trajectory and even internalized as part of a subjectivity, akin to an active stream of consciousness. Furthermore, virtual agency can be reembodied (an actualization at one remove) through the physical agencies of a sensitive performer. It is important to note that such interpretations are not just subjective projections but can be intersubjective (shared) inferences that are stylistically and strategically warranted by specific features of a musical work. From the perspective of a composer, aspects of virtual agency may be staged or enacted through various means that I demonstrate and explain in the chapters that follow.

The experience of virtual agency in music is not equivalent to the kind of agency one personally (subjectively) experiences when donning a virtual-reality headset. Virtual-reality technology attempts to reproduce the illusion of a place, or better, an interactively navigable space that is responsive to the actual movements of one's sensorimotor system (in this case, primarily the eyes, oriented by directing the head, along with purposeful movements of the hands, arms, and legs). The virtual reality of a soundscape might provide a change in sound dynamic and quality as one distances oneself from its virtual source, but true sonic interaction is more complicated to achieve. Whereas sonic illusions of real-world sounds have long been available through recordings, spatially enhanced by speakers and surround sound in theaters, these earlier virtual realities lack a coordinated aural interactivity. Although one may turn one's head to hear somewhat differently, one cannot directly manipulate the sound through movement. Nor might one escape an approaching sonic agency, or occlude the sound of a dangerously looming agent, other than by breaking the illusion—for example, by leaving the theater or turning off the stereo. While it is true that experimental installations in museums may offer limited kinds of interaction, for example by allowing a participant's movements to affect the electronic production of sound (transducing the energies of one's movements into parameters of sound), these kinds of experiments more often allow the participant to interactively create a uniquely personalized soundscape rather than to imaginatively enter and identify with the energies in an already composed soundscape (such as that presented by the sounding of a musical work).[2] The creative interpretive acts that a listener brings to a musical work generally do not involve changing its sounds (unless the listener is also the performer, as explored in chap. 8).

Thus, it is imaginatively interactive participation (experienced by the listener and potentially staged by the composer), rather than a virtually real interactive participation as just described, that I investigate in this book under the rubric of virtuality.

Five Engagements with Virtual and Fictional Agency

To further explore the possible kinds of engagement with virtuality and fictionality in both artifacts and artworks, I invite you to participate through your imagination in the following five scenarios.

1. As a builder in ancient Egypt, you imagine a pyramid—visualizing its virtual existence. Through a series of actions, a pyramid is finally actualized—you can see and touch it. But when you think of your pharaoh, soon to be laid out with extensive accoutrements in a chamber inside his monumental tomb, you can also virtualize the pharaoh's voyage to the afterlife. This is a virtuality that you have no power to actualize, except in the vividness of your belief. Yet, your belief sanctions the imaginative virtualizing of that next life.

2. As a twenty-first-century entrepreneur, you imagine and help design a video game that, when it is manufactured, exists as an actual product that can be purchased and manipulated by consumers. But its purpose is to recreate a virtual reality. As a player, you enter into the game's virtual environment, move a visualized character (an avatar) with whom you can identify, and share its virtual agency with a degree of actual control. You thereby interact with a fictional world with carefully constructed elements and effectively conditioned movements that have to a large degree been preactualized (and constrained in advance) by the game's creators. But suppose that increasing identification with your avatar leads you to an unhealthy obsession with the virtual-fictional world in which your actions appear to have real meaning. As you lose yourself in a virtual subjectivity, you do not realize that you have allegorized the game as psychologically real, in some sense meeting a deeper existential need beyond the virtual fiction of the game.

3. As an avid movie lover, you attend a screening of *Ruby Sparks* (2012). You enter a dark theater and submit to the initial presuppositions of this experience: an illusion on screen that appears perceptually real with little effort on the part of your imagination. The digital sequence of pictures appears to be actualized as a perceptual reality. You seamlessly transform this fast sequence of frames into a perceived analog continuity that allows you to experience the perceptual illusion of seeing actual movement in a real world. But you focus instead on the perception of actual people (the actors), whose previous movements have been recorded and transmitted through a perceptual illusion and whose identities have also been transformed into virtual beings in a virtual world. These virtual agents then inhabit roles as characters in a virtually presented fictional world, and you are led by degrees into accepting the virtual reality of a fictional tale (with which you will interact primarily through your imagination). You repress your awareness that what you are seeing is a recording of a past reality (the time when actual people were being filmed), and you accept the convention of the unmarked, present temporality offered by the fictional story (even as it may also be staging events as both past and future, in its own temporal realm).

Not unlike the video game (or the pyramid, for that matter), the movie's production was actualized as an artifact through many prior and interactive acts of creative virtualizing—here, through the various dimensions of multimedial production (writing, designing, staging action, directing shots, etc.). Compared with your active interventions directing an avatar in a video game, your present interaction with the movie's virtual world and fictional story may appear passive. And yet you may find yourself reacting even more strongly, perhaps even existentially, when watching the movie, an engagement that may lead to a particularly intense experience of subjectivity.

As you enter the fictional world of the characters in *Ruby Sparks*, you begin to discover further levels of (fictionalized) virtuality. You may begin to identify with the fictional protagonist, a novelist, who so vividly imagines his own virtual-fictional character (Ruby Sparks) that she miraculously manifests as an actual human being (within the movie's virtual fiction), having the same characteristics with which the writer has fictionally endowed her. You may further identify with the writer's existential crisis as he thinks he is delusional. You may then marvel at the apparent (fictive) miracle of his best friend's ability to see and interact with Ruby as a real person. Later, you may begin to identify empathetically with Ruby as she suffers her own existential crisis—a tragic recognition of her own fictional existence within the writer's world.

Throughout the film, you are invited to accept the premise of a virtual-fictional world within the initial fictional world of characters in the film, in which one character's literary creation can become an actual person within his world and can also appear as real to others. The complexities of fictional and virtual levels continue to mount as the movie progresses, and you may wonder how much this fictional world can possibly be like your own, since its (fictive) actualizing of a writer's virtual-fictional character exceeds the actual constraints of your own world. Yet, as you react to the seemingly real and plausible plight of these virtual and fictional characters, each takes on an emotional reality in your virtualizing and fictionalizing subjective engagement with them. And you discover a remarkable phenomenon—your considerable ability to imaginatively identify through/with, or feel deep empathy alongside, or compassionate sympathy (or perhaps even disgust) for, the characters of the writer and his Ruby. They may appear, seemingly transparently, to have become real to you as actualized human agents, regardless of their degrees of embedding within the fictional and virtual worlds of your (and their) imagination.

4. These deeper effects do not arise merely from the perceptual illusions of seeing real people's movements recorded on film. Reflecting on your childhood experience of animated Disney cartoon characters, you realize that what you responded to were simulations of human gestures and movements. Even though the cartoon characters were mimed by clearly nonhuman, nonreal figures, they spoke (and sang) with recognizably human voices. Thus, despite their cartoonish images, you were able to identify with them as virtually embodied human agents with actorial roles in a drama, and as a result, you experienced, along with or for them, appropriate and (for you) actual emotions.

5. Viewing the film *Avatar* (2009), you are delighted to find levels of film fiction and virtuality combining with the worlds of fantasy familiar to you from their construction in video games. Pandora is a virtual world actualized in the fictive world with an ecology that parallels your own (plants and animals with features derived from ones in your world) but with very different

forces at work (mountains can float and an energy/life force is spiritually transferred from the humanoid inhabitants to animals and trees through the bonding of gangliar tendrils). Since the animated humanoid characters of Pandora are created through a process of motion and performance capture (multiple points on real actors filmed with multiple cameras), you experience a closer simulation (as compared to either the cartoon or the video game) of motivated human movement and emotional facial gestures that support the (actual) human voice correlated with each (virtual-fictional) character. Thus, the virtual appears infused with the actual, leading to a strange phenomenon that has been described as the "uncanny valley," the increasing discomfort we feel in encountering robots or automatons when they come somewhat close to replicating actual people in appearance.[3] The Pandorans, with their unsettling similarity in size and shape to humans, yet clear differences in other respects, may trigger an aversion in you that undermines to some degree your comfort in identifying with them, as opposed to the much easier identification you find possible with characters that are not as closely human in appearance (e.g., Mickey Mouse).

There is yet another level of virtual agency, thematized in the fiction of the movie's plot, in which living humans can (through a transfer of brain function) enter Pandoran bodies and operate through them, much like the avatars in video games—hence the title of the movie. The humans must gradually learn to use those bodies, and their own cognition negotiates with the capacities of the enlivened Pandorans, whose bodies obviously have not forgotten how to move (keep using your imagination, here!). Ultimately, a mystical transformation (via gangliar bonding) allows one such avatar to become more fully Pandoran, thus bridging the gap between a virtual and an actual Pandoran (within the virtual-fictional world of the movie). You may find yourself identifying with this character (the protagonist in the fictional drama) largely through the power of the emotions that are staged by the drama and expressed by the characters—and in this way you may overcome the uncanny gap through the power of a shared virtual actorial agency. You may also slip into a sentimentalized emotional engagement with an enacted virtual subjectivity that, on leaving the movie theater, you may begin to criticize, self-reflectively, from the perspective of your actual subjectivity—even as you ruminate on the experience of wonder that the film has managed to evoke, in enlarging your subjective awareness of these (virtual) possibilities.

Having exercised your virtualizing mind with these five scenarios, I trust I have opened your awareness to the complexities of virtual agency that you have experienced in the past, or can imagine experiencing in the future. Even if you are not able to actualize the virtual in real life (as in the case of a pharaoh's afterlife), you have the capacity to realize it in your imagination, in the virtual and fictive worlds of video games and films, with a wide range of interactive options and intensities of engagement.

Presuppositions for a Theory of Virtual Agency in Music

Turning to music, we can find many of these same imaginative capacities being adapted to a medium that does not so obviously display its internal agents. However, a basic presupposition underlying my theory of virtual agency is that humankind's cognitive capacities to hear music as expressive, and thus as expressed by a virtual source with which humans can identify in some fashion, have been in place since the earliest records of human responses to music: from the Hebrew Bible (Jubal's lyre, Miriam's harp) to Greek theories of ethos. Changes in musical styles have created new possibilities for virtual agency (e.g., the staging of virtual actors within dramatic and narrative frameworks and the premising of a more complex virtual subjectivity), but the embodied response to musical energies as actantial in a virtual environment, as akin to human agents in their gestures and their associated emotions, and as suggesting an inspired subjectivity, are all arguably present in monophonic Western music at least as early as the chants of Hildegard of Bingen. The evidence is to be found in the notes (their rhythmic and pitch contours, motives, and modal trajectories) as well as their sung embodiment, textual specification (praise, petition), and spiritual transcendence (here, as identification with, or participation in, God's cosmic universe). Remarkably, an actorial dimension also emerges in Hildegard's mystery play or opera *Ordo Virtutum* (*Order of the Virtues*), made explicit by the actual human embodiment of virtual characters portraying textually and dramatically explicit roles. Ranging further, the music of the trouvères and troubadours stages an imaginative (tropological) interaction between secular and sacred virtual agencies as well as projecting narrative agency, and these clear agential associations are further strengthened in both sacred and secular spheres by motets, madrigals, and spiritual songs throughout the Medieval and Renaissance eras.

The history of how more complex conceptions of musical subjectivity emerged is typically written to reflect contemporaneous philosophical framings of human subjectivity, from Marsilio Ficino to René Descartes, Immanuel Kant to Arthur Schopenhauer, Friedrich Nietzsche to Theodor W. Adorno. Compelling approaches to the emergence of subjectivity may be found in Gary Tomlinson's (1999) account of the metaphysics of voice throughout the history of opera, in Jairo Moreno's (2004) account of (increasingly embodied) musical thought from Gioseffo Zarlino to Gottfried Weber (the dialectical construction of a listening subject as implied by various theoretical representations of a musical object), and in Daniel Chua's (1999) account of music's increasingly independent subjectivity (among other capacities) in the turn toward "absolute music." His speculative history, as rewarding as it is in tying music's subjectivities to both cultural and philosophically defined conceptions of music and the self, may also underestimate the potential of earlier listeners, who may well have experienced virtual subjectivity in music but whose abilities could not have been fully elucidated or conceptualized at the time. Mark Evan Bonds (2014) traces this history of the absolute across the entire range of Western music.

Might composers indeed have anticipated philosophers and theorists in their staging of subjectivity? Susan McClary (2004, 2012) considers this possibility in her studies of subjectivity in the sixteenth-century madrigal and the seventeenth-century sonata, respectively.[4] Moving to the eighteenth century, might Johann Sebastian Bach have endowed even his purely instrumental music with virtual embodiment and spirituality in ways that only later theories can fully reconstruct?[5] If so, should expressive interpretation of his music be limited to those passions that were only vaguely being theorized in his time? And turning to the nineteenth century, might Franz Schubert have explored multiple, errant, or alternate subjectivities in his *lieder*—as Lawrence Kramer (1998) claims, while drawing on the music itself as primary evidence?[6]

My analytical interpretations analogously presuppose cognitive capacities and at least a basic level of robust subjectivity as having been available to composers and listeners throughout the entire scope of Western music history. Although I certainly acknowledge a range of more specific subjectivities and emotional experiences to be found in various emotional communities throughout European history, I cannot undertake that more detailed investigation here.[7]

I propose a fresh inquiry into the potential for virtual agency to be staged by music on its own in two senses—not only as exceeding the limits presupposed by contemporaneous philosophies and theories but also as existing in musical works distinct from the agency of those performers who manifest them in various ways. I fully acknowledge the often overlapping roles of performers and composers in their quest to stage an experience of agency. However, the experience of virtual agency is also warranted by a deeper reconstruction of musical styles and works, beyond the incomplete specifications of notations, theories, or performance traditions. I propose such virtual agency even in the absence of verbal evidence of its envisioning by composers, or manifestation by performers (contemporaneous or later). Thus, I offer new interpretations, based on the kinds of musical evidence that a new theory can bring to light. And I shed new light on interpretations that are already generally shared, offering alternative explanations.

With respect to repertoire, I limit myself primarily to composed Western art music, with a focus on instrumental tonal music from J. S. Bach to Johannes Brahms, although I include forays into post-tonal music, early music, and interpretations of texted and programmatic works. My central concern in choosing music examples is to elaborate a theory of agential levels or functions that can be helpful to historians and theorists researching more closely the musical practices of various eras and styles throughout the history of Western art music—practices I consider to be expressively motivated. Although my interpretations inevitably reflect my current aesthetic engagement with historical musical works, let me stress that the speculative framework for virtual agency developed here can be adapted to support more historically contextualized investigations of these and other musical styles and works. As a necessary complement to my theory of virtual agency, I draw on theories and explanations for musical expressive meaning developed in my earlier work. Indeed, this book may be understood, retrospectively, as the third part of a trilogy on interpreting expressive meaning in music (preceded by Hatten 1994 and 2004).

In developing this theory, I pursue several intersecting questions. First, what kinds of inferences are involved when listeners interpret virtual agency, from actants to agents, actors, and subjectivity, and from the narrative to the performative? Second, how have composers found means to support such inferences, in effect staging these various kinds of virtual agency? Third, how can listeners and performers understand emotional expression more effectively through the multifocal lens of virtual agency?

Virtual agency, as noted, is to be distinguished from the actual agency of composers and performers, whose intentional actions respectively create music (typically as notated, to some extent) and creatively manifest music (typically as significant sound). Virtual agency may be inferred from the implied actions of those sounds as they move and reveal tendencies within music-stylistic contexts. Beginning with gestural energies (interpreted within tonal and metric frameworks that constitute their virtual physical environment), I explore the embodiment of analogues to human intentional actions and reactions—how such virtual musical agents achieve and sustain their identities across change, understood as emotional and psychological growth or development of an actorial protagonist, and how various virtual actors can fulfill roles in dramatic (or narrative or even lyric) trajectories. I then explore how these levels of agency begin to blend the virtual and actual, as when listeners integrate virtual agency into a more personal subjectivity (guided by that virtual subjectivity staged in, or inferred from, the music). I further demonstrate how composers have found means to stage virtual narrative agency in their works and how performers can further enhance (or distort or in other ways negotiate) virtual agencies by projections of their own (actual) agencies. Thus, although my central focus is on those inevitable perceptual and cognitive inferences concerning virtual agents, made by stylistically competent listeners in their role as actual agents, I also explore the contributions of composers and performers (as actual agents) to the staging and projection of virtual agency, both in the score and beyond.

My interpretations imply a certain kind of listener, which I would frame here as a stylistically and strategically competent listener—one who can hear what is strategically achieved by a work conceived within the constraints and possibilities of stylistic principles. I have long defined style as "that competency in symbolic functioning presupposed by a work of art" (Hatten 1982), which has the advantage of defining style as other than an inventory of common types or (conversely) a set of distinctive features or (behaviorally) a summary of choices. Instead, an emphasis on competency suggests that a musical style is more analogous to the combination of grammar and poetics presupposed by a literary style. My emphasis on symbolic functioning is broad enough to embrace both principles and constraints (the latter conceived more as regularities than as rules) as well as both the formal/structural and the expressive/emotional motivations for those forms and structures. But the hypothesis of a competent listener need not entail a prescriptive interpretation; there are far too many ways that even a competent listener may traverse the formal-expressive trajectories available in a musical work. In chapter 6 I theorize aesthetically warranted emotions as issuing from composed expressive trajectories, and as guided by stylistic competencies (including topical and intertextual imports). But I also leave considerable room for individual listeners to hear in individual ways and to negotiate their personal subjectivity with the virtual subjectivities they may hear staged in a work (as suggested by my description of the interpretations of three imagined listeners in interlude II).

By conjecturing that a composer stages virtual agency, wittingly or unwittingly, I am also invoking a stylistically competent composer who works (more or less consciously) in a stylistic language. Charles Rosen, in his construal of the Classical style as itself an artistic achievement, is overly dismissive of "the mass of minor composers, many of them very fine, who understood only imperfectly the direction in which they were going, holding on to habits of the past which no longer made complete sense in the new context, experimenting with ideas they had not quite the power to render coherent" (1972, 22). Although I have not defined style in this way (on the basis of artistic value), it is certainly the case that a small number of composers helped forge those principles and hierarchies that ultimately constitute the language (or better, semiotic system) by means of which we come to understand the works of a given historical period, such as Rosen defines for the Classical.

As for the audacity of presuming to interpret expressive meanings, I share something of the pragmatic stance that Rosen enunciates with respect to the problem of a work's unique expression: "It is a contradiction essential to a work of art that it resists paraphrase and translation, and yet that it can only exist within a language, which implies the possibility of paraphrase and translation" (1972, 22).[8] Although I cannot pretend to resolve the philosophical complexities of artistic expression, I can at least provide some helpful guidelines for interpretation. One comes from Peirce's concept of type-token relationships. For expression, I would claim that the uniqueness of a token's expression draws from, even as it expands on, the common expressive range of its type. Markedness theory (Hatten 1994, 34–44) offers yet another means of tackling the relative specificity of expressive meaning—the unmarked term of an opposition (B) has more general meaning against which the marked term (A) carves out a more specific meaning (which in turn helps us identify the "not-A" generic meaning of the unmarked term). As my interpretations illuminate, such basic principles can help us conjecture further meaning in a more rigorous fashion. But I also acknowledge the ultimate mysteriousness of expression that presents what is more like a numinous symbol than an expressive signified (as explored in my interpretation of a Schubert string quartet theme near the end of chap. 5).

I must also acknowledge a bias in my choice of examples that, for the most part, draw from what are already highly valued works of music. This is also a pragmatic decision—I do not have space to acquaint the reader with less-familiar music and still accomplish my interpretive and theoretical goals (although I have included music of my own composition, or recomposition, where it could best illustrate a point). However, I welcome other scholars' productive incorporations and adaptations of the theory of virtual agency for other repertories, including popular music.[9]

Finally, I regret not having the expertise to pursue implications of virtual agency for gender (beyond the brief discussion of examples from Robert Schumann and Hector Berlioz in chap. 4 and 5), gender orientation, race, religion, nationality, and marginalized communities or cultural groups. Much important work is being done in these areas, and I trust the basic concepts of virtual agency may be of use for these studies as well.

Precedents

The theory of virtual agency presented here builds on (and in many cases departs from) significant theories of virtual, fictional, and actual agency in the interpretation of Western art music by music theorists and musicologists over the past forty-plus years: Edward T. Cone's (1974) groundbreaking theory of implicit and virtual agents controlled by an overarching persona, understood as an experiencing subject; David Lidov's (2005) somatic and Peircean account of musical gesture (originally published in 1987); Fred Maus's (1989, 1997) animistic and dramatic agencies—and their at times indeterminate status; Carolyn Abbate's (1991) "unsung voices"; Marion Guck's (1994) "analytical fictions"; Steve Larson's (1994, 2012) description of musical forces; Eero Tarasti's (1994) Greimassian account of musical actoriality and modalities and his later (2012) account of the existential *moi* and societal *soi* in music; Scott Burnham's (1995) insights into presence (voice) and subjective engagement in Beethoven; Anthony Newcomb's (1997) explorations of action and agency in Mahler; John Rink's (1999) perspective on the performer as narrator; Andrew Mead's (1999) physiological metaphors for "bodily hearing"; Naomi Cumming's (2000) Peircean framing of the relationship of musical gesture, voice, and subjectivity; Arnie Cox's (2001, 2006, 2011, 2016) mimetic hypothesis and its entailments; Byron Almén's (2008) theory of musical narrative; Roger Graybill's (2011) and Edward Klorman's (2016) theoretical reconstructions of agency in chamber music; Lawrence Zbikowski's (2002, 2008, 2012, 2017) exploration of musical analogues for human actions; Matthew BaileyShea's (2012) querying of agential sources; and Seth Monahan's (2013) four levels of musical agency as found in theoretical discourse about music. I refer to contributions on agency from dissertations by my students Michelle Clater (2009), Tamara Balter (2009), and Ian Gerg (2015) as well as dissertations by John Peterson (2014) and Cora Palfy (2015). Along with the work of Cumming and Lidov, Peircean approaches that have influenced this study include Vincent Colapietro's (1989) investigation of Peirce's concept of the self (including the important role of the imagination) and Paul Kockelman's *Agent, Person, Subject, Self* (2013), whose four constructions prompted my own, rather different levels of virtual agency for music.

This study also develops virtual agency as emerging from the persona theory forwarded by music philosophers Jerrold Levinson (1990, 2006), Jenefer Robinson (2005; Karl and Robinson 1997; Robinson and Hatten 2012), and Aaron Ridley (2007), which counters critiques of the persona by Stephen Davies (1997) and Peter Kivy (2009). These critiques are often directed against a naïve straw agent, a persona modeled too heavily on literary fiction and too intentionally bound to the composer's own subjectivity. By providing a wider range of options, I hope to defend listeners' inferences of agency as more than external props without sufficient warrant in the music. I also want to foster a clearer conception of what specific inferences listeners may actually be making when they hear in terms of a "persona"—a loaded term that I avoid whenever possible, substituting from a set of more carefully focused concepts.

My work prior to this more comprehensive study has demonstrated gestural agency as distinct from environmental forces in music, explored the role of emotion in forming subjective agency, speculated on the range of agential types, considered agential identification as relevant to categories of narrative, examined shifts in level of discourse along with other indicators of staged narrative agency, and finally, offered some perspectives on performative agency (see Hatten 2004, 2006a, 2009a, 2010a–c, 2012a–e, 2014a–b, 2015a–b, 2016a–b; Robinson and Hatten 2012). What each of these studies, as well as those by other scholars, clearly exposes is the need for a more comprehensive theory of virtual agency, including the evidence for our inferences of agency at various levels, how we move smoothly among levels of agency (as also addressed by Monahan 2013 for references to agency in theoretical discourse about music), how we engage as listeners with our inferences of virtual agency, and how those inferences help us understand and appreciate music in its interacting structural and expressive dimensions.

While we need a common language to ascertain agential inferences, if only to clarify how much we are claiming about virtual agency in various musical contexts, I cannot pretend to offer an answer that will resolve every conflict. As Maus (1989, 1997) rightly cautions, there are times when our inferences of agency are at best indeterminate. But I trust that my theoretical account of virtual human agency in music will enable such questions and arguments to be more productively framed and interpretive claims to be more clearly stated.

My study is primarily theoretical, and thus I assume a great deal of historical style competency for which I cannot fully argue (see Hatten 1994 and 2004 for some of those arguments). I address the consequences of this theory, however, not only for historical but also for cognitive investigations into the emergence of virtual agency in musical listening and interpretation—as part of musical understanding in the broadest sense. Given the limited reference to agency or subjectivity (despite considerable interest in embodiment, on the one hand, and a potential persona, on the other) in major collections devoted to music psychology and cognition (Hallam, Cross, and Thaut 2009) and music philosophy (Gracyk and Kania 2011), respectively, a theory that proposes to bridge cognitive and philosophical concerns while providing evidence for the theoretical and historical emergence of virtual agency in music would appear to be timely.[10]

Overview of the Book

Given the somewhat complex set of terms involved, I offer a prelude that lays out in some detail the structure of the theory, beginning with its roots in my theory of musical gesture (2004). A foundational chapter follows, addressing agency as a part of our more general cognitive apparatus. Chapter 2 is devoted to an extension of Larson's (2012) theory of musical forces, in order to incorporate virtual musical environments that help define virtual actants as they contribute to inferences of human agency. Chapter 3 addresses the issue of embodiment, already extensively theorized by Cox (2016); I go further by exploring what might be understood as the virtualizing of embodiment (including what I have coined as "enmindment") as listeners imaginatively (re)construct virtual human agents. Chapter 4 explores some of the ways in which composers have staged virtual identity and helped to ensure the persistence of an initially identifiable virtual agent. I elaborate a fresh concept of musical *melos*—with special attention to techniques that enhance the integration of melody with counterpoint, harmony, and motive—as support for the continuity of agents through the unfolding of a musical discourse.[11] I also briefly address actorial roles as complementary to the already extensive theorizing of actoriality by Tarasti (1994) and Márta Grabócz (1996). Interlude I bridges the gap from embodiment to subjectivity. Chapter 5 then explores virtual subjectivity from a number of perspectives, beginning with an argument for basic features of human subjectivity as implied already in sixth-century philosopher Boethius's *The Consolation of Philosophy*. Chapter 6 extends these considerations, focusing on emotional interpretation and experience. Chapter 7 explores virtual narrative agency as the staging of narrator-like effects in music and goes further by considering the composer as a narratizing agent. Chapter 8 offers examples of the agency of (actual) performers in their various interactions with virtual agency. Chapter 9 integrates the approaches of the previous chapters through a summary analysis and interpretation of levels of agency in Frédéric Chopin's Ballade in F Minor, op. 52, with attention to the expressively motivated form of this work. A second interlude takes a brief look at the different ways contemporary listeners might understand levels of virtual agency with respect to the *Adagio cantabile* theme from the second movement of Ludwig van Beethoven's Piano Sonata in C Minor ("Pathétique"), op. 13, by way of posing a challenge for cognitive and empirical approaches to musical meaning. Chapter 10 then examines several related issues with bearing on virtual agency, including the radical perspectives afforded by some twentieth-century music. Finally, the postlude considers the consequences of virtual agency for those disciplines that have a stake in explaining music, from its sources to its interpretations.

Notes

1. More broadly, Peirce's concept of virtuality is foundational to his doctrine of signs as well as his conception of mental capacities (see Esposito 2017 and Skagestad 2017 for brief accounts). Gilles Deleuze ([1966] 1988, [1972] 1994), building on Henri Bergson's pioneering work, has expanded the virtual into a theory of consciousness derived from the experience of time. I do not follow this line of thought, since my aims are considerably more modest from a philosophical standpoint, but for helpful summaries, see Shields 2003, Pearson 2005, and (with application to music) Hasty 2010. Further speculative accounts and definitions of virtuality have since appeared in *The*

Oxford Handbook of Virtuality (Grimshaw 2014), suggesting both the viability and the variability of the concept.

2. Granted, the boundaries are permeable. One could imagine various provisions for feedback that would allow the user some degree of cocreation, manipulating the resources of a preexisting soundscape (a possibility opened up, if not fully explored, by the soundscape designed by Edgard Varèse and Iannis Xenakis for the Philips Pavilion at the 1958 World's Fair in Brussels).

3. Masahiro Mori ([1970] 2012), a Japanese robotics expert, identified this phenomenon in 1970. His concept was first translated as the "uncanny valley" by Jasia Reichardt (1978). Interestingly, as the constructed body more closely approximates humanlike appearance (and behavior), the discomfort dissipates and one can again experience unclouded empathy.

4. As McClary observes, "During the seventeenth century, pleasure, desire, and the body became crucial preoccupations in most cultural enterprises, and the music of this period yields innumerable simulations of precisely these qualities, even if treatises do not address them (the silence of seventeenth-century writers concerning these issues should not seem surprising; after all, musicologists only began acknowledging these elements in the 1990s)" (2012, 6).

5. For Bach's instrumental counterpoint, see Yearsley 2002, and for Bach's vocal music, see Chafe 1991.

6. Extending his claim in *Music as Cultural Practice* (1990) that music can shape rather than merely reflect culture, Kramer notes that his "focus is on the songs as examples of cultural practice, not as autonomous artworks" (1998, 7) and further argues that "the recurrent possibility of a certain kind of interpretation is itself a kind of fact, a mode of evidence" (8).

7. For an account of the changing history of musical emotions both as expressed and as experienced, I direct the reader to Michael Spitzer's book-in-progress (tentatively titled "A History of Emotion in Western Music"), which draws on studies of emotional communities as developed by Rosenwein (2006, 2016) and others.

8. The concept of expression as "intransitive" (Wittgenstein [1933–35] 1960, as further developed by Richard Wollheim [1968, 82]), and thus beyond paraphrase or translation, is ultimately (and impressively) upheld by Roger Scruton, despite his awareness of the type-token distinction, as stemming from Peirce and as developed for music in Hatten 1994, 44–56 (see, e.g., Scruton 1997, 8n6).

9. For applications to popular music of gesture and topics, respectively, see Echard 2005 and 2017.

10. In the latter collection, Robinson (2011) develops her theory of the persona, drawing on Levinson's work (1996, 2006). Saam Trivedi distinguishes his concept of "animating" music from actually hearing in terms of a persona that, in his view, is "philosophically *distinct* . . . from the music" (2011, 230; emphasis in original). And Malcolm Budd considers the concept of a persona as dispensable, since it adds nothing to the "mirroring emotional response" of a listener who is following expressive features of the music (2011, 240–41).

11. For an earlier perspective on music as discourse, see Agawu 2008.

Prelude: From Gesture to Virtual Agency

In the conclusion to my 2004 book, *Interpreting Musical Gestures, Topics, and Tropes*, I summarize several links between gesture, expression, and agency in music:

> In our gestural encounters with music, both evolutionary history and individual
> human development have ensured that we will connect with the expressive—
> we can hardly force ourselves not to attend to significant energetic shaping as
> affective—but this sense of embodied expressiveness in music is enhanced by our
> ongoing engagement with the implied agency behind thematic, rhetorical, and
> dialogical gestures. In addition to recognizing gestures' expressive properties,
> and co-experiencing their synthesis through an embodied sense of action within
> the virtual environments of meter and tonality, we can identify at least one
> fundamental agency as created and sustained through the developing variation
> of a thematic gesture. We will experience its independent "life force" within
> gravitational fields, but also as an emerging individual subjectivity defined by
> interactions with other agencies (at least in those musical styles that treat thematic
> gesture as the "subject" of musical "discourse"), and the journey of that agency will
> create a trajectory—a dramatic arc and an outcome—as a unique realization of an
> expressive genre. (Hatten 2004, 290)

Moving beyond this preliminary statement, I have fashioned a theory of agency that embraces gesture and emotion as part of a more comprehensive theory of musical meaning. This chapter briefly outlines the theory, beginning with its grounding in gesture and affect.

Musical gestures may be characterized with respect to five functions: spontaneous, thematic, dialogical, rhetorical, and tropological (2004, 134–37).[1] We can find examples of each of these gestural functions in the opening measures of the first movement from Ludwig van Beethoven's Piano Sonata in F Major, op. 10, no. 2 (see example P.1).

Beethoven begins with a relatively spontaneous gesture, injecting an individual energy into a somewhat conventional, galant-style opening gesture, perhaps also alluding to opera buffa. This initial gesture is defined (foregrounded and segmented) by the articulated release and following rest, which also implies a rhetorical break, by which I mean the marked disruption of an unmarked flow—in this case the disruption of sonic continuity. The spontaneous gesture receives

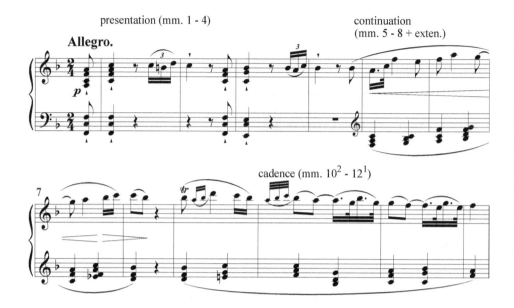

Example P.1. Beethoven, Piano Sonata in F Major, op. 10, no. 2, first movement, first theme (mm. 1–12).

a dialogical response in measure 2 with the turn figure on the pitch C (where the first gesture ended)—already implying an emergent discourse. After initial foregrounding, the first gesture is fully thematized when it is subsequently returned in measure 3. (Foregrounding and use are two primary criteria for thematization.)

When measures 3 and 4 are heard, in turn, as a response to measures 1 and 2, a new thematic level emerges as the now-foregrounded two-bar unit is dialogically responded to in measures 3 and 4. The rhetorical breaks created by the rests have become thematized through consistent use. They have, in effect, been absorbed into a larger thematic unit—as unmarked articulations rather than as marked disruptions. But their loss of rhetorical force does not entail a loss of the thematized potential of a rhetorical break, and that potential will be fulfilled at the end of measure 8.

But first, a new gesture appears in measure 5, and its continuous texture is marked in opposition to the now unmarked broken continuity of the first four-bar unit. Although contrasting, the new gesture is also related to the first gesture (by developing variation of the rising third) and thus can be interpreted as another kind of dialogical response that further implies an emerging thematic discourse.

The subtle recontextualization of the opening gesture (the rising third) is tropological as well as developmental (an example of developing variation's own power to create an emergent discourse). The troping of gestures is supported by the troping of several topics in bar 5's merger of (1) fanfare arpeggiation enhanced by the noble/heroic dotted rhythm; (2) the singing style achieved by the lyrical melody with its expressive rubato (a regular rhythmic displacement often referred to as Mozart rubato); and (3) the projection of that melodic line above a chordal accompanimental texture that alludes to a hymn or chorale.

Already by measure 5, then, we have considerable structural evidence for a thematized gestural discourse that has exploited all five of my functional categories. Furthermore, some kind of agency is suggested or implied by each of these functions: spontaneous (the composer's injection of energy, fitting a unique human gesture to a stylized musical context); thematic (a constructed entity possessing energy and an affective character, implying an individual virtual agent, and subject to coherent development, implying a virtual actor); dialogical (two virtual actors sharing a discursive context); rhetorical (a marked disruption outside of an otherwise unmarked continuity, perhaps suggesting an external or even narrative agential source); and tropological (a merging of different agential/actorial properties into a higher, individual synthesis, implying virtual subjectivity).

If we consider the affective character of these gestures, we can call on still other features as evidence: for example, direction, dynamic force, density, and degree of metric and tonal stability. I hear the initial gesture's soft, tonically grounded, upbeat/downbeat rising third as tentative (since soft), contented (since major, with two root-position tonics) yet playful (due to the staccato articulations), and mildly provocative as a proposal (implied by the rising-third inflection, akin to the intonation of a question). Indeed, it may be hard *not* to hear the speech-act sense of this gesture as part of its affective character.[2] By using the metaphor of a speech act in considering the gesture a tentative proposal, I am incorporating the intonation and ultimately the voice of a human agent as part of that gesture. But even if the gesture were heard as merely contented, that affect alone would imply an agent who expresses an emotion, or possesses a mood, of contentment.

In developing the initial agential commitments of my 2004 theory of gesture, I explore how gesture may best be understood as part of a more cohesive and comprehensive theory of virtual agency in music. Stimulated by Seth Monahan's (2013) proposal of four levels of agency in the analytical discourse of music theorists, I propose four rather different levels to speculatively account for listeners' inferences of virtual agency in music.[3] In order of most basic to most complex, these levels proceed from (1) unspecified virtual actants to (2) virtual human agents to (3) their ongoing actorial roles in lyric, dramatic, and/or narrative trajectories and, finally, to (4) their transformation as parts of a larger, singular consciousness or subjectivity that is negotiated by each individual listener. These four levels guide the coherent interaction of musical forces, gestures, topics and tropes, embodiment, identity, and the continuity of musical discourse. Furthermore, they lead to the expression (not merely representation) and ongoing development (not merely succession) of virtual emotions and thoughts, both as motivated by virtual situations in virtual worlds and as enriched by self-reflection. Focusing mainly on Western composers of purely instrumental tonal music, I explore various compositional strategies that help to project these levels of virtual agency.

Although not the only way listeners may productively hear and appreciate music, virtual agency provides a coherent grounding for understanding music's ongoing affective meaning as subjective expression, not merely as objective representation of a series of expressive states. Given purely instrumental music's inability to reference a specific situation in the real world, a theory of virtual agency must also address how listeners bring their own human experience to an engagement with music's intentional expressive designs.[4] Rather than conceiving of purely instrumental music as abstract sonic design—a tendency stemming from Eduard Hanslick in the nineteenth century and hardening into formalism in the twentieth—I offer a semiotic bridge from music's virtual energies to their expressive significance for actual listeners: as actions and reactions, urges and reflections, feelings and thoughts, and the blending of these into a larger subjectivity.

Transformative Inferences for a Theory of Virtual Agency

I propose four transformative inferences that lead, respectively, to each of the four stages of agency already described: virtualizing moves ascriptions of agency into the music itself, enabling musical energies to be understood as actions by an as yet unspecified virtual actant; embodying is crucial to interpreting an actant (or combination of actants) as a virtual human agent (with human gestures and emotions); fictionalizing enables us to understand virtual agents as virtual actors that have roles to play in a story that unfolds in the music's virtual world; and interiorizing transforms those competing strands in a singular consciousness—that is, virtual roles become parts of a larger subjectivity with all that entails in terms of psychological or spiritual interpretation. My hypothetical reconstruction of these levels and inferences moves logically up the scale of complexity, but the actual cognitive processes involved and their precise orderings are undoubtedly far more complex.[5] I also want to emphasize that listeners need not progress through these stages of agency to experience a sense of subjective identification with music.[6]

Virtualizing an Actant

Virtualizing is emergent from, though still dependent on, several lower-level capacities by means of which we initially perceive and interpret sonic emissions:

a. "Gestalt perception" (of a coherent imagistic and temporal shape) refers to the capacity to understand a sonic emission as having significant character and ongoing shaping (as an imagistic and temporal gestalt) and thus possessing identity as an event.
b. "Cross-modal generalization" (as an energetic profile) refers to the capacity to infer a sonic event or sequence as having or at least projecting an expenditure of energy with an equivalent profile in any sensorimotor area. As I have argued for gesture, the sonic event is intermodal in its energetic shaping through time.

c. "Generative" (from a source) refers to the capacity to infer some generative source for a coherent emission of sonic energy.

d. "Individuating" (as a focal identity) refers to the inference that a sonic event has sufficient coherence or particular dynamic projection as to suggest a singular activating source, which might thus be identified (as opposed to a diffuse source, as in the case of the wind).

e. "Effect" (leaving a trace) refers to the inference that a sonic event exhibits a trace of the energy expenditure by some individual source and thus is its effect.

f. "Action" (performed by an actant) refers to the inference that a sonic event trace may be understood as an action by some (unspecified, but individual) actant and that the action may be revelatory of that actant's identity.

If we want to infer any dynamic event as an action, we must presuppose an actant—simply defined as whatever it is that acts. For music, a default assumption is the actual performing agent who is producing the sound. Even when performers are not physically present to the eye, a sound can still be considered as emanating from an actual source either directly, in the case of the voice, or more indirectly, in the case of an instrument. Those actants are nonetheless actual.

But another kind of inference, which is the critical starting point for my theory, is the capacity to imagine a virtual agency in the sounds themselves. Thus, a music-internal action implies a virtual actant. The inference here is that an action finds its source virtually in the music itself and not just in an actual performer. Here, musical styles and compositional strategies provide various kinds of support for such a remarkable inference. In my 2004 book on gesture, I describe a "temporal gestalt" (101) cognitive capacity that enables us to hear a sequence of pitches not as beads on a chain but as a singular flow of energy—hence, we can hear a virtualized "energetic shaping through time" (102) as though it were the movement of a supported energy through space. This capacity, which we take for granted (and rightly so, since it has such deep evolutionary roots), is the basis for our experience of both movement and gesture *in* music.

To hear movement through time may seem to be an easy inference, since sound depends on transmission in a series of waves. But we can also readily hear implied movement through space. Again, the default inference would be an actual emitter moving through space—as when early humans linked otherwise disjointed sounds into the trace of an individual predator stalking them. But with music, we can imagine the sounds themselves as capable of implying their own energetic source and spatial-temporal location in a virtual world (environment) of tones. This is the profound imaginative leap of virtualizing, and it can occur prior to specifying any actant as a virtual human agent. Strictly formalist listeners might not virtualize in this way (although they may be unaware of the extent to which they actually do); instead, they may enjoy various energetic gestalts as they enter a complex structural hierarchy or web of relationships roughly corresponding to Eduard Hanslick's "tonally moving forms" ([1854] 1986, 29).[7]

Further evidence, however, provides continuing support for a progressively imaginative simulation. At the most basic level, a series of pitches whose frequencies are progressively wider are heard as going down. And strong accents are typically heard as oriented downward. Why? Because those sound directions correspond most closely, analogically speaking, to our experience of weight in the physical world—we are subject to the force of gravity that orients our environment in terms of up and down, as Steve Larson (2012) has exhaustively demonstrated. Thus, we readily construct a virtual environment (Hatten 2004, 115–18) in sound that is based, at least minimally, on those dimensions.[8] Music that has both tonal and metrical organization can further stabilize a virtual musical environment by providing clear platforms, as Larson puts it, toward which pitches are pulled gravitationally, to mention just one of his forces. The alternation of *up*beats and *down*beats enshrines in our theoretical language the embodied feel of meter's virtual physical environment, one that is constantly being refreshed, as it were, by the recurrence of each subsequent downbeat.

Embodying a Virtual Agent

Having access to a virtual musical environment with such clear directional constraints, composers could begin to suggest virtual agential energies through the contradiction of, for example, the force of virtual gravity. A leap upward would feel motivated by an injection of virtual agential energy, thereby supporting the continuity of an individual virtual agent moving through a virtual environmental space.

The following series of inferences guides the listener from an unspecified virtual actant to an increasingly humanly characterized virtual agent:

g. Independence (inferred from the countering of virtual environmental constraints) implies an individual virtual agent.
h. Intention (interpreted as the willed overcoming of constraints) implies a purposeful, acting agent.
i. Gestural character (including the affective qualities of an event's energetic shape) implies a virtual feeling agent.
j. Agential identity (a recognizable set of qualities) implies an agent with specific characteristics.

But identity must somehow be preserved. Thus, we need still further inferences:

k. Persistence or continuity (which involves interpreting change as growth) refers to a virtual agent's ongoing development, which may initially be understood as emotional growth. Given the complexities of human agency, we may make further inferential leaps to psychological or spiritual growth, or character development, not unlike the *Bildungsroman*, a genre of novel that features the gradual education and maturation of the protagonist.

The interpretation of energetic traces as independent agencies need not require continual bottom-up inferences. Once we have made the imaginative leap to hearing a virtual agent, we do not need to constantly reconstruct the sequence with every event. Furthermore, a virtual agent may be inferred even when a line "gives in" to music forces, as Larson (2012) phrases it. As I have demonstrated (Hatten 2012d), dynamics, rhythms, accelerations, and accents may emphasize a virtual agent's movement toward a platform that is already implied by musical forces (see chap. 2). Either way, we can hear the independence of agential energies. A musical line or melody that has temporal continuity also supports continuity as a series of actions by a singular source—hence, the continuity of the virtual agent it presupposes. But melody is merely the most basic of agential inferences. Counterpoint can also be motivated by the desire to project a singular agent through what I call refractive counterpoint, in which countersubjects are derived from the subject. In fact, the entire musical texture may take on an integrative agential character. In my keynote for the XII International Congress on Musical Signification in 2013 (Hatten 2015b), I introduced *melos* as an appropriate term for this integrative agential flow. *Melos* is the path or passage of our focal attending when we listen to a musical discourse.[9]

Further evidence for virtual human agency, as opposed to mechanical or animal virtual agency, may be found in the qualitative character of musical events as full-fledged gestures, which I define as significant and affective energetic shapings through time (Hatten 2004, 97). What makes a gesture immediately affective, and hence humanlike, is its distinctive dynamic shaping of energy, whenever it is analogous to the body's physical expression of some action or emotion.

As soon as we hear the gesture as embodying virtual human agency, we begin to expect the continuous persistence of that agential identity, and still other compositional strategies can support that inference. Continuity of identity may be associated with a motive or thematic gesture that continually evolves through a work, perhaps through developing variation, as Arnold Schoenberg first theorized. Here, we infer change as growth. If change is too great to be absorbed as growth, we may then infer a second agency (with all kinds of possibilities for its interaction with the first). However, the continuity of virtual experiencing may also be sustained by any of the other elements analyzed by music theorists, such as a harmonic progression or the opening up of new vistas through voice-leading projections modeled by Schenkerian analysis. The "will of tones"—to borrow Heinrich Schenker's (and Arthur Schopenhauer's) productive metaphor—suggests not only those musical forces that Larson theorized but also those seemingly willful, since independent, movements that agential melodies appear to enact when countering the virtual environmental constraints of tonality. Following this thread still further, we can interpret either willful agency that appears to decide, often spontaneously, on contra-environmental paths or else reactive agency, in cases where seemingly external forces act on a virtual agent in ways that may thwart or hinder its independent action.

At this point, we may encounter difficulties in making sense of a potential proliferation of agential inferences. Edward Cone helpfully distinguishes between "temporary" and "permanent" agents (1974, 89), and Fred Maus (1989, 1997) perceptively notes that agency in music is often indeterminate. However, as each analyst brings to bear evidence for agential identification, differences in assignment can be contested in ways similar to debates about musical structure and expression—interpretations that may not be any more determinate. What makes for a compelling agential interpretation, as with any interpretation, is that it can account for those events that appear most unusual: for example, departures from expectations of style or genre, as in the Beethoven theme with which this chapter begins.[10]

Fictionalizing Virtual Actors

At the beginning of some Classical works, we may find extreme contrasts, premising dramatic conflict through what I call dialectical themes. Here, contrasting musical gestures may suggest opposing virtual agents, setting into motion a dialogical interaction that may also develop over time. Such ongoing developments, whether of singular or multiple agencies, serve to create an agential discourse. And the more oppositional the contrast, the more likely we are to interpret it agentially in terms of dramatic conflict. Such contrasts help motivate a third major inference, fictionalizing, in which virtual agents take on roles as virtual actors in a fictional story enacted in a virtual world. The various inferences supporting a fictionalizing move from agents to actors may be outlined as follows:

l. Contrast (implying another agent) implies an encounter between two virtual agents.

m. Interaction (as in alternation or imitation) implies a dialogical role (and further self-identification) for each virtual agent.

n. Conflict (the dramatizing of contrast) implies basic roles such as protagonist and antagonist.

Two more inferences are closely related to those roles:

o. Identification (the recognition of a central agent) further implies the listener's identification with a virtual agent's role as a protagonist.

p. Perspective (taking the viewpoint of a central agent) implies the listener's capacity to interpret the energies of a protagonist as reflecting either willed actions or reactions to other agents.[11]

These inferences are all part of the progressive unfolding of a

q. dramatic trajectory (a dramatized series of events leading to an outcome), which may be understood as a fictional story within the virtual world of the music.

Just as actions in virtual worlds have virtual physical consequences, in that the virtual agent must overcome physical forces such as gravity, actions within fictional stories have dramatic consequences, spawning other actions or reactions and leading to outcomes that ground the kinds of narrative archetypes explored by Byron Almén (2008) and addressed by the narrative theories of Márta Grabócz (1996, 2009) and Eero Tarasti (1994).

Understanding virtual human agents as dramatic actors means that we can conceive of their fictional situations as sufficient to motivate an ongoing experience of emotions. In other words, virtual agents virtually experience emotions in their fictive worlds, and thus we can relate to those emotions directly rather than hearing music as merely—in Peter Kivy's (1980) phrasing—"expressive of" such emotions. Virtual agents can be understood as actually expressing emotions that are motivated by virtual events in their dramatized fictional worlds. We not only appraise their emotions, but as we make increasingly engaged inferences, we conjure virtual agents that evaluate their own situations within these virtual worlds and fictional dramas.

Interiorizing Virtual Subjectivity

The fourth level of inference in my theory, subjectivity, is that point at which virtual actors become parts of a larger subjectivity, components of a consciousness that at times may, in the case of a conflictual issue, be of two minds. By this inferential stage, the continuity of the music (as an ongoing *melos*) interiorizes its agencies into currents of thought and feeling, fashioning a larger subjectivity akin to the thinking and feeling Self—a consciousness that can reflect on its own thoughts and feelings. The virtual actors at this stage undergo interiorization in several senses.

r. Sublimation (internalizing as ideas): Although separate virtual actors may appear to lose their identity as characters in a drama and merge into a single virtual consciousness, they nonetheless maintain their dialogical status as competing trains of thought and feeling within that consciousness.

s. Allegory (interpreting further or deeper meanings): By understanding music's virtual environment as interiorized in the mind and actorial roles as parts of one's larger Self, the virtual drama can unfold in one's psyche like a stream of consciousness, leading to various possible outcomes such as those found in dramatic trajectories at the actorial level.[12]

t. Romantic irony (self-reflectivity): Self-reflectivity is achieved by means of shifts among levels of discourse that imply commentary or, in the case of romantic irony, outright dismissal of an ongoing discourse (and the consciousness it implies). Evidence for self-reflective thoughts and feelings may be found in the musical staging of narrative agency, in which a virtual narrator appears to comment on the discourse. At the level of subjectivity, such a narrator may be understood as the protagonist's higher thoughts, reflecting on his or her own experience. Local clues for what I call "shifts in level of discourse" (Hatten 1994, 174–75) include rhetorical gestures that break the unmarked flow of the discourse, fermatas and their musical extensions, insertions of the recitative chord or other markers of recitative, and certain parenthetical insertions.

Interiorization may lead to the further inference of

u. spiritualization (metaphysical interpretation), referring to those kinds of experiences that are loosely gathered under the concepts of the spiritual, metaphysical, and transcendent. Through this kind of interpretation, one may achieve a greater sense of personal identity, or one may willingly sacrifice a sense of personal identity while merging into a greater realm of significance (as in Eastern religious thought).

Although subjectivity merges actors into a larger consciousness, implied actors need not lose their interactive roles. An antagonist that acts against a protagonist may still play a potent role at the subjective level, as emblematic of the tragic, for example. But the advantage of subjectivity as a stage in inferring virtual agency is that it completely engages the listener in a massively parallel experience guided by the music but referentially situated by the listener/interpreter, and merging into a meaningful flow of "feelingful thought."[13]

Engagement and Participation

As interpreters (actual agents, whether engaged as listeners, performers, or composers), there are several ways we participate in constructing the virtual agency of a given work and in developing the competency in virtual agency that we bring to other works. First, we constantly compare a virtual agent's virtual experience to our own in terms of actions and emotions. Thus, engagement involves a

v. negotiated identification, by means of which interpreters' own experiences can help provide referential grounding for expressive meaning. For example, a listener may identify with a protagonist, and endow that virtual agent with greater emotional force by comparing its virtual expression with actual situations in which the listener has experienced similar emotions. Furthermore, a listener may choose varying degrees of engagement with the virtual agencies being inferred, from relatively complete identification (feeling through or with) to the increasingly greater psychic distance implied by empathetic sharing (feeling alongside), sympathetic reaction (feeling for), and completely unsympathetic rejection (feeling against). Ideally, however, the listener will at least competently track and (even if neutrally) recognize the nature of a virtual agent's fictional experiences and follow these through the discourses and dramatic trajectories that a composer has staged, whether or not the listener becomes directly emotionally engaged.[14] Such engagement, however subjectively personal it may appear, is often aesthetically warranted by tonal styles in which expression is strongly foregrounded—at least from the time of early opera in Western music.

Engagement can also lead to

w. enhancement, or personalized further development, in one of two ways: First, the music may suggest experiences and situations that go beyond those a listener can bring to the work—thereby potentially expanding the listener's consciousness and possibly providing still further expansions on subsequent listening. The listener can begin to hear and understand more as the music enables the listener to imagine new experiences. Jenefer Robinson (2005) has made this kind of emotional education part of her theory of music's expressiveness, although she relies on the older model of a persona, as first applied to music by Cone (1974) and developed further by philosophers such as Jerrold Levinson (1990) and Aaron Ridley (2007).[15] Since music philosophers such as Stephen Davies (1997) and Peter Kivy (2009) have written rather dismissively of the concept of a persona, the multiple levels of inferences I outline here may help clarify more precisely which inferences are at issue in any discussion and perhaps disarm criticism directed toward an unnuanced conception of agency as persona. A second way we participate in constructing virtual agency is by understanding enhancement in the sense of the listener's imagination going further along its own personal pathways yet still channeled by the music's trajectory. Here, the listener may take the lead in further interpretation, adapting the music's implied meanings to her own needs through further allegorizing or spiritualizing.

Moving beyond the subjective, we find that music also fosters

x. sharing, as interpreters communicate with each other and further develop each other's experience, whether in participatory rituals, informal conversations about the music, or more formal instruction.

Such sharing promotes intersubjective confirmation or modification of one's interpretations and leads ultimately to

y. codification, or the semiotic establishment of stylistic meanings as shared cultural meanings that emerge from intersubjectively understood strategies (gestural, syntactic, topical, and tropological).[16] For music theorists, this means theories, analyses, and interpretations that are intersubjectively established as valid (if not exclusive) by experts working at all levels of the chain of inferences outlined here. Eventually, this intersubjective agreement can lead to a body of relatively objective stylistic and cultural

Table P.1. Levels of inference for virtual agency in music, as emergent from various actual sources and agencies

Level of inference for virtual agency	Actual source or agency (examples)
Interiorizing virtual subjectivity	Presumed intentions of actual composer
Fictionalizing a virtual actor	Sociability among actual performers
Embodying a virtual human agent	An individual, actual performer
Virtualizing a virtual actant	A sound source, actual vibrations

meanings, perhaps approaching what Lawrence Zbikowski (2017) has developed under the rubric of a "musical grammar."

Table P.1 illustrates rough parallels and emphasizes differences between virtual and actual agents based on the transformative inferences I have outlined here.[17]

Conclusion

As suggested in the preceding discussion, some of the indeterminacy we sense in trying to account for agency in music may be due to the inadequacy of our theoretical language. My theoretical outline leads from the sources of forces that, as actions, presuppose actants to more humanly embodied agents endowed with quasi-physical and emotional capacities to actors who realize individual roles in expressive, dramatic, and narrative trajectories and, ultimately, to what I call subjectivity. The latter is, in effect, a mode of consciousness that is negotiated between a virtual subjectivity that integrates all (or nearly all) the events in a musical work and the corresponding subjectivity of a given listener. That interpreter may identify with, and in the process enhance the richness of, what amounts to a flow of feelingful thought. At this level, subjectivity also appropriates rhetorical moments, such as sudden gaps of silence, which may enable or enhance reflection and self-awareness.

Although the agential category of virtual subjectivity involves a greater admixture of an actual listening agent's subjectivity, it will remain virtual in a very important sense—as part of the working imagination of the listener. This is the case even when it draws on, evokes, and further enables the integration of music's virtual agencies with specific contents of the imagining listener's past and present experience. Subjectivity includes not only individual actions and emotions but their consequences; the development and growth of these emotions leads to the self-reflexivity that merges all these processes into a higher consciousness of value and meaning and that contributes to our sense of Selfhood. Thus, music not only suggests a virtual *Bildung* but guides the listener's application of that *Bildung* to his or her own growth and individuation as a passionately thinking and actively feeling Self.

Having offered this condensed outline of the theory, in the next chapter I turn to a more detailed examination of the issues pertaining to our understanding of agency in general. I demonstrate how inferences of virtual agency in music draw on our experiences in interpreting the source of energetic forces in the real world, including the relationship between more objective and more subjective interpretations of agency.

Notes

1. Briefly (as becomes clearer in my later application), a spontaneous gesture is an individual/original/creative mapping of a human expressive gesture to a sounding form; a thematic gesture is akin to a motive but draws on a synthesis of its gestural features (not merely pitch and rhythm)—it is similarly foregrounded and focal as developed in a musical discourse; a dialogical gesture is one that appears to respond to another gesture; a rhetorical gesture is one that breaks the unmarked flow of the musical discourse; and a tropological gesture is the result of a blend between characteristics of two different gestures.

2. The concept of a "speech act" (Austin 1962; Searle 1969) applies to speech utterances that are *doing* something (performing an act) rather than merely *stating* something. Thus, a "tentative proposal" is "performative" in this sense—it is a request that calls for a response (which Beethoven provides dialogically in mm. 2 and 4 and even more dramatically in mm. 5ff.).

3. Monahan's (2013) outline of levels of agency is hierarchical—higher levels subsume lower ones. The analyst (level 1) reconstructs the agency of a (hypothetical) composer (level 2), who has created a work-persona (level 3) that comprises various individual agential elements (level 4). My theory is primarily concerned with the fourth level, subdividing it into a set of inferences that lead to virtual actants, agents, actors, and ultimately, subjectivity—the latter only loosely corresponding to Monahan's level 3. I address actual analysts and composers (Monahan's levels 1–2), along with performers and listeners as they interface with the virtual, near the end of this prelude. Monahan's (2013) critique of my 2004 agential approach to the first movement of Op. 132 was a helpful impetus for my own further development of agency. Realizing that I needed to make my agential attributions more precise, I began to expand my previous work on gesture in order to detail the considerable number of inferences entailed by a more complete theory of virtual agency.

4. I do not mean to imply that purely instrumental music is not situated within historically, culturally, and personally contingent contexts, but that nonprogrammatic music does not clearly reference them. And even in the case of programmatic indications by the composer, we tend to draw situations from our own experience to make instrumental music's expressed emotions more relevant for our lives.

5. Although the series of inferences outlined in this prelude are speculative, they present a set of explanatory challenges that I trust will be more thoroughly addressed by cognitive scientists and music psychologists. I use "inference" here as a very general label for those complex semiotic processes by which listeners move from one kind of knowledge to another; I do not assume that every such process is equivalent to a propositional or rational or even conscious inference but rather that some mental processing must be involved. I recognize that the myriad competencies involved in musical understanding are not easily teased out into testable components, and I do not present this theory as more than suggestive in terms of its components. I would, however, also caution that cognitive approaches cannot presume to explain (or constrain) by scientific methods those potential meanings that accrue from historical,

learned, and aesthetic behaviors. Hence, I defend as equally appropriate the speculative, philosophical, semiotic, hermeneutic, and at times ad hoc approaches that music theorists, aestheticians, and active musicians bring to bear in attempting to explain musical meaning.

6. Naomi Cumming, for example, offers a convincing Peircean account of subjectivity that relates gesture to voice leading and the (singular) voice of a (virtual) persona in the music by noting the complex syntheses of different kinds of signs. As she observes, "Reference to a 'musical persona' is one way of capturing this notion of a specific character without a particular name—a complex and novel synthesis of signs, occurring either within a theme or over a longer span of time" (2000, 223). In chapter 4 I offer a complementary approach to the integration of musical elements (as *melos*). Cumming's compelling argument that the persona is (virtually) *in* the music further emphasizes the importance of a listener's encounter with that agency. As she elaborates, "The idea of 'persona' (or of complex 'character') does well in suggesting an individuality of affect and agency, which demands to be encountered in order to be known, and which cannot be simply paraphrased or summarized. . . . [The persona] 'belongs' to the music itself, and it is not a personal [composer's or listener's] 'expression' in any direct way. As an element of the music as 'other,' it can be encountered, confronted, or discovered in the process of listening, not simply experienced by a listener as an image of his or her own subjective desires. . . . [The] persona is truly 'other,' not merely a projection" (223–24).

7. For a critique of Hanslick's view of expression in music, see Hatten 1994, 231–36.

8. The concept of a virtual environment enables us to experience a "virtual, experiencing body" (Hatten 2004, 116) that is active within that environment.

9. See chapter 4 for a more detailed discussion of *melos*.

10. For an extended example of this approach, see Hatten 1994, 9–28.

11. I should add here that these inferences may be made by a listener, but they may also be strongly manipulated by a composer's choices (see the discussion of Dmitri Shostakovich's opera *Lady Macbeth of the Mtsensk District* in chap. 7).

12. Marianne Kielian-Gilbert offers an especially compelling account of how allegorical inferences can work: "Allegory implies parallel stories that don't usually meet: a story and its characters . . . amplify 'real life' (and vice versa). . . . At some point one experiences a moment of identification (of familiarity and repetition) to make the connection—a sudden 'shock' or identification links the fictional story to a potential 'real-life' outcome in a special way not understood or thought about before" (2010, 221).

13. My admittedly awkward coinage of "feelingful thought" may serve to remind the reader of the unfortunate binary between emotion and reason inscribed in our language.

14. See further discussion in chapter 1, summarized in table 1.3.

15. Briefly, Cone's theory includes various implicit and (for instrumental music) virtual agents under the control of a (complete) persona that is not equated with the composer but rather with an "experiencing subject" (1974, 84). His "virtual agents" are tied to instruments (or combinations of instruments) that "assume roles as virtual characters" and "appear to move freely" (88). However, "unlike real characters, . . . instrumental agents move on a purely musical, nonverbal plane, and they communicate solely by what [he calls] symbolic gestures" (88). With respect to my own theory, Cone's "complete persona" roughly corresponds to my virtual subjectivity, and his agents to my virtual actors (in their personalized instrumental roles). But Cone also provides for a more actantial level in noting that "an implicit agent can be any recognizably continuous or distinctively articulated component of the texture: a line, a succession of chords, an ostinato, a pervasive timbre" (95).

16. For a more extensive consideration of intersubjectivity as relevant to agential interpretation, see Palfy 2015.

17. The interaction of actual and virtual agents in Wolfgang Amadeus Mozart's chamber music is implied in Edward Klorman's (2016) theory of multiple agency. Dean Sutcliffe (2013) develops a notion of sociability as a kind of actual agency (at the actorial level) among performers in Classical chamber music as conditioned by (virtual) agential clues in the music.

1   Foundations for a Theory of Agency

The primary locus of agency for human perception and cognition is the re-constructed source of a perceived expenditure of energy. Agency is most relevant for humans and other sentient beings when that source can be understood as concentrated in an individual or entity responsible for a motivated expenditure of energy. When agency is not immediately apparent to the senses, more than one inference may be required. For example, the movement of the wind is so dif-fusely motivated that it is generally not practical to ascribe agency to a singular source. We make exceptions for localized winds emanating from the action of a fan (for which wind is the primary function) or a jet engine (for which wind is a secondary consequence of propulsion). Earlier human cultures, however, gave in-dividual agency to the diffuse natural winds that we experience when outdoors. The ancient Greeks invoked a supernatural individual (Aeolus, the god of wind) to personify that agency. Today, weather reporters typically invoke the causal agency of a meteorological entity (e.g., a cold front) to help explain the source of a prevailing wind. These examples suggest that the agents we infer need not be ac-tual, living individuals, but they can also be conceived as virtual constructions, whether in the form of a god (Aeolus) or in the shape of a theoretical entity (a cold front) that stands for an actual, proximal cause.

It is also possible to assume a placeholder for potential agency in the absence of sufficient clues (or interpretive imagination), whereby we neutrally assume a source without constructing a particular or individual agency for it. I call this unspecified source of energy an actant. When a given force is presumed, for whatever reason, to have an unspecified but concentrated motivating source, that force is considered an action. Defined in this way, actions and actants are mutu-ally implicative—you cannot have one without the other.

A given force may also have a given direction. If both source and direction are fully explicable by one or more physical or mechanical causes not directly involv-ing an individual intention, we remain at the level of the actant. Ascribing human agency occurs only when there is evidence that the action could be willed, or in-tended, at some point in the chain of causes and effects. For example, an inter-nal combustion engine causes a car to move in the direction that its wheels are pointed. The engine is individualized (a particular engine) but not intentional. For intention we require a human agent who starts the engine and applies the gas. Thus, the actions of a car have not simply causes but actants, and in this case one of the actants is also an intending agent (the driver).

Energetic shaping through time (Hatten 2004, 109) may also provide evidence of human agency, especially if we add the criterion "interpretable as significant"— in other words, intelligible, and perhaps intelligent, with respect to some intention, whether or not the presumed gesturing agent is consciously aware of that intent. Thus, degree of conscious intent on the part of an agent is subject to interpretation, ranging from witting to unwitting communication or signification.[1]

Agency may be transferred along the lines of transmission of a corresponding energy. We tend to ascribe agency to an immediate, individual force, especially in cases where the ultimate source of the force may be diffuse. Thus, semiotically speaking, I would not typically say that the force of gravity caused an object to strike my head but rather that an apple falling from a tree hit me, taking the convenient shortcut that relegates the source to the closest impinging individual actant (that is why we consider Newton's inference of an underlying physical force to be so remarkable). However, if the source agency is obviously an individual, especially a sentient one, and readily observable, we generally have no trouble moving back up the chain of causes and effects in understanding that source as being the responsible agent. Suppose we are watching a game of pool: a player sends energy through the cue stick, which transmits it to a cue ball, which transmits it to another ball, which may produce an intended result. Although the immediate action propelling a struck ball may be traced to the energy transmitted through the cue ball, the chain of energy transmission is easily traced perceptually to an original, individual motivating force, and thus we consider the player as the intentional agent, just as we saw the driver as the intentional agent moving the car in my earlier example. For humans, then, semiotic attribution of agency typically involves a sentient being that may set into action various tools (such as a cue stick in billiards) or intermediaries in order to attempt and possibly achieve an ascertainable result.

The ascription of subjective agency, as opposed to brute or objective cause and effect, is typical of animals as well as humans; in reacting to energy expenditures of an unknown source as though from other sentient beings (potentially threatening, in the case of predators), we also localize and attempt to identify the source of those forces that may have an impact on our survival. Here, gestalt laws of pattern completion and good continuation serve to stitch together fragmentary perceptions into functionally coherent individuals moving intentionally (e.g., from glimpses of a striped pattern moving through the tall grass we may interpret a stalking tiger). When, however, humans ascribe agency to energetic shapes, such as gestures (or music) that they know to have been produced by other humans, the ascription of performative agency is even more compelling, whether or not the energetic shapes are seen or heard in close proximity to their producer. Such inferred, intentional agency tends to persist, to have identity across time and change, whether the inferred agent is active or passive (i.e., interpreted as producer or receiver of energy).

Table 1.1 summarizes these and other means by which we move from objective, physical inferences to subjective, agential inferences with respect to the

Table 1.1. Aspects of agency as interpreted (objectively and subjectively) by humans to account for the source (and significance) of perceived and focal energy expenditures

Objective		Subjective
Source		
Diffuse, general	→	Focal, individual (action by unspecified actant—e.g., machine, natural, supernatural, human)
Nonsentient	→	Sentient (embodied—e.g., animal, human)
Connection		
Causal (cause-effect)	→	Intentional (by specific agent; motivation-achievement)
Force		
Energy	→	Will
+ Direction	→	Striving
+ Intensity	→	Desire
+ Result	→	Intended goal (i.e., teleological)
Continuity		
One-time force (isolated event)	→	Preserving an identity, persevering (as actor—i.e., continuity of agent across change, as active or patient)

source, connection, force, and continuity of energies as perceived and experienced in the world.

These basic principles of attributing agency also apply to our understanding of music, as table 1.2 displays. Even when speaking of a disembodied musical gesture, a sonic energetic shaping through time that we may hear without an observed source, we generally assume an actual human agency comprising one or more performers who have provided the physical energy and intention required to produce the act we call a musical gesture in sound. Why should that be, when we know that machines may also reproduce notated sounds synthetically without human performance? Generally, we hear subtle cues in recordings that signify both the more flexible realizations of human gestures (i.e., lacking strict mathematical proportionality) and the expressive potential of such irregularities (i.e., coordinated with significant aspects of musical organization). Mechanical intervention—whether by means of impressions on a piano roll that are then sonically realized on a player piano or through digitalization and reproduction on a Bösendorfer Synclavier—often reproduces enough human nuance to enable a listener to infer a human performer (even one long deceased, as in the case of the Synclavier's digitalized realization in sound of piano rolls made by George Gershwin).

In the case of a purely mechanical realization of a score (i.e., mechanical production from notation through a midi interface), we may nevertheless assume agency, if not in the performance, then in the composition itself—the creative

Table 1.2. Some types of agency with reference to music

Actual agents

Listener
Performer (with performative agency [Hatten 2004])
Composer
Teacher/coach

Virtual agents
Persona (e.g., the "composer's voice" [Cone 1974])
Subjectivity (as integrative, self-reflexive consciousness)
Narrative (staged by "shifts in level of discourse" [Hatten 1994])
Actors (with roles in a dramatic trajectory)
    Internal, principal (e.g., "protagonist" [Hatten 2004]); stable identity (active or reactive)
    External (e.g., "Fate")
Agents (with human characteristics)
    Primary
    Secondary (Clater 2009)
Actants (prior to agential identity)

---

agency of the composer who fashioned the score. However, if the score is the result of an algorithm, as in David Cope's (2001) fascinating computer programs that emulate musical styles in their generative capacities, we will perhaps be fooled in our ascription of composer agency. If we are knowledgeable enough, though, we may move still further up the chain of agency to Cope himself as the intentional agent configuring the algorithms that guide the sonic output that simulates a composer's musical style. Even more problematically, however, the actual agencies of performer and composer may coexist, or merge, as in the case of improvisation, when the performer takes on a somewhat compositional or creative role.[2]

I have noted some of the subtle cognitive and semiotic bases for attributions of actual agents, even when not physically present as part of a perceived action. Here, I develop the idea that we have adapted these evolutionarily refined capacities to infer not only once-removed actual agents (such as performers or composers) but also virtual agents that may only be implied by composed (notated) or performed (sonically realized) musical gestures. "Virtual" in this context means any actant or human agent (or actor or subjectivity) that can be inferred as producing intentional musical actions (gestures and the like), reacting to implied forces or other agents, revealing intentions, and experiencing thoughts and emotions. I suggest that this capacity to infer or construct virtual agencies as implied by the music's own events need not result in the intentional fallacy of attributing every expressive effect in a musical work to the expression of a composer or a performer (which are clearly the first defaults in interpretation, and thus not so much fallacies as predictable human responses). Virtual agency provides a more neutral playing field for the composer, who is freed from the direct responsibility of being the individual who is feeling the emotions expressed by various virtual agents. Instead, the composer may fabricate a virtual world in which virtual agents take that responsibility. And a performer may reanimate that world by manifesting it in sound, by actually embodying those forces and intentions implied by virtual musical agents.

To restate this point, we employ many of the same perceptual mechanisms and cognitive strategies to ascribe virtual agencies in composed or artistic worlds as we do to ascribe agency in the everyday world.[3] Productive forces within a musical work may therefore be interpreted, along the lines of our experience in the natural world, as either diffuse or individual, as sentient or not, and as humanly intentional or not. For example, if a composer creates an undulating contour to suggest waves, the resulting sonic shape may simply imply a diffuse physical source within the virtual realm of the musical work. But just as one may ascribe supernatural agency to wind, one may ascribe an external agency to these musically simulated waves (perhaps at first defaulting to a generalized Nature as a hypostatized natural source of energy). The agitation of those waves may then suggest the agitation of a virtual human agent. Finally, through a similar process by which we infer emotion from movement (i.e., movement as implying agency and the character of that movement implying the emotive state of that agent), we may arrive at an interpretation of a natural wave force as personified. We thereby move beyond generalized Nature, applying agency to a specific individual (e.g., an angry god) or to a more specified force (e.g., the restlessness of Fate). The agency implied by a musical gesture need not always be a virtual human one, but it will likely be interpreted in human terms, in the sense that we will attribute intentionality to the source and an emotional charge to its forceful manifestation.

Musical Gesture, Emotion, and Agency

I have defined musical gesture as energetic shaping through time that is understood as both affective and significant (Hatten 2004, 125). Affect (emotion) and significance (meaning) are inextricably woven into any human gesture, creating what I consider to be an emergent expressive meaning. In music, however, human gestures must be negotiated with harmony, melody, motive, meter, and other relevant stylistic elements. Even Béla Bartók's negative cadences, in which he slides downward in a nontempered glissando gesture of rejection, typically begin from a pitch that is included in the tempered set of twelve pitch classes.[4] Thus, any interpretation of expressive meaning must take into account the semiotic contribution of all the elements integrated into a given musical gesture.

For example, the opening motto of Ludwig van Beethoven's Piano Sonata in E♭ op. 81a (*Das Lebewohl*), features a gestural stepwise descent that by itself might suggest a prolonged sigh (example 1.1). But the topical reference is that of horn fifths, and the symbolic significance of the figure is that of distant longing (in music iconography, the horn call in the Romantic forest), evoking emotions such as regret in the face of absence (Rosen 1995, 117). Harmonic implication in the two-voiced horn-fifth gesture is the relatively closed progression I–V–I^6 with

Example 1.1. Beethoven, Piano Sonata in E♭ Major, op. 81a, first movement, motto theme (mm. 1–2).

the relatively closed trajectory of stable-unstable-stable. Its motto-like concision contributes to its symbolic significance as an emblem, foregrounded and succinct. The figure appears as it would on the natural horn, in the major mode; thus, its use here might seem to contradict the warranted expression of sadness when facing the departure of a friend (note the text setting of "Le-be-wohl" ("fare-thee-well" would be an approximation in English). However, the undercutting insertion of C in the bass turns the I⁶ harmony into a deceptive vi chord, and the sudden swerve to a minor submediant in place of a major tonic enacts an expression of poignancy that is like a sudden stab of sadness—a staged moment of dramatic recognition that expresses an emotion rather than merely evoking a mood.

But whose gesture is this? Is the virtual agent also the creative agent (here, Beethoven) hiding behind a mask as a persona? In such an interpretation, we might identify emotionally with Beethoven, and through the representation or expression of his presumed sadness, we might experience our own sadness. But we could also interpret the horn call as being produced by an unidentified, more purely virtual agent in a distant, virtual location; the emotion we feel might then be in reaction to that virtual agent's (perhaps unwitting) act in producing this sonic symbol from afar, which we might further interpret as having the significance of an oracular utterance. Furthermore, we might share some sense of empathy with the virtual utterer of this horn call—not unlike the protagonist at the end of Franz Schubert's *Winterreise* who empathizes with a blind hurdy-gurdy player and appropriates his song as emblematic of the protagonist's own grief. This leads to a central question: Where might we locate the agency of our own emotional responses to musical gestures?

The very question highlights the interdependency of agency, gesture, and emotion. Figure 1.1 offers a preliminary model of these relationships. Once a virtual agent is embodied by the music and given subjective identity in the musical discourse, that identity may be understood as actively producing (as immediate agent) some gesture or, alternatively, as receiving (as immediate patient, or better, recipient of) the energy of a musical gesture—and perhaps also actively engaging with another agent, depending on the context. If we interpret the virtual agent as receiving the gesture, then another human agent or source (whether natural

Musical Work	Listener

Gestures	Levels of engagement

energetic + style-coded
gestalts: syntheses:

dynamics	topics	1. mere **recognition** of virtual emotions
articulation	schemata	
pacing/timing	modules	2. actual emotion: **sympathetic**
contour	harmony/voice leading	feeling *for* (e.g., pity)
texture	melody/motive	or *against* (e.g., disgust)
tempo	rhythm/meter	
timbre	form	3. actual emotion: **empathetic**
		feeling *alongside* a virtual agent

4. actual emotion: **coexperiencing**
feeling *with* a virtual agent
or *through* one (complete **identification**)

$\boxed{\text{virtual emotion}}$

(as **expressed** by a **virtual agent**,
not merely *represented* by one)

Figure 1.1. Preliminary model for the interactions among gesture, virtual emotion as expressed by a virtual agent, and the range of actual emotions potentially experienced by a listener.

or mechanical) must be inferred as having produced the gesture received. Furthermore, the recipient role presupposes the prior establishment of an already stable agential identity that, like a human character or human being, may be understood as persevering across considerable change in expressive gesture. The listener, at least in the case of Romantic music, will tend to identify with a central virtual agent who apparently both produces and receives—both acts and is acted on. I call the agent or character with which we tend to identify the principal internal agent (which takes on an actorial role in the current theory), and I call any agency that acts on the internal agent (also actorial, in the current theory) an external agent (Hatten 2004, 225). Internal-external here refers to the perspective of that agent with which we identify, but both are within the virtual-fictive world of the musical discourse.

If gestures are the means by which we infer agency, how do we infer a singular internal agency across the variety of gestures that may be understood as either produced or received? I address this question in the following chapters, giving special attention to the means by which a virtual agent/actor's identity and its persistence are staged (chap. 4). In addition, I also explore shared subjectivity (Hatten 2004, 231–32), first through our identification with an inferred virtual agent and then through the coherent integration of more than one virtual agent or actor into a single virtual subjectivity (chap. 5–6).

But what leads us to ascribe embodied agency in the first place? In her dissertation Michelle Clater (2009) builds on Eero Tarasti's (1994) Greimassian-based theory of modalities to help infer agency. In short, if one can detect a modality (of action or being) in a gesture (such as "doing" [*faire*] or "having to do" [*devoir faire*] or "being able to do" [*pouvoir faire*] or "willing (wanting) to do" [*vouloir faire*] or "knowing how to do" [*savoir faire*]), then one has evidence of a sentient (and presumably human) agency. To the degree that these modalities of action include modalities of feeling, one has still further evidence.

In the context of the Requiem texts, whose settings by Hector Berlioz and Gabriel Fauré are the basis of Clater's interpretations, it is not hard to distinguish acting agents from reacting "patients," or recipients of actions. However, even with clear textual evidence for these agential types, Clater is able to distinguish primary from secondary agents based on their relative dominance. She also analyzes the individual gestures of complex musical passages into their more basic actants prior to their clear consolidation into higher level agents, a process I theorize more fully in chapters 2 and 3. It can be difficult to detect modalities consistently and to know what features cue each modality. An alternative strategy is to triangulate among interpretations of gesture, emotion, and agency, where more secure knowledge of one or two can help in inferring the remainder.

On the left side of figure 1.1, I roughly divide the more immediate energetic parameters of a gesture from the more learned, stylistically coded dimensions. However, a competent listener synthesizes all these elements into a unique amalgam with affective character. Without benefit of virtual agency, we might conclude that an emotional state is merely represented by a musical gesture. However, since gestures as energetic shapes imply some original source for their energies, we are led to ascribe agency, which in turn leads us to perceive affect as expressed emotion rather than represented expressive states (a distinction to which I return later).

Nonetheless, the listener may experience a range of actual emotional experiences with respect to the virtual emotions expressed by a virtual agent (as shown on the right side of fig. 1.1). Most closely and intricately, a listener may coexperience the expressed emotions of the virtual agent, perhaps identifying with by living through that agent. A listener may also maintain various degrees of reserve in responding to a virtual agent—either empathetically feeling alongside (yet not fully identifying with) or sympathetically feeling for, as in the case of pity, or feeling against, as in the case of disgust. Or the listener may not be aware of any actual emotions, even while fully recognizing (and even appreciating) the emotions being expressed by one or more virtual agents.

Furthermore, it is possible that a listener might coexperience through, without necessarily fully identifying with, a virtual agent. A listener may choose to map a virtual agent's presumed dramatic trajectory completely onto his own personal experiences, effecting a kind of para-experiencing of the emotional plot of the music's trajectory. Or a listener who chooses not to invest personal emotion in a virtual agent's expressed states, instead critically assessing or appreciating the emotive expressiveness of the work, may nonetheless use that evaluation as a springboard for engaging with other dimensions of the work: its superior craftsmanship or its solemn beauty. And these emergent meanings may themselves entail higher-level emotional responses. For example, when the protagonist in the movie *The Shawshank Redemption* (1994) locks himself in the warden's office and broadcasts the letter duet from *Figaro* over the PA system to the prisoners in the yard, the work is received as an almost supernatural emanation of pure beauty without concern for the foreign words or unknown dramatic context, as evidenced by the voice-over description of the scene by the narrator (another prisoner in sympathy with the protagonist).

Interpreting the Gesture-Emotion-Agency Triad

A brief musical example addresses some of the possibilities—and problems—of gestural-emotional-agential interaction for interpretation. The familiar opening of Beethoven's *Tempest* Piano Sonata in D Minor, op. 31, no. 2 (example 1.2), features a succession of gesture-agency-emotion syntheses.[5] The first gesture, a rolled chord, is topically a first-inversion recitative chord that implies human agency, yet its "chord of nature" treatment suggests the profound agency of Nature as source. Thus, an interpretation of expressive meaning might (tropologically) combine "anticipation of intimate discourse" with "profundity" to suggest an oracular agency with near supernatural power.

The transformation of that arpeggiation to the bass motive in measures 21 and following brings with it a dramatic gestural energy that readily suggests the *tempesta* topic, cueing either a fateful external agency or a tragic-heroic energetic response to Fate.[6] Depending on which way we interpret the agency of this bass motive, we may either react against the inexorable quality of Fate or coexperience a heroic struggle within a larger subjectivity. Beethoven tips the balance by providing a dialogical gestural response, the chromatic turn figure played by the left hand crossing over the right. Now, the expressive character of the gesture suggests a fearful or anxious response to the bass motive, and thus it becomes easier to assign external agency to the bass and internal agency to the treble. Emotionally, we may choose to identify with (and even experience) the treble agency's pleading character as well as experience that virtual human agency's reaction to the fateful agency expressed by the bass. And we may also infer a broader subjectivity encompassing both agencies as warring forces within a single virtual subjectivity.

In this brief example, we can see how the interaction of gesture, agency, and emotion (as expressed, experienced, or reacted to) enables us to triangulate meaning, helping to compensate for any less-than-determinate members of the triad. This simple model also respects another difference by distinguishing between emotions expressed by the work and emotions experienced by the listener, the latter either through identification with or reaction against a virtual agent's gestural projection of emotion.

Virtual and Fictional Agencies

In both the introduction and the prelude, I distinguish between virtual and fictional with respect to agency. The virtual, on the one hand, is understood

Example 1.2. Beethoven, Piano Sonata in D Minor, op. 31, no. 2, first movement (mm. 1–24).

against the backdrop of the actual; it includes the everyday process of imagining an outcome that one then proceeds to create.[7] We are evolutionarily conditioned to understand virtual events as potentially realizable, or virtually effective in ways the actual might be. The fictional, on the other hand, is opposed to the real, in that a fictional character may only actualize a contrafactual or possible world (or even an impossible world)—one that must never be confused as being a real world. Although fictional worlds may achieve remarkable verisimilitude to reality (people may look the same, they may act realistically, etc.), fictional worlds do not share certain critical entailments of the real world. These entailments include the following:

1. The survival imperative—events in one's life (as opposed to fictional events) must be evaluated with respect to the survival of the agent; responses must be weighed accordingly. A loud shot in a theater may actualize our startle reflexes and we may even duck as the result of a sudden, protective reflex, but once we cognitively evaluate the shot's fictional source on stage, we are not compelled to seek cover. Similarly, a grieving musical passage does not demand that we grieve in equal measure.
2. The existential imperative—people in one's life actually exist; fictional people (and events) exist only in the imagination and (normally) only for the duration of the fictional world.
3. The significance imperative—life events have meanings that radiate out to recontextualize the significance of other events. Fictional events, on the other hand, touch our lives only tangentially. This is not to deny the capacity of fictional events to help us change the way we think, but they serve rather as catalysts for the imagination.
4. The consequentiality imperative—events continue to impinge (to varying degrees) on one's life, whereas fictional events need not have an impact beyond the frame or dramatic context of their occurrence. Although events in powerful works of art may affect us more than events in our actual lives, we can usually tell the difference with respect to reality.

Fictions, in turn, make their own demands:

1a. The make-believe-as-if-real contract—we accept fictional characters and events by making believe they are real and reacting to them as if they were, within the constraints of those imperatives entailed by reality (outlined in the previous list).[8]
1b. The make-believe-though-clearly-fantastic contract—we accept fantasy characters and events by imagining (or trying to imagine) a world where their interactions are plausible.
2. The verisimilitude contract—though this can be violated for expressive effect, we expect that a work's characters and environment will have some degree of verisimilitude with respect to our experience of the real, physical world, such that we can participate vicariously through the virtuality of fictional agents.
3. The selectivity contract—regardless of degree of verisimilitude, we don't expect fictional agents to be represented in terms of all the functions of actual humans but only those that are relevant to the plot or dramatic premise of the work. Violations of this contract are generally short-lived in the world of art (e.g., movies that show every bodily function, or every tedious event in everyday life), although even everyday events can be transformed

Table 1.3. The opposition of Fictional and Factual as distinct from
the continuum of Virtual to Actual

FICTIONAL	(as opposed to)	FACTUAL
VIRTUAL ———————	(on a continuum to) ———————	ACTUAL

into art by revealing the deeper subjectivity of the characters, as in the
works of Anton Chekhov.

4. The nonviability contract—we accept that fictional characters do not live in
the real world—even fictions based on real-life personages.

5. The consistency contract—we accept that fictional worlds will play by their
own rules and choose whatever degree of verisimilitude their creators
choose but that they will do so consistently enough to create a degree of
predictability (although some film fantasies or science fiction may violate
this to expressive effect).

Although "fiction" is often used to describe those worlds that go beyond real-world plausibility, "fantasy" is the preferred term. Consider the genre of science fantasy (e.g., the novels of James Morrow), which is categorically distinct from science fiction. Verisimilitude to reality is also violated in the subgenre of magical realism, as in Gabriel García Márquez's *One Hundred Years of Solitude*.

Virtual worlds may be understood as both imagined and imaginable, as both humanlike and actualizable. We can identify with virtual agents and their virtual worlds as well as sense their physical actions within a virtual environment. Fictional worlds are often virtual worlds in this sense. Writers are frequently given this sage advice: make sure that readers can identify with your characters. But again, the crucial distinction captured by the term "fictive" is the distance between fiction and fact, whereas the distinction captured by the term "virtual" is the closeness between virtual and actual. We have machines to deliver virtual reality, but the closest we can get to the more paradoxical category of fictional fact is in the realm of creative nonfiction, a genre exemplified by works such as Truman Capote's *In Cold Blood*.[9]

Table 1.3 maps the opposition of Fictional to Factual (despite various illusions and deceptions, an event is usually understood as one or the other) alongside the continuum of Virtual to Actual. The colloquial locution "it's virtually an X" is often used to mean that something is almost something else or that something is almost finished—which reflects the graduated continuum of virtual to actual in everyday parlance. For music, a virtual agent may possess various actual features (energetic attributes) that help us determine its existence, as virtualized, in a musical discourse. Furthermore, a performer can to some degree actualize those virtual energies and agencies. Degrees of determinacy in implied agency may also reflect this continuum.

Dreams are virtual yet also fictional in the broader sense just described, which I have not reserved for intentional, literary fiction alone. Dreams, however, often draw on real people and events in one's life and thus have the capacity for provoking intense engagement, even to the point of actualizing the virtual through immediate and even life-threatening physiological responses. One might have a heart attack provoked by the virtual reality of a dream without the world (and characters) of the dream ceasing to be fictional.

In a sense, everything we experience may be considered as real in that we experience it. Nevertheless, we find it helpful to keep separate any reality that is once removed, as in fictional worlds of art where imagination can play or make-believe but has an escape hatch to return to reality unscathed. As vulnerable as we may feel when identifying with a protagonist in danger, we also know at some deeper level that we are safe. Tragically, however, victims of real violence may at times default to unhelpful behavior (closing one's eyes or ears, trying to return to a better reality) that was initially entrained as a strategy to escape from fictional violence.

Believability is not always characteristic of our experience of reality. No one wants to believe in an early death—if it looms, it may appear as fictional to us as any story. Nor is truth a reliable criterion of reality. Real behavior is often riddled with misdirection and outright deception. A key difference is that fictional behavior, even when it appears (virtually) to have the same entailments as real behavior, will not persevere beyond the imagined sustaining of the fictional world. Plays end and we go home; as moved as we may be, we need not attend to the needs or fear the actions of any of the fictional characters when we wake up the next morning.

Four Scenarios of Engagement with Degrees of Virtual Agency

Artists may not choose to implement greater degrees of mimesis, embodiment, or plausibility to capture a sense of vividness, but each of these can contribute to anchoring our sense of reality by enabling us in some way to actualize the virtual in our own lives (e.g., by actual emotional responses). Compare the following cases involving virtuality:

1. A video-game player (a) moves a warrior avatar (b) in a fictional world. The avatar is cartoonlike in appearance and clearly lacks convincing embodiment of motion (staggered running, full-body turns, etc.). Yet by moving the avatar through space and activating its fighting, the player cements her identification with this virtual self and permits a degree of actualized, independent behavior within the limits of the virtual world of the game.
2. A reader (a) follows the actions of a character (b) in a novel. The character's full appearance is not completely described by the author, and the character is not rendered visually on the cover by an artist. The reader imagines and fills out for himself a suitable description of the character's appearance but follows that character's adventures without being able to intervene in any way. Nevertheless, the character's situation and the author's

description of emotional reaction to an event in the plot is so plausibly created that the reader engages empathetically with the character, perhaps even identifying with it.

3. An audience member (a) at a "realistic" monodrama interacts with the rhetorical questions that an actor (b) fires at the audience and finds herself in a kind of intersubjective dialogue with the fully embodied agent of the playwright's imagination. The embodiment of the actor playing the role and the engagement with the audience (breaking the fourth wall) encourage not so much an identification with but a response to an "other" who is actualized and appears "real," at least for the duration of the scene.

4. An audience member (a) at a piano recital hears emotionally passionate music emerging from the instrument while the head and trunk of the pianist (b) remain motionless. Although the pianist might be inwardly embodying the virtual agency in the music, by declining any visual gestural engagement, the performer forces the listener/viewer to actualize the virtual agency in his own aurally engaged imagination.

Figure 1.2 provides a matrix in which we can situate agency in these four cases among the three axes and along the continuum of each axis: an axis (x) indicating degree of embodiment; an axis (y) indicating degree of identification, from a Self to an Other; and an axis (z) indicating whether the virtual agent is being inferred from appearance, interaction, or imagination.

Based on these axes, we may understand the video-game player (1a) as embodying the avatar (1b) as a virtual Self through identification via appearance and even more via interaction. In the case of the reader (2a), embodiment through identification with a virtual-fictional Self (2b) relies less on appearance or (direct) interaction and more on imagination. For the audience member (3a) at a "realistic" monodrama, the actor (3b) is embodied as an Other through appearance and more radically through interaction. And finally, the audience member (4a) at a piano recital attempts to embody through imagination the virtual agential Self (4b) in the music while the pianist remains a disembodied Other whose appearance forces the listener to bypass the pianist as an agential (actorial) representative of a virtual Self (despite the fact that the pianist may well be shaping the musical gestures that aurally support the listener's imaginative construction of a virtual Self within the music).

The music that I analyze also exemplifies a range of possible modes of identification, though none so radical as that of the video-game player, who is actually moving an avatar as an extension of her real volition, adapting to the fictional context of the virtual world in which the avatar has certain (limited) humanlike capacities (and a few extended, nonhuman capacities as well). Perhaps improvisation on a standard tune comes closest to this model of limited executive freedom on the part of a performer, but the listener rarely shares that degree of executive freedom.

There are special cases of virtual musical agency in which performers are far from being transparent vehicles of virtual musical agency, as in the extreme example of the pianist who appears relatively impassive (case 4). Philip Rupprecht

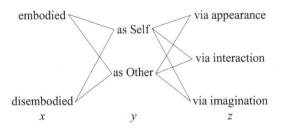

Figure 1.2. Matrix of degrees of (x) embodiment, (y) identification, and (z) mode of inference.

analyzes two examples in which performers take on more active roles. In Thea Musgrave's Chamber Concerto No. 2, an instrumental agent (the violist, "Rollo") projects an actorial role, which listeners infer from the work's dramatic trajectory, and which Rupprecht interprets as "an implicit narrative of class hierarchy" (2013, 209). In Harrison Birtwistle's *Verses for Ensembles*, performers are given "consistent musical identities" through their physical actions on stage as "player-agents" not necessarily tied to specific instruments, and they function as "stage performers of a wordless secret theater" (210). Similar performer-agents, individuated as actors to varying degrees, are found in theatricalized works of Mauricio Kagel, Luciano Berio, György Ligeti, and Dieter Schnebel (190), and—I might add—those of Peter Maxwell Davies, George Crumb, and Karlheinz Stockhausen.

Conclusion: From Objective to (Inter)Subjective

Foundational considerations for any discussion of agential inference are causality, motivation, movement, source of energy, direction of energy, goal, and (intentional) action. As a preliminary summary of how humans infer agency in everyday life, table 1.1 contrasts more objective with more subjective interpretations of the energies we perceive and experience in the world. Although that outline may suggest that our inferences are always at the level of the actual and the real, quite often in life those inferences are merely hunches based on an imaginative (re)construction of a coherent virtual world. What distinguishes real life from fiction (along the lines of the entailments outlined earlier) is that we constantly check to confirm our perceptions and inferences about the real world (often by comparing with others' perceptions and inferences) and act accordingly in ways that guarantee our survival (including not only physical but psychological and spiritual well-being). Those same strategies of agential inference may also be employed when we listen to music. In effect, we coadapt our agential inferences to an aural realm that appears very different from the real world but that will prove to have sufficient means of supporting agential inferences that are both virtual and fictional.

Notes

1. In considering unwitting gestures, I go beyond Adam Kendon, who argues that human gestures must be intentional: "A gesture is usually deemed to be an action by which a thought, feeling, or intention is given conventional and voluntary expression. Gestures are thus considered to be different from expressions of emotion, involuntary mannerisms, however revealing, and actions that are taken in the pursuit of some aim, however informative such actions may be" (1981, 28). See also Hatten 2004, 112, and Kendon 2004, 7.

2. Bruce Ellis Benson (2003) exhaustively explores these possibilities in his philosophical study of musical improvisation.

3. Steve Larson (2012, 1–2) emphasizes this point with respect to interpreting forces in music in terms of analogous physical forces in our environment (see chap. 2 for further discussion).

4. See, for example, the glissando negations of first-theme phrases in Bartók's String Quartet No. 6, first movement (mm. 30 and 35). The term "negative cadence" is my coinage, referring to those events that are gestural endings of phrases but that fail to resolve in a tonal sense. Negative cadences may be found in the works of Claude Debussy as well as Arnold Schoenberg (see chap. 10 for both a negative cadence and a negative interrogatory cadence in Schoenberg's Op. 11, no. 1).

5. For a more extensive interpretation of this sonata, see Hatten 2009a.

6. For more on *tempesta* as a topic (replacing the less precise *Sturm und Drang*), see McClelland 2014.

7. For a Peircean treatment of this argument, see Colapietro 1989.

8. For more on make-belief as an approach to meaning in the representational arts, see Walton 1990, and for its application to music, see Guck 1994.

9. This genre even has its own literary journal, *Creative Nonfiction*, founded in 1993 and published in Pittsburgh. Editor Lee Gutkind's definition of "creative nonfiction" is deceptively simple: "true stories well told." See Gutkind 2012.

2 Virtual Environmental Forces and Gestural Energies: Actants as Agential

Steve Larson's (2012) metaphorical application of physical forces to explain continuities in melodic and rhythmic patterning is one of his signature contributions to the field of music theory.[1] In my 2004 book on musical gesture, I cite his evidence for musical forces as part of a virtual physical environment with reference to which listeners can experience or infer embodied agency. I also briefly introduce agentially motivated motion, consider momentum as a supplement to his concept of inertia, and suggest the possibility of virtual musical friction (Hatten 2004, 115–16).[2] In this chapter, inspired by Larson's own quest for analogues and metaphors of motion in music, I expand on those initial speculations.[3]

Consider how we hear music when we infer Larson's musical forces of gravity, magnetism, and inertia. A melody "gives in," as he puts it, to these musical forces, and throughout his work he offers compelling examples of the typicality of such motion. Gravity, by analogy to our human experience, is the tendency to descend to a stable platform (stability here determined by tonal context). Magnetism is the tendency to move in either direction to the closest stable pitch in a given collection's alphabet, or scale. And inertia is the tendency of a given state, process, or patterning to continue. These forces can be mutually supportive, or they can counteract each other. In example 2.1 a stepwise descent from scale degree $\hat{4}$ to $\hat{3}$ in C major is impelled by both gravity (descent to a stable platform) and magnetism (moving toward the closest stable pitch—here, a half step away). Continuing by step to tonic exemplifies inertia (in tandem with gravity in this example) but contradicts magnetism, since E descends to D, a whole step away, instead of returning by half step to F.[4] Continuing stepwise motion past the tonic C to B further exemplifies inertia in that the downward motion tends to continue, here with enough force to push past a stable platform. But in this example, the magnetism of B to resolve to C may then be understood as counteracting both inertia and gravity: overcoming inertia by changing direction and overcoming (earthbound) gravity by reversing the natural downward pull. This brief example illustrates only the most basic application of the theory.

Larson also annexes Heinrich Schenker's prolongational levels: when a pattern of pitches moves as a unit (e.g., in the case of a sequence), both the pattern

Example 2.1. Larson's musical forces. Arrows indicate the directional forces of gravity (G), magnetism (M), and inertia (I).

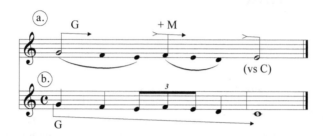

Example 2.2. Musical forces are constrained by patterning (motivic, *a*, and rhythmic, *b*), which predicts alternative closures for the same pitch pattern.

Example 2.3. Musical forces are constrained by harmonic motion; the root of a chord creates an alternative platform for gravity (F in the second measure).

Example 2.4. Musical forces cannot account for an upward leap, which counteracts magnetism (M), gravity (G), and inertia (I).

and its structural pitches will be constrained by Larson's three forces. Example 2.2 demonstrates how distinct patternings of the same six pitches, highlighting different structural pitches, can thereby imply alternative continuations to a seventh pitch.

The hierarchy of tonal patterns also enables a listener to shift among relevant gravitational platforms depending on the governing harmony. For example, if an implied harmonic root shifts from C to F, the gravitational platform will shift accordingly. In example 2.3 a melody descends by arpeggiation, implying continuation of the tonic arpeggiation to E, but the shift of harmonic underpinning produces an alternative gravitational platform, F, which provides a stronger goal for the melodic descent.

Voice leading, in a Schenkerian sense, also reveals a hierarchical tonal orientation for Larson's forces. Indeed, the diatonic tonal system helps create what I term a "virtual environment" in which movement can flow to a point of repose (Hatten 2004, 115). For Schenker, the patterns by which contrapuntal lines move inexorably to closure are the *Ur*-forms that contribute to the coherence of tonality, which may be understood as a hierarchy of resolutions—or, in Leonard B. Meyer's memorable phrase, a "hierarchy of closures" (1973, 89).

But melodies also exhibit at least some degree of freedom, which listeners can infer whenever a line does not give in to one of the three forces that Larson has theorized. Consider example 2.4. What might a listener infer when hearing an upward leap in a tonal melody, a move that immediately counters both gravity and magnetism? And what if this happens at the very beginning of a melody, thereby counteracting the inertia of stasis as well? If, as I suggest, we imagine a virtual environment in which Larson's three forces constitute environmental constraints, then such a leap would require additional energy, and the requisite energy cannot be provided by the three musical forces if it contradicts each of them. Instead, we are compelled to infer some kind of agency capable of generating what might be called initiatory energy—the hitherto unaccounted force necessary to overcome the inertial stasis of the first pitch, the gravitational pull that would press the pitch downward, and the magnetism that would compel it to move instead by step (not by leap) in whichever direction was closest or most stable. This brief example suggests that the tendency to hear musical motion as embodied depends on our hearing a succession of pitches as motivated by an energetic agency that can counteract as well as give in to the virtual environmental forces of gravity, magnetism, and inertia.[5]

But inertia has nothing to say about agency. It simply describes the persistence of an object's motion (or lack thereof). How is it that momentum is achieved by an independent agent? Consider another basic example, that of a melody that ascends by step. In its embodied interpretation—for example, as "climbing upward by step"—we understand that climb to have required energy. Magnetism may provide an assist along the way, tipping the balance whenever the option is a half step up instead of a whole step down. However, starting from tonic, a half step will occur only between $\hat{3}$ and $\hat{4}$ and then $\hat{7}$ and $\hat{8}$. Once a stepwise process begins to emerge perceptually (by the time we hear the third pitch), an interpretation of climbing implies an injection of agential energy sufficient to achieve momentum, which the *Shorter Oxford English Dictionary* defines as "the quantity of motion of a moving body" and more generally (figuratively) as "strength or continuity derived from an initial effort" (Brown 1993, 1811). The concept of musical momentum similarly implies that there must be some source of energy ("initial effort") capable of overcoming inertial stasis, and sufficient energy clearly cannot be provided by Larson's three forces to explain certain kinds of upward melodic motion, including upward leaps. Only after having achieved momentum can an unimpeded continuation of consistent motion (whether by step or by arpeggiation) reflect an analogue to the physical law of inertia. The initiating energy resulting in momentum must therefore be inferred as having its source in a presumed agent (whether human or not).

Meyer hints at momentum in *Explaining Music* when he introduces the concept of a reversal as a kind of deflection that "change[s] the implications generated by the initial, primary patternings" (1973, 119):

> Particularly when they tend toward uniformity, so that no decisive points of structural stability are established, *patterns develop a strong internal momentum.* In such cases, a marked, unequivocal break in process is needed if closure is to be effective and convincing. Since as a rule such uniform patterns take the form of linear sequences, reversals generally involve a skip followed by a change in the direction of the motion—from descending to ascending, or vice versa. (119; my emphasis)

This "break in process" as a means of countering the nonclosural momentum created by patterning reflects a principle that Meyer learned from Barbara Herrnstein Smith's *Poetic Closure* (1969).[6] By stating that "patterns develop a strong internal momentum," however, Meyer clearly suggests that momentum arises from the implicative force of a pattern. What is missing in Meyer's account is an agent (as opposed to a disembodied pattern) as source of that energy—and ultimately the implied option on the part of that agent to move in a new direction whenever there is a break in the process (e.g., a reversal).

What Meyer suggests by momentum, then, is pattern implication, and thus it is similar to Larson's inertia but at the level of the pattern and its structural pitches. Meyer draws his concept of pattern implication from the gestalt law of good continuation, as does Larson. And both go further, emphasizing not only continuation but completion. As Larson phrases it,

> Experienced listeners of tonal music expect melodic completions in which the musical forces of gravity, magnetism, and inertia control operations on alphabets in hierarchies of elaboration whose stepwise displacements of auralized traces create simple closed shapes. (2012, 110)

Larson goes beyond Meyer, however, in elaborating rules (formulated as algorithms) that can predict listener expectations for melodic continuation and completion in various tonal contexts.

But it is my concept of musical momentum, with its implied injection of initial energy by an agent, that is missing from both Meyer's and Larson's accounts. Such agential energy must be implied at a level sufficient to overcome not only the inertia of an object at rest but also such virtual environmental forces as gravity, in order to achieve continuity of motion. Furthermore, an isolated upward leap, as in example 2.4, loses its initial momentum if it does not generate another leap in the same direction. The inertia of an object in motion, then, may be understood as the result (not the cause) of sufficient energy having been invested earlier by an agent. That energy must be such that the object could plausibly have achieved the motion that will then tend to continue. The law of inertia with respect to motion assumes such prior achievement; all that inertia predicts is the continuation of achieved momentum in the absence of any impedance. Although we might incorporate the implication of pattern continuation into an enlarged concept (what might be labeled "implicative momentum"), the embodied formulation of such patterned processes still presupposes an initial investment of energy sufficient to establish a motion (by the pattern) that can then be continued (e.g., by sequencing).

But having achieved a certain momentum, will a musical motion simply continue unimpeded through a neutral environment? Or will it require a continual investment of energy to be sustained? A sense of winding down when sustaining energy begins to decline can be interpreted as the attenuation of initial momentum. The third movement of Ludwig van Beethoven's String Quartet in B♭ Major, op. 130, offers clear examples of such winding-down effects, as I argue elsewhere (Hatten 2004, 35–52). One is found in the third measure (m. 69) of example 2.5, a chromatically side-slipping sequence that suggested to Leonard Ratner (1980, 391–92) the winding down of a clockwork mechanism.[7] I would interpret his mechanical image allegorically as the breakdown of willed energy on the part of a virtual human agent.

In the physical world, friction is the effect of any environmental medium (e.g., air) that acts as a drag and slows down achieved momentum (inertial motion). A constant infusion of agential energy is required to counteract environmental friction in order to maintain a given motion. Is there a virtual musical effect akin to friction that functions as an environmental constraint alongside Larson's musical forces? A melody climbing up from tonic may require initiatory energy and implicative momentum to override gravity, but the tonic left behind would not typically be felt as frictional impedance to an ascent. However, if the tonic continues to sound as a stationary pedal point, its ongoing stasis might be interpreted as creating a drag-anchor effect on the rising melodic line, which must invest extra agential energy not only to climb but now to struggle upward against the inertia implied by tonic stasis. Oblique motion between two voices beginning on the same pitch or pitch class will generate dissonance with the first diverging step, and this dissonance between gradually expanding lines may further suggest the frictional effect of an environmental element that impedes the motion of an agent. The extra expenditure of energy required to overcome friction in addition to gravity may be reflected musically by increased dynamics in the score.

Example 2.5. Winding down of energy in Beethoven, String Quartet in B♭ Major, op. 130, third movement (mm. 67–69).

But the pedal may in turn be heard as an agent in its own right, with its own pull, so to speak.[8] The drag-anchor analogy need not assume that the pedal is part of a neutral environment of physical forces. Especially when sustained under an obliquely rising line, it may be interpretable as an opposing agential force that has been introduced into the virtual environment. As an example, consider the opening of Johannes Brahms's First Symphony (example 2.6, only string parts shown), in which the pedal C may be interpreted as an external agency, akin to Fate, against which the ascending voices are struggling to emerge and free themselves. Further agential friction is generated by contrary motion in this example. However, once we infer agential energy, we have moved beyond the analogue of

Example 2.6. Friction as an opposing agential (actantial) force: pedal point versus rising theme in the opening of Brahms's First Symphony (mm. 1–4, string parts only).

a physical environment into the more complex realm of interacting (hence, actorial) agents. Instead of friction, then, we might in this case interpret agential conflict as the more appropriate analogy.[9]

Now let us consider the implications of Larson's analogy involving magnetism. The degree of closeness of pitches in a given alphabetized collection determines their degree of attraction. But attraction is not only attributable to closeness; it also is attributable to the degree of stability of the two available pitch continuations (compare gravity, where a more stable pitch is interpreted as the platform). Thus, in C major, a chromatic F♯ is pulled magnetically to G, not to F♮, even though scale degrees $\hat{4}$ and $\hat{5}$ are equidistant (in equal-tempered tuning) from the chromatic pitch ♯$\hat{4}$.

What if the weight of a structural scale degree were conceived as analogous to physical mass? Larson's force of magnetic attraction, focused in centers of stability for the style, might in that case have been subsumed under the more global force of gravity. But as Larson points out (2012, 22–23), the physical environment for our bodies is not that of outer space, where mass determines degree of gravitational attraction (ignoring for purposes of this analogy Albert Einstein's and Stephen Hawking's more precise theories). Since we do not experience the local gravitational mass of smaller bodies or objects, Larson (2012, 95) metaphorically captures this musical force by analogy with the experience of magnetism (and by further analogy, with common metaphors of magnetism as forms of personal attraction, whether charismatic or physical).

Virtual Environmental Forces and Gestural Energies 53

Example 2.7. Repulsion as a contramagnetic force generated by contrapuntal dissonance.

Physically, the closer iron approaches a magnet, the greater the attraction; analogously, the closer a pitch approaches a center of relative stability (e.g., by half step instead of whole step), the greater the pull toward that center (leading to a resolution into that center).[10] The center need not actually be sounded—it exerts its force within the virtual environmental field established by tonality.[11] But one might note that when hearing C♯ as a chromatic passing tone moving between two scale degrees, C and D, the C drags on C♯ even while the D pulls on it. C and D have equivalent half-step attractiveness to C♯. But C would be more stable than D in the key of C major; thus the drag would be greater than the pull. Conversely, D would be more stable than C in the key of G; thus in that key the pull would be greater than the drag.[12]

The opposite of attraction is repulsion, which Larson touches on briefly in his discussion of magnetism: "Magnets (if you reverse the poles) can also repel each other" (2012, 95). Repulsion in music analogously presupposes two agents possessing a reciprocal magnetic power. Thus, the suspension in example 2.7 implies two independent voices in the right hand.

This analogy resembles the one involving friction. Here, an agential reaction against a sounding center of relative stability (which may also imply an opposing agent) produces a dissonance that repels the other pitch and forces it to move in an opposite direction from the initial agent. The prototype for this kind of agential repulsion is the 2–3 suspension.[13] In measure 2 of example 2.7, F moves closer to the opposing agent E, but instead of magnetism drawing E into F (the more stable local pitch), a dissonant repulsion forces the E to move in the opposite direction, toward D. If the dissonance first produced is a minor second, as here, the force of repulsion will be felt as correspondingly greater than in the case of a major-second dissonance—further supporting the analogy with magnetism.

Interestingly, effects akin to repulsion do not depend entirely on closeness. Consider the suspension illustrated so expressively by Mozart in his "Confutatis" movement from the *Requiem* in D Minor, K. 626 (example 2.8). Here, the "voca me" features a major third moving to a perfect fourth, which in triadic tonality is heard as a dissonance. The originally stable C is thus repulsed by the upper voice F, and C in the lower voice gives way to B. Remarkably, the acoustically greater dissonance of a diminished fifth that results is an acceptable resolution of the nontriadic dissonance of a perfect fourth, since the diminished fifth represents two chord tones in the implied dominant-seventh chord. Of course, as a tritone

Example 2.8. Repulsion as contramagnetic, from a P4 dissonance to a d5 resolution (within the implied V⁶/₅ harmony). The outer voices then resolve by magnetism (M) to respective platforms in the tonic.

the diminished fifth must also resolve, and here Larson's magnetism nicely captures those forces drawing B and F to their respective platforms. I would simply add that the diminished-fifth interval itself (a higher-level pattern) is also drawn into the more stable major-third interval, C–E, providing further evidence that stability and not solely proximity is crucial for the effect of magnetism. In effect, 1̂ and 3̂ are magnetized by their tonal stability in the style.

Table 2.1 summarizes the forces or effects that I have discussed thus far, interpretable respectively as reflecting a virtual environment (column one), contextually created by an opposing virtual agent (column two), or arising from a central virtual agent with sufficient energy to counteract environmental or other agential forces (column three).

We can now consider further interactions of these forces. Gravity presumes a (lower) stable platform, like the earth beneath our feet, to which pitches are drawn. The inertia of a descending motion (i.e., sustained agential momentum without any braking or acceleration) will result in an impact. Is it possible for the platform to absorb the shock of a gravitational impact? Consider the various kinds of impacts on a platform (such as the tonic) in cases of uninflected (unbraked) inertial contact, as shown in example 2.9. These impacts may indicate the platform's relative rigidity as well as the force of the inertial descent (which may be greater than presumed gravity would warrant, depending on the degree of already-achieved agential momentum). A hardened platform (*a*) will result in either a hard bounce or, as here, a splat; a soft platform (*b*) may be inferred from a gentle rebound or reverberation;[14] a more permeable platform (*c*) will allow a descent just past the platform before recapture by magnetism (recalling the playground game Red Rover, in which defenders' linked arms form a line to absorb the force of an attacking body; the line may bulge but nevertheless hold, forcing the body back to the original point of impact).

But the descent may also be modified by agential intervention—for example, by some kind of willed braking, as shown in example 2.10. Composers have several means of implying the braking of energetic momentum, ranging from *decrescendo* (*a*), implying a decline in the dynamic energy required to sustain momentum against friction, to *ritardando* (*b*), indicating a decline in momentum as implied by slowing down. Other braking devices include durational expansions (*c*), motivic liquidations (*d*), ornaments (especially the anticipation found in *e*), hemiola, and so forth. With sufficient braking, any inertial tendency to bulge beyond the platform can be neutralized.

Virtual Environmental Forces and Gestural Energies 55

Table 2.1. Various proposed musical forces and their implied source(s)

Virtual environment	Contextual agency	Virtual agent (subject, protagonist)
Gravity: force that pulls downward toward some platform		Initiatory energy: force needed to leap or step against gravity or magnetism or to counter inertial stasis
		creates
Inertia: not a force; rather, an acknowledgment that momentum from a virtual agent will tend to continue unless impeded by other forces		Implicative momentum: the further injection of energy needed to build up to a continuous motion, which can then imply inertia; may be a simple process (e.g., a line) or a pattern (e.g., a sequence)
		which may require
	Friction: drag/pull (may imply a second virtual agent)	Further force to overcome environmental forces or agential conflict
		possibly involving
Magnetism: attraction toward a stable center; decreases with distance (may imply a second virtual agent)		Repulsion: resistance against that center, forcing a second virtual agent to move

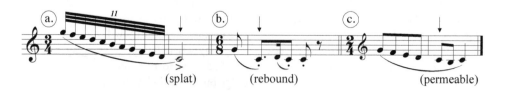

Example 2.9. Various impacts imply differing degrees of rigidity among gravitational platforms.

I have demonstrated ways in which the counteraction of musical forces can provide a strong trace of a willful agency—allowing for a sense of agential free will while moving within the constraints of a virtual environment's field of forces. I now consider the possibility that virtual environmental forces, as inferred from the fluctuations through tonal space of a common-practice melody, can themselves be manipulated to reflect a kind of agency—perhaps even willfulness on

Example 2.10. Agential braking of momentum prior to impact with a gravitational platform.

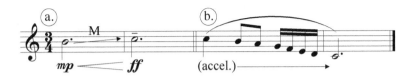

Example 2.11. Intensification of virtual environmental forces implying agential will.

the part of that agent. This claim would be provocative in its extreme form: once we began to hear music as agential, *all* actions could be interpreted as continuous reflections of willed or received energies by the subjective agent. But how might such a presupposition affect interpretation? An implied agent would be able to "own" or even "will" (as opposed to merely "give way to") environmental forces by adding agential energy to the very movements implied by those forces. In example 2.11, a crescendo (*a*) on a leading tone might imply willful resolution to the subsequent tonic, suggesting the power of an agent and supplementing the force of magnetism. An accelerated descent (*b*) might supplement the effect of gravity, implying a forceful action by the agent to ground an arrival. An agent cannot enhance inertia, however, since inertia is not a source of energy but rather the lack of impedance by the environment to either an object's continued motion or stasis. But an agent may easily appear to increase momentum by any of the musical means familiar to us—especially by the directness of an *accelerando*.

Rhythm and meter also respond to and/or reflect musical forces. Larson devotes a lengthy chapter to this phenomenon (2012, 136–79); here I simply mention the effect of the virtual environment created by meter (see Hatten 2004, 117; 2015a) in which we can experience an embodied sense of up versus down.[15] Meter accomplishes this over and over, which might suggest that all metric music flows, in the trivial sense of alternating downs and ups, and thus already implies motion. But meter's establishment of a more stable virtual environment can perhaps be

Example 2.12. Willful metric reorientation of the rhythmic motive that opens the third movement of Brahms's Third Symphony. The measures on the left (*a*) are rhythmically normalized in 3/8 meter. The measures on the right (*b*) are as notated by Brahms and justify the expressive crescendo.

defended by analogy with the constant perceptual refreshing accomplished in vision by the saccades, or ever-adjusting eye movements, that occur even when we think we are focusing on a particular spot. The bar-by-bar refreshing of a virtual environment enables us to experience gravity not only tonally but metrically as a continuous field reinstantiated by each downbeat. Once again, we can venture agential action from the energy implied by rhythms that do not conform to the metric environment. A compelling example (see Hatten 2004, 117) is found in the opening theme from the third movement of Brahms's Third Symphony. The first three measures (*a*) in example 2.12 show the melody as rhythmically normalized in 3/8 meter; the last three measures (*b*) display the theme as Brahms actually composed it. In Brahms's version there is a metric contradiction when the dotted-rhythmic upbeat motive recurs in the second bar, now positioned on the downbeat. The stretching of the previous pattern that engenders this contradiction is clearly expressively motivated (even if we cannot describe the effect adequately in words). The feeling of riding a wave may describe the loss of grounding created by the metric displacement of the motive in its second occurrence along with the expansion that extends its first statement. The expansion suggests gestural yearning, which in turn implies agential will—perhaps wanting to hold on too long (to a feeling). How might we then interpret the contradiction between agential yearning (the suspended motive) and environmental inexorability (the downbeat)? A given performance might add enough willful dynamic energy to the second anacrusis such that we hear the virtual agent insisting on the environmental inexorability of the downbeat—perhaps enhancing the effect of yearning with that very insistence while still experiencing a kind of stomach-wrenching loss of gravity. These decidedly mixed physical sensations might be further interpreted as creating a sense of existential uncertainty. But even if we cannot decide whether this or another interpretation best conforms to our reconstruction of the movement's energetic forces, we nonetheless have a better means of explaining the effects of each interpretation—and perhaps explaining our preference for one over the other. The sense that each is compelling in its own way further enriches the interpretive potency and freshness of this movement.

Example 2.13. Environmental musical forces as implied in an atonal score. Schoenberg, *Drei Klavierstücke*, op. 11, no. 1, opening theme (mm. 1–3). Used by permission of Belmont Music Publishers, Los Angeles.

Thus far I have confined my discussion to tonal music. Larson extends the same principles to the interpretation of musical forces in tonal jazz (2012, 233–37). Could the theory be further extended to post-tonal music? Consider one of the landmarks of emerging atonality, the first of Arnold Schoenberg's *Drei Klavierstücke*, op. 11 (example 2.13). Absent the scale-degree information given by common practice tonality, we cannot assume built-in environmental forces such as those hypothesized by Larson for a tonal hierarchy. Thus, any implications of forces leading to expected pitch outcomes must be earned by the work itself. Interestingly, it is possible for each of Larson's musical forces to be locally activated. Gravity pulling down to a platform pitch need not imply a traditional tonal center but simply a locally asserted pitch. Magnetism as a kind of attraction between pitches will be more heavily dependent on proximity, since the magnetic power of stability within a tonal hierarchy is absent. The effect of stability may be approximated in an atonal context by gestures that recall appoggiaturas or suspension figures. For example, the melodic movement from F to E in measures 2 to 3 suggests a rearticulated suspension, but the presumed resolution is unusual in that E is actually more dissonant with respect to the accompanying chord than the suspended F. The familiar gestural pattern, however, allows us to hear E as an implied goal tone despite the absence of consonant resolution. Finally, inertia, as the tendency of events or patterns to continue, is relevant for any linear movement (understood as a vector combining direction and force), as well as for any (roughly) sequential patterning (e.g., the descending third plus second pattern that is sequenced irregularly—by developing variation—in the top voice in mm. 1–3).[16] The sequence would suggest implicative momentum with an original agential source of energy.

I return to tonality for a final example of my own composition, the beginning of which I have foreshadowed in examples 2.3 and 2.7. In the opening measures of example 2.14, one may hear a virtual agent giving in to virtual environmental forces, but by the second system, the agent begins to express itself in opposition to that lulling environment.[17] At any rate, I hear (and compositionally intended) a sense of comfort and well-being in the first four measures, which is correlated with the melody's unproblematic "giving in" to environmental forces. The

Wordless Carol
a siciliana for Steve Larson

Example 2.14. Hatten, "Wordless Carol," a siciliana for Steve Larson.

suspensions may suggest a hint of conflict (the repulsion discussed earlier), but their immediate resolution in an overwhelmingly consonant tonal context contributes to a sense of being enfolded. The lullaby-like, siciliana-based metric and rhythmic features help support this interpretation. In the subsequent measures, the melody appears to willfully counteract the easy concession to environmental constraints and instead begins to project itself energetically, as implied by the large leaps in the melody. If we hear the willfulness of an agent as motivating this change in melodic contour, we may experience a corresponding expressive shift from well-being to emotional urgency. I interpret this willful projection as a kind of restless yearning, made poignant by the more plangent dissonances. The short piece then returns to an acceptant "giving in" to environmental forces, leading to a gentle close.

It is not hard to extrapolate from this example to countless tonal works in which agency is inferred from such flexing of melodic muscle, interpretable as increased emotional expressiveness. Such marked moments are at the heart of expression, whether found in Bach, Mozart, Chopin, or Mahler.[18] Understanding musical forces and their interaction with agential energies is one key to unlocking the mysteries of musical meaning, a project that was close to Larson's heart. "Wordless Carol" is dedicated to his memory.

A global musical affect—for example, a tragic mood or emotional modality—can also affect the virtual agent's experiencing of the virtual environment. For instance, one might speak of the "gravity" of grief. The D-minor slow movement (mesto) of Beethoven's Piano Sonata in D Major, op. 10, no. 3, creates such a heaviness of grieving in its opening theme that it appears to intensify the virtual gravitational field. By contrast, the joyful lightness in the opening of the finale to Beethoven's String Quartet in C Major, op. 59, no. 3, creates such a sense of elation that even the initial downward gestures of the fugal subject seem not to ground themselves, and the theme appears to escape the downward pressure of virtual tonal gravity even as the subject escapes the virtual metric gravity of downbeats as goals.

* * *

To summarize, many kinds of evidence support inferences of virtual human agency in tonal and metric instrumental music. I emphasize cases where the force-field constraints of tonality and meter may appear to be overcome by what we can hear as agential energies, but the thwarting of implication can occur at other structural levels as well. These include Meyer's pattern implications, the implications of various harmonic progressions, and the implications of harmonic-contrapuntal structuring at various levels, as featured in a Schenkerian analysis. Thwartings of normative behavior may suggest a willful agency, but if the disruption is strong enough, the virtual agency implied may be other than the prevailing one. In other words, sufficient contradictory force may imply an opposing agent and indeed an opposing actorial role in a larger drama. I explore this level of agency further in chapter 4.

Agency revealed by such perturbations of virtual environmental forces, or denials of implication at any level, may be characterized (or modalized) in terms of willfulness, suggesting freedom and sufficient strength (energy) to overcome normative constraints. Composers are constantly exploring such denials of implication for their expressive force; Meyer first theorized the importance of emotion arising from expectation (1956) and later implication (1973) when these were denied or deferred. What is added to the concept of implication itself is the motivational energy provided by an inferred, virtual (human) agent.

But the energy of a virtual agent may also be inferred from the dynamic shaping of a musical event, regardless of its implications, whenever it may be heard as analogous to a human gesture. By defining musical gesture as affective and significant energetic shaping through time (Hatten 2004), I emphasize many of the elements that may be imputed to a virtual agency: movement considered as action, emotional expression as revealed through that action, and the coherence of that action as goal-directed, thus presumably intentional. Indeed, what holds a gesture together for a listener is its functional coherence as a plausible movement with a plausible motivation toward a plausible goal. This mutually reinforcing evidence leads naturally to our experience of gesture as the fusion of action and expression, a fusion embodied in a virtual agent.

As discussed earlier, meter contributes to our embodied experience of a virtual environment, but it does so in a way that is dramatically different from that of tonality. In effect, meter's oscillation of downbeat and upbeat creates a constant refreshing of our perceptual field, like the saccades of the eyes that constantly refresh and fine-tune our visual perception from a series of image flashes. Tonality may seem to be a relatively constant background field, but motives occur in the foreground, and their metric placement (within a metrical force field) contributes a vital part of their gestural embodiment and expressive meaning.

Motives are also constantly being regenerated by repetition, variation, sequence, and the like, but not as consistently as meter refreshes its virtual environmental field. Furthermore, motives are often subject to acceleration or deceleration, either through literal diminution or augmentation, or through the accelerating effects of fragmentation. The agency that motives and gestures initially imply also encounters a dilemma: on the one hand, a motive or thematic gesture must be sufficiently discrete to be grasped as a coherent unit. This occurs through various forms of segmentation and foregrounding, involving rhythm, texture, dynamics, register, and the like. Along with the dynamic shape of the gesture, its individuation and identity must be established by such foregrounding. On the other hand, a virtual agent, just like a thematic gesture, must somehow preserve its identity across time. Thus, its refreshing must occur at a higher level than the recurring cycles of meter.

That next level engages with increasingly longer spans of memory. As Meyer (1973) demonstrates, what he calls "conformant" relationships (motives, themes) must recur often enough such that the ear can remember their shape and compare them with slightly different versions to discover an underlying "sameness" (as virtual agential identity) that emerges from an embodied (thematic) gesture. Perhaps a better term at this point would be "continuity"—since the discrete segment will now be the "grain" of a continuous process at a higher level (see Hatten 2004, 239). Again, Meyer's (1973) discussion of continuity and closure offers a comparable hierarchical model, but a more flexible model for thematic gesture is provided by Schoenberg's concept of developing variation; by helping to ensure a continuous thematic discourse, developing variation supports the continuity of an inferred virtual agency.

Before their increasing focus on motivic-thematic-gestural discourse in music, however, composers employed more basic means to secure musical continuity: through continuous timbre, texture, or line (melody), or some combination of these (creating the contrapuntally integrative *melos* I explore in chap. 4). Indeed, at every level (or in every dimension) the continuous is made up of discrete elements that form its "grain."[19]

But consider affect, which emerges from both consistent and nonnormative musical behavior, and which can range from euphoric to dysphoric. How is it possible that affect can contribute to the creation and preservation of a virtual agential identity if it appears to be all over the map? First, affect provides evidence of human relevance and significance. Second, a composer can direct affective states (moods) and expressions (emotions) as part of a coherent dramatic trajectory or narrative plot such that a virtual agent can plausibly be understood as both expressing and experiencing a series of moods and emotions—and perhaps changing or developing in response to those experiences (Robinson 2005; Robinson and Hatten 2012). I return to this topic in later chapters.

Finally, there is a kind of entrainment effect for virtual agency that is analogous to that for meter: once one commits to a meter or a virtual agency, it is robust in preserving the filter or lens through which we find coherence in what we perceive. It takes a significant (and hence potentially contra-agential) effort to break up our identification of (or with) an ongoing virtual agent. We have a propensity to make even contrasting gestures and affects part of at least a minimal story: that of the ongoing adventures of a protagonist, say. But before elaborating that actorial level in chapter 4, I turn in chapter 3 to the crucial grounding of embodiment, by means of which we endow virtual actants with human agency and coherent identity.

Notes

This chapter is drawn in part from Robert S. Hatten, "Musical Forces and Agential Energies: An Expansion of Larson's Model," *Music Theory Online* 18, no. 3 (2012), http://mtosmt.org/issues/mto.12.18.3/mto.12.18.3.hatten.html. Since then, John Peterson has elaborated on several of the ways through which we may infer intentional agency, including "gesture, contradiction of musical forces, unexpected event, change of state, repetition/restatement, and conflict" (2014, 44). See also Rebecca Thumpston's (2015) work on agency in twentieth-century British cello music.

1. As Larson gathered converging evidence for his theory of musical forces, I was honored to help shepherd his resulting book, *Musical Forces: Motion, Metaphor, and Meaning in Music*, to publication in January 2012. As early as 2003, during his residency in Bloomington, Indiana, I had shared with him some of my own conjectural expansions to his theory from the perspective of my work on gestural agency and its energies.

2. Steve graciously credited some of these ideas in two sections from the last chapter of *Musical Forces*. In "Forces and Intention" (2012, 315), he mentions my characterization of his musical forces as environmental as well as the relationship between those forces and "a perceived or implied *source* of gestural [agential] energy" (Hatten 2004, 115–16; emphasis in original). In "Other Forces" (Larson 2012, 320), he notes my suggested addition of musical friction to his set of musical forces (Hatten 2004, 116).

3. For an additional extension of Larson's theory of musical forces, see BaileyShea 2012. Larson briefly notes the prior work of theorists on "metaphors of motion and forces" (2012, 2). Chief among these was Ernst Kurth (1886–1946), who pioneered what is today referred to as musical energetics (Rothfarb 2002). Kurth speculated, with the tools of early twentieth-century psychology and philosophy, about tonal space (including a potential analogue to gravity), melodic and harmonic energy, and tensions produced by a concept of musical movement. For helpful summaries, see Rothfarb 1988 and Tan 2013.

4. However, if we take harmony into account and assume that D and F are locally stable as members of a V^7 chord, then D would be more stable than F (the seventh), and hence D's greater stability might make it magnetically more attractive despite its slightly greater distance from E.

5. See note 2 for Larson's acknowledgment of such agential "intention."

6. As Meyer acknowledges, "The vital importance of closure in the articulation of forms and processes was made clear to me by Barbara H. Smith's book, *Poetic Closure: Or Why Poems End* (Chicago: University of Chicago Press, 1969)" (1973, 81n2).

7. I examine mechanical virtual agency in chapter 10.

8. Compare Matthew BaileyShea's (2012) use of the term "pull."

9. Or, in BaileyShea's (2012) terminology, we might interpret the pedal as a nonsentient "elemental force."

10. Larson clearly defines magnetism "so that it describes the attraction of any unstable pitch to the closest stable pitch" (2012, 92), as discussed earlier (see also note 4).

11. Larson (2012, 55) cites Jamshed J. Bharucha's (1984) distinction between tonal hierarchies (independent of pieces in which they occur) and event hierarchies (ordered with respect to the time of the piece within which they occur). My "virtual environmental field established by tonality" would be an example of a tonal hierarchy.

12. An evaluation of dragging versus pulling may be useful as a refinement of the experience of magnetism as it interacts with gravity.

13. As Larson notes, "The analogy to a string of 2–3 suspensions, in which two voices seem to push each other away each time they are a step apart, might be a good example of this phenomenon" (2012, 95).

14. Alexandra Pierce (2007, 120–35) has theorized a nuancing of timing in performance that allows for reverberation in the finishing envelope of arrival gestures. Reverberation then becomes the first stage in the juncture required for elegantly embodied transitions between phrases.

15. For more on the embodiment of meter and the importance of "focal impulses," see John Paul Ito, forthcoming.

16. For further discussion of the entire eleven-measure theme, see example 10.1.

17. To hear my recorded performance, go to example 14 at http://mtosmt.org/issues/mto.12.18.3/mto.12.18.3.hatten.html.

18. See, for example, my interpretation of marked expressive moments in the slow movement of Mozart's Piano Sonata in F Major, K. 533, in chapter 6.

19. For more on this conception of continuity, see Hatten 2004, 239–66, which examines textural continuity (e.g., perpetual motion) in the Classical style and explores moves toward textural and thematic plenitude as a compositional strategy, notably in Classical fugues.

3   Virtual Embodiment: From Actants to Virtual Human Agents

Whenever listeners interpret a musical movement as an action, they are inferring a virtual actant as an individual source of the force, whether specified as human or not. Virtual agency is humanized whenever the listener can infer actions as willfully intended, expressed, or experienced. In chapter 2, I demonstrate how traces of humanlike agency may appear whenever we interpret sequences of pitches as willful movements overcoming the constraints of those virtual environmental forces associated with tonality and meter. But that is just one way in which actants can take on more human characteristics. In this chapter I investigate how virtual agents can be virtually embodied with other human attributes. Virtual embodiment is to be distinguished from the kind of embodiment other scholars have been exploring of late, in which listeners and performers exhibit corresponding musical energies in their own bodies as they listen and perform. Specifically, virtualizing as an imaginative inference entails a degree of separation between virtual musical agents and their actualizing sources (e.g., performers). It may indeed seem paradoxical that virtual embodiment involves the capacity to disembody (detach) from actual agents prior to reembodying (and "enminding") virtual human agents in virtual-fictional worlds. I illustrate this process with a speculative historical account of how virtualizing would have become an essential key to musical understanding, especially with respect to instrumental music. I then explore a wide range of musical elements that support the human (re)embodiment and "enmindment" of a virtual agent. Following a brief consideration of the relationship of body and mind in the construction of our sense of self, I conclude that our reconstruction of a coherent virtual agency in music owes much to strategies we routinely employ in constructing our own coherence as a self-aware person. Finally, through analysis of a complete prelude by Johann Sebastian Bach, I demonstrate how embodied virtual agency can help integrate gesture and emotion, grounded in stylistic understandings but sensitive to rhetorical strategies, into a coherent (if flexible) interpretation of virtual emotional experience. From the standpoint of this early synthesis, chapters 4–6 delve deeper into the issues of agential identity, perseverance, actorial roles, subjectivity, and—once more—emotion.

Historical Precedents for Virtual Embodiment

A starting point for virtual embodiment is our capacity to identify with actual human agents who are singing and perhaps dramatically gesturing. Emotional contagion, moving with the music, and singing or dancing are obvious signs of such engagement.[1] Before fixed roles were established for performers and well before the advent of musical notation, listeners were capable of various forms of participation, communally sharing spontaneous (or ritualized) expressions of joy or sorrow. These forms of coparticipation may well have benefited from the sensorimotor input of mirror neurons, triggering imitative actions based on previous familiarity.[2] Thus, there are rich implications for the development of a virtualizing capacity, even in the presence of actual agents. If actual agents are not present to the eye and virtual movements have to be inferred from sound alone, our sensorimotor system has sufficient intermodal capacities to allow us to imagine the source of sounds and many of the characteristics of actual agents producing them (male vs. female, large vs. small, euphoric vs. dysphoric).[3]

But with the rise of orchestral ensembles, instrumentalists were seated in regimented rows that severely limited individualized motions even when these were visible (and they could be obscured when orchestras were positioned below the stage in an opera house). For listeners, this progressive disembodiment of the actual agential sources may have helped encourage a comparable (and compensatory) reembodiment of those sources as virtual agents. For example, a group of orchestral violinists playing the same sequence of pitches would support a cognitive shift of imputed agency from that of a single performer to the merger of several performers' energies in creating a single line—metaphorically, a single voice. To be sure, multiple singers also realize a single "voice" in a choral work—but the variety of vocal characteristics among even a single voice category (e.g., soprano) is such that one can hear a kind of timbral heterophony suggestive of a communal agency. Indeed, the congregational role of chorale singing could also support a sense of communal envoicing from a liturgical perspective. By contrast, increasingly well-trained orchestral violins could create the illusory merger of sound into a singular voice, and the absence of verbal text would further support the cognitive shift toward hearing that voice in terms of its virtual agency.

The identification of a melodic or contrapuntal line as a voice, however, is a telling metaphor in that it acknowledges the primordial role of the voice in communicating the nuances of human emotion. Through the intonation curves of speech and various paralinguistic gestures of the voice, speakers intentionally communicate, and unwittingly reveal, much of the emotional force and meaning behind their verbal utterances (see Hatten 2004, 106–7, 131–32). It is not surprising, then, that instrumental performers (and instrument builders) would attempt to mime the expressive features of the voice. Along with dynamics, contour, articulation, and timing, instruments such as the violin can create an individuating vibrato characteristic of a human voice while also capturing some of its emotional qualities. Thus, a violin soloist could also virtually suggest an actual singer (see Cumming 2000, 24–28).

Despite such means of capturing vocality, including declamatory prosody and expressive intonation, Western music (whether vocal or instrumental) exhibits several marked differences from speech. Discrete pitches and rhythms based on regular divisions are not as obviously speechlike. The degree of repetition in tonal music exceeds that of any spoken language, even if echoed to some extent by meter and rhyme in oral poetry.[4] Listeners, then, were able to hear the human expressiveness of musical lines not only by recognizing the miming of speech gestures but by virtualizing a set of stylistic conventions that moved beyond such intonations.[5] I explore several of these conventions (primarily tonal and metric/rhythmic) in chapter 2, noting their strong grounding in analogues to human movements (not necessarily human sounds). The challenge to hear in this way was also spurred by the progressive disembodiment of actual performers as (ensemble) instrumentalists in the ways just noted.[6] This physical disembodiment helped foster a compensatory reembodiment or virtualizing of agents as implied by the sounding notes themselves.[7] Reproducing the rhythmic/metric grooves of dance types was yet another gestural inheritance of purely instrumental music (Zbikowski 2008, 2012). And still other avenues for embodiment in instrumental music were provided by musical topics and their dramatic deployment in various expressive trajectories (Hatten 1994, 2004).

The seemingly abstract stylistic conventions of tonality and form underlying purely instrumental sonatas, however, led to a telling reaction by contemporaneous listeners who experienced difficulty in making such an imaginative leap into the virtual. When Bernard Le Bovier de Fontenelle (c. 1750) famously posed the question "Sonate, que me veux-tu?" (Sonata, what do you want—or ask—of me?[8]), he was essentially seeking access to meaning in performances not illuminated by texts, programs, or the full gestural embodiment of, for example, a standing solo violinist (as opposed to the more limited gestures of seated chamber instrumentalists). Without the capacity to enter imaginatively into virtual worlds where virtual human agents could be heard as experiencing, expressing, and acting, how could one begin to account for such strange emanations by nearly disembodied sound-producers (to put the case most brutally)? Fontenelle's question is revelatory of the lack (by some contemporaneous listeners) of a crucial competency—or set of competencies—in virtualizing actantial energies into embodied agents and actors and internalizing the subjectivity of their expressive journeys.[9]

We might also blame this virtualizing gap on the performers Fontenelle heard, if indeed they lacked the capacity to humanize (by reembodying) the virtual agency implied by the music as opposed to a more mechanical reproduction of notated sounds.[10] As violinist Giuseppi Cambini observed in 1803,

I have always thought that he who said, sonata, what do you want of me? was right only because the musician who produced and executed the sonata was at fault. . . . Had it been otherwise, that man of wit would not have had the time to take exception; he would instead have cried out, sonata, you touch me . . . you move me! ([c. 1803] 1972, 22, cited in Le Guin 2006, 276n25)

Thus, a competency in hearing virtual agency need not have required expert tuition; it might have been entrained by listeners who could follow the actual embodiment of a skillful performer and more readily make the transfer involved in imaginatively hearing virtualized agents capable of humanlike behavior.

Arnie Cox (2006, 2016), with his mimetic hypothesis and extended exploration of the ways we are humanly attuned to music (as evidenced by our irrepressible tendencies to move to the music we hear), has assembled an impressive array of biological, psychological, and cognitive evidence illustrating the ease with which we can hear and respond to music in an embodied way. His research further grounds my own work on interpreting human gestures in music.[11] But my brief introduction to embodiment thus far suggests that to hear virtually goes beyond directly embodying music's energies (i.e., in one's own body). A listener is also able to distill a virtual embodiment that is not always—or necessarily—actually embodied in performers (or listeners).[12] That initial distillation should not be confused with abstraction, since its aim is not to objectify but rather to subjectify.[13] Distilling by performers is, of course, one way of instilling qualities of human embodiment into virtual agents, but it is not the only way. As I argue in chapter 2, listeners have the capacity to hear an imagined virtual world in which (reembodied) virtual agents operate within a virtual environment constructed by the music itself. This is the crucial move from actual to virtual in the realm of purely instrumental music; a listener is able to displace identification from those living beings producing the sound to those virtual human agents inhabiting the sound, in the world of sound itself.[14]

An immediate rejoinder to this claim is that one may hear chamber music as a conversation among equals, an analogy formulated in various ways beginning in the 1770s, including a remark by Johann Wolfgang von Goethe in 1829 (Klorman 2016, 20–21). The turn-taking of parts along with ensemble cueing by performers enact a continuous dialogical discourse that was viewed as analogous to a conversation.[15] More recently, these insights have been theoretically refined with the positing of "imaginary musical agents" by Roger Graybill (2011, drawing on Maus 1997), "sociability" by Sutcliffe (2013), and "multiple agencies" by Klorman (2013, 2016), in order to capture the interactive and even competing roles that are assumed by virtual agents who become, in effect, virtual actors in the musical discourse.[16] But virtual agents or actors need not correspond to actual performers for at least two obvious reasons.[17] First, there would be too many instances of simultaneous "talk" to emulate a rational conversation (Sutcliffe 2003a, 187). Second (as Graybill [2011] emphasizes), our imaginative construction of a virtual agent may easily shift to encompass contributions by more than one of the actual performers. For example, when the first and second violins play in parallel thirds, we may opt to hear the doubling as an enrichment of a single virtual agency, instead of a duet between two agents. Thus, although the performers' gestures may make the virtual dialogical element of the music more vivid, competent listeners may also focus on other dialogues as created within the music—for example, two pairs of instruments may project only two dialoguing "voices" instead of four.

Cues for Virtual Embodiment

Reembodiment involves distilling sound from that produced by an actual performing agent and instilling it as virtualized in terms of an agency that moves within the music.[18] But reembodiment still depends on the cueing of some degree of human verisimilitude with respect to at least some aspect of human experience. From the lowest levels upward (although even lower levels may involve cultural as well as biological or physiological motivations), a listener's inferences will include the following:

1. The interpretation of one or more actants as implying parts of a single virtual agent by miming the physicality of a human agent—moving, and hence acting or reacting, within a realm of virtual environmental forces (as discussed in chap. 1–2)
2. The interpretation of a musical gesture as energetic shaping through time with kinetic and affective qualities akin to those of actual humans in any sensorimotor modality (as further elaborated in Hatten 2004)
3. The interpretation of a musical line as a voice having intonations and affective qualities akin to those of actual human vocalization including, but not limited to, speech (e.g., a melody played by a violin, as elaborated in Cumming 2000)
4. The interpretation of a directed motion to an eventual arrival or resolution as a virtual agent's intentional, willed effort to reach a destination or achieve a goal (as elaborated by Schenker)[19]
5. The modality with which such virtual being is expressed, or virtual actions are undertaken, by which degrees of will, ability, or belief (as in the Greimassian modalities introduced by Eero Tarasti [1994]) are ascribed to a virtual human agent
6. The emotions that are heard as evoked and simultaneously understood as being expressed by a virtual human agent (as elaborated in Robinson and Hatten 2012)
7. The extent to which a virtual human agency appears to cohere and sustain an identity across change, interpreting some change as internalized growth and persisting throughout a work (e.g., through motivic developing variation, as part of a musical discourse)

The first six inferences would be sufficient to make an immediate connection with a musical event, gesture, or progression as analogous to characteristically human qualities. But the seventh inference is crucial in its concern for those means by which a composer or listener can sustain a given virtual agency, analogous to a singular virtual human agent, throughout a movement or entire work.

In addition to these processive means by which musical events can cue and over time entrain listeners to hear imaginatively in terms of virtual agency, we can add certain stylistic and genre-based conventions that may presuppose such hearing in advance:

8. The contribution of textures with their preestablished conventions of fore-grounding (e.g., a melody-and-accompaniment texture may foreground the melody as a singular agential voice; an imitative texture may fore-ground a dialogical relationship among actantial or agential voices)[20]
9. The contribution of certain topics with their preestablished general expressive meanings and agential implications, with respect to points 1–6 (e.g., a sigh or *pianto* figure implies a sigher, a *Ländler* implies a rustic or less-sophisticated agency, and a hymn topic implies a spiritually oriented agency)
10. The contribution of conventional genres imported topically, with their already established types of agency (e.g., a sonata may appropriate a concerto's textural oppositions, implying an individual in dialogue with a more collective agency)[21]
11. The presuppositions of lyric, dramatic, narrative, and epic modes that imply particular human agents:
    a. Lyric implies an individual subjectivity expressing itself.
    b. Dramatizing the lyric implies an internal conflict, as basic to drama, in a lyric utterance.
    c. Dramatic (as in a concerto or sonata or symphony) projects the dialogical and implies not only actoriality but the interaction of two or more agents.
    d. Lyricizing the dramatic (as in a solo sonata) deepens the emotion of a single agent or implies that a dramatic interaction is between or among parts of a single, all-embracing subjectivity (i.e., an internal struggle within the agent).
    e. Narratizing the dramatic implies a narrative agency, as staged by the work, that orders the temporal sequence of events or comments on the enacted drama (see chap. 7). This agency may also imply a self-reflective subjectivity.
    f. Epic implies not only a narrative agency but at times a mythic consciousness (as one kind of subjectivity). As a genre, the epic may also introduce lyrical and dramatic elements.

In the next two chapters I explore still other ways in which virtual actorial roles and a more comprehensive virtual subjectivity can further support an interpretation of virtual embodiment.

Virtualizing, Embodiment, and "Enmindment" in Human Life: Constructing Our Sense of Self

To what extent does the experience of our own body as it relates to our sense of self prepare us for the leap to imaginatively embodying a virtual human agent in music? Are there things our bodies do on their own that seem to contradict our sense of self as being in control of our own bodies—in effect, counteracting the naïve assumption that our bodies act only according to our will? If we have experienced such gaps within our own, otherwise functionally integrative body-mind-self, we may be more willing to grant the emergence of virtual agency whenever the energies of sounding music separate themselves from the performances of actual agents.

The autonomic nervous system keeps our heart beating and our lungs breathing, whether or not we are aware of these functions. Our muscular reflexes are traces of an evolutionary engine geared toward our survival, preceding and at times even circumventing our direct will. If we inadvertently touch a hot stove, our hand jerks back before the message of pain can make it into our consciousness. A tap just below the bent knee evokes a response that may appear humorously ungrounded by any conscious will or intention. To take a less pleasant example, most of us cannot will ourselves to vomit without physical or medical intervention. Thus, when one vomits, the act appears to lack the willed intention of the self. How might one experience it? I have the disorienting sensation of being carried along on the surge of my body's independent purging reflex. This experience might place my sense of embodiment at peril, in that I experience a paradox of two agencies in my "divided" self, simultaneously responding to (as patient) that which my own body has enacted (as agent) without my conscious willing (as agent), but with my unavoidable coparticipation (as . . . what?).

Philosophers have rightly sought to downplay the binary opposition of mind and body (along with a different binary, between reason and emotion), but such common cases force us at the very least to reframe duality as that between consciousness of the self as willing and controlling (through the central nervous system) one's body and acknowledgment of the body as having its own actions that can ignore or override (through the actions of the autonomic nervous system) one's conscious, willing self. Such overriding suggests the evolutionary wisdom of reflexes: they can respond to the environment with a speed and deliberation (and determination) not always ensured by the conscious will.[22]

The autonomic system can thus accomplish what it would not be safe to presume individuals could effectively will—for example, the unimaginably painful effort of giving birth. How strange that one of the most important events ensuring survival of our species, that of giving birth, should be largely out of a woman's direct control (labor is experienced, not directly willed), despite her coparticipation in the act (by pushing) and her enabling of the act (by Lamaze breathing and other forms of mental relaxation that free the contracting muscles from interference). It is easy to assume that what we experience as under the control of our will is fundamental to our sense of self. Instead, the body's capacity to control *us* during times of extreme survival stress should be clearly evident.

The conscious will is not to be dismissed as being an evolutionary loser in such immediate battles with the body's reflexes, however. The will has the ability to extend the body's capacities in ways we have yet to understand. We hear anecdotally of parents, apparently superhumanly empowered by the determined will to save their children, able to lift impossibly heavy objects off their children's bodies. Or there is the apocryphal story of a prisoner in the Stalinist era who refuses to die, despite being exposed to extreme cold in the Siberian wastes. Is this the flip side of embodiment, for which we should invent a new word? Perhaps "enmind-ment" would serve. Might conscious thought (motivated by a will to survive) galvanize the body with apparently superhuman power, and could this in turn enhance our sense of self? Or is this yet another example of the body finding its own means of exceeding itself? Granted, in the case of superhuman lifting, the brain can send neurochemicals that prompt the endocrine system to supply the muscles with enough adrenaline to exceed their normal load. While this is a safe, materialist explanation (assuming it to be true), it also suggests that an emergent power of the will (as "mind over matter") conditions our awareness of embodi-ment as subject to the conscious mind. (Of course, this flooding of chemicals may also be the result of another reflex, triggered by our conscious appraisal of danger but ultimately beyond our conscious control.)

The lesson to be drawn from these extreme cases is that our sense of self must ultimately be constructed by our imagination to accommodate the gaps between an at-times independently functioning body and an at-times emergent con-sciousness. Richard Hallam goes as far as to claim that "our common-sense idea of self as some sort of entity is a human construction, in effect, a virtual reality" (2009, 3). He suggests linking embodiment with a sensed person (as opposed to a self) and construing that person as "a kind of hybrid entity, a biological human being who comes to be perceived by others and who perceives her or himself in ways that are shaped by the society in which they live" (5). The construction of this person, then, would add social interaction and dialogue to the equation.

We need not be scientists or philosophers to recognize that there are still gaps to be explored between the will of the body and the will of the self or person. What is remarkable is the way consciousness attempts, and usually succeeds, in constructing an integrated self or person that we can sense as possessing a coher-ent identity. Having become masters at this virtual, constructed, and emergent integration of our actual parts, we can then draw on this integrative competency in interpreting musical energies as actantial, embodied into virtual agents that in turn have the character of integrated selves acting within a virtual environ-ment. A virtual agent is thus emergent in its capacity to go beyond its embod-ied limits by being "enminded" with intentionality and other aspects of human subjectivity.

The human self is also emergent in its capacity to imagine (plan, project, fan-tasize) in such a way that humans are able not only to construct a sense of self but to create what they need to sustain that self from what is afforded by the world around them—whether by imagining the planting of crops or the taming of ani-mals or the building of shelters or the creation of social structures.[23] We can draw on these same imaginative capacities whenever we interpret music, using them to reconstruct the virtual and fictional worlds that a particular musical work implies—and constructing our notion of a virtual self that emerges from those more automatic functions of music's actantial body.

The capacity to imagine virtual emotions and affective encounters has not only a biological but also a cultural history enhanced by language and literature (from oral to written storytelling and from chronicle to history and fiction) and further strengthened by unions of music and words—in song, religious/musical ritual, or opera. These all provide motivations for hearing (and creating) instrumental music as involving virtual agents that mime action or reaction and experience emotions or thoughts in trajectories of human significance. I pursue some threads of that history in chapter 5.

Degrees of Emotional Embodiment and Identity: Compositional Strategies as Stylistically Grounded and Aesthetically Warranted

Although listeners can easily imagine virtual agents and worlds for any music and lose themselves in such subjectivizing of the music, how might composers of particular musical works constrain and direct such imaginative participation? And how might listeners reconstruct the emotions of virtual agencies presupposed by the strategies of a musical work and its style? Granted that any listener is also warranted to go further in developing the significance of these virtual emotions for their "actual" lives, I have nevertheless argued for what I call "aesthetically warranted emotions" (Hatten 2010a; see also chap. 6) as a subset of the wider range of emotions that listeners actually experience. Here, I want to make an analogous argument for stylistically and strategically warranted virtual agents and worlds; these warranted contexts serve to constrain the range of interpretations that are freely and often rather subjectively constructed by listeners. In so doing, I assume a degree of intersubjective agreement for stylistically warranted emotions. But I anchor my claims in evidence and prior reconstructions of the compositional strategies previously outlined, including musical forces and agential energies, style types of gestures and topics, conventions of genres and modes, and the extraordinary resources of tonality—all as contributing to the embodiment of a virtual agent through emotion.

Embodiment through Emotion: Bach, Prelude in E♭ Minor, WTC I, BWV 853

An example serves to illustrate how these musical elements provide mutually supportive evidence for the embodiment of virtual human agency through an analogous expression of human emotion. I argue that this agency undergoes a process of emotional development in a dramatic trajectory, leading to a virtual subjectivity that encompasses both internal and external agency.[24] I have chosen a relatively early example from common-practice tonal music, Bach's Prelude in E♭ Minor from the first book of the *Well-Tempered Clavier* (example 3.1), in part to emphasize how much is already available for interpretation as early as 1722.[25]

The emergence of an expressively marked opposition between minor and major mode as a convention in the eighteenth century does not mean that a minor mode work is merely "sad." Its expressed emotional states or activities may range further, from poignant reflection or ritualized grieving to personal suffering, but other musical oppositions are required to make those finer

Example 3.1. Bach, Prelude in E♭ Minor, WTC I, BWV 853.

distinctions.[26] For example, the meter of the Prelude in E♭ Minor is triple, and a competent listener will hear the topical influence of the sarabande, which by the time of Bach had become a dignified dance in slow tempo (made slower here by the choice of $\frac{3}{2}$ instead of $\frac{3}{4}$ meter). The sarabande meter, topically imported into this arialike prelude, contributes its own associations of high dignity and solemn seriousness.[27] The melody's dotted rhythms would likely have been performed more sharply, as double-dotted, drawing on the conventions of the French overture, another imported topic that contributes its own associations of high ceremonial nobility and seriousness. These stylistically conventional topics, overlapping and mutually supportive in their expressive associations, provide sufficient redundancy to ensure the basic emotional purport of the prelude. The blending of aria (split into a dialogical duet in mm. 4³ff. and mm. 17ff.), sarabande, and French overture topics constitute a purely musical trope in which a unique expressive meaning is emergent—and such tropes may lead to more specific emotional interpretations as well as more distinctive emotional interactions.[28] For example, the shared dignity of these topics suggests a virtual agent who is not inclined to extreme outbursts (although the expressive force of large or dissonant melodic intervals indicates an extremity of arialike expression that is being moderated by the decorum of chordal accompaniment, at times suggestive of a hymn in sarabande meter). Our empathy for such a virtual agent may lead to even greater emotional involvement.

The expressed and embodied state of sadness at the opening is thus aesthetically warranted, although in the first two measures it is at first a relatively generic sadness, perhaps experienced initially as a relatively unmarked mood. Sadness quickly becomes more nuanced, and hence marked as more emotional, through the use of specific dissonances long associated with visceral expressions of sadness, such as those created by suspensions and marked leaps to appoggiaturas. The stepwise, descending resolution of these marked dissonances creates the conventional *pianto*, or sigh figure (as in the suspensions circled in mm. 3 and 13), and the discontinuous resolution of dissonance to consonance (for the 7–6 suspensions circled in mm. 9 and 11) creates an emotionally freighted expressive declamation characteristic of eighteenth-century *Empfindsamkeit* (the expression of deep sentiment).

76 *A Theory of Virtual Agency for Western Art Music*

The unfolding emotional journey is marked by still other conventional features of the style. Modulations to the minor dominant (B♭ minor) in measure 10 and subdominant (A♭ minor) in measure 17—as opposed to the more hopeful major mediant and submediant (G♭ and C♭ major, only briefly hinted in mm. 5–6)—help sustain the tragic character of the discourse, as well as the embodied emotion of a virtual agent expressing grief in melodic response. Even the home key of E♭ minor, in a well-tempered tuning, would sound more dissonant than in today's equal temperament and hence could exacerbate the expression of grief.

To summarize thus far, although the dignity of the opening hymnlike accompaniment may suggest a degree of reserve on the part of a virtual agent experiencing profound sadness, the arialike prelude's ongoing tragic trajectory is strongly marked by unusual events that further enhance the *empfindsamer* character of the music in ways that suggest the active responses of a virtual agent. Implications denied often have expressive effects (Meyer 1956, 1973; Huron 2006). When implications are denied in the prelude, the listener is not only surprised but may share in the apparent suffering of a virtual agent. Those denials are intensified when achieved by sudden reversals or other rhetorical gestures, which I have defined as those events that break the unmarked flow of the musical discourse (Hatten 2004, 135–37). Thus, instead of merely sharing the general mood or experiencing the lower-level emotions of a ritualized grieving by both individual and choral voices, we may experience a more intense feeling of emotion prompted by a series of wrenching shifts. This process can lead us to interpret the prelude as expressing the less predictable fluctuations of a very personal experience of profound sadness. Granted, we do not know the cause of this sadness, but we can share, intersubjectively, the trajectory of its working out as the dramatic mise-en-scène of a virtual human agent, one who is feeling genuine human emotions.[29] In the case of a solo piano piece, it is natural to identify this virtual agency with the "suffering" expression of the performer, who actualizes and manifests the emotion embodied by the virtual agent. In turn, listeners can enactively imagine or simulate that grief to varying degrees in their own emotional responses.

Among the surprises that heighten the emotional intensity of the prelude are several marked uses of the diminished-seventh sonority. By itself emblematic of angst, the sonority is used twice to create unexpected tonal shifts (as opposed to typical common-chord modulations): first to A♭ minor on the downbeat of bar 17 and then back to E♭ minor at bar 20 (following the cadence in A♭ minor on the downbeat). Near the end of the prelude (bars 32–35), a four-bar expansion of the diminished seventh as vii°⁷ in E♭ minor follows a rhetorical shift that displaces the vii°₄ of iv in measure 31 (the intensification is enhanced by the nonsyntactic shift of harmonies as well as by the diminished-seventh sonorities themselves). Temporal expansion of the vii°⁷ is expressively complemented by registral expansion outward to create an unmistakable (and, within the context of this style, nearly unbearable) gesture of emotional intensification, leading to an expressive climax on a high C♭ in the solo voice at the end of bar 35.[30]

Throughout, textural changes also create hints of recitative, interpretable as a more intimate mode of expressive discourse, in those passages where the accompaniment is sparser. The colorful Neapolitan-sixth chord (bar 26) is used not only conventionally to mark an impending cadence but rhetorically to mark a shift in texture toward more direct discourse (note the rests in the left hand that leave the solo voice isolated). The shock of this Neapolitan can be interpreted as a moment of sudden insight—perhaps even tragic recognition—in a dramatic trajectory where the virtual agent has become a virtual actor or protagonist.

The cadenza-like elaboration of the solo line (during the rests in the accompaniment following its Neapolitan and V_2^4 interjections) leads to a high C♭ in bar 28 in clear anticipation of the later climax in bar 35. This poignant dissonance is barely resolved to B♭, however, before the high solo register is brutally undercut by the return of the chordal texture midway through bar 28 (note that the V_2^4 in m. 27 is left unresolved). The implacable cadential chords may be interpreted as a marked harmonic interruption of the soloist's climactic plaint, suggesting in turn an external agency with the power to disrupt the emotional trajectory of the protagonist by means of an intrusion of inescapably tragic reality. The accompanimental chords have emerged here from their initial state as unmarked, objective background (enhancing the virtual environment with a mood of tragic grieving) and taken on the role of a more independent, external agent acting in dramatic or dialogical opposition to the internal agent implied by the solo melodic voice.[31] Within the model of a tragic drama, this external agency could be identified with Fate and its E♭ minor goal as inexorably tragic. The deceptive cadence in measure 29 would then function not merely structurally, to delay the expected perfect authentic cadence, but expressively, to heighten the protagonist's anguished attempt to avoid that reality—here, by means of an exceedingly poignant 7–6 suspension (B♭ to A♭) in an inner (alto) voice, suitably surrounded, as if trapped, by the fateful cadential progression that it just barely evades.

An expressive plot (here, tragic) and a virtual agent (here, in the actorial role of a protagonist who is expressing emotions of great sadness while suffering disruptions that lead to heightened states of feeling) are mutually supportive and stylistically grounded interpretations. A listener initially simulating or experiencing in imagination the sad mood of this prelude may become emotionally engaged by the various means that Bach employs to intensify that mood. With investment in an ongoing emotional drama, the listener may continue to identify with an implied protagonist (virtual actor) and more deeply experience the process of unfolding emotions correlated with those that the implied protagonist is expressing or experiencing. Bach's marked rhetorical gestures offer clear evidence of his intent to intensify key points in the expressive drama. Furthermore, the listener's emotional response may provide clues to those important events, even when that listener is unaware of their structural significance.[32]

A performer (as an actual agent constrained by an interpretation of virtual agency in the music) may bring out still other features that may be interpreted as unique expressive gestures (tokens of stylistic types). And a listener who hears and sees a live performance may find some aspects of the virtual protagonist viscerally embodied in the physically contained but strongly conveyed anguish of the performer (see chap. 8). But even if one is listening alone over headphones, one can empathize with the virtual agent in the music, whose expressions of profound sadness and anguish unfold not only before us but in us. Although this is not the only way one may experience the music, it helps explain powerful emotional responses to the piece as a result of listeners identifying with a virtual agent who serves as the imaginative embodiment of those emotions.

Conclusion

Virtuality transcends physical embodiment in life as well as in music—both depend on a connectedness with the body even as they go beyond it to create a (virtual) self. A virtual human agent in music is cognitively constructed, and that construction is often based on the listener's attribution of expressed emotion. Other cues for virtual human agency include the use of conventional topics, individual treatments of dissonance and tonal progression, and virtual embodiment of agential energy via melodic contour, dynamics, rhythm, or other less conventionally mediated shapings of the surface. Embodied actants (potentially willful exertions against a virtual environment of musical forces) afford the emergence of virtual agents, but virtual agents also draw more deeply on conventions of a musical style to acquire the expressive forces they appear to embody. Similarly, virtual agents' actorial roles need not be conceived as equivalent to literal characters in a drama (although there are certainly precedents in opera, and the use of operatic topics such as recitative or aria can further that association). Actorial roles can also be interpreted (interiorized) as streams of virtual thoughts/emotions "acting" within a virtual agent's subjectivity or consciousness—and further actualized by a listener's own contribution of experience, which lends situational grounding, reference, and motivation. These points are elaborated in the following chapters, which explore the compositional staging of levels of actoriality and degrees of subjectivity.

Notes

1. Arnie Cox (2016) has extensively explored the physical evidence for what he calls the mimetic hypothesis (founded on conscious and unconscious imitation of motor actions in the production of musical sound, with further engagement through motor imagery). Music based on song and dance, but also any music that suggests goal-directed motion, is especially conducive to this kind of embodiment in the listener. I explore still other kinds of embodied inferences here, but I direct the interested reader to his significant study for further details on physical motivations for interpreting musical motion and affect. See also my comments on the embodiment of gesture in music (Hatten 2004, 131–32).

2. See a brief review of this literature by Cox (2016, 23).

3. For more on intermodality, see Hatten 2004, 100–101, and Cox 2016, 17–18, 45–46.

4. Elizabeth Margulis (2014) explores the implications of music's various forms of repetition.

5. Russian music theorist Boris Asaf'ev (see Tull 1976) makes a similar point in theorizing the historical move from music-gestural intonations (expressively miming speech inflections) to *melos* (melody that is grounded in its own metric and rhythmic frameworks) but without developing a theory of virtual agency. See chapter 4 for my expansion of the concept of *melos* beyond a single line or voice to embrace the continuity of musical discourse.

6. The historical process of disembodiment continued well beyond the seventeenth and eighteenth centuries. As Nicholas Baragwanath has pointed out, Adorno (1981, 72ff.) viewed Wagner's orchestration as both a subjectivization of sound ("the transformation of the body of instruments into the voice of the composer's individuality") but also a desubjectivization ("since its tendency was to render inaudible whatever might give a clue to the origins of any particular sound") (Baragwanath 2005, 61). Thus, in Adorno's construal, Wagner "actually destroyed the individual voice of the bourgeois subject, the solo instrument" (62).

In a fascinating study, Carolyn Abbate explores the artistic uses of intentionally disembodied voices (such as when the character singing is not seen) throughout the history of opera, with special attention to its importance in Symbolist styles. Effects can range from a projection of authority, especially one coming from a supernatural realm, to instances of doubt, illusion, or the heightened sense of an ineffable symbol (2001, 153).

7. This is not to discount the various more literal embodiments of listeners who move to the music, as in Cox's (2016) mimetic hypothesis, but to further explore the role of the (virtualizing) imagination, which Cox approaches through a hierarchy of image schemata embedded in conceptual metaphors. See interlude I for a closer consideration of conceptual metaphor.

8. Beverley Jerold notes that the phrase may be "an abridgement of the common idiom *Que veut dire cela?* (What does that mean?)" and thus a plausible translation might be "Sonata, what do you mean to me?" (2003, 150).

9. Still other competencies might have helped Fontenelle better understand what was happening in the sonata around 1750. Danuta Mirka (2014) provides an exhaustive account of eighteenth-century writings on affect and what we now theorize as topics, which go well beyond the basic notions of imitation that Fontenelle might have encountered in reading Charles Batteux's *Les Beaux Arts réduits à un même principe* (The fine arts reduced to a single principle; 1746). But the beginnings of topical transformation via dances can be found, as Mirka (2014, 11) observes, in Mattheson (1739) 1954, 161.

10. Jerold (2003, 151, 156) attributes the lack of meaning to empty virtuosity, a common complaint among informed listeners about performers of solo sonatas in the eighteenth century. Another set of complaints centered on orchestral performances: poor in execution, lacking in rhythmic coordination, overly loud, with forced tone quality.

11. For my own arguments along this line, see Hatten 2004, 93–204. Cox's application of his theories to explain the cognitive bases for my agential and expressive interpretation of the opening of Franz Schubert's Piano Sonata in A Major, D. 959, is highly instructive (2016, 143–45).

12. This ability to hear the bodily in music became a critical aesthetic principle for August Halm (1869–1929), as Lee Rothfarb has explored. "Korperlichkeit" (corporeality) for Halm was "a necessary trait for musical effectiveness, and an

important criterion for assessing music-aesthetic value" (2005, 123). In sketches for a letter to Heinrich Schenker (February 1–6, 1924), Halm referred to corporality as "reality, the actual manner, the gesture, type of movement"; in journal notes Halm likened Beethoven's rhythm to "visible gesture" (123). And (as Rothfarb summarizes) with respect to melody, corporeality is manifested "in thematic gestures whose contours trace distinctive shapes in music's imaginary space, resulting in the impression of depth, something metaphorically tangible" (123). Halm's interpretation of corporeality in Anton Bruckner, whom he championed for a spirituality grounded in corporeality, influenced music theorist Ernst Kurth's (1931, 8–9) later observation of an "illusion of corporeality" through "the incursion of psychic processing forces" (as cited in Rothfarb 2005, 123, n12).

13. I elaborate on aspects of virtual subjectivity and its negotiation with a listener's own subjectivity in chapter 5.

14. Of course, there are several ways in which a performer can reinsert, and reassert, herself in this negotiation, as I explore in chapter 8.

15. The conversation metaphor has received extensive critical examination by Barbara Hanning (1989), Mara Parker (2002), Gretchen Wheelock (2003), W. Dean Sutcliffe (2003a), Elisabeth Le Guin (2006), and Edward Klorman (2016).

16. The conditions for inferring virtual actors are examined in chapter 4.

17. For a helpful discussion of these and still other problems with the conversation model, along with proposals for alternatives, see Klorman 2016, 113–27.

18. David Lidov first introduced this idea as a general principle of semiotics: "The abstractive, transformational, and compositional process by which sound takes shape and motivation from the body but transcends it to become music is representative of a general semiotic phenomenon. In acquiring signs, sensations and impulses formed in and of the body transcend it to become mind" (2005, 147). With respect to gesture, Lidov views somatic (bodily, gestural) signs as evolving "from a mode of reaction to become a mode of ideation" (153), in effect, "sublimating the obvious meanings of the musical body" (153). If gestures are iconic and indexical in themselves, when they "are manipulated by composition, they lose their expressive transparency; they become symbols" (157). But I would argue that the specificity of gesture is largely preserved in that negotiation through reembodiment in virtual agents, not just through remanifestation by actual performers. In my 2004 book (122–23) I develop this argument by proposing, in place of the abstraction of gesture to mechanically manipulated motive, a thematic gesture whose emergence does not lose its gestural character. In this book I consider virtualizing as the means by which we distill the bodily into virtual agential action, reaction, emotion, and other expressed meanings. Granted, there is still a negotiation involved with the music-stylistic or syntactic, and I respect Lidov's insights into the evolution of icons and indices into symbols. Furthermore, I introduce a notion of "enmindment" to capture this aspect of Lidov's "transcendence" from body to mind. Compare Cumming 2000, 225ff., on the layering and coexistence of gestural and voice-leading signs.

19. This is already implied by Schenker's metaphor of the "will of tones" (*Der Tonwille*; [1921–24] 2005) and his virtualizing of pitch structures, specifically motives, as musical agents or actors. Nicholas Cook (2007, 105) suggests that Schenker may have been influenced by the personification of ornament in art by Aloïs Riegl in his *Stilfragen, Grundlegungen zu einer Geschichte der Ornamentik* (Problems of style: Foundations for a history of ornament) (1893). Cook cites Schenker's similar observation for music: Schenker finds "the motifs in ever changing situations in which their characters are

revealed, just as human beings are represented in a drama" (Schenker [1906] 1954, 12, cited in Cook 2007, 105).

20. I explore some ways that even the dialogical may merge into a single actor/ subjectivity through refractive counterpoint in chapter 4.

21. Floyd Grave (2001) discusses this phenomenon with respect to Haydn string quartets.

22. A striking example of this phenomenon is the so-call fear circuit (LeDoux 1996, 163) discussed by Robinson (2005, 47–52). LeDoux discovered that auditory stimuli reaching the auditory thalamus follow two neurological pathways: (1) they are sent directly to the amygdala, and (2) they are also sent to the auditory cortex, where the sound is first cognitively identified and then sent to the amygdala for emotional assessment. The fear circuit is the initial, direct signal to the amygdala, which more efficiently leads to a response, whether or not the response is warranted by subsequent cognitive appraisal. Having this faster system has obvious survival advantages, since being mistaken is better than being late in responding to a threat.

23. Or the fashioning of stone tools—see Tomlinson 2015, as discussed in this book's postlude.

24. With reference to actorial roles and subjectivity, I am anticipating the concerns of the next two chapters.

25. This example, expanded from my own analysis, is drawn from Robinson and Hatten 2012, with permission of Jenefer Robinson. I have revised our prose account to de-emphasize "arousal" (a theoretical perspective in which the music arouses emotion in a listener). I critique some arousal theories at the end of chapter 6 and again in chapter 10.

26. I provide examples of the strategic growth of markedness in Hatten 1994, 39–43, 76–80. Basically, further marked oppositions may subdivide one term of an original marked opposition, thereby further specifying meaning within that term.

27. Johann Mattheson (1739, pt. I, chap. III, par. 118) appears woefully out of touch in his assessment of the sarabande's expressive associations: "This species expresses no passion other than *ambition*" (cited in Lenneberg 1958, 65). His simplistic opposition of interval size as correlating with affect is also contradicted by the opening melodic contour of this prelude, which dramatizes the affect of grief by its arialike leaps. As Mattheson (1739, par. 56–57) writes, "Since, for example, joy is an *expansion* of our vital spirits, it follows sensibly and naturally that this affect is best expressed by large and expanded intervals. Sadness, on the other hand, is a *contraction* of those same subtle parts of our bodies. It is, therefore, easy to see that the narrowest intervals are the most suitable" (cited in Lenneberg 1958, 51–52; emphasis in original). Mirka translates "vital spirits" (*Lebens-Geister*) as "animal spirits" because of Mattheson's reliance for his theory of musical affect on Athanasius Kircher's *Musurgia universalis* (1650), "according to which affects are caused by the so-called animal spirits flowing in nerves and stimulating physiological processes such as blood circulation" (Mirka 2014, 10). But Mattheson's and contemporaneous philosophers' inconsistent taxonomies of emotion throughout the eighteenth century (see Schmitter 2006, sec. 2.2) cannot help us interpret Bach's more refined capacities to express emotion, even if they provide secondary evidence of the ways that his contemporaries might have conceived emotion. Therefore, I have not based my interpretation in this chapter on various treatises but rather on a stylistic competency that scholars have begun to reconstruct as much from the music itself as from its incomplete description by theorists and even composers. This is not to deny the importance of a history of musical emotions but simply to acknowledge that the enormous project is only now being comprehensively undertaken (in a book-in-progress

by Michael Spitzer). This is also not to deny the importance of Mattheson in other arenas—for example, his contribution to musical rhetoric, as helpfully interpreted (and expanded) by Laurence Dreyfus (1996); or his contribution to the concept of topical transformation, as highlighted by Mirka (2014, 11).

28. For more on the concept of troping in music, see Hatten 1994, 161–96; 2004, 217–24; 2012e; and 2014b.

29. Note that we can identify with a single virtual agent as emotional protagonist or virtual actor throughout this prelude, even though we recognize the potential existence of other virtual agents (as implied by the chordal accompaniment, for example) that may interact with that agent in various ways.

30. David Lidov (personal communication) suggests that since the mechanical sequencing of the bass no longer motivates harmonic change, its less humanized melody might also suggest the emergence of Fate. This makes sense, although the prolongation of a vii°⁷ also occurs as a means of intensification in mm. 17–18, where the duetting of bass and soprano, and hence their dialogical role within a single subjectivity, is clearer. In mm. 32–35, I hear a prolonged, agonized, obsessively repetitive, and inner agential struggle in the bass, reflective of the virtual agent's subjectivity, and when the soprano takes over from the bass in m. 35, I hear an outer expression of anguish before the fateful agency of the cadential $^6_4$ chord in m. 36 closes the door.

31. I develop these basic categories of agency in Hatten 2004, 225–26. See also chapter 1.

32. This is a key point that Robinson (2005) emphasizes in her theory of expression.

4 Virtual Identity and Actorial Continuity

Whether acting or reacting, moving or reflecting, one way a virtual agent persists across musical time is by assuming a role in a dramatic trajectory. The transformative inference for this actorial level of agency is fictionalizing, which typically involves interpreting a virtual agent as akin to a protagonist or antagonist in a story. To summarize the three inferences thus far, virtualizing involves hearing actions and emotions as arising from sources within the music (the medium itself)—as virtual actions by virtual actants. Embodying virtual actions and emotions means hearing (at least some of) them as possessing humanlike agency. And fictionalizing involves hearing a story in which those virtual, embodied agents can play individual roles in an ongoing trajectory with an outcome of some sort (whether that story is played out within essentially lyric, dramatic, or narrative modes). Note that the emphasis on fictionalizing rather than narratizing places the focus on the nature of the agency involved while accommodating differences among lyric, dramatic, and narrative modes.[1]

Although music can tell stories in a limited sense, it is better at expressing a dramatic sequence of emotions within a coherent temporal frame of events. The engines of tonality and thematic development help us track a tonal work as an allegorical journey. Dissonance followed by resolution, or thematic departure followed by return, may be developed into dramatic schemes that also incorporate the Aristotelian hinges of reversal and recognition. Expressive genres, such as the tragic to transcendent, suggest archetypal plot types with basic actorial roles (protagonist, antagonist).[2] For example, within a military topical mode, it is typical to experience a hero's active struggle leading to triumph or tragedy (or perhaps to a subtler state of resigned acceptance). The pastoral mode offers lyrical states of reflection in which dissonance is muted and threats are subsumed within an all-encompassing calm or state of grace; it supports a more interiorized, reflective agency. The comic mode, inspired by comic opera, offers an imbroglio in which carnivalesque high spirits lead to complications that are eventually unwound and resolved, suggesting an externalized, active agency. It is also easy to imagine various combinations of these archetypal stories, but when a composer attempts to overstretch the frame, presenting too many crises and too many breakthroughs (as in a Lisztian tone poem with too many "arrival $\frac{6}{4}$s"), then the model of a single dramatic story begins to break down. In that case the more appropriate analogy might be a novelistic, even picaresque journey—displacing the Aristotelian norms of a single drama in a single time or place.[3] In compensation, a more complex subjectivity can emerge from the mixing, expanding, and compressing of these archetypes.

Much of the history of Western art music may be viewed as an account of composers finding musical means to support virtual actorial hearing throughout the course of a movement or work. Although humans have a natural tendency to fabricate stories in order to make sense of often random sequences of events, I would argue that coherent event sequences as composed within Western musical styles warrant the fictionalizing of virtual, embodied agents that undergo dramatized expressive journeys. However, agential fictions were not easily earned or staged by composers, especially for purely instrumental music. The history of their achievements is analogous to the history (and psychology) of the acquisition of various visual artistic styles, as brilliantly surveyed by Ernst Gombrich (1960). In this chapter I similarly explore historical works in light of their expansion of our cognitive capacities for aural interpretation. More specifically, I interpret compositional innovations as motivated by attempts to guide listeners toward certain kinds of agential (and hence expressive) interpretations. I begin with a brief overview of the conditions for a fictive trajectory, drawing on Byron Almén's work on musical narrativity. I then explore some of the technical means by which composers might initially project an agential identity and subsequently preserve that identity across change (which can be interpreted as growth). Although multiple lines or voices imply multiple actants, composers have found ways to integrate these strands into a coherent discourse. As we will explore, the interaction of multiple actants is often coordinated by the establishment of a singular (if complex) agential identity sustained within an actorial role throughout a work. This consolidation of actants into agents demands the skillful integration of multiple dimensions of harmony, counterpoint, and motivic development. The resulting integration creates what I call *melos*—the ongoing thread (or multistranded cable) of a musical discourse—which I examine at length.

To summarize, a dramatic discourse can help consolidate multiple actantial lines into a central agent with the actorial role of a protagonist facing various antagonistic agencies. And just as various actantial lines merge into a single agent, various actorial roles can be embraced as parts of a single subjectivity—in effect, parts of an overarching consciousness (as chap. 5 and 6 explore).[4]

Narrativity and Fictional Trajectories

By invoking fictional trajectories, I may appear to be suggesting that music should be heard literally in terms of characters in a story.[5] While this may be true of programmatic works in the nineteenth century, purely instrumental music from Bach to Brahms does not require literal or literary programs to achieve fictional trajectories. Indeed, as Almén (2008) claims, musical narratives need not be indebted to literary ones (e.g., they need not presuppose a narrator or specific characters). Furthermore, the underlying engine of narrative in music (which for Almén embraces dramatic and even lyrical modes) is not so much a plot as it is a "transvaluation" in the ranking of one entity with respect to another, specifically that of an established order and a potential transgressor (Almén 2008, 50–51; see also Liszka 1989, 71). And these roles may be filled by musical events of any size. Transvaluation means that the relationship of the two entities is conflictual and that either the order or the transgressor will emerge victorious—that is, with a higher rank.[6] Since any musical event may be construed as establishing an order (either positively or negatively valued) and any musical conflict may be construed as establishing a transgressor (either positively or negatively valued), it is possible to construe a basic narrative even in the absence of characters analogous to those in literary stories. This is a significant breakthrough for establishing musical narrativity on its own terms. Embracing transvaluation in the broadest sense enables music's dramatic trajectories to be enacted free of mediating programs. Lyric modes or genres may thus be seen as narrative with respect to the trajectories of tonality, theme, texture, and the like. Even a short character piece such as Chopin's Prélude in G Major, op. 28, no. 3, may be interpreted as narrative in this sense (Almén 2008, 3–10).

But musical fictions still require agential identification. Drawing from the work of literary theorist A. J. Greimas ([1966] 1983), both Liszka and Almén consider these agents as assuming roles, which Greimas terms actantial, because of their abstraction from actual characters in a given story and their status as more universal categories (e.g., protagonist, antagonist). Despite the risk of terminological confusion, I reserve the term "actant" for the first stage in my theory, prior to the inference of human agency. Liszka's and Almén's actants thus correspond to my actors, with the emphasis on their fictional roles. Although actorial roles may appear to be abstract at times, I prefer to interpret them as distilled from concrete musical actions (recall the related discussion of distillation with respect to embodiment in chap. 3).

What I examine here, under the rubric of fictionality, is how roles are often filled by virtual agents as virtual actors in fictional dramas. It is worth reiterating that these virtual actors need not be defined as (literal or literary) characters, although they are often appropriated in that way for the fictions of programmatic instrumental music, as well as for the fictions of operas. Furthermore, such roles need not be tied to their initial musical instantiation (e.g., as a theme or motive); listeners quickly distill roles from a compelling musical discourse, and roles can move quickly into the more fluid realm of virtual subjectivity. However, even in the absence of clearly identifiable fictional characters, we may infer fictional roles, and those roles may often be characterized with generalized terms such as protagonist or antagonist, helper or sender. Greimas adapts these labels from the original typologies of Vladimir Propp ([1928] 1968), who discovered similar invariant roles in his work on Russian fairy tales.

Establishing Agential Identity

Actoriality in music is not simply a matter of assigning a role; it begins with the establishment of a clear agential identity. Once a virtual human agency is embodied (perhaps by a musical gesture, perhaps by a characteristic theme), its identity must somehow be sustained in order to fulfill any kind of role, dramatic or otherwise. We must then ask how such a defined or particularized human agency can persist across musical time. How, in effect, can an agential identity persevere amid a constantly changing stream of events? A virtual agent takes on characteristics of a virtual actor only when those conditions can be met in the temporal stream of a musical work, which imposes significant demands on music's resources. I begin by exploring these fundamental conditions as they are addressed in nineteenth-century music before turning to the equally ingenious solutions of eighteenth-century composers. My interpretations explore how agential identity can be shaped and then sustained across various spans of musical time.

Schumann, Carnaval, Op. 9

Robert Schumann gave these dances and character pieces various titles that suggest revelers at a masked ball (a mask evokes the original Latin meaning of "persona," the mask through which actors spoke in late Roman theater). The identity of each character need only be created and sustained for the length of a short number, since there is no extended dramatic role for most of them. Rather, these characters appear in a series of tableaus.[7] But we shall see that Schumann moves in rather interesting ways beyond the simple identification of an agent with a theme.

The piece entitled "Chopin" may indicate an intention on Schumann's part to virtualize the actual composer, Chopin, but it is only through miming the characteristic piano texture of a nocturne in the style of Chopin that Schumann is able to reference his friend (example 4.1). Preserving the identity of this virtual "Chopin" is achieved through the ongoing pastiche of a nocturne. The association is doubly metonymic in that both compositional and performing styles stand in for the named, actual person (based, to be sure, on his established persona as composer and pianist). But Schumann may also be disguising himself as a composer wearing the mask of Chopin throughout this exquisite pastiche.[8]

The pieces titled "Eusebius" and "Florestan" more directly reference Schumann's literary-musical personas, the reflective and passionate alter egos, respectively, of Schumann himself. Schumann enacts "Eusebius" through a characteristic mode of expression—soft, slow, and dreamy (example 4.2[a]). The "floating" subdivisions of seven against four eighths and a turn figure emblematic of self-reflection suffice to capture the virtual expression of this persona. Schumann achieves the preservation of an actorial role (with only minimal tonal drama) by the simple device of varied repetition.

"Florestan" (example 4.2[b]) offers a more complex tableau with hints of an internal dramatic trajectory. Beginning and ending unstably on a minor-dominant-ninth sonority expanded by tempestuously agitated figures, Schumann in effect stages Florestan's sudden entry and equally precipitate exit from the scene.

Example 4.1. Schumann, *Carnaval*, op. 9, "Chopin" (mm. 1–4).

Example 4.2. Schumann, *Carnaval*, op. 9. (a) "Eusebius" (mm. 1–4). (b) "Florestan" (mm. 1–10).

A sudden modulation from G minor to V^7 of B♭ major in measures 7–9 underlines an unexpected calming of the passions, perhaps suggesting a bipolar identity. But this sudden change is also extreme enough to be interpretable as the intrusion of another, external agent. A few measures later, the same modulation is enhanced by a more specific association: the fragmentary quote of a waltz from Schumann's own *Papillons*, op. 2. As with stylistic pastiche, quotation makes reference to

Passionato

Example 4.3. Schumann, *Carnaval*, op. 9, "Chiarina" (mm. 1–4).

an actual individual by metonymy. Here, the metonymy goes further, implying that Florestan is a virtual projection of (at least one aspect of) Schumann's own personality. Preservation of Florestan's identity across change (modulation and tempo modification) is coordinated by distinctive phrase structure and the use of developing variation, two of the means that can preserve the association of a motive with an agent/actor.

Although by this point Schumann has established the premise of one character or mask (persona) per piece, pairings prove possible. In this case the spilling over of "Florestan" into "Coquette" (in B♭ major) may suggest that the earlier B♭ major moments were foreshadows of a particularly distracting (feminine) actor.[9] "Coquette," with its teasing grace notes, projects an appropriately coy entrance for this virtual agent. But the tableau lasts only as long as a simple characterization can be spun out (not nearly as long as "Florestan"), and this agent is only an actor in a minimal dramatic unit.

With "Chiarina" (example 4.3) the issue of musically staging an actual identity is further problematized. Chiarina is Schumann's secret name for Clara (his distant beloved at this time), and thus we might expect a feminine theme—gender-coded along the lines of the waltzlike "Coquette" but presumably with a more serious or elevated quality. Instead, we find a waltz whose impassioned expression is more akin to Florestan's. The metrically displaced, inner-line descent helps project an emotional struggle as marked by appoggiaturas against the waltz downbeats, charged diminished-seventh harmonies, and registrally expanding texture (as if his passions were tearing him apart). Thus, a more plausible interpretation of agency is that of the tormented lover Florestan (a persona of Schumann) reacting to the (unrepresented) agency of the eponymous Chiarina (Clara). This displacement proposes another potential plot unit or at least a dramatic subtext: we hear "Schumann" in his projection of feelings for "Clara," and thus we can infer the role of "Schumann" as that of a passionate lover whose feelings are as yet unfulfilled. But *Carnaval* as a whole does not directly fulfill this dramatic premise: the ongoing tableaus instead suggest the blurred scenes of a masked ball as represented fictionally

Virtual Identity and Actorial Continuity 89

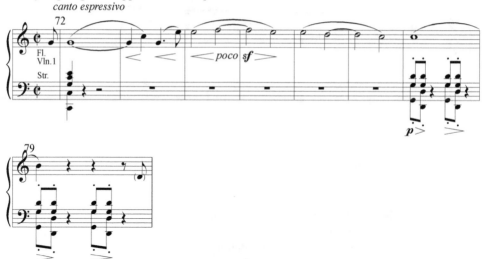

Example 4.4. Berlioz, *Symphonie fantastique*, op. 14, first movement, idée fixe (mm. 72–79 only).

by Jean Paul Richter in *Flegeljahre*, an 1804–5 novel that Schumann had read and admired.[10]

Berlioz, Symphonie Fantastique

It is to Hector Berlioz that we must turn for a more novelized (though still discontinuous) sequence of scenes. Berlioz's autobiographical account is well known: he witnessed a Shakespearean performance by the English actress Harriet Smithson and was so transfixed by her (actorial) character that he took to stalking and eventually marrying her, with predictably disastrous results. But what of the famous *idée fixe*, the theme that Berlioz claimed represented Harriet in his initial program for the work?[11] Not unlike "Chiarina," it is the lover's reaction to his beloved that is being expressed. The musical element most closely associated with Harriet's own virtual-actorial identity appears to be the lyrical melody itself. But note how it begins (example 4.4) with a fanfarelike intervallic contour (a masculine-encoded motive associated with heroic nobility) followed by a sequence of sighs whose appoggiaturas clearly suggest Berlioz's own emotions in reaction to Harriet. And in the accompaniment there are unmistakable signs of human heartbeats, both excited and irregular, as befitting the disturbed emotional state of an entranced lover. The obsession is clearly that of the self-aggrandizing Berlioz, and to the extent that we hear the melody as Harriet (or her fictive representative), it is as a vision placed on a pedestal, a projection enhanced by the opening fanfare figure expressing the male gaze in its self-absorbed reification of an objectified love.[12]

It is but a short step from *idée fixe* to *leitmotif*, and it may be instructive to compare Richard Wagner's use of *leitmotifs* in *Der Ring des Nibelungen* (*The Ring of the Nibelungs*) for objects that also imply actorial agency.[13] Consider the so-called spear motive associated with Wotan. Iconically, the motive has a single directional descent, and this straight-line contour is intermodally similar to the shape of the spear. Indexically, the force of that direction and, symbolically, its topical dotted-rhythmic (heroic) impetus metonymically signify Wotan's power and authority.

The spear is where Wotan carves his contracts, and when he breaks his promise, there will be severe consequences. Thus, the descent of the motive takes on further symbolic associations by allusion to a tragic lament bass. Its inexorably continuous descent suggests fate, and the initial dotted rhythm adds a touch of authority. Together, these features suggest Wotan's authority and his ultimate tragic destiny. With one motive Wagner is able to achieve so much: we hear Wotan's possession of power, but we are also cued to his ultimate possession *by* that power, especially when it is abused. The troping of meanings in this one *leitmotif* gradually accrues for a listener who hears it in a series of significant dramatic contexts. Thus, its identity—anchored to an unmistakable motivic shape—takes on two roles in the larger drama. It stands both for Wotan and for something beyond Wotan—the fateful authority of his world's order.[14]

Siegfried's horn motive is also clearly metonymic in its signification, indexing Siegfried's own power (his youthful vitality) and his association with Nature (the horn also metonymically references the forest). Symbolically, the diatonic horn motive enters into a consequential opposition between diatonic (associated with innocent, natural, and heroic simplicity) and chromatic (associated with richer human emotions and complex/tragic subjectivity).[15] The musical opposition helps fix Siegfried's identity as naïve hero and establishes the role he will play as pawn in a drama beyond his comprehension.

An actorial role may not always present itself as virtually human. Although referencing objects, Wagner's operatic spear and horn nevertheless virtually embody strong human energies, and those characterizing energies are readily associated with their owners. Thus, Wagner's endowment of humanlike qualities in the musical representation of these objects enables them to project humanly expressive, actorial significance in the drama.

Sustaining the Discourse through Topics: The Continuity of Agency

For music without text or (implied) program, topical associations are one effective means of sustaining a discourse in which agents are interpretable as actors. Another means, already suggested by the thematic (and topical) transformation of a *leitmotif*, is the continual evolution of thematic material. Arnold Schoenberg identified a more developmental technique of thematic evolution, which he called "developing variation" ([1947] 1975).[16] He associated it with Brahms, whom he considered more progressive than Wagner, although both composers exploited the technique. Another set of techniques that help sustain an actorial discourse is the enhancement of a single line through techniques I refer to as expanded melody, refractive counterpoint, and agentially motivated counterpoint. Finally, the creation of dramatic scenarios at both local and global levels provides a stable framework in which agential roles can develop the way individuals grow and develop in life (as well as in novels or plays). I review each of these techniques in the sections that follow.

Mozart's Topical Discourse: Piano Sonata in F Major, K. 332, First Movement

Expanding a Classical theme's phrase structure (as we see with the Beethoven theme in this book's prelude) opens up space for a small dramatic scenario (and indeed often provides the spark for that drama). The first theme of Mozart's Piano Sonata, K. 332, creates a dramatic agential discourse through a play of topics and their troping.[17] Troping entails not only the interaction and merging of meanings but the interaction of actants/agents to create a robust actoriality.

As labeled in example 4.5, the first four bars of K. 332 present a *Ländler*-like theme (¾ meter, half-plus-quarter-note slurred rhythmic gestures) in a singing-style texture (melody with Alberti-bass accompaniment), with typical pastoral features (pedal point, a harmonic turn to the subdominant, even a hint of yodeling). These various topics readily merge as compatible members of a larger pastoral trope, implying a singular agency composed of the various actantial features comprising each of the individual topics. A rhetorical gesture is created in measure 4 by a sudden sigh and interruptive rest, although the sigh might be interpreted more convincingly as expressing a foot-stomping gesture, typical of the *Ländler* as danced.[18]

The next four bars introduce a dialogically oppositional topic, the learned style, as marked by imitative texture and suspension (with galant decoration). Its actorial role in this miniature drama is perhaps interpretable as high-style mockery: a parody that also dismisses the opening melody by reversing its yodeling leap of a sixth.[19] The final four bars achieve cadential closure while also dignifying the dance topic as a galant minuet (higher in style than the more rustic *Ländler*).

What justifies hearing this theme as the expression of a single actor rather than two or even three? Developing variation links the opening four bars with the dismissive mockery of the learned parody, but a common theme is also characteristic of dialogue between two agents. Should we simply concede that, in this case, agency is indeterminate? One might argue from the standpoint of performance that a solo sonata implies a solo agent. But a more convincing argument is that the dramatic discourse appears to support a single actor as protagonist, and it is a singular agency that is sustained, even on its encounter with an antagonistic (mocking) external agency.

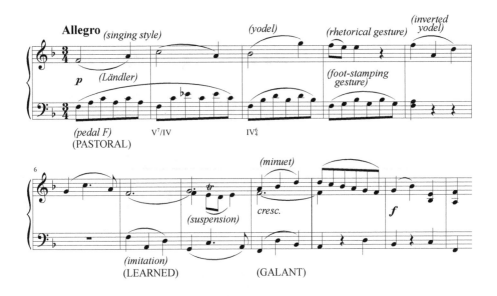

Example 4.5. Mozart, Piano Sonata in F Major, K. 332, first movement, first theme (mm. 1–12).

Example 4.6. Mozart, Piano Sonata in D Major, K. 311, second movement, first theme (mm. 1–4 only).

Topical Opposition in Mozart's Piano Sonata in D Major, K. 311, Second Movement

In the opening theme from this slow movement (example 4.6), sudden *forte* chords disrupt a pastoral-lyrical theme, suggesting the dialogical tutti of a concerto. Here, two different actorial levels are more clearly implied and sustained by subsequent textural-dynamic oppositions. Interestingly, the tutti may itself be heard as communal (in the sense of a collective noun, a single entity made up of parts rather than multiple agencies).

Example 4.7. Beethoven, Piano Sonata in E♭ Major, op. 31, no. 3, first movement, first theme and counterstatement (mm. 1–17).

Dramatized Topical Discourse: Beethoven's Piano Sonata in E♭ Major, Op. 31, No. 3, First Movement

Consider the series of disparate topics that form the opening theme of this sonata (example 4.7).[20] The sequence in mm. 1–8 proceeds from pastoral fanfare (ii⁶₅), ombra (ii⁶₅ to vii°⁷/V), heroic (arrival ⁶₄), and buffa (V⁷ to I). Given their contrast, these topics might suggest four different actorial roles. However, there is a clear dramatic progression when dark moves to light (ombra to brilliant breakthrough on an arrival ⁶₄). There is also a clear dramatic link between the heroic ⁶₄ and the Romantic-ironic dismissal enacted by the subsequent V⁷–I, which undercuts the cadence texturally, dynamically, and topically.

Consider, as well, the logical harmonic progression of this dramatic theme. Although the progression begins *in medias res* as an "auxiliary progression" (to use Schenker's terminology), it nonetheless progresses according to all the rules of voice leading—even while flouting stylistic expectations for topical and textural consistency. Does the continuity of the harmonic progression support the continuity of a single virtual actor? Or should one interpret the theme as a mini-drama with four distinct characters, each leading the music in a distinct, oppositional direction? The latter might best respect the social comedy characteristic of the Classical style, but I think Beethoven's humor emerges from a higher-level commentary on the progress of an individual protagonist. The varied repetition of this theme (a counterstatement launching the transition) supports an interpretation of higher (hence potentially narrative) agency by further extremes of registral shifting, undermining even the heroic arrival $^6_4$ in measure 15.

A Dialectical Theme: Mozart's Symphony 41 in C Major, K. 551, First Movement

Chapter 5 shows how such conflicting actorial roles can often be integrated as part of a single overarching subjectivity through an interpretation that interiorizes their conflict. But again, composers must find the means to nudge a listener's inferences in this direction. The treatment of the dialectical opening theme of Mozart's *Jupiter* symphony (example 4.8[a]) is instructive in this regard. It is easy to hear two virtual actors in the opening measures—one authoritative, the other appearing to respond with gentle yearning. However, in the counterstatement (example 4.8[b]) Mozart immediately reduces the authority of the first gesture by giving it a *piano* dynamic; he then provides a scalar link to connect it with the second gesture. Does Mozart want us to merge these two agencies into a single actor? And if so, do we hear the first one merge tropologically with the second? Or does this passage suggest integration into a single actor/subjectivity with two sides, as it were? The productive tension between the dialogical and the integrative is perhaps best preserved by the latter interpretation, which interiorizes without overly resolving or subsuming the opposition.

A Larger Dramatic Trajectory: Schubert's Piano Sonata in A Minor, D. 784, First Movement

An emerging dramatic trajectory can help orient a listener's identification of a central agency through its actorial growth. The first movement of Schubert's sonata projects a drama whose protagonist is characterized through the expressive associations of topics: the tragic, lamenting funeral march (mm. 9ff.) and the "stoic heroic" dotted-rhythmic chains of $^6_3$ chords (mm. 28ff.) give way to a moment of doubt (the *pianissimo*, B♭ to G descending-third motive, obsessively repeated three times in mm. 47–49), "willfully" reversed by a heroic *fortissimo* fanfare (mm. 53–54 and 57–58). Its alternation with a softly acceptant cadential $^6_4$–V^7 prepares a pastoral, hymnlike second theme that proposes resolution in an illusory key, the major dominant instead of a more Classical minor dominant.[21] But when the half-note to eighth-note ostinato gesture from the opening returns in the second theme to progressively disrupt the serenity of the pastoral hymn, whose agency is it? The motive originated with our protagonist as part of the funeral march topic, but now it subverts the protagonist's attempt at solace. Should we simply consider its role as that of an antagonist, perhaps tragic fate, within a tragic expressive genre typical of minor-mode sonata-form movements throughout the nineteenth century? Or might it be possible to hear this agency

Example 4.8. Mozart, Symphony No. 41 in C Major (*Jupiter*), K. 551, first movement. (a) First theme (mm. 1–4 only). (b) Counterstatement (mm. 24–27 only).

as though it were part of the protagonist's psyche, as a repressed trauma that suddenly breaks through the subject's defenses? If the latter, then agency has moved beyond mere actoriality and is beginning to look a lot like consciousness itself—a subjectivity inferred from the musical discourse as a whole.[22]

Developing Variation, the *Grundgestalt*, and the Persistence of Agential Identity

"Developing variation," Schoenberg's term for the gradual evolution of a theme from a motive or from one theme to another theme provides a ready-made analytical tool for establishing the persistence of an identified motive through the growth of a theme and its unfolding discourse. But to pursue the evolutionary metaphor, are we tracking the emergence of a new species (change) or the development of a given individual (growth)? The second theme that evolves logically from a first theme may not strike us as preserving the actorial identity associated with the first theme—rather, the two themes may suggest contrasting identities that are related (by means of a common derivation) but are nevertheless dialogical. But is the second "derived" from the first?

Schoenberg conceived of the *Grundgestalt*, or basic idea (literally, the "ground form") as that source from which a thematic or motivic discourse is derived.

A *Grundgestalt* is typically expressed as a pitch cell, intervallic set, or pitch contour. A *Grundgestalt* can also be a rhythmic motive, as in the *Hauptrhytmus* (roughly, "leading rhythmic motive") that Alban Berg develops so ingeniously in *Wozzeck*, act III, scene 3. I have expanded the concept of a *Grundgestalt* in my work on thematic gestures to include even "secondary" parameters (e.g., articulation) that might contribute to gestural identity (2004, 178, 214, 289–90). Positing a *Grundgestalt*, however, does not predict the gradual evolution throughout a work that results in a discursive and dramatic trajectory of motivic or thematic transformations. Nor does it give us information as to how these transformations should be heard as relating to each other. Rather, it merely acknowledges their common derivation from a primordial shape. Nonadjacent transformations at distant points along the evolutionary chain may appear to have little in common, even when the linkage among consecutive elements is convincing. In other words, by the time you get to the end of the chain, the last shape may be quite different from the original shape.

Suppose we include the notion of generativity in our concept of the *Grundgestalt*, as in the case of a generative cell? This new metaphor captures the growth of an individual but, as it were, from the inside out. Substitute DNA in the metaphor and you have a good sense of this kind of nonagential unfolding into a complete individual body. In this case we could still presume that an identity is gradually being constructed and that the completion of the movement or work achieves a completely bodied virtual individual. But the concept of agency seems to disappear if the process is predetermined.

What happens if we consider a theme (with clear initial identity) as implying a virtual human agent? In this case we need a somewhat different model than a generative *Grundgestalt* with its range of possible derivations set in advance. From the perspective of a virtual human identity, ongoing change (whether achieved by developing variation or other means) may be interpreted as internal (psychological) growth, and the end state may not be motivically relatable to the first. Instead, the focus might be on a virtual agent gradually gaining psychological integrity and ultimately achieving a fully realized individuality.

This perspective on agency, by which an individual (virtual agent) undergoes a process of change as psychological or spiritual development, implies that the virtual individual is an active and willing participant in the unfolding—indeed, that the virtual agent is understood as encompassing the motive, embodying its energetic shaping and evolution. As the thematic discourse unfolds, the virtual agent may take on an actorial role as the protagonist in an ongoing drama, akin to the *Bildungsroman* or various heroic dramas. By contrast, social comedy may involve exchanges among several roughly equivalent actors whose goal is perhaps a more harmonious sociability. This alternative is suggested by many string quartets or other chamber ensembles and has been well documented recently by Dean Sutcliffe (2013) and Edward Klorman (2016).[23]

As in the case of human agency, an actor is not merely an inevitable recipient of the processes that we might analyze in music through developing variation. Rather, if the agent's identity can persist across change, then that agent is also involved in the negotiation of its own development. The agent's growth may come about through overcoming resistances (initially as a virtual actant within a virtual environment), through other humanlike emotional experiences (as a virtual human agent), or through dramatic encounters (as a virtual actor engaging with other actants, agents, or actors). In the following section, I examine how composers from Bach to Brahms have found ways to mobilize and integrate various musical parameters in the service of a single agency—perhaps as a protagonist in an emotional journey, perhaps internalized with other (oppositional) actorial roles as parts of an overarching virtual subjectivity.

Melos as Level of Attending: Sustaining Virtual Agency through Musical Discourse

In addition to developing variation, composers have discovered other means to sustain a virtual agent through a series of unfolding musical events. Drawing on continuities of meter and tonality, composers can sustain agency through harmonic progressions and melodic implications and through negotiations with the schematic, expressive, and dramatic entailments of form and genre. Allanbrook (1992) highlights Leopold Mozart's image of the *filo*, or thread, that is roughly equivalent to the unfolding of a musical work's ideas, conceived linearly as a train of thought. It is this metaphor that I expand on, moving from melody and motive to a more broadly conceived integration of multiple strands into an agentially motivated musical discourse.

The average listener typically attends to melody as the most prominent thread of continuity: it is what one whistles and identifies as being the essence of a song. Evolutionarily speaking, melodies, along with rhythmic patterns, are the earliest threads of continuity in music. Melody may be elaborated into heterophony or acquire an ostinato rhythmic shape as found in many musical cultures. What marks the historical development of Western music, however, is the evolution of a notational system that enabled the coordination of separate melodies into more or less constrained sequences of intervals, energized by a periodic oscillation between consonance and dissonance. Thus, by way of the invention of rule-guided counterpoint, we can trace a path toward harmonic syntax and triadic tonality, coordinated with metric patterning (all presuppositions for the virtual environments found in most of the music I analyze in this book). Whereas non-Western musical traditions can encompass an enormous degree of complexity in a wide variety of multistranded music, Western musical traditions afford a greater hierarchical and syntactical control over various concurrent strands, which can assist the composer in integrating them into larger agencies, actorial roles, and an all-embracing subjectivity.

Indeed, the inferences of virtual actants, agents, and actors that I have described thus far would have become unmanageably large without some means of coordinating these implications into coherently unfolding processes. Consistent tempo, meter, and rhythmic texture suffice to provide a stable background (and background mood), but virtual emotions require greater foregrounding, focus, and situational/dramatic contextualizing (illustrated earlier in examples from Bach and Beethoven). Achieving a coherent musical discourse inevitably involves many diverse components, as Kofi Agawu (2008) has extensively explored.[24] Thus, a theory of agency must address the integration of several diverse components: from the gestalts of humanly agential gestures and motives to the syntheses of tonally implicative melodies, the developing variation of generative motives, the coordination of harmony and counterpoint, the Schenkerian extensions of progressional spans, and the long-range trajectories of tonal-formal schemas. All must work together to produce an internally logical and psychologically plausible discourse. The term that I employ to refer to this multileveled but integrative discourse is etymologically linked with "melody"—namely, *melos*.[25] However, *melos* encompasses, in the sense I intend, far more than melody; it embraces all the intertwined strands that are designed to capture the (style-competent) listener's focal attention during the course of a work.[26]

The term *melos* originated in Greek music theory, and it was already somewhat integrative, combining melody with its associated text and movement. Thomas Mathiesen draws from Aristides Quintilianus in summarizing the concept:

> Music in [the] sense of a performing art was called melos . . . by the Greeks. A distinction was made between melos in general, which might be no more than an instrumental piece or a simple song, and perfect melos . . . , which comprised not only the melody and the text but also highly stylized dance movement. . . . Melic composition . . . together with rhythmic composition . . . is the process of selecting and applying the various components of melos and rhythm to create a complete composition. (1999, 25–26)

For Greek theory, then, *melos* appears to apply both to a genre (simple song) as well as to a category of musical elements (in contradistinction to rhythm). Despite some ambiguity in this description, it appears that *melos* began as what we would consider melody, only to take on further associations.

Interestingly, Boris Asaf'ev (see Tull 1976) adapted the term *melos* to refer to those music-gestural intonations based on metrical rhythms (as opposed to speech rhythms); hence, he considered *melos* as a historical stage in the progression toward melody, emerging in Italy in the seventeenth century (Monelle 1992, 276). My concept of *melos* is not historically delimited in this sense, although Asaf'ev also applied the notion as part of his conception of symphonism, as a term for the continually unfolding process he advocated as part of his prescription for Soviet realist symphonic composition.[27] In my own usage, *melos* refers to the continuity of coordinated musical elements in a work as they unfold to produce a coherent musical discourse. Arising from melody and its gestural and energetic inflections (and already synthesizing all the secondary parameters of expression, such as dynamics, articulation, tempo, and pacing), this continuity in time expands in space to embrace compound melody, thickened melody (through heterophony or planing), counterpoint (as refracted or agentially motivated), and (since melody for tonal music is already harmonically generated) harmony itself, including such functions as a contrapuntally supportive bass line or directed progressions that enhance agential energy, as in Ernst Kurth's kinetic and potential energies ([1913] 1973, 122). *Melos* includes the expressive associations of sonority types and the use of harmonic overtones to enhance melody. *Melos* further absorbs into its integrative sweep both thematic and topical unfolding. It is, in effect, the union of musical elements into a directed stream of musical discourse, ultimately corresponding to a stream of musical consciousness.

This integrative *melos* is nevertheless capable of virtual freedom, as we have already seen in the striking departure in measure 5 of Beethoven's opening theme from Op. 10, no. 2. Composers have explored various ways of appearing to break up (while nevertheless sustaining) an evolving discourse. As enacting a sudden shift in thought, such disruptions may be understood as essential characteristics of human consciousness and subjectivity, as well as inevitable results of the staging of drama as conflict. In addition to the low-level contesting of virtual environmental forces (moving from actantial to agential energies), composers explore the breaking up (rhetorical disruption) and deferred realization of implications, arising from

1. stylistic voice leading (at various levels),
2. strategic pitch/motivic patterning (from sequences and varied repetitions to more subtle evolutions along the lines of developing variation),
3. meter and hypermeter (producing rhythmic and metric dissonance) (see Krebs 1999),
4. phrase design (producing hybrids and more loosely knit phrase structures via expansions and compressions) (see Caplin 1998; Rothstein 1989), and
5. formal genres (producing hybrid genres and other "deformations") (see Hepokoski and Darcy 2006).

The flow of *melos*, then, may be conceived as an ongoing nuancing of Leopold Mozart's basic "thread," enlarged to encompass an entire musical discourse—whether that discourse is conceived as Goethe's musical conversation among equals, an unfolding thematic argument, a dramatic trajectory, an expressive genre, a narrative, or some combination or complex expansion of these. As the focus of listening attention, the *melos* of a work captures and consolidates all the parameters of musical construction into an ongoing thread, or better, cable of closely intertwined threads. This consolidation into *melos* is conditioned by, if not entirely motivated by, agential expression. The integrations that we find in *melos* are thus indicators of those syntheses by which listeners infer a larger virtual subjectivity as expressed by the music and as further enhanced through their personal experiences in interacting with what is virtually expressed by the music.

In the next section I concentrate on one area of special interest to a theory of virtual agency—namely, some ways in which counterpoint in Western music developed to expand (thicken) the melodic thread (whether viewed as melody or subject), refracting its motivic content, and in general reflecting the motivations of a virtual agent. These processes enabled listeners to hear multiple lines or strands of the texture as coherent parts of a singular virtual agent, actor, or ultimately, subjectivity.

Agentially and Expressively Motivated Counterpoint

The use of parallel motion is found in early descant in fourths, and this kind of troping suggests that refracting a single line was already a motivating force prior to the gradual separation of counterpoint into distinctive voices. A much later procedure called *gymel* (from the Latin *gemellus*, or twin) suggests still another motivation—the expansion of a single line into two parts. *The New Harvard Dictionary of Music* defines gymel as follows:

> In English counterpoint of the 15th and 16th century, the temporary splitting of one voice part into two of equal range; also the name of each of these two parts. The term first occurs in Continental manuscripts, in connection with anonymous voices added to a piece by John Dunstable. . . . The first English references to gymel (also called *semel*) are in the treatise of c. Pseudo-Chilston (ca. 1450) and in the Eton Choirbook (late 15th century). . . . Later composers who made use of gymel include John Taverner, Christopher Tye, and Thomas Tallis. The term was no longer employed after the late 1560s. (Randel 1986, 359)

I mention these precursors because the technique—in part motivated as a way of proceeding from the known to the new, as found in Medieval troping—also reflects how composers could relate the new to the old while preserving some aspect of the original voice's agential identity.[28]

By the time of Bach, other means had emerged that more clearly reflected a conscious intention to unify an entire texture into a coherent discourse, often by motivically saturating multiple voices with the substance of an original one, as achieved by imitative counterpoint. In addition, structural parallel consonances, often enhanced by sequences, could combine even motivically or topically diverse ideas into a singular agential flow.[29]

The history of counterpoint is complementary to that of tonal harmony in one fundamental sense: whether coordinating the succession of intervals or triads, each is a means of integrating the flow of multiple voices while at the same time supporting individual expressive contributions to that flow. Although initially we may hear each line as an unspecified virtual actant in terms of its energetic flow, its gestural qualities may also imply a more humanlike virtual agent. Textures with multiple lines (especially those in which voices imitate or offer complementary responses) may imply a dialogue among virtual agents as actors. And we may ultimately hear the emergent musical fabric in terms of a singular subjectivity with a coherent expressive purport. What I explore here, from the perspective of virtual agency, are some of the strategies employed by Bach, Haydn, Mozart, and Beethoven that can enhance both the independence and the interdependence of contrapuntal voices, leading to their emergent synthesis as *melos*. These strategies, in other words, are means of achieving focal agential identity, discursive actorial continuity, and integrative subjectivity, all in the service of heightened expressive meaning.[30]

Although the techniques of counterpoint can create surface expressive effects, they may also serve as a scaffolding that helps to integrate the expressive contours of more freely independent melodic or motivic lines into a unified discourse—free composition built on the framework of strict counterpoint, to use Schenker's imagery. Just as rubato achieves its most striking effects against a steady metric hierarchy, so the individual expressivity of different lines may be more effectively projected against the background of an integrative contrapuntal framework.[31]

Topical Integration: Bach's Fugue in A♭ Major, WTC II, BWV 886

Bach uses counterpoint to harness extreme thematic or topical contrasts, as seen in the opening of the Fugue in A♭ Major, WTC II (example 4.9). Raymond Monelle singles out this fugue for its radically different topics: a galant subject that "comes from the world of the trio sonata" (2000, 199), and a countersubject with a descending chromatic line invoking the ancient *passus duriusculus*, which Monelle describes as expressively "pathetic, painful, distressed, tender, sorrowful, [and] anxious" (199). Monelle first presented the merger of these two topics as illustration of a musical trope, a concept I introduced at the Helsinki conference where we first met in 1988.[32] There, I argued that a musical trope creates an emergent meaning, akin to metaphor *in* music, from the interaction of two often incompatible stylistic types in a single functional location. I might also have considered the opening of the A♭ fugue as an example of a "discursive trope" (Hatten 1998, 197), in the sense that the two thematic ideas are not only individuated as virtual agents but also coordinated in dialogue as virtual actors. Their coordination is easily demonstrated contrapuntally—subject (answer) and countersubject create, and are supported by, an underlying scaffolding of parallel thirds (more accurately, alternating thirds and sixths with implied 7–6 and 2–3 suspensions at the end). Moreover, the unified direction of that stream of intervals signifies not only a common discourse but a unified purport—or perhaps two ways of looking at the same thing—that helps integrate their contrasting virtual agents into a singular virtual subjectivity at a higher level of the musical discourse.

Remarkably, hearing this way begins to alter our perception of the presumably dysphoric *passus duriusculus*, since we can also hear the passage emergently as a sequence of euphoric thirds and sixths with embellishing chromatic passing tones.[33] Thus, the underlying contrapuntal scaffolding promotes a harmonious merger of subject and countersubject into a higher expressive unit—an "expressive invention," to adapt Laurence Dreyfus's (1996) concept of Bach's contrapuntal inventions.[34] Here we see how counterpoint can override topics, or at least contextually nuance them. However, we might also experience a counterpoint among two levels of interpretation in which topics are both individuated and coherently integrated—as accomplished by Bach's contrapuntal feat of textural and topical synthesis.

Example 4.9. Bach, Fugue in A♭ Major, WTC II, BWV 886 (mm. 1–5¹), voices on separate staves, displaying contrapuntal intervallic structure between answer and countersubject.

Refractive Counterpoint: Bach's Sinfonia in E Minor, BWV 793

Example 4.10(a) illustrates another, rather different approach to agentially motivated counterpoint. Here, the subject has no comparable rival—instead, the counterpoint is freely derived from the substance of the subject itself by means of a technique I call "refractive counterpoint" (Hatten 2015b, 315).[35] This strategy is further enhanced by the surface use of parallel thirds and sixths as a more obvious means of integrating two voices into a single line. When Bach does introduce a rhythmically more active countersubject, it is also clearly derived from the subject's already derived countermaterial, and it functions as a *Fortspinnung* in sequential diminution (example 4.10[b], mm. 14ff.). This plausible countersubject takes over as a second subject for a developmental middle section before it ultimately liquidates in the *dubitatio* of a vii°⁷ (shown in the first bar of example 4.10[c]) that prepares for a coordinated tonal and thematic return in E minor. The initial motive on its return appears to inaugurate a three-voice stretto (the ultimate in refractive counterpoint), but the stretto is only hinted at. Furthermore, the return soon intensifies into a "crisis" vii°⁷ *in extremis* (the extreme registers in m. 42). This framing of the return by diminished-seventh chords undermines both tonal and thematic stability and lends the refractive motivic stretto a sense of utter desolation. A final contortion of the motive leads to a last-minute Picardy third. The positive effect of this sudden ending on a major tonic suggests an act of grace, one that exceeds the agential power of a struggling virtual protagonist.

Bach has also deepened the subjectivity of his implied virtual protagonist through developing variation of the initial motive, culminating in the derivation of his second subject. The modulatory path of that derived subject in the middle section further enhances a sense of agential development and contributes to the overarching dramatic trajectory of the sinfonia.

A Contrapuntal Drama: The Allemande from Bach's Partita in D Major, BWV 828

Motivic derivation of a counterpoint is not necessary to achieve an integration of lines into *melos*. Consider one of the more contrapuntal dances in the Baroque

Example 4.10. Bach, Sinfonia in E Minor, BWV 793. (a) Measures 1–5[1]. (b) Measures 13–18[1]. (c) Measures 37–44 (end).

suite, the allemande shown in example 4.11. In this excerpt a 5–6 syncope generates a sequence that integrates contrasting melodic contours above its underlying contrapuntal scaffolding.[36] The allemande, a stylized dance in binary form, features an expressive move to a climax at the end of the first half. Here, the left hand executes the 5–6 syncope, enacting a stepwise ascent in staggered sequence that is enhanced by chromaticism in the bass. The right hand elaborates freely around

Example 4.11. Bach, Allemande, Partita No. 4 in D Major, BWV 828 (mm. 19–24, end of first part), displaying contrapuntal intervallic structure of the sequence in measures 19–20.

the structural tenths that also ascend stepwise with the bass (D–F♯, E–G♯, etc.). The melody's freer melodic agency is further elaborated with 4–3 suspensions on the first and third beats of each measure. Tonally, the passage modulates from D to A major, and the initial expressive effect of positive uplift arises from the integration of the melody with the progressive, stepwise "urging upward" in the sequential accompaniment.[37]

On gaining the new tonic, A, Bach reverses direction in the bass in measure 21 and steps down through an octave plus a leading tone. The tenor is still rhythmically staggered but features a less systematic relationship with the bass. Meanwhile, the upper voice accelerates rhythmically with sixteenth-triplets; from beat 3 of measure 21 it sequences upward in half-bar units with more anguished diminished-seventh drops; in beats 3 and 4 of measure 22, the upper voice compresses to quarter-bar units. The climax of this wedge motion between outer voices occurs at the registral extremes of G♯ and B on the downbeat of measure 23. This moment is part of a brief vii°⁷ harmonic crisis that evades resolution by deflection to vii°₃⁴ of V on the second beat before eventually subsiding into a V⁷–I resolution.

Although the 5–6 sequence comprises only the first two bars of this excerpt, the subsequent stepwise descent of more than an octave may be heard as developing-variational in its reversal, extension, and further intensification (*Steigerung*) of the original sequential activity.[38] Notice how the initial positive ascent, made urgent by chromatic passing tones in the bass, now takes on a more disturbing character with directional reversal in the left hand and diminution in the right hand. Plangent diminished-seventh melodic reversals exacerbate the progressive ascent in the right hand, and the sequence accelerates to a climax with maximal dissonance at registral extremes. This highly coordinated *melos* enables a listener to hear three different voices as parts of a larger, singular subjectivity—moving purposefully toward a shared series of goals and thereby enacting an interiorized dramatic discourse. The plot of this dramatic discourse features analogues with Aristotelian reversal (of direction and mode) and recognition (via diminished-seventh crises that delay the ultimately tragically climax) leading to an eventual, if temporary, resolution.

Shaping an Expressive Climax: The Slow Movement of Haydn's Piano Sonata in C Minor, Hob. XVI/20

Haydn's use of the 5–6 syncope also supports wonderfully expressive climaxes. In this slow movement (example 4.12), the sequence supports an expressive melodic duet in contrary motion that is also staggered rhythmically on the surface through a notated rubato. The 5–6 underlying sequence in measures 47–50 is enhanced when the tenor is extended to create 7–6 suspensions. The head of each descent in the upper voice also forms parallel tenths, as we saw in the Bach Allemande.[39] Haydn's four-bar sequence enfolds the contrary motion of a one-bar invention into a larger, stepwise ascending pattern. The coordination of these diverse lines merges their individual contours and agency into a larger virtual subjectivity that is enriched by the energetics of its actantial component lines, creating a multidimensional expressive depth.

A Textually and Thematically Integrative Melos: Mozart's Symphony No. 40 in G Minor, K. 550, Second Movement

Mozart's later works increasingly illustrate the kind of derived or refractive counterpoint seen in the Bach Sinfonia in E Minor but now in service of a galant style in which developing variation also plays a significant role.[40] The E♭ major slow movement from this late symphony (example 4.13a) is a stunning example of how an integrative *melos* can emerge not only from the integration of counterpoint but from its further integration with other textures—notably, melody and accompaniment. In the opening theme of this sonata-form movement, an unusual layering of voices spins out a continuously enriched texture (in effect, a textural crescendo). The first measure offers what appears to be a minimal repeated-note melody in the violas with a minimal accompaniment in the cellos and basses; the second measure reinterprets that melody as a contrapuntal subject

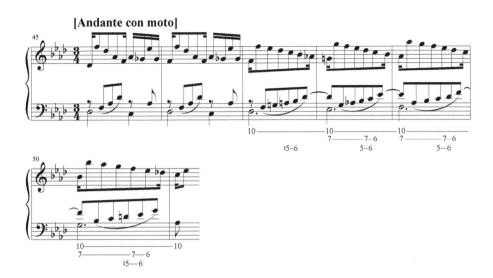

Example 4.12. Haydn, Piano Sonata in C Minor, Hob. XVI/20 (C. Landon 33), second movement (mm. 45–51^1), displaying contrapuntal intervallic structure of the sequence in measures 47–51^1.

that receives stretto imitation (again, the ultimate in refractive counterpoint) in the second violins. The suspension against the violas adds emotional tension. At the same time, the sparse accompanimental bass begins to take on contrapuntal significance as a chromatic line. Its role appears to have become that of a countersubject against the static subject, contributing a sense of unsettled desire against that staid, repeated-note motive. By the third measure, the violas finally resolve their suspension (now 4–3 against the bass), and the third entry of the imitative melody creates, with the bass arrival on B♭, a full dominant-seventh harmony in E♭ major. The violas continue to move, echoing the bass line in the previous measure and leading to a cadential trill. By the downbeat resolution to tonic in measure 4, we have kaleidoscopically experienced nearly every kind of texture: straightforward melody and accompaniment, imitative counterpoint with a chromatic countersubject, and a textural build to a single harmony, the dominant seventh.

But the texture continues to expand with the addition of the horns, echoing the repeated-note subject as though it were a fourth imitative entry. This echo overlaps the continuation in which the violins now merge in octaves with a new melodic gesture, a leap down to a chromatic incomplete neighbor, sequenced to create parallel tenths with the doubled viola/cello/bass voice (harmonically, IV to I^6). The gesture is accelerated and broken in the next measure, which introduces yet another motive, an ascending third featuring a Scotch snap in thirty-second-note rhythm. The immediate repetition of this figure has all voices supporting the leap to the sigh. The cadence in measure 8 completes a cyclic return to galant

Virtual Identity and Actorial Continuity 107

Example 4.13a. Mozart, Symphony No. 40 in G Minor, K. 550, second movement, first theme (mm. 1–19).

texture: melody and accompaniment, with a parallel-third chromatic collapse from $\hat{5}$ to $\hat{2}$ over $\hat{5}$ in the bass.

The consequent phrase of this compound period allows for further display of learned skill in a more fully contrapuntal texture. The melody that we have been entrained to hear as a subject now enters in textural inversion in the bass, doubled in the horn, and the series of answering imitations leads to a 2–3 suspension in the lower voices. The lyrical line in the first violins now emerges into a full-fledged countersubject that is clearly derived from the bass line in measures 1 and 2. The chromatic line from measure 2 is now augmented in the first violin, suggesting a countersubject, but one that is extended to accommodate all three imitative entries of the repeated-note subject. The continuation from measure 12 also features textural inversion when compared with measure 5, but now a new countermelody dialogically responds in looser contour inversion.

The cadential phase of the consequent is expanded from one to four measures, and it features the Scotch-snap figure's budding thematic emergence via developing variation, sequencing its thirds down by thirds (and thus arpeggiating the harmony) while being supported by the accompanimental (or are they fully contrapuntal now?) eighth notes. Measure 17 adds another countermelody that expressively enhances the move toward the cadence, and that melody is also extended, by lyrical arpeggiation and timbral counterpoint, to effect a merger of harmony with melody (even as it reduces the previously foregrounded Scotch-snap figure). Thematized harmonic arpeggiation then merges into a harmonic cadence.

The second theme simply shifts to B♭ in the next measure for its presentation phase, and developing variation is further in evidence. But I now skip to its continuation phase, as seen in example 4.13b, where the Scotch-snap motive is transformed into a two-note sigh that emerges as a continuous idea. It descends on every eighth note to elaborate the penultimate V/V, before a galant resolution to V. Instead of launching a consequent, however, Mozart shifts harmony in measure 28 over the F in the bass to a G♭ $\frac{4}{2}$, interpretable as IV$^4_2$ of D♭ as the next harmonies slide down to V$^4_3$ and then I in D♭ major.

This harmonic shift sets up a remarkable return of the opening subject in measure 29, integrating two full statements of the previously fragmentary accompanimental voices. The passage from measures 29 to 32 marks a culminating textural and thematic fulfillment (perhaps a "galant invention," to further expand Dreyfus's concept): the repeated-note subject, with closer stretto overlap in measure 30, is integrated both with the complete pattern of accompanimental eighths in the bass (two per bar) and with the completed Scotch-snap sequence of descending sighs. The effect is a Classical version of what in the Baroque might have been a triple fugal integration had all three motivic elements been prepared as subjects or countersubjects. Instead, these are individual, actorial components of a galant texture that has finally achieved its definitive form. The thematic and textural plenitude of this passage is expressively fulfilling as three agential strands merge into a complex subjectivity that is experiencing something akin to bliss.[41] But tension builds as the sighs begin to inject a note of desperation, inflecting the enhanced yearning of the tighter stretto in measure 30. Emotional instability is held in check by the imperturbable harmonic bass line, sequencing upward by step in two-bar harmonic units: I–V, then ii–vi, in D♭ major. The resultant expressive intensification is not merely the result of a sequential *gradatio*, however; it also emerges from the spectacular troping of three distinct, actorial emotional expressions, here integrated into a virtual subjectivity experiencing a welling up of emotion. The intensity of this emotion would appear to be capable of breaking through the galant propriety of sensibility, but Mozart keeps holding back, maintaining a *piano* dynamic despite the textural crescendo, to prepare for a suitable rhetorical-dramatic gesture. And that carefully anticipated gesture

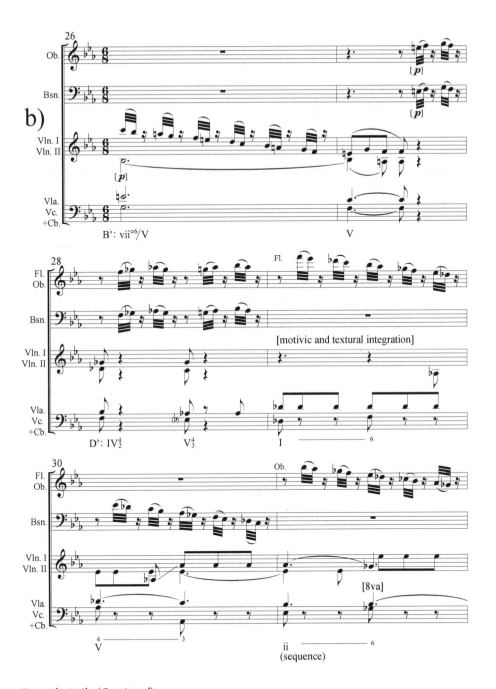

Example 4.13b. (*Continued*)

Example 4.13b. Mozart, Symphony No. 40 in G Minor, K. 550, second movement, continuation of second theme (mm. 26–36¹), with motivic and textural integration in measures 29–32 and rhetorical-dramatic swerve in measure 33.

suddenly appears in measure 33, overwhelming the listener, *subito forte*, with full orchestration. The E♭ minor sonority is hypercharged with a dissonant added sixth, C♭, grinding against B♭ in the upper winds. Note that the original subject now plays the role of pulsating accompaniment, rhythmically intensifying the psychological force of this surprisingly dissonant harmony. Although the harmony owes its existence to counterpoint (the dissonance is thematically motivated by the contrapuntal suspension in bar 2), the singularity of texture at the point of arrival now further integrates the voices into an overwhelming outburst of emotional pain, dramatically motivated as a moment of tragic recognition by a virtual actor whose profound subjectivity is thereby revealed.

The remainder of the passage reveals Mozart's deft reinterpretation of the added-sixth dissonance as IV$^6_5$ for a brief expansion of G♭ major, understood as ♭VI of B♭, leading to an ultimately positive cadence in the key of the second theme.[42]

Agentially Motivated Contrapuntal Anomalies: The Freude Theme from Beethoven's Ninth Symphony

I move forward thirty-six years, from 1788 to 1824, to examine how agentially motivated counterpoint may also help explain some rather unusual violations of contrapuntal propriety. Example 4.14 presents the bassoon countermelody against the violas' melodic presentation of the Freude theme from the finale of Beethoven's Ninth Symphony. This passage has always affected me deeply; the agency of the bassoon line appears to interact both empathetically and individually in relation to the communal agency of the hymn presented in the violas and cellos. The bassoon countermelody is rather unorthodox in its contrapuntal relationship to the melody in the violas (doubled in the cellos). Note several apparent "errors" from a textbook perspective: merging to unisons or octaves in mid-phrase in measures 117, 118, 121, and 129; and a bizarre shift from a seventh to a unison in measure 122 and again in measure 130. These moments of mid-phrase merger cause the bassoon line to lose a sense of agential independence as it fuses briefly with the hymn—note the striking parallel unisons in measure 127. Of course, timbral contrast preserves the bassoon's identity, but this on-again, off-again merger of pitches is agentially motivated in that it enacts a variable subjective identification with the moral and spiritual sentiments expressed by the hymn. (I would argue that those sentiments are already topically earned, prior to the addition of text in the later vocal presentations of the hymn.)

The other contrapuntal improprieties suggest a greater independence of the individual agent in variable opposition to that communal sentiment. For example, the displaced parallel thirds in measure 120 result in parallel perfect fourths—an unusual but still clearly refractive counterpoint. Note also the refractive support that the bassoon line receives from the contrabasses (e.g., parallel tenths in measures 117 and 118 and elsewhere), which suggests an intermediary agency (perhaps a helper role, to draw from Greimas's categories).

I interpret the entire passage as enacting the subjectivity of an individual of the Enlightenment (the bassoon) who both empathizes with (shares) and also comments on (diverges from) the communal spirit of the hymn theme (the violas and cellos) while also experiencing support from a similarly attuned agency

Example 4.14. Beethoven, Symphony No. 9 in D Minor, Finale, *Freude* theme, variation 1 (mm. 116–131), displaying unisons and parallels between melody (violas and cellos) and countermelody (bassoon). Note also the refractive counterpoint between bassoon and basses.

(the basses). The effect is so moving because of the intricacy of this dialogical encounter—part independent, part supported, and part fully immersed.

Summarizing Melos *and Actoriality from Counterpoint*

In these examples from Bach, Haydn, Mozart, and Beethoven, I illustrate several ways in which counterpoint can:

1. Enhance the freedom and hence the expressive individuality of lines as virtual actors
2. Coordinate and synthesize those expressive individualities into a larger *melos*, with a singular expressive purport, suggesting a complex virtual subjectivity

These compositional strategies include:

a. refractive counterpoint, as in drawing from the same motivic substance and contours of a given line;
b. contrapuntal scaffolding, by means of which even topically oppositional lines can merge into a discursive trope;
c. a counterpoint of contrasting textures and textural strands, as in the Mozart example, in which the textural strands are themselves undergoing developing variation and shifting roles; and
d. "violations" of (expressive exceptions to) contrapuntal "rules" (learned regularities), as in the Beethoven example, which further individuate and clarify the role of a virtual actor (bassoon), and whose interaction with another (communal) actor (violas) is thereby foregrounded.

These strategies constitute some of the means by which composers have adapted the highly constrained structures of counterpoint to help stage the expressiveness of virtual agents/actors in music. They ensure ongoing agential identities, coordinate actorial roles, and ultimately foster an interpretation of virtual agents/actors as parts of a singular virtual subjectivity.

Other Innovative Mergers of Melody and Harmony

In addition to these strategies for merging individual lines into an expanded *melos*, Bach and later composers explored other ways to accomplish a merger between a singular melody and its harmonic support. One common strategy was to create a melody out of a chordal arpeggiation—in effect, linearizing harmony. Another was to bring out a melodic line from the voice leading between arpeggiated harmonies (nonconsecutive steps creating a melodic step progression). And if the arpeggiation implied a contrapuntal sequence (e.g., 7–6), then the counterpoint could be heard as a compound melody with arpeggiated harmonic filling.

A more complex textural strategy was to alternate attack points between melody and arpeggiated chordal accompaniment, creating fleeting lines in the accompaniment that might occasionally imitate or respond to the initial melody. This texture is related to *stile brisé*, a technique that served to counteract the quick decay of the harpsichord as well as bring out potential inner voices by arpeggiating harmonies into separate attack points. The broken-out lines could highlight a step progression or provide hints of contrapuntal voice leading in dialogue with, or in imitation of, the main melodic line.

One can find many examples of these linear and motivic enrichments of harmony in Bach's keyboard suites, and the technique is masterfully extended by Chopin and Brahms, as we shall see.

Bach, Courante from the French Suite No. 1 in D Minor, BWV 812

The melody and harmony in the first two measures of this courante (example 4.15) are derived from the opening of the previous dance, the allemande. In the courante, the melody splays down from a structural A with passing and neighboring tones filling out the tonic arpeggiation; the accompaniment mirrors (and emphasizes) this arpeggiation in contrary motion. The upper-voice A is easily heard as moving to B♭, both as voice leading and as step progression, and the descending arpeggiation from B♭ is stemmed as a separate voice. Meanwhile, the stemming in the left hand has already divided the accompaniment into two voices. By measure 2 an extra voice in the alto supplies a decorated 4–3 suspension. One might construe these emergent (and added) voices as examples of a melody that is prismatically refracting into three voices, in effect generating its own harmony. In turn, the accompaniment is also diffracting into counterpoint and even melody: having emerged as a contrapuntal tenor voice in measure 1, that voice now vies for melodic attention by imitating the melody from measure 1. In the free texture of this courante, Bach is generating a network of relationships that, for all the ingenious surface individuality of its emergent lines, sounds like a singular and coherent *melos* because of a clearly audible, gradually unfolding derivation. Here, motivic developing variation meets generative texture, and arpeggiation conceived as a process of melodic generation mediates the otherwise stark textural opposition between foregrounded melody and backgrounded accompaniment. While fugues may be more technically constrained in their mediation of melody and harmony into continuous thematic counterpoint, this courante is no less sophisticated in its generation of material, featuring a careful calibration of melodic and linear emergence.

This is *melos* of a kind that may have inspired Haydn's textural innovation in the Op. 33 string quartets, as celebrated by Charles Rosen (1972, 116–17), whereby a melody can become accompanimental, and an accompanimental figure can emerge as melodically foregrounded, all in the same short phrase. Both Bach and Haydn are creating a continuously unfolding discourse, but whereas Bach often generates his discourse from a single idea, Haydn often puts more than one motive into dialogical play.

Composers who learned from Bach and Haydn realized the potential of varied textures that could bring together melody and harmony in new and surprising ways, creating fresh integrations in the thematic discourse. Rather than simply working within the textural archetypes of homophony (whether chordal or melody-and-accompaniment) and polyphony (whether imitative or not), they pioneered other ways to merge line and harmony. And these explorations afforded still other ways of hearing multiple energetic strands of material (lines, voices) integrated into a singular agential identity. Ultimately, such an enriched agential identity could support the further characterization of a virtual actoriality, as in the examples presented earlier in this chapter. The newly woven textures could promote a depth of interrelationships that in turn could model an ever more complex virtual subjectivity.

Example 4.15. Bach, Courante, French Suite No. 1 in D Minor, BWV: 812 (mm. 1–3^1).

Chopin, Prélude in D Major, Op. 28, No. 5

The fleeting emergence of melody from harmonic arpeggiation is well illustrated in Chopin's Prélude in D Major (example 4.16). Here, it is an inner voice that sighs, alternating (as often in Beethoven) between diatonic and lowered sixth scale degrees. Beaming and accentuation reveal Chopin's conception of voices and their projection. At measure 5 the suspended texture breaks into a fascinating integration of harmony and melody as parallel tenths are broken by alternating leaps to fill in harmonies (fractured arpeggiations), creating a loose give-and-take between the hands.

Chopin ventures a nearly pointillistic fragmentation at the climax, measures 13 and 14, where the upper voice features the broken continuity of a step progression while lower voices split into three supportive voices, registrally maintained, with just enough step progression and regularity of rhythmic hocketing to provide patterned continuity. Without a theory of virtual agency, however, one might be hard pressed to find a mimetic counterpart to this bewildering dispersion of pitches. Although the voice leading supports a singular, if fragmented *melos*—which in turn implies a singular agent—the passage demands a broader conception of agency. I suggest an interiorized subjectivity (elaborated in the next chapter) that can embrace the splintering excitement of these alternating points, analogous to a sparkling consciousness of thought that appears to be going everywhere at once—while nevertheless proceeding along a single discursive path. A powerful emotional situation might engender such a prismatic refraction as suggesting multiple reactions. Perhaps Chopin fractures his texture to spin off a similar profusion from a single emotional charge.

Brahms: Intermezzi in E Major, Op. 116, No. 4, and Op. 119, No. 1

Brahms was the great inheritor, primarily from Schumann but also from Bach and Chopin, of the textural enrichment of *melos*, which might be considered an underlying project for an extraordinary series of essays in thematic interwovenness: the late character pieces for piano, Opp. 76 and 116–119. Stephen Rings (2012) has already demonstrated how imitative or learned enhancements in these

Example 4.16. Chopin, Prélude in D Major, op. 28, no. 5 (mm. 1–17).

works are expressively motivated, often creating highly expressive climaxes.[43] Thus, I concentrate here on other textural means by which Brahms creates innovative integrations between melody and harmony.

One striking textural process reveals Brahms's unfolding use of diminution to achieve integration—a developing of variation, if you will. The Intermezzo in E Major, op. 116, no. 4, begins with a thematic idea that is already a merger of harmony and melody, via arpeggiation and a linear, upper-voice, chromatic passing tone (example 4.17). But this initial gesture is immediately answered by another

Example 4.17. Brahms, Intermezzo in E Major, op. 116, no. 4 (mm. 1–25).

melodic candidate, the wistful sigh from G♯ down to C♯ in the right hand. The left hand immediately takes on a supportive role, splaying upward in fused melodic harmony and responding with a contrary-motion gesture as if offering positive support. The upper-line melodic kernel eventually grows into a stepwise, sighing cadence (mm. 3–4), and on varied repetition, a small climax (m. 9) in which the two hands are coordinated (though still exhibiting grouping dissonance) for a complete measure.

But these are just the first steps in Brahms's remarkably integrative development of an actantial duet that has already become an internalized colloquy. A brief contrasting middle sustains the phrase discourse through both linkage technique (the echo of the cadential sigh from m. 10) and developing variation (the figuration incorporating the expansive sighs from mm. 2–4). But this section also pursues textural integration via parallel thirds between the hands in measures 13 and 14. When the theme returns, the splaying arpeggiation technique (as described earlier in the Bach Courante example) is applied to the melody in the right hand in measures 16 and following, filling in and rhythmically delaying the descending, expansive sighs. The splaying deftly splits into two lines but harmoniously lands on a third. This diminutional, arpeggiated elaboration integrates the dialogical play between hands, rhythmically and harmonically overlapping with the arpeggiation in the left hand. In measures 20–22 the return of measures 6–8 is varied further: now the upper line descends by stepwise sighs, and its landing is rhythmically offset from the splayed inner line, giving that line more prominence.

The most extraordinary effect, however, is yet to come, and it involves an internal stretching of the *melos* and an interiorizing of its temporality that is unprecedented. In measure 23 the climax from measure 9 is stretched as the splayed line takes on contrary-motion independence by mirroring the climactic ascent. Then, a sudden drop in dynamics suggests that the overlapping imitation of three-note descents between these two lines is occurring inside the temporality of the discourse—a kind of reflective musing, if you will. The parenthetical effect is confirmed by the sudden increase in dynamic back to *forte* and the continuation from the climactic E left hanging in measure 23 with contrary-motion support by the splayed line. This rupture in the fabric of an implied thematic discourse moves inside the expanded actorial climax to carve out a brief, interior moment of reflection—a move from external actorial drama to the complex subjectivity of inner awareness.

Limits of space prohibit a detailed examination of many other cases where Brahms has conjured an original relationship between melody and harmony, fusing them to a singular texture and agential identity.[44] But I cannot neglect the most celebrated of Brahms's splaying themes, that of the opening of the Intermezzo in B Minor, op. 119, no. 1 (example 4.18). This was one of the intermezzos that Brahms sent to Clara Schumann in May 1893, preceded by a letter in which he emphasizes the foregrounded, melodic significance of the splayed arpeggio:

Das kleine Stuck is ausnehmend melancholisch, und "sehr langsam spielen" ist nicht genug gesagt. Jeder Takt und jede Note muss wie ritard. klingen, als ob

Adagio

Example 4.18. Brahms, Intermezzo in B Minor, op. 119, no. 1 (mm. 1–8).

man Melancholie aus jeder einzelner saugen wolle, mit Wollust und Behagen aus besagten Dissonanzen! Herr Gott, die Beschreibung wird Dir Lust machen!

(The little piece is exceptionally melancholy, and "to play [it] very slowly" would not be saying enough. *Every* bar and *every* note must be played ritard[ando], as if one wanted to suck melancholy from *every* single one, [drawing] pleasure and contentment out of [each] dissonance. Lord God, [my] description will make you eager to play it!) (Litzmann 1971, 228; my translation and emphasis)

The remarkable nature of this integration of harmony and melody comes from the fact that the tonic chord keeps arpeggiating by thirds past its root, creating an implied em^9 (iv^9) in B minor. One could imagine a prototypical 2/8 version deleting the last two notes in measure 1 and featuring a rooted tonic; however, Brahms's extended descent through two more thirds creates an effect akin to slipping away from both (metric) time and (tonal) space. The further sense of temporal stretching, emphasized by the careful attention to *"every* note" in Brahms's note to Clara, may suggest an early move toward interiorization, a virtual subjectivity ruminating over deepening pools of potential reflection, if you will. Have we reached a point in music history where virtual subjectivity can be staged in five notes?[45]

Displaced and Refractive Melody: Debussy's "Il pleure dans mon coeur," L. 60, and Fauré's "Clair de lune," Op. 46, No. 2

Claude Debussy and Gabriel Fauré, in songs composed about the same time to different poems by the same poet (Paul Verlaine), independently pioneered a song texture in which the singing voice is initially displaced from a melody

Virtual Identity and Actorial Continuity 121

that is focal to the *melos*, thereby opening another dimension of subjectivity.[46] Both composers begin with a lyrical melody that is foregrounded in the piano alone; however, it is only sung as a melody by the voice in Debussy's setting (e.g., in mm. 23ff.). As in Schumann's "Am leuchtenden Sommermorgen" (see chap. 5), where a postlude features the "voice" in the piano, such "unsung melodies" (Abbate 1991) can suggest interiorized, subjective thought/emotion. Their strongly foregrounded appearances guarantee agential identity as part of a lyrical protagonist's inner reflection. What I explore here, however, is how this vocal melody interacts with the music given to the singing voice.

Debussy's singer begins before the piano melody ends, but the voice "line" is more declamatory than lyrical at first, with its oscillation between G♯ and B; its repetitions of G♯ echo the piano's background textural oscillation between D♯ and B that represents the rain (example 4.19). Fictional rain is an external agency that is made internal through both verbal metaphor (comparing the rain to tears, such crying symptomatic of pain in one's innermost being) and musical developing variation. The combination of the singing voice with the lyrical line in the piano suggests the singer's actorial role in providing textual commentary—perhaps reflecting the weariness suggested by Verlaine's "s'ennuie" in measures 32 and 33. The virtual actor's true inner state is revealed by the piano's more emotional melody. But even this melody does not so much enact as poetically suggest a deeper emotion through the power of wistful reminiscence.[47]

Together, the three elements of the musical texture, combined with the poetic text, blend in a trope of complex subjectivity—a sensory perception of rain, doubly personified as tears and unceasing ennui. Debussy interiorizes deep feeling but represses its full outward expression, as suggested by his "triste et monotone" instruction to the singer in measures 4 and 5. We might interpret the effect as dramatic irony if the protagonist were unaware of his true feelings. But the metaphors and musical-textural mergers may warrant a further move from the actorial level to a more comprehensive virtual subjectivity if the listener engages directly with all these layers of simultaneous awareness and their potential for emotional development.

Verlaine's metaphors are more sweeping in "Clair de lune," in which the implied lyric narrator first compares the beloved's soul to a party of masqueraders dancing to the lute in a moonlit garden, then develops the poetic conceit by suggesting that the beloved is no more sincere than the *masquers*, and no more aware: "Ils n'ont pas l'air de croire à leur bonheur" (they don't have the appearance of believing in their happiness). A synesthetic blending serves as transition to the "quiet" moonlight: "Et leur chanson se mêle au clair de lune" (and their song mixes with the moonlight), "Au calme clair de lune triste et beau" (the calm light of the moon, [both] sad and beautiful). The moonlight is perceived as deeper truth in its implied revelation as a trope of sadness and beauty. The paradoxical emotion is echoed when the moonlight makes the fountains sob with ecstasy. Sexual imagery is further troped with the deep sense of regret for true feeling—both of which the speaker realizes he cannot have from his beloved. The repetition of "jets d'eau" (fountains) places them

Example 4.19. Debussy, "Il pleure dans mon coeur" (Verlaine; mm. 1–10).

"parmi les marbres" (among the marble statues), and in a sense, the speaker merges with the still, silent rebuke of these Classical emblems of beauty and truth.

Fauré begins with a theme in the piano (example 4.20[a]) that is set with the texture, rhythm, and modal harmony of a simulated performance in a fictional garden (although the figuration introduced in m. 5 is more evocative of a guitar

Example 4.20. Fauré, "Clair de lune" (Verlaine). (a) Measures 1–5. (b) Measures 12³–17.

than a lute). The modal melody (Aeolian) with its multimodal accompaniment (Dorian, with a Picardy third) cues a mysterious otherness—in the past, imagined, and hence suitably allegorical. Although stylized with the fictive performance of dance music, the piano melody nevertheless has an evocative air akin to Debussy's, here suggesting mixed emotions.

The voice does not enter until the *leitmotivic* melody has sounded a second time, overlapping with the guitar figuration first heard in measure 5 (example 4.20[b]).

Example 4.20. Fauré, "Clair de lune" (Verlaine). (c) Measures 26–30. (d) Measures 39–47.

Similar to Debussy's protagonist, Fauré's more narrative protagonist appears to be commenting on the texture rather than expressing a feeling—the declamatory, syllabic style also refracts (echoes, and occasionally joins with) the upper line in the piano (recall the Beethoven Ninth Symphony example, where the bassoon did something similar). Together, the voice and the piano dance, but at different levels of the discourse—the virtual agent/actor here assumes a narrative and somewhat objective distance in describing the scene.

At measure 26 (example 4.20[c]) the piano melody returns, but unlike Debussy, Fauré does not allow his virtual actor (the role played by the singer) to identify with the seductive melody in the piano. Instead, the singer continues to comment on the unnatural party with ironic disdain (note the musical oxymoron—a Picardy raised third as part of the setting of "le mode mineur"). And, as in measures 13–17, the singer also refracts the pitches of the recurring, *leitmotivic* melody.

But with the turn to the moonlight (example 4.20[d]), Fauré marks the singer's lyrical line as *expressivo e dolce* to enhance the emotional effect of this pure, natural, and revelatory ("clair") light. The modal mysticism of the piece is preserved even as it magically shifts character to a transcendent E♭ Lydian and arpeggiation in the piano evokes a wash of moonlight. The key metaphor, the troping of "triste et beau," is clinched by an appropriate thematic merger when the piano's original melody is recalled, also *dolce*, with its original pitches transformed by scale-degree variation to fit within E♭ Lydian (mm. 42–44). The absorption of the piano's melody into a thematic section where the protagonist is engaging with personal feelings suggests another agential cue—the beloved, in the guise of the piano melody, here floats through the protagonist's mind, perhaps as an idealized *idée fixe*.

Conclusion

From the problematized or masked identities of literal characters to actorial roles and the expanding of a protagonist's emotional journey as a kind of interiorized subjectivity, I have explored the staging of agential identity and its perseverance in a variety of musical incarnations. The demands of staging a continuous musical discourse require consolidation of multiple musical strands into an integrative *melos*, and that continuous *melos* could have inspired—but certainly served to enable—the integration of actants into singular agents, the ongoing identity of those agents as actors, and their potential merger as parts of an all-embracing subjectivity. It is to the complexities of creating and sustaining virtual musical subjectivity that I now turn.

Notes

1. I explore types of narrative agency more extensively in chapter 7. Marion Guck (1994) applies to music Kendall Walton's (1990) investigation of "involvement" in the representational arts, examining degrees to which various theorists create "stories"

to address their engagement with musical works in ways that go beyond a formalist analysis of structures.

2. For more on expressive genres and their trajectories, see Hatten 1994, 74–90.

3. An "arrival $^6_4$" (Hatten 1994, 15, 22) is the rhetorical effect of a cadential $^6_4$ chord that emphasizes resolutional clearing to tonic. Although above a dominant in the bass, an arrival $^6_4$ need not resolve like a cadential $^6_4$; instead, it may be heard rhetorically as a breakthrough that launches a theme in the tonic, ennobled by its presentation above a dominant "pedestal," as in the second theme from the first movement of Beethoven's Piano Sonata in C Minor, op. 111.

4. Although I develop my concept of *melos* along different lines, my argument has some affinity with Edward Cone's speculations on the synthesis of musical elements required to infer a complete persona: "The musical persona is implied, not by any single component or progression, but by the interaction of all of them, by the comprehensive line of the whole. Above all, the persona is realized in the total rhythmic life of the composition, for the composite rhythm, more than any other musical element, controls the interrelationships of all motifs and progressions" (1974, 110). My integration of various actorial roles as parts of an overarching subjectivity also has some affinity with Cone's observation that "all roles are aspects of one controlling persona, which is in turn the projection of one creative human consciousness—that of the composer" (114). My turn toward virtual subjectivity, however, differentiates a virtual consciousness from Cone's "composer's voice."

5. Even Eduard Hanslick ([1854] 1986), in chapter 7 of *On the Musically Beautiful*, relates themes to characters in a novel while nevertheless insisting that musical content is inherently immanent, a point noted by Thomas Grey (2011, 365). Recall Heinrich Schenker's comparable observation with respect to motifs mentioned in chapter 3, note 19.

6. There are four basic narrative archetypes (Frye 1957, 162; see also Almén 2008, 64–65) that are structurally defined by the four possible outcomes in the resolution of that conflict, based on the listener's identification with (valuing of) either the order or the transgressor in any such conflict (see table 7.1 and the accompanying discussion in chap. 7).

7. An interesting exception to this perspective is developed in a recent article by my student Clay Downham (2016), who argues that Schumann's compositional persona acts as a controlling agent, via his two musical personae (Florestan and Eusebius), to direct the action of each character.

8. Lawrence Kramer also emphasizes the inversion of gender in Schumann's portrait of Chopin as "a feminine persona for the masculine Schumann who impersonates him in drop-dead note-perfect style" (2002, 115).

9. Kramer suggests these interpolations are references to Eusebius, with their adagio tempo and dreamy introspective character serving as evidence. From that perspective, "Florestan may . . . be said to contain Eusebius as an inner double" (2002, 112). As he summarizes with respect to identity, "there are no selves, only impersonations" (112).

10. An English translation of the masked ball chapter in *Flegeljahre* is provided by John Daverio (1997, 493–501) in his biography of the composer.

11. Berlioz later withdrew the initial program, but only after it was too well known to be ignored.

12. Cone claims that "the Beloved never actually appears in the first movement—indeed, it is not clear whether she appears anywhere in the story, except in the fevered brain of the artist" (1974, 90). Stephen Rodgers explores the "relentlessness of the artist's passion for his beloved" in Berlioz's cyclic return to the *idée fixe* in the first movement: "Her

image changes as his obsession grows more intense, just as the thematic cycles change as they are repeated" (2009, 93).

13. For a detailed study of the *leitmotif* that illustrates its integration of thematic and associative meanings, see Bribitzer-Stull 2015. See also Thorau 2003 for a comprehensive account of the history and ideology behind leitmotivic analysis, as well as its potential for interpretation.

14. Pyotr Tchaikovsky uses a similar stepwise descending motive (minus the dotted rhythms that have already appeared in the initial horn fanfares) as part of an invocation of tragic fate in mm. 5–7 of the introduction to his Fourth Symphony, op. 36 (1877). The intertextual reference of the descending scale to Wagner's spear *leitmotif* would not have gone unnoticed. The fanfare portion of Tchaikovsky's theme is used somewhat leitmotivically at dramatic junctures in the first and last movements.

15. This opposition is highlighted by Eero Tarasti (1978).

16. Developing variation involves more than thematic derivation from a *Grundgestalt*, as I argue later. For Brahms's own appropriation of Wagnerian techniques, see A. Peter Brown 1983.

17. The opening theme of this sonata is rich in topics, as Wye Jamison Allanbrook (1983, 1992, 2014) has demonstrated. My contribution to the discussion, drawn in part from Hatten 2014b, includes identifying still other topics, explaining how these topics combine into tropes, and furthering a virtual agential interpretation. Allanbrook topically interprets the first four measures as "cast in a simple singing style—a pathetic aria performed by a soprano accompanied by an Alberti bass" and the next four measures as a "parody of learned counterpoint" (2014, 111). However, her interpretation of the "comic surface" does not lead her to support an agential interpretation: "The impulse to posit a single guiding voice behind this expressive polyphony or to assign personae to the expression of the disjunct *mimēmata* [mimetic representations] creates a superfluous layer of reference—an extraneous anthropomorphizing that enables analysts to overlook the often radically variegated mimetic content of the representations or the disparate points of view from which they are made in order to imagine a conversation between recognizably consistent participants" (117). The remainder of this chapter addresses some of these valid concerns.

18. See McKee 2014, 176, on this aspect of the *Ländler*.

19. My identification of at least an allusion to yodeling in the melodic contour at the beginning of this theme is supported by a description of the *Ländler* by dance scholar Mark Knowles: "The dance was performed to 3/4 time music, usually to the accompaniment of singing or yodeling. . . . The lilting melodies and use of wide leaping intervals in the music, especially evident in yodeling, gave rise to deep swinging movements and lifts in the dance" (2009, 21).

20. This theme is also analyzed in Hatten 2004, 168–69.

21. This analysis is elaborated in Hatten 2004, 187–95.

22. Almén's "psychodynamic" interpretation of Schubert's Piano Sonata in B♭ Major, D. 960 (2008, 139–61), proposes a similar strategy by interiorizing (my term) a dissonant conflict between actants (in my sense) as a "tragic flaw" within a single subject (specifically, the low G♭ to F trill in m. 8 that perturbs the serene first theme).

23. See also my review of Klorman in Hatten 2017a.

24. David Lidov also offers a compelling account of musical discourse: "The interplay between the representation of gesture and its formal contextualization creates discourse—a representation of think*ing* as action" (2005, 138; emphasis in original). But, as Lidov concludes, discourse works in both directions: "When groups of notes

are performed in a manner that brings out their gestural characters, that is, performed expressively, the entire musical structure is transformed from a merely rational construction into an expressive construction. At the same time, the rational construction of the music parlays the representations of gesture into an elaborate discourse" (144).

25. I introduce the term *melos* in Hatten 2015b, but it is more richly developed here.

26. Music philosopher Aaron Ridley's (1995) "musical melisma" is a rough approximation; Naomi Cumming's (2000) Peircean development of a synthesis of signs into a complex signification is also relevant here.

27. For more on Asaf'ev's conception of *melos*, see Mott 2018.

28. Medieval troping involved the addition of words, music, or both to an established liturgical chant. As I have observed elsewhere, this "purely material interpolation might be seen as figural in the sense that the new text or melody served to inflect or enlarge upon the sense or significance of the original. . . . But the troping of meaning was probably secondary to the primary urge of church composers to open up new areas for musical development, while not presuming to an originality unrelated to the canonical chant repertory" (1994, 314n4; see also Hoppin 1978, 144).

29. In this chapter I offer an admittedly more "presentist" (Christensen 1993) perspective on agential and expressive motivations for counterpoint, but one that is nonetheless legitimately historical in taking as its primary documents the music itself. Contemporaneous treatises that purport to explain contemporary practice are often either not representative of that practice or woefully incomplete in their approach to its expressive motivations (as I note in chap. 3 with respect to my interpretation of the Bach Prelude in E♭ Minor). As Ian Bent (2002, 581) has observed, a "new body of theory" emerged in the latter part of the eighteenth century (after Bach's death), from C. P. E. Bach and Friedrich Wilhelm Marpurg to Johann Philipp Kirnberger. These theorists conceived of counterpoint not from the pedagogical treatise of Johann Joseph Fux but from the standpoint of current practice in harmony and voice leading. Their approach to counterpoint was, according to Bent, "based on the music not of Palestrina but of J. S. Bach (who repudiated species counterpoint, and started his pupils with four-part figured bass writing)" (581). In this spirit of constantly revising speculative theories to reflect actual practice, I offer a closer interpretation of evidence for agential integration as grounding a clear expressive purport in music not only by Bach but also by those composers who would follow his lead.

30. David Yearsley (2002) advances a rather different approach to what I would consider more holistic meanings of counterpoint in Bach's music. He traces a range of cultural associations for canon and invertible counterpoint, including allegories of heavenly music as anticipated from the deathbed, self-ironizing plays with genre and style, and the modeling of mechanistic devices. Although my focus is on the expressive contours of the music itself, my expressive interpretations need not be in conflict with those potential cultural functions or associations that Yearsley explores. For example, my interpretation of the learned style in Classical music as having an "authoritative" correlation (Hatten 1994, 87) reflects the prestige that counterpoint held in the Baroque as the highest art of human imagination, and thus why it would be the most appropriate kind of music to honor the dying or memorialize the dead.

31. Cumming illustrates the synthesis of expressive gesture with voice leading in her illuminating analytical interpretation of the Adagio movement from Bach's Sonata in G Minor for Solo Violin, BWV 1001. Her summary as it relates synthesis to a persona is worth quoting at length: "The bringing of gestural events into the aural perspective of a tonal purpose is an act of 'synthesis' between different kinds of signs, which, for a

listener highly attuned to the tonal level of organization, might lead to the expressive moment being heard as an ephemeral or passing event, and thus as carrying less affective weight. . . . The 'persona' can be apprehended as a complexly formed yet singular character, whose synthesis as 'one' is an ongoing process in musical time, responsive to new information as it is heard, and thus mutable in its emergent qualities—a highly expressive gesture in one moment being quickly contained by a perception of unfolding directional lines, only to reappear at a later time" (2000, 232). My examples explore other forms of synthesis in Bach's counterpoints, but our aims are complementary.

32. My paper was subsequently published as "Metaphor *in* Music" (Hatten 1995). I refined the concept and incorporated it into chapter 7 of *Musical Meaning in Beethoven* (Hatten 1994, 161–72). A further elaboration of the theory of troping with respect to topics appears in Hatten 2014b.

33. Hearing the chromatic descent in the context of major mode also supports a more positive interpretation.

34. According to Dreyfus, an invention is not the subject alone but rather the complete contrapuntal progression as it recurs throughout a work in various contrapuntal inversions and other transformations: in effect, a "patch of inventive 'work,'" to use Dreyfus's colorful characterization (1996, 12).

35. A version of my analysis of this sinfonia first appeared as Robert S. Hatten, "Melodic Forces and Agential Energies: An Integrative Approach to the Analysis and Expressive Interpretation of Tonal Melodies," in *Music, Analysis, Experience: New Perspectives in Musical Semiotics*, ed. Constantino Maeder and Mark Reybrouck (Leuven, Belgium: Leuven University Press, 2015), 315–30.

36. Eugene Narmour (1977) has traced the 5–6 sequence as a style type throughout music history, and—I might note—it plays a role in coordinating individual lines into a singular expressive *melos* as late as Schoenberg's *Verklärte Nacht* (Transfigured night) (see, for example, mm. 378–80).

37. A series of "reachings over" in the soprano (e.g., F♯–A–G♯) further enhances the sense of uplift in this sequential ascent.

38. *Steigerung* (intensification by degrees; gradation) along with repetition are figures of attention that Bach biographer Johann Nikolaus Forkel (1749–1818) discusses in his *Commentar* (1777). As Matthew Riley observes, "Forkel says that it is most effective when a crescendo is combined with the gradual development of new ideas and progressions" (2004, 138). In the allemande, sequential intensification through registral ascent serves as the *Steigerung* at the end of the first part. *Steigerung* typically occurs as a culminating effect at the end of Baroque movements (or sections), and it may include textural and thematic complexity (e.g., stretto) as well.

Goethe further developed the concept of *Steigerung* to characterize turns toward a more intense lyrical poetic style within a work. As Michael Spitzer notes, Goethe's concept "blend[s] biological development, spiritual growth, intensification of feeling, and lyrical efflorescence in a single metaphor" (2004, 295).

39. And the melodic line reaches over more extravagantly than in the Bach Allemande, with a yearning octave leap spilling down by step to the next tenth against the bass in subsequent measures.

40. For another example of Mozart's use of developing variation in a late work, see the analysis of the slow movement of K. 533 in chapter 6.

41. For more on the expressive and structural significance of plenitude as both topic and premise, see Hatten 2004, 43–52.

42. The shadow of E♭ minor (this time as a mm⁷ chord) will return as a tragic reminder in the closing group of the exposition, providing a striking example of Mozart's developing variation of a rhetorical gesture.

43. Indeed, the overarching theme of the collection in which Rings's essay appears, *Expressive Intersections in Brahms* (edited by Heather Platt and Peter H. Smith), is that there are expressive motivations behind all innovations or departures from the norm with respect to genre, form, and patterned structures of melody, harmony, and counterpoint in Brahms's works.

44. For example, the bizarre Intermezzo in E Minor, op. 116, no. 5, in which harmony acts as brief coloration, an over- and under-tone penumbra surrounding the two-note, initially stepwise, contrary-motion melodic particles in the two hands. Or the Intermezzo in E♭ Minor, op. 118, no. 6, in which the arpeggiation of a diminished-seventh chord appears to be derived from the minor third outlined by the descending, stepwise melodic line. This piece may well have inspired Schoenberg's own textural derivations of harmony from melody (motive); its wonderful climactic overlapping return of the A theme is an effect Schoenberg would emulate in his *Klavierstücke*, op. 11, no. 1.

45. Rings (2012) notes the subtle canon between soprano and bass in mm. 4ff. that supports a more systematic integration of *melos* in the continuation of this theme. Its immediate echoing effect also supports a sense of inward reflection characteristic of subjectivity (see chap. 5). Another example of melodic-harmonic integration occurs in the B section of Op. 119, no. 1, a D-major theme that recalls the E-major opening of Op. 116, no. 4. The accordion-like alternation of extrema in the right hand creates a mirroring effect, as though the opening third were splayed in both directions in this refractive melody.

46. Debussy's song was composed between 1885–87 but only published in 1888. Fauré's song is dated 1887.

47. For more on Debussy's "rhetoric of suggestion," see Thompson 2018.

Interlude I: From Embodiment to Subjectivity

Having established the potential of virtual actants to combine into agents and actorial roles in chapter 4, I turn in chapter 5 to the consideration of actorial agents as interiorized threads of thought in a larger, virtual subjectivity. For this interiorization to take place, the interpreter must have some means to move from more literal (or imagined) kinds of embodiment, as theorized by Arnie Cox (2016) and as discussed in chapter 3. Virtual subjectivity is not so much embodied as it is spiritually (and spiritedly) infused with the transmuted (and transfigured) energies of music. These form trains of "feelingful thought," which in turn can lead to profound, emotionally freighted reflections. In other words, a virtual agent may be conceived not just as a virtual body but as a distilled part of the virtual subjectivity or consciousness implied by the music.

Unfortunately, we do not have a clear theoretical language to substitute for embodiment when virtual subjectivity is so distilled (I suggest "enmindment" in chap. 3), but artists have sought to reach this level in various ways. Anton Chekhov's plays are filled with examples of the subtlety with which he could convey, through otherwise plain language, a dramatically charged situation that reveals deeper subjective awareness, to some extent recognized by the characters but to a greater extent experienced by the audience, as drama critic Richard Gilman has demonstrated. He notes how, in Chekhov's *Three Sisters*, "the characters never announce who or what they are but simply speak and behave. . . . They make themselves known at every moment, but *the important knowledge is chiefly of interiority*; we have to follow their signs, using the stuff of our own experience as a guide" (1995, 166; my emphasis). This subjectivity is filled with longing, which we must infer even in the absence of Chekhov's characters' direct expression, and it is one of his most powerful aesthetic effects.

For music, even virtual agents who urgently will their virtual actions or actively express their virtual emotions may not be telling the whole story. The merger of individual agents into a larger entity has been explored in terms of a "work-persona" (Monahan 2013) or the persona of the "composer's voice" (Cone 1974). I instead theorize this merger of virtual agents in terms of their interiorization as components of an individual, virtual subjectivity.

The next chapter explores in more detail this process of virtual actors becoming interiorized as trains of thought within a larger consciousness. I begin here by emphasizing how "enmindment" can occur already at the beginning of a work, apparently bypassing the need for prior embodiment of individual agencies or actors. This powerful subjectivization speaks to the important role of virtualization in our experience of music, even when it appears to evade those "actual" sources of embodiment arising from the experience of shared gestural shapes or energetic profiles.

Consider the opening of the andante from Johannes Brahms's Piano Quartet in C Minor, op. 60 (example Int.1).[1] Although one may experience emotion as expressed by the contours and dynamics of the opening gesture, much of the specificity of that response may be traced to musical conventions that build on and nuance the physically gestural energy of the opening *melos*. Certainly, there is a majestic descent followed by an energetically enhanced ascent, but the richness of virtual emotion draws on higher levels of musical engagement with the implications of mode (major), descent in thirds (a style type for Beethoven as well as Brahms), and harmonic mixture (the C♮), which inflects the shift to a neighboring harmony (a parenthetical half-diminished seventh) before returning to a glowing E major. Energetics can account for a gracious, spacious, and generous descent followed by a noble (dotted-rhythm) ascent, but notice that even my characterization of the descent and ascent involves inflections acquired from conventional stylistic elements. In other words, the synthesis of elements that make up this rich thematic gesture, while implying a virtual experiencing agent, nevertheless do not reduce to embodiment in a strict sense—that is, as derived from "moving to" the energies of the melodic contour or its intensification by a dotted rhythm and a shift of direction.

Indeed, as a listener I already feel myself experiencing a subjectivity that is closer to spiritual consciousness: reflective, interiorized, and as though a subtle metamorphosis had already been accomplished by the transmutation of higher musical understandings from lower energetics. An experiment may help reveal the difference. Try the same contour and rhythm with radically post-tonal melodic and harmonic constituents and see if anything like the same effect is produced by contour and rhythm alone.

So how does this transmutation occur? What helps us make the leap to full subjective consciousness as informed by emotional qualities that further contribute to a higher state of reflective awareness? Might it already be a habit, a practice that has been inculcated through our experiences of previous works by Brahms, by the Romantics, by Beethoven, by others—how far back in music history should we go? If this is an aesthetic competency inculcated by Western music and enhanced by successive styles, how can we nevertheless ground it in musical and cognitive realities? As soon as the correlations of energy to movement are exhausted at lower levels, must we turn to metaphor?

Invoking metaphor is certainly one way of introducing cognition that can be emergent from literal movement. But consider a similar maneuver that weakens, for me, Nelson Goodman's (1968) otherwise brilliant theory of exemplification and expression in the arts. First, he observes that exemplification is

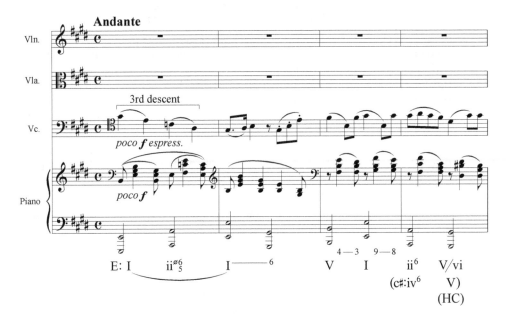

Example Int.1. Brahms, Piano Quartet in C Minor, second movement, first theme (mm. 1–4 only)

signification by possession of features (e.g., a red sample signifies red by possessing the property of redness). Next, expression is defined as "metaphorical exemplification," in that signification is based on the metaphorical possession of features. But what is the basis of this metaphorical possession? How can we decide whether a claimed metaphorical possession is in any way warranted? Clearly, we need the warrant of a symbol system, or style, as Goodman realizes in his subsequent article, "The Status of Style" (1975). But again, how do we establish the "warrant" afforded by any given style? I believe it is through careful reconstruction of the principles, correlations, and interpretive strategies of style considered as a competency in symbolic functioning presupposed by a work of art (Hatten 1982, 1994). Thus, for the Brahms example, we need not limit ourselves only to readily embodied aspects of movement and contour; we may also include the semiotically earned contributions of mode, mixture, harmony, and so forth, which nuance contour and rhythm (and dynamics, pacing, and articulation) into more complex syntheses worthy of the complex emotions and reflections of consciousness.

Note an interesting theoretical reversal here: we tend to think of Leonard B. Meyer's (1989) "secondary" or "statistical" parameters (dynamics, pacing, and articulations) as nuancing harmony and tonality, but in terms of subjectivization, it is harmony and tonality that endow these energetic shadings with deeper content.[2] Nevertheless, as I demonstrate in my work on musical gesture, even secondary parameters can be thematized as primary (Hatten 2004). And furthermore, they may be our default guides when the syntax of tonality in a work becomes either too complex or too deformed to be immediately interpretable within the style presupposed by that work. Thus, dynamics, pacing, and articulation are faithful clues to embodiment that can also help us make the leap to new forms of subjective experience or reflective consciousness.

Melody is a curious parameter in that it includes both the dynamic contouring of pitches and the tonal voice leading of pitch classes. Raw contour is invoked in my Brahms example, with mode, mixture, and neighboring harmonic functions relegated to a "higher" musical level of style. Melody, fascinatingly and often frustratingly for a staged theory of agency, combines both raw contour with stylistic voice leading and harmonic implications at the start (and further merges with the *melos* of an entire texture). Thus, Steve Larson's (2012) very basic musical forces already imply the virtual environmental contributions of tonality for both gravity (implying a stable platform) and magnetism (half-step attraction implying voice-leading function). But recall that Larson's "force" of inertia does not require or presuppose tonality—it is simply the observed tendency of a process/pattern (or its absence) to continue (or persist), unless impeded (or energized) in some way. Thus, pitches, when melodized as contour and durational patterning, are amenable to Larson's force descriptions (and my virtual agential energies) and can directly evoke mimetic/energetic correlations leading to experiences of embodiment, even in the absence of tonality's voice leading or meter's conditioned rhythms.[3]

But to return to the issue of embodiment: What kind of embodiment is focal for Cox's (2016) mimetic hypothesis? Primarily, it is the way a listener can literally (and then imaginatively) embody the energies of the music being heard. Granted the existence and strong plausibility of such a mode of listening, might there be a difference between that mode and one in which the listener infers a virtual agent who is virtually embodying a virtual experience of those energies? Might those virtual experiences be interpretable as virtual emotions being expressed or experienced by that virtual agent? In other words, *how do we position the actual listener with respect to the virtual agent*? This may seem not to be an issue when we speak of a listener identifying with whatever emotions and psychological journeys she may infer from the music. In such a case, the listener may appear to function *as* the virtual agent experiencing music's expressions. But consider the important distancing implied by empathy and, even more obviously, sympathy. Here, the emotions evoked, triggered, and selectively experienced by the engaged listener may not be equal to (as in the case of identification) or equivalent to (as in the case of empathy) but indeed divergent from (as in the case of sympathy) those that may be inferred as experienced by a virtual agent. The divergence may be either positively sympathetic (pity) or negatively unsympathetic (disgust).

What does this wrinkle entail for a theory of embodiment? Might it suggest that along with finding ways to explain how we can actually move *to* the music, we might also (at the same time) need to explain how we move *against* the music? Or, to put it less oppositionally, how might we explain the listener's negotiation of personal subjectivity with the virtual subjectivity being developed by the music? And might that negotiation already be at issue from the start?

Let's return to the Brahms example. Suppose (as was actually the case for me) a listener experiences an emotionally wrought frisson already in the opening two bars of the music as it is being performed without any direct correlation of movement to contour or rhythm and without any imagined "movement" being part of the conscious experience? Has the transmutation of sound into emotion simply been processed so quickly that one is not consciously aware of the stages of mimesis? Might there be shortcuts, both cognitively and aesthetically practiced, that enable one to instantaneously "be" in the music, bypassing the more obvious "moving with the music" stage? If so, this would not be surprising. When we become accomplished readers, we no longer move our lips as we read informational prose quickly.[4] Instead, we grasp meaning at a more transparent level of consciousness as the signs constellate into emotional syntheses or feelingful discourses without requiring minute attention on lower levels of construction. In other words, perception driven by the search for meaning can override bottom-up processing. And this same phenomenon may be understood musically as the power of subjective engagement with emotional-reflective meaning to override (not merely enhance) lower-level physical responses of the directly correlative kind studied by Cox.

If we can at least imagine this powerful kind of engagement, then why does it not always have such spectacular effects? In my own experience, the Brahms movement came as an encore right after hearing a piano quartet by Antonín Dvořák that offered (to me) none of that immediate emotional engagement at a profound level of subjectivity (although to be fair to Dvořák, I've always experienced it with his *Dumky* trio). Is there also an immediate sense of quality that somehow acts as a trigger? I have proposed as a suggestive analogue the very different modality of taste (Hatten 2004, 3). We instantly synthesize into flavor what a chemist must analyze in assessing any recipe that combines many different ingredients. We are cognitively primed to accomplish these instantaneous blendings into the "trope" of a given flavor. Similarly, we may perhaps understand the Brahms movement, within the subjective present of its opening gesture, as sufficiently complex and rewarding on first hearing.

But there is no easy way to establish such syntheses. They do not submit to the kinds of cognitive tests that we might design for lower levels of more obvious embodiment—the "moving to music" that Cox's mimetic hypothesis initially explores. Instead, we must rely on the speculative theorizing of musical expressive meaning that has grown in such intensity over the past thirty years. We have plenty of tools now to make those assessments, progressing from more obvious meanings to the plausibility of more complex blends, as most spectacularly illustrated in the theory of troping (Hatten 1994, 2004, 2012e, 2014b), with which I demonstrate music's own means of achieving creative syntheses akin to metaphor or creative contradictions akin to irony.

Here I distinguish my approach to musical metaphor from George Lakoff and Mark Johnson's (1980) approach to conceptual metaphors (see also Lakoff 1987).

Given the linguistic formulation of conceptual metaphors, their explanatory force is heavily laden from the start with a corresponding linguistic-conceptual organization—despite the claimed bodily source and motivation for the linguistic formulations. The complex character of Lakoff and Johnson's supposedly primal metaphors is due to their conceptual abstraction through language.[5] Cox begins to resolve this issue through a hierarchy of image schemata embedded within conceptual metaphors. I would go further along this line, replacing conceptual metaphors with expressive schemata (analogous to the use of this concept in Gjerdingen 2007 and Byros 2012, 2014), that would be generalizable from musical shapes rather than simply applied from the top down. I would then reserve the concept of metaphor for its original poetic sense, as describing those creative acts, syntheses, or blendings of music's own materials into complexes that can trigger elaborate acts of interpretation on the part of listeners who are already primed to enter into profound engagements with emotions and subjectivity. Indeed, troping in this sense is perhaps the mind's most significant and characteristic activity. Thus, subjectivity, as actively engaging with (virtual) worlds and interiorly reflecting on itself, may be staged most compellingly by those musical works where complex, creatively tropological syntheses suggest the workings of our highest forms of consciousness.

Notes

1. For a more rigorous, extended analysis of this movement, see Robinson and Hatten 2012. The observations I make here are entirely my own.

2. The "true content" for Heinrich Schenker (1930); see Hatten 1994, 113.

3. I explore this possibility further in chapter 10 with an analysis of a theme by Arnold Schoenberg.

4. Granted, we may savor the slower experience of vocalizing movements when reading poetry aloud to appreciate its phonetic music—those subtleties created by rhyme, alliteration, assonance, duration, and accent.

5. This problem would appear to be mitigated by Lakoff and Johnson (1999) in their provision for a "cognitive unconscious"; see also Johnson's emphasis on image schemas as neither "mental" nor "bodily" but rather "contours of what [philosopher John] Dewey called the body-mind" (2007, 139). As Johnson summarizes, "Only when image schemas are seen as structures of sensorimotor experience that can be recruited for abstract conceptualization and reasoning . . . does it become possible to answer the key question: how can abstract concepts emerge from embodied experience without calling upon disembodied mind, autonomous language modules, or pure reason" (141). However, in *Interpreting Musical Gestures, Topics, and Tropes*, I note Sunny Y. Auyang's critique of Lakoff and Johnson's (1999, 54–58) neural modeling hypothesis (as cross-domain neural connections, akin to metaphor) in that it presents a rather "rigid notion of embodiment" and there is "no evidence that the projections [from sensorimotor areas] preserve entire activation patterns that are recognizable as sensorimotor inference or metaphors" (Auyang 2000, 90, cited in Hatten 2004, 299n7). Auyang argues that the isomorphism in Lakoff and Johnson's "metaphors" requires higher-level cognitive work, hence a more theoretical than metaphorical modeling (2000, 92).

5   Staging Virtual Subjectivity

We have seen how the source of a force may be interpreted as a virtual human agent either willing an action (as implied by movement that overcomes environmental constraints) or experiencing an emotion (as foregrounded by rhetorical gestures or unexpected swerves that break the unmarked flow of a background mood and imply a corresponding reaction by a virtual agent). Freely willed physical actions, inferred from their degree of free movement against constraints, offer one concrete analogue for the more abstruse philosophical notion of free will. With respect to subjectivity, however, it is *virtual* freedom that counts. A virtual subjectivity may be able to feel and think freely, even when unable to act freely (whether constrained by extreme environmental forces or antagonistic external agencies, as in the dramatic sphere of tragedy).

In this chapter I explore the staging of subjectivity from the liberating freedom of an actively emergent theme by Beethoven to the inescapable confines of an obsessively interiorized theme by Schubert. But before returning to close analysis and interpretation, I want to step back and reflect on the history of subjectivity from an unusual vantage point.

Components of a rich human subjectivity experienced in the past, albeit not explicitly recognized or fully theorized as such, may be reconstructed from the beginnings of written history.[1] If one can establish the existence of these components, one can then argue that creators and interpreters of music not only had access to key aspects of subjectivity but might have found means to express or experience them virtually in their music. Although philosophers place varying constraints on the historical emergence of aspects of human subjectivity, I would argue that a crucial component, self-awareness, was already clearly signaled by Socrates in his famous dictum, "the unexamined life is not worth living."[2]

Significant Components of Western Subjectivity: An Example from Boethius

Free will may be experienced subjectively (and virtually) as the freedom of the mind to imagine and feel deeply, even when the capacity to act is severely constrained. This was the case for the remarkable Roman scholar and translator Boethius during the last year or so of his life when he was a political prisoner before his execution under the reign of Theodoric. Struggling with despair, Boethius nevertheless composed a literary and philosophical masterpiece, *The Consolation of Philosophy* ([524] 2008), during his incarceration. Described as a "prosimetrum (a prose work with verse interludes)" (Marenbon 2013, sec. 1, par. 3), Boethius's *Consolation* was translated and studied for a thousand years, both inside and outside Medieval schools and Renaissance academies.[3] Boethius's literary and philosophical musings are highly revealing about the construction of human subjectivity at this early point in Western history. His basic but profound ways of thinking about the Self were, I argue, available to composers and listeners throughout the history of Western music, although the musical means by which composers could stage comparable effects were only gradually acquired. Prior to the explicit staging of virtual subjectivity in music, however, listeners were already engaging with music through their own subjectivity as they negotiated its significance through their own experience and capacity for growth.

When we begin reading the *Consolation*, we immediately sense its deeply human motivation: Boethius is struggling with utter despair and seeking ways to manage and transcend the spiritual hardships of his loss of active freedom. First, we find his imagination soaring beyond the confinement of prison: Boethius virtually experiences freedom of thought as part of a rich subjectivity that discovers it need not be bound by any circumstance. Just such imagination would empower composers, some of whom found ways to overcome even encroaching deafness to achieve an inner freedom of virtual hearing. This capacity for imaginative freedom, however, is also available to listeners, and it is most evident whenever we internalize and engage with a virtual agent's expressive journey as our own.

Second, we encounter an allegory of that imaginative freedom as framed within dialogue. As Seth Lerer observes, Boethius "develops the pedagogic dialogue found in the works of Plato, Cicero, and St. Augustine into a dramatic narrative of self-awareness" (2008, xiv). The notion of self-awareness achieved through an inner dialogue is akin to how listeners access a richer subjectivity in music through the dialogue of virtual agents in a virtual environment, or as virtual actors that take on roles understood as parts of a listener's own consciousness. Self-awareness as dialogical is fundamental to this transformation, which ultimately involves a dialogue between music's virtual subjectivities and the listener's own.

Third, at Lady Philosophy's demand, Boethius apparently agrees to dismiss the poetic muses whose inspiration has fueled his laments and thus led to his depression. Lady Philosophy allegorically offers philosophy (moral understanding) as a palliative, and eventually a cure, for his depression. But despite what might first appear as a pragmatic attempt to move from the weaker emotionality represented by poetry to the stronger moral intellection represented by philosophy, Boethius continues to alternate poems with prose, thereby rejecting any naïve opposition of the two. He creates a synthesis of passionately embodied thoughts whose moral and expressive power are enhanced by his interwoven lyrics. Poetry and its muses are revealed to be capable of higher realms of subjective feeling, especially those that ennoble the spirit by transcending the slough of depressive feelings.

Similarly, we find music's virtual subjectivity able to encompass more than mere emotions or their development; music can also develop a virtual realm in which moral and philosophical feelings and thoughts are possible. For example, abnegation, understood as overcoming the tragic through positively resigned acceptance, would qualify as a moral emotion, one that is staged virtually by Beethoven in a number of ways, especially in his late works.[4] A related moral emotion is the sense of nobility that emerges from positively resigned acceptance, as suggested already in the first two measures of the *Adagio cantabile* movement from Beethoven's Piano Sonata, op. 13.[5]

Fourth, although Boethius recognizes (through the voice of Lady Philosophy) that "anger is helpless, fear is pointless, and desire is all a delusion," he acknowledges that "if you want the physician's cure, you must bare your wound" ([524] 2008, 10). In other words, part of the awareness that Boethius must achieve to realize healing is a full expression of the experience of suffering. Analogously, we can observe that the emotional effects of music go beyond mere gushing or wallowing in grief, since the processing of intense emotions in music can lead to a purging or cathartic effect of full awareness, part of a richer subjectivity that can both fully experience as well as sublimate suffering through its virtual expression in music.

Fifth, Lady Philosophy reproves Boethius with the diagnosis that he is "torn by grief and anger and self-pity, and each of these pulls [him] in a different direction" ([524] 2008, 22). Here, the implication is of a subjectivity that can be multiple in its emotions, and hence potentially incoherent, despite its singular source in an individual consciousness. Similarly, music may present "an image of shattered subjectivity" (McClary 2000, 119) that may nevertheless (*contra* McClary) be interpreted virtually as a struggle among competing actorial agents within a single (virtually integrated) consciousness. This is the basis for my own interpretation of the first movement of Beethoven's Op. 132 (Hatten 2004, 267–78), where external, fateful/tragic forces are in dialogue with an internal protagonist-actor, and where together they constitute a singular virtual subjectivity with which listeners can identify.

Sixth, just as the question-and-answer aspect of Boethius's constructed dialogue serves a kind of therapeutic function, it also allegorizes the self-reflectivity (and even self-reflexivity[6]) that characterizes human subjectivity in its bootstrapping efforts to transform from one psychological state to another. For Boethius, that bootstrapping helps him rise from his despair at the vagaries of Fortune and a perception of the world as meaningless to a firm conviction in the moral justness of the universe as immune to the inevitable caprices of chance. For music, the inner struggles implied by conflicting actorial roles that are embraced by a single subjectivity also enable that virtual subjectivity to experience a profound sense of moral growth and understanding, one that follows the trajectory of emotions expressed and developed throughout the course of a musical work. A listener can be engaged by both virtually participating in and actually reflecting on the dramatic trajectory of an existential emotional struggle that leads to a transformative outcome (as in a symphony by Mahler).

Seventh, Lady Philosophy urges Boethius to draw on his past, his books, and "the ideas in them, the opinions and principles of times gone by" ([524] 2008, 21). Here as elsewhere we find a vision of a historically informed and explicitly intertextual subjectivity. As Lerer puts it, Boethius has an image of life as "a library of the imagination" (2008, xvii). And Boethius exemplifies that intertextual sense of history through his own allusions to "Homeric and Virgilian epic, Ovidian love poetry, [and] Senecan tragedy" (xvi). Thus, subjectivity has a cultural past, and that past—as exemplified by the insights of those who came before—can and should inform present consciousness. For music, I have noted the importance of intertextuality as a means of enhancing the expressive depth of passages in Beethoven (Hatten 1985; 1994, 196–201), and Michael Klein (2005) has further developed the concept of intertextuality to embrace, for modern listeners, relevant intertextual connections that enhance our understanding of a given musical work from the perspective of later works, not just prior ones. Thus, for contemporary listeners the virtual subjectivity of a musical work has a future as well as a past.

Finally, Boethius in effect believes himself into belief: he writes himself into a conviction that he holds by virtue of his having envisioned it and expressed it in language. Thus, from the allegorical we have access to the actual. We can transfer the allegorical force of a virtual subjectivity's musical struggle by applying it to our own lives. We may experience an actual catharsis (as Aristotle first theorized from the practice of Greek dramatists) as a result of our subjective engagement with the virtual argument, struggle, or passionate trajectory of a philosophically, morally, and psychologically profound drama in music. And all of this can occur even in purely instrumental music, through the help of compositional strategies that explicitly stage such trajectories.

I should add that Boethius offers evidence through his own, already rich subjectivity of what would come to be intersubjectively shared and understood in Western culture as a profound self-awareness. Although music scholars know Boethius primarily for his more technical contributions to the history of music theory, in his last and most personal work we find a model for subjectivity that may well have informed composers' awareness of subjectivity in its potential to be staged and experienced in music.

Subjectivity in the History of Western Music

As a literary influence on music's development of a relatively independent staging of subjectivity, one would not likely mention *The Consolation of Philosophy*. There are far too many more direct examples in the musically set poetry of the trouvères and troubadours, Medieval composer Guillaume de Machaut's own poetry that extends the courtly love tradition, or Petrarch's self-reflective sonnets of the Renaissance. But Boethius's Neoplatonic orientation may well have inspired Dante's *La Nuova Vita* and Lorenzo de' Medici's sonnets, each accompanied by their own Neoplatonic commentary that links the emotions and images of their poetry to philosophical and moral situations that inspired them. It was

Lorenzo's friend, the poet Poliziano, who wrote the first poetic *Orfeo* to be set to music (around 1500). And Poliziano's *Orfeo* was forerunner to the Florentine Camerata's own Neoplatonic vision of expression, as developed a century later, in monody and opera (including their own musical realizations of the legend of Orpheus). The Camerata's vision would be developed by Claudio Monteverdi into a wider-ranging style capable of still more vivid expression of human emotions. In his last opera, *Poppea*, Monteverdi's stylistic options enable him to musically embody both the moral emotions so poignantly expressed by Octavia and Seneca and the sensual ones so seductively exposed by Poppea and Nerone.

Between Poliziano and the Camerata, the era of the late Renaissance madrigal provides further evidence of the power of music to stage subjectivity—indeed, the subjectivity of a virtual agent who is torn between conflicting emotions, as in Petrarch's poetry. Susan McClary (2004) demonstrates how the multiple voices in madrigals from Jacques Arcadelt to Monteverdi could portray, simultaneously as well as in close succession, a variety of emotions and thereby stage a complex subjectivity. By a striking analogy with popular gospel, doo-wop, and boy group collectives in our own day, she suggests how unproblematic our capacity to experience this multiplicity could be: "Like madrigal ensembles, [these popular singing groups] feature *simulations of complex interiorities*: rational grounding in the bass, melodic address in the middle, ecstatic melismas on the top" (4; my emphasis).[7]

McClary also makes a strong case for finding evidence in the music itself—historical documents equally worthy of interpretation and just as capable of doing cultural work. Through a series of close analyses, she demonstrates that "music often yields a somewhat different chronology of issues such as subjective formations or conceptions of the body than would a study based solely on written documents" (2004, 6).[8] As one example, McClary states, "Over the course of a good century, madrigal composers anticipate Descartes in performing the crucial break with traditional epistemologies, plunging musical style and thought into an extraordinary crisis of authority, knowledge, power, and identity" (6). Thus, early modern subjectivity in music begins, for McClary, nearly a century before its typical designation with the beginnings of monody and opera in 1600.

With my example from Boethius, I have illustrated some of the key components of a rich subjectivity that was available at least a thousand years earlier in Western history. Erich Auerbach (1953) goes still further in his comprehensive history of literature's attempts to portray human subjectivity as psychological realism. He notes the greater depth of emotion and motivation in the Hebrew Bible's realistic portrayals of human individuality, whereas Homer (or the Greek oral poetry tradition) offers more stereotyped representations of Greek heroes. Plutarch, in his *Lives of the Noble Romans*, contributes not merely a chronicle of life events but sufficiently deep psychological insight into his subjects that, centuries later, Beethoven would credit Plutarch with having taught him resignation.[9] Indeed, by the time Western music provides enough evidence for historical reconstruction, I would argue that humans were already endowed with components of subjectivity, as found in Boethius, at least cognitively comparable to our own (if perhaps not as complex). This is not to deny the extensive cultural enhancement and refocusing that would continue to form distinct historical subjectivities. Rather, I propose a common substrate of capacities available for exploration by individual creative composers, whether or not particular aspects were focal to their own cultures. Indeed, by the time of Shakespeare (roughly 1600), a vast store of human emotions and self-awareness was available from which musical styles could continue to draw throughout subsequent centuries.[10]

Thus, self-aware subjectivity, already available in various configurations from the beginnings of Western culture, is a capacity that enables listeners to virtually experience a range of moral feelings, thoughts, and actions in music. Compositional strategies such as those explored in chapter 4 further promote the identity, continuity, and coherence of a more singular agent's musical discourse—interiorizing contrasts as inner conflicts and integrating change as growth. It is this depth of subjective experiencing of music that empowers purely instrumental music whenever, and to whatever degree, it sheds the scaffoldings of religious ritual, social dance, song texts, theatrical dramas, and other explicit cues for situating its virtual agencies.

Historically, we find theorists eventually attempting to attribute "characters" to the actorial roles of dialogically interactive musical events in purely instrumental music, as seen in Jérôme-Joseph de Momigny's (1805) interpretation of characters in a Haydn symphony (see Bent 1994, 130–40).[11] However, the stories that listeners may be tempted to tell in weakly "programmatizing" these works are only surface manifestations of deeper allegories. Purely instrumental music is often more concerned with the inner realm of subjective experience and growth (even when that experience is framed within a comic mode of social interaction, as in the late eighteenth century[12]). As I argue in chapter 4, virtual actoriality is possible without nameable characters; it should not be surprising, then, to discover that virtual subjectivity can dispense with an identifiable persona.

Theorizing Virtual Subjectivity: Hildegard and Beyond

The incorporation (or staging) of various degrees of virtual agency in historical musical styles should not be confused with what was already happening in human listeners' own subjective engagement with music. Throughout the Medieval era, listeners would have had the capacity to engage in deeply subjective and spiritually profound ways with monophonic chant. The music of Hildegard of Bingen (1098–1179) holds tantalizing clues to techniques that could enhance and even direct listeners' engagement with virtualizing, embodying, fictionalizing, and interiorizing.[13]

The abbess Hildegard of Bingen's creative individuality emerged only in her early forties; she viewed what we would consider to be her rather independent emerging subjectivity primarily in terms of obedience in response to the inspiration of God. A few have conjectured that her explosion of creativity is explicable as a symptom of migraine or stroke (see Singer [1928] 1958; Sacks 1992).[14] Others have more charitably viewed her breakthrough as motivated partly by righteous anger at the injustices of a patriarchy (both sacred and secular) with which she was beginning to compete in both voice and power.[15] A full acknowledgment of her considerable artistic gifts, however, must include a closer examination of the music itself.

Although Hildegard lacked formal academic training in music, she was taught by monks and had access to the library in the double monastery at Disibodenberg (Gebuhr 2012, 51). Her own spiritual subjectivity soon found voice in her original poetic texts and musical settings. As Ann Gebuhr elaborates,

> Her music was intrinsically a part of her life and her relationship to the cosmic God of her visions and her heart. She wrote eloquently about the role of music as creating and carrying the "essence" of the word much more than "merely" the literal fact of the text. For her, music and text were united as one within the unity of the whole created universe. (2012, 64)

Indeed, when one listens to the freer *ambitus* of her chants and spiritual songs, one hears the kind of gestural energies that I have previously associated with human yearning or striving. In the context of religious texts, that desire may best be interpreted as spiritual: mapping the praise and petition of her texted prayers onto the body's energetic vocal projections of joy and hope through the contours and motivic coherence of what I would recognize as an emerging musical-spiritual discourse.[16]

Margot Fassler's expressive interpretation of formal features in Hildegard's chants offers further evidence for subjectivity as afforded by the music. Use of extensive melismas enables self-reflective "rumination" over significant words in the chant (1998, 164). The use of large- and small-scale repetition (165) along with scaffolding on a preexistent chant (166) could support virtual subjectivity as building on a past (both within the new chant and intertextually prior to it), thereby enriching that experience. These are hallmarks of Boethian subjectivity, and it is remarkable to find them being staged so effectively as early as the twelfth century.

In the fourteenth century, Machaut's motets mark another high point in the history of integrating words and music into complex subjectivity. They display highly sophisticated means of portraying the sentiments of love simultaneously in religious and worldly contexts (Robertson 2007; Lavacek 2011). This troping of sacred and secular forms of love, which one may find already in the music of the trouvères, would continue to enrich French vocal music in the seventeenth century (Gordon-Seifert 2011).

Along with early Western music's semantic scaffolding of text, the bodily scaffolding of dance was another means toward music's more independent virtual agency (see Leppert 2007). Richard Hoppin notes that dance songs "may sometimes have been played by instruments alone, although in manuscript sources they exist only as songs" (1978, 349). One dance, the *estampie*, does occur as both an instrumental piece and a poetic form. Along with building on the actual agency of bodily dancing, musical processes provided another source for attribution of agency. The canon emerged from the folk practice of singing rounds (as in *Sumer is icumen in* [Summer has arrived], found in a thirteenth-century manuscript) in a process that was virtualized agentially in the instrumental *chace*, as seen in four examples from the Ivrea Codex (c. 1360) at the papal court in Avignon. As Hoppin observes,

> The name was probably intended as a description of the way one voice chases another in a musical canon. Slightly later terminology shifted the emphasis from the pursuer to the pursued and gave it the name *fuga* (flight). The double meaning of the word *chace*—a simple pursuit, or a hunt—undoubtedly suggested the use of canonic technique to depict hunting scenes, and one of the Ivrea pieces does depict such a scene. (1978, 370)

Here we find virtual *actorial* agency as a primary motivation for the development of a technique that will later be associated with more structurally conceived counterpoint practices—as canonic imitation.

Associations from both dances and texted music would continue to enrich the purely instrumental repertoire historically. Notably, the *galanterie*—eighteenth-century characteristic dances—were beginning to be imported topically. As inserted into other, more abstractly conceived genres, dances provided immediate referentiality and emotional resonance.[17]

One purely instrumental genre that may appear to have been independently conceived as a virtual-actorial genre is the concerto, in which the emerging role of the soloist reflects the evolution of individualized subjectivity in the eighteenth century. The principle of concerting instrumental forces independent of text can be traced to the polychoral responses explored by the Gabrielis in the late sixteenth century in Venice's San Marco.[18] The *concerto grosso*, a Baroque genre developed in the seventeenth century, emphasized a smaller concertino group isolated against the larger tutti: the eventual focus on single soloists in the eighteenth century marked an increasingly individualized (and hence subjective) agency, responding both collaboratively and conflictually with opposing orchestral forces in an allegory of the individual within society.[19] The notable virtuosity of a soloist-composer such as Niccolò Paganini or Franz Liszt would begin to suggest an extrahuman, supernatural agency embodied in the performer. But Liszt's actual agency as a virtuoso also enhanced the powerful virtual subjectivity that he was learning to stage in his solo concerto compositions with piano and that he would transfer to other genres such as the tone poem.[20]

Chamber music also displays an evolving relationship among virtual agents. Early Haydn string quartets are treble dominated, featuring the first violinist as soloist carrying the burden of the thematic discourse. By the time of Haydn's Op. 33 quartets, as Charles Rosen (1972, 116–17) has perceptively noted, the thematic discourse is more equally distributed among the four players, with the added effect of subtle transitioning mid-phrase: what begins as thematic may turn into accompaniment, and vice versa.[21] Goethe's image of the string quartet as a conversation among equals is perhaps best conceived in terms of the virtual agencies expressed in these works, even as actual sociability is realized in their performance.[22]

From vocal rounds to canons, from the imitative motet to the instrumental ricercar and ultimately the fugue, from responsorial psalms to dialogical forces and voices in concertos and string quartets, and from (often sung) dance music to stylized and topically imported dances, we have seen that composers had many sources from which they could draw on to achieve a semiotically grounded virtual agency and actoriality for instrumental music. With the powerful dramatic resources of tonality, composers could begin to explore a range of shorter- and longer-term goals that would far outstrip the periodicities and predictabilities associated with vocal and dance genres.

Thus, when Fontenelle posed his rhetorical question, "Sonate, que me veux-tu?" the query may also have signaled a crisis for many eighteenth-century listeners, precipitated by instrumental music's increasing independence from obvious social functions. This new music presupposed a listener who could be entrained or otherwise instructed in the ways sonatas, or any nonprogrammatic instrumental works, could imply virtual agency through sophisticated tonal and thematic processes, not merely through topical importations of basic features from vocal and dance music. The issue was not an entirely new aesthetic competency in subjective engagement but rather an engagement with a new, more internally musical staging of virtual subjectivity.

Subjectivity before Philosophical and Aesthetic Theories of Subjectivity

As I have suggested in my brief and highly selective historical surveys, virtual agency was capable of subjective depth well before the nineteenth century. Already, the Enlightenment had fostered a reliance on individual freedom and free thinking as well as individual feeling and sensibility.[23] Such an enhancement of subjectivity could not help but be incorporated by composers (if not already anticipated by them), whether through spiritual alignment with the church (as in the case of dramatized and individually expressive spiritual agencies in Bach's Passions) or through more individual explorations that could complement or even threaten conventional religion (as in the case of Beethoven's turn toward Promethean and pantheist agencies).

What is fascinating about the history of musically staged subjectivity is how composers are able to configure musical styles in order to enact a variety of individual and complex forms of subjectivity—especially in purely instrumental music that is to some degree divorced from physical identification with bodies and voices (characters acting in an opera, singers embodying roles, or dancers manifesting actions). And as Wye Jamison Allanbrook (1983, 2014) and others have shown, topics and other style types provided embodied linkages to help secure an equivalent engagement with instrumental music at both surface textural and deeper syntactical levels.

We should not assume, however, that the history of aesthetic and philosophical evaluations of music's capacities for subjectivity adequately capture either those musical discoveries or (just as importantly) contemporaneous listeners' capacities for engaging subjectively—from the standpoint of their own stylistic competencies—with what was available to them in a musical work. To reconstruct this potential, we must go beyond the histories of both aesthetics and work reception to recover that which may yet have gone unnoticed, not only by philosophers who were not stylistically competent musicians but also by competent musicians and theorists of the time who may nevertheless have lacked crucial structural/analytical and hermeneutic/interpretive resources for the task.

Historical accounts of philosophical and aesthetic attempts to understand contemporaneous music in terms of its emerging subjectivity (among other aspects) are found in Daniel Chua's *Absolute Music and the Construction of Meaning* (1999).[24] The philosophical understandings of absolute music that Chua explores in critical writings from Friedrich Schlegel in the nineteenth century to Theodor W. Adorno in the twentieth provide, however, but one strand of the history of potential interpretations of that music.[25] I propose another strand, one that focuses on how contemporaneous musicians, as opposed to philosophers, might have engaged with their own music (whether or not they were fully able to articulate or theorize their usage). Whereas Chua uses music to reflect or reveal crises in philosophical conceptions of emerging subjectivity, I envision how listeners in any era were fully capable of engaging, through their own richly developed subjectivity, those virtual agencies that were implied already in earlier musical styles. I touch base with the Schlegel-to-Adorno history of emerging subjectivity, but more from a music-theoretical than an ideological perspective.

My approach is not the strictly formalist/structuralist one by means of which analysis has been critiqued as unwittingly supporting an absolutist ideology. Rather, the meeting between my approach and aesthetic philosophers such as Adorno is in that middle ground so elegantly prepared by Scott Burnham in his studies of Mozart's grace (2013) and Beethoven's heroism (1995), and by Allanbrook in her studies of eighteenth-century topics (1983) and the comic surface in Mozart (2014).[26] Michael Steinberg (2004) perhaps comes closest to articulating the virtual aspect of subjectivity that I develop here, although his examples begin historically with Mozart and are more concerned with the emergence of the modern subject.[27] But there is much overlap in our claims with respect to what I call virtual subjectivity. As he observes, "Insofar as music can be understood to possess a quality of simulated agency, it would appear to achieve a condition of subjective experience for itself" (2004, 4).[28]

What I envision with respect to virtual subjectivity, then, is a historically informed yet theoretically and hermeneutically enhanced exploration of what it was possible to hear—and to be engaged with (inter)subjectively—in music. Perhaps not surprisingly, many of the claims aestheticians forward for Romantic music have clear precedents in Bach as well as in Mozart. But the ways in which subjectivity was aesthetically constructed have clearly changed over time. Indeed, recent scholarship explores how modern subjectivity emerged in the face of crises that may have undermined the very coherence of the subjectivity I am proposing as a substrate to our understanding of all Western music.[29] The next section addresses this issue, arguing for a basic level of subjective consciousness that embraces those capacities found already in Boethius and demonstrating its relevance for the interpretation of tonal music. I propose a shared sense of subjectivity that is robust enough to have persisted over the last fifteen hundred years of Western music, despite the very real crises to which the modern subject has been exposed and to which it has responded with such resiliency. I set my proposal against the backdrop of those crises.

Crises of Subjectivity

Behind every theory of subjectivity that laments the loss of the self or subject, there is a presupposition of some coherent living being or process that has suffered that loss. Regardless of how one constructs one's subjectivity (or has it constructed from the outside or through some negotiation between inner and outer forces), there is always a being to, through, or in place of whom subjectivity is posited. Regardless of what we might consider as normal subjectivity (even when the "norming" is insidiously performed by cultural institutions such as those Michel Foucault has devastatingly deconstructed[30]), we can at least agree on the extreme cases: that humans who kill themselves due to the terror of a completely fractured mind/self/being are at the sad end of a continuum of subjectivities. As we move to the other (hypothetical) extreme, we encounter a range of surviving beings with their variously experienced but relatively robust subjectivities, even if these are problematized by the various social or subconscious forces that philosophers have argued to be implicated in our very conception of subjectivity.[31] The Self, however delimited and denatured it may be conceived in its historical "development," persists due to the psychic conditions necessary to our very survival, and its complete loss would be equivalent to death (not only of the individual but also of the species). Thus, the biological and psychological reality of consciousness entails that awareness by means of which an individual is able to act not only to survive but to thrive in the world. If an individual experiences feelings of contentment or even happiness, it may well be an indication of some degree of evolutionary success in that quest.[32] Such a (relatively) robust subjectivity is here presupposed as the ground of my speculations about the design, self-awareness, intentionality, and capacity for independent action attributable to that consciousness—and as a fundamental grounding of my claims for music. Thus, for the tradition of classical Western art music from at least the Baroque through the extended nineteenth century, I rely on a baseline cultural conception of the subject as an independent individual capable of (and owning) independent thought and feeling; able to learn, grow, and develop in response to the world; and possessing some degree of independent agency in the world. Furthermore, the robust subject has a self-reflective awareness and a central identity as a willing, acting, and feeling Self. It has the capacity to hold multiple, even conflicting positions without threatening its underlying sense of coherent self-hood. It has the capacity to experience transport from the perspective of a central identity experiencing a different state of being. And it has the capacity to identify more or less empathetically with a range of "other" selves, both actual and virtual.

However, Klein (2015, 122–23) presses Foucault's claim that human agency is ascribable to institutions, which create individuals.[33] From a Lacanian perspective, language (as another such institution) also has the power to define who we are. As Klein summarizes, "We do not use language, language uses us" (126).[34] I would counter that we can recognize the multifarious and often conflicted realm of an individual's consciousness in that it maintains its coherence from the perspective of a singular, individual subjectivity. Although I offer a baseline set of characteristics for a robust subject, my focus is on the means by which composers are able (wittingly or unwittingly) to stage such a singular consciousness (with which we can identify, virtually) by means of analyzable and interpretable musical strategies. Thus, although the problems of human subjectivity continue to intrigue and haunt philosophers, I hope to provide sufficient evidence for the (virtual) staging in music of those basic aspects of subjectivity found already in Boethius.[35]

As for the role of the Symbolic in Lacan's theory, I do not discount its force, and Klein's exposition of the Symbolic has deepened our understanding of the various kinds of questions that can be posed by given works of music. His interpretations of Chopin and Debussy, for example, demonstrate the extent to which a Lacanian conception of subjectivity can not only affect a modern listener's interpretations but provide insight into the compositional process itself.[36] My emphasis, however, is on the capacity we have, or imagine ourselves to have, to freely choose among alternatives (even if, for Lacan, all the choices have already been predesigned within the Symbolic). My alternative to the limitations of Lacan's Symbolic, then, is to conceive of culture, language, gesture, and (musical, artistic) style in a less radical sense, as overlapping semiotic systems (prior to their presumed folding into the Symbolic) that not only constrain certain choices but afford countless others—choices that only retrospectively appear predetermined. As much as we are formed by our entraining in culture, gesture, and language, I believe composers, performers, and listeners can consciously and independently choose to go further, educating themselves in the complexities of a musical style by apprenticeship with a master, tuition within a conservatory or school, or self-tuition by studying and modeling exemplary scores. And as much as discourses of or about music may help define the cultural conception of an artist, the inner will and drive of that individual typically moves through and beyond the models and resources of styles, realizing an emergent creativity that could not have been predicted in advance.

Thus, I argue that musical styles constrain, but they do not overdetermine compositional choices. Instead, musical styles afford, as in philosopher Wilhelm von Humboldt's succinct formulation for language, infinite creativity from finite means.[37] Musical styles provide endless affordances and virtual worlds for the imagination, worlds within which unpredictable choices and original venturings may occur. As heard in the opening themes of Beethoven's Piano Sonatas, op. 10, no. 2 (discussed in this book's prelude), and op. 22 (introduced later in this chapter), a composer can create means to portray or stage the very kind of freedom he brings to his compositional venturings. Not only are composers able to choose among multiple implicative paths suggested by tonal configurations; they may at any time play the wild card of a rhetorical gesture (that which breaks the otherwise unmarked flow of the music), thereby introducing the unpredictable. Such unprepared disruptions of continuity mime our reaction to life's unexpected outward events as well as our inward experiences of sudden psychological shifts. Indeed, any spontaneous musical gesture (unpredicted by the style, even if immediately negotiated within its constraints) may refresh or expand the resources of a musical style. Such bodily gestures may have their origin outside of music (whether culturally entrained or individually achieved), and yet they may be accommodated within the realm of a tonal system.

Although human freedom itself may appear to be a delusion from certain philosophical perspectives, the semiotic fact remains that it is an essential way we think about ourselves. And a virtual sense of individual volition can be both composed and heard (interpreted) in music. It is through an emergent sense of music's virtual human capacities that an individual listener is able to imaginatively (virtually) merge her consciousness and its fund of experience with that of the virtual consciousness being embodied or "enminded" by the music. What is fascinating with respect to this enminding is the way in which the virtual in music moves listeners from embodiment to imagination, such that we can interpret emergent ideas or thoughts as having been grounded in the body even as they are interiorized in the mind. Thus, in engaging with music, we continually reaffirm our own subjectivity's capacity for thinking passionately or reflecting on feelings—and we thereby find ourselves effectively bridging the presumed divide between body and mind, emotion and thought.

Staging Subjective Freedom: The Emergent Theme

I define "emergence" as that which is not predictable from a prior state (either of organization or of our understanding of the levels of that organization)—hence something that is emergent is new and demands a new level of explanation. This is in accord with the scientific sense of emergence, in which human consciousness is emergent from biology, chemistry, and physics. A reductionist view, by contrast, attempts to describe what are claimed as emergent phenomena entirely in terms of lower levels of organization or explanation. My critique of Lacan's Symbolic, for example, could be framed as a critique of its reductionist claims about human freedom. My insistence on free will as a marker of human subjectivity reflects my commitment to the emergent capacities of human consciousness. Individuals can suddenly act in ways that are not predictable in terms of their previous behavior; if their actions are to be rationalized after the fact (whether as choices or inevitabilities), then an emergent level of explanation is often required.

My concept of musical troping (Hatten 1994, 2014) is one example for which meaning is emergently understood as more than the sum of its parts. Here, the parts are those juxtaposed musical events or topics that spark a creative interpretation along the lines of metaphor or irony. Such emergent meaning is fragile (it may not spark for a given listener), it is fuzzy (it does not have clear boundaries), and it is distinctive, if not unique (it cannot be easily translated or paraphrased). Philosophers (e.g., Roger Scruton) who view musical expression itself as unique (hence intransitive, in Richard Wollheim's sense) are, in effect, highlighting expression's emergent status (see Wollheim 1968; Scruton 1997). A more practical approach to musical expression (at least for those of us who do attempt a preliminary paraphrase, as one step toward more complex interpretation of creative expressive events) would be to view such events as amalgams of old and new, familiar and unfamiliar elements. Here, the type-token distinction first proposed by Charles Sanders Peirce enables us to preserve the uniqueness of the token while recognizing the identifiable contributions of its potentially multiple type affiliations.[38]

One way a composer can stage virtual freedom is by reproducing the conditions of emergence, by enacting freedom from virtual environmental and structural constraints, and thereby suggesting the freely willed actions of a virtual agent. Though (at least initially) unpredictable, such actions will spark a new level of (emergent) understanding that in turn captures the fragile, fuzzy, and distinctive meaning of this virtual musical expression.

Back to Beethoven: Op. 10, No. 2, First Movement, First Theme

What kinds of cues can help dramatize the interiorizing move from the everyday to more profound states of subjectivity? Return to the opening theme (mm. 1–12[1]) of Beethoven's Piano Sonata in F Major, op. 10, no. 2 (reproduced in example 5.1[a]). Here, Beethoven creates the illusion, or grants the virtuality, of subjectivity not only as freedom from the mundane but as a corresponding spiritual release into a realm of experience that is both more internalized and more profound. He even stages a brief moment of self-reflection (the break between mm. 8 and 9). Although these strategies involve the kinds of extreme shifts we see in the opening of the Mozart K. 311 slow movement (example 4.6), there is a more explicit reference here to a prototypical phrase structure, one that is productively evaded as a dramatic shift cueing subjective freedom—and there is a greater sense of exhilaration that emerges from the experience of that freedom.[39]

In measure 5 we find a change of texture and theme that shifts from a normative continuation of the sentence structure implied by the first four-bar presentation phase with its Mozart-inspired statement-and-response schema.[40] Example 5.1(b) is my composed realization of a faux-Mozart, eight-bar prototypical sentence (here ending on V, as antecedent to a compound period). The conventional motivic acceleration in measure 5 climaxes in measure 6, and measures 7 and 8

Example 5.1. Beethoven, Piano Sonata in F Major, op. 10, no. 2, first movement. (a) First theme (mm. 1–12¹) as composed by Beethoven. (b) First theme recomposed in measures 5–8 to suggest an eight-measure prototypical sentence serving as the antecedent of a compound period (not shown in its entirety).

provide a grounding cadence (with a playful echo of the triplet motive in m. 8). My realization preserves the *buffa* implications of the presentation while still drawing on the destabilizing continuation's developmental power to dramatize. Rounding off to a half cadence implies a larger-scale symmetry and balance that would be achieved at the sixteen-bar level, as well as a conventional phrase structure within the otherwise unmarked galant style of the Classical era.[41] Although agency is still present, subjectivity is rather limited by the somewhat mechanical motivic development and conventional phrase structure.

By contrast, Beethoven's continuation (example 5.1[a], m. 5) declines the buffa topical gambit in measures 1–4 and instead "takes flight" by radical shifts of texture and topic as well as register.[42] The "new" idea that takes flight is developed through an accelerated stepwise motion to a more elaborately worked-out climax that expands the conventional eight-bar sentence to twelve. Provocatively, at the very moment where we might otherwise have expected a cadence (m. 8), a harmonic swerve to the subdominant is broken off by a rhetorical silence. This momentary repose allows us to reflect on this extraordinary freedom that has now affected harmonic syntax as well as phrase construction. The unsupported subdominant appears to have lifted us away from all tonal responsibility. The momentary pause also develops, as thematic, the rhetorical rests found in the basic idea. Reflection is justified as an interiorizing inference here, since the resumption of the subdominant in its exact register and spacing marks the moment as parenthetical. A "continuation of the continuation" picks up where the previous continuation left off, injecting new agential energy with the leap to a registral apex in measure 9 and further intensifying the expressive energy by pressing downward to an appoggiatura crux enhanced by an expressive turn figure in measure 10. Only at this point does the psychic energy subside into a more conventional cadence, although the melodic integration of both dotted rhythms and sighs serves as fitting denouement.

In effect, Beethoven has staged not only a sense of freedom but an almost ecstatic release—as though he were miming a sudden turn of thought that had led to an emotional epiphany. Notice how I have tried to combine these analogues of thought and emotion into a singular experience of a psychic breakthrough. It is in this sense that Beethoven's staging of freedom merges a philosophical, moral depth with a dramatic, emotional peak.

Although we cannot always know what may have inspired Beethoven's own subjective experience—its referential or situational grounding—we can follow the precise contours of that virtual experience and fill it with appropriate content from our own fund of experience. Or perhaps we can realize a new experience that takes us out of our own embodied routines to a realm of ecstatic revelation. I venture such extravagant language to make a point—that something truly special is being staged in this theme, which has quickly earned a level of subjective freedom and emotional exaltation, transcending conventional structure to enact an analogous transcendence of consciousness.

This, I would claim, is what Beethoven's theme is about. It coordinates various types of gestures and levels of virtual agency in a sophisticated way to achieve its expressive effects. There is no contemporaneous theorist who could have accounted for, much less explained, all the expressive effects that I reconstruct from evidence in Beethoven's score, even as these effects depend on departures from (or expansions of) the kinds of structures the theorists of the time were attempting to explain.[43]

To summarize, a simple set of correspondences supports the sudden accessing of a more profound level of subjectivity in this theme:

1. The shift in measure 5 is interpretable as a freely willed escape from the overly conventional opening.
2. Its movement to a higher register suggests that the escape transcends the mundane. (Note that my conventional version in example 5.1[b] also enacts an escape, but as comic release—spilling over with continuous triplets. Interestingly, the comic can also emerge from sanctioned social transgression.)
3. The momentary break in measure 8 allows us time to reflect on what has just transpired, and that self-reflection adds to its significance.
4. The eventual climax and overflow result in a complete twelve-bar unit that has eclipsed, in its expressive intensity and engagement, the initial four-bar unit's implication of an eight-bar sentence structure. This displacement into another realm of heightened expression thus mimes a shift from one mode of thought to another—a more profound realm of experience that "displaces" the original.

Thus, it is aesthetically warranted to interpret Beethoven's theme as explicitly staging virtual subjectivity by enacting both freedom and self-reflectivity. The listener's spirit can indeed soar, since it experiences its own freedom as a kind of release from conventional constraint. The rhetorical gestures by which Beethoven breaks the unmarked flow of the discourse serve as traces of the imaginative freedom by which a subjectivity can move beyond the laws of nature, logic, and contingency to find greater expression through an individualized trajectory. That trajectory may appear willed yet also have an aspect of grace—of being granted, like a sudden vision or insight that one seizes on and follows through to its completion, even after a momentary gasp of awe (the subdominant break) that provides a brief, sublime moment of awareness on the way to expressive fulfillment.

Furthermore, the virtual subjectivity being staged here is one that must also find a way to integrate surprising novelty into a coherent unfolding discourse—analogous to the psychic integration achieved by a robust (unfractured) subjectivity. In this example a Schenkerian analysis of the upper line would discover the basis for a more integrative continuity: an incomplete structural descent, as initiated in measures 1, 3, and 5 ($\hat{5}$–$\hat{4}$–$\hat{3}$), first overlaps the launch of the new texture in measure 5 and then is eventually completed in measures 11 and 12 ($\hat{2}$–$\hat{1}$) after an admittedly extravagant deferral (mm. 5–11). However, completion occurs an octave higher, in the "freer" register achieved by the extravagant interruption. Thus, the theme is still somewhat open, since the upper line's resolution did not take place in what Heinrich Schenker would call the "*obligate Lage*" (the original and hence obligatory register required for definitive resolution).[44]

Beethoven, Piano Sonata in B♭ Major, Op. 22, First Movement, First Theme

Compare Beethoven's similar staging of subjectivity in the opening theme of the Piano Sonata in B♭ Major, op. 22 (example 5.2). Here, the presentation phase is evocative of Haydn; its terse motive recalls the opening of Haydn's Piano Sonata in E♭ Major, Hob. XVI/49.[45] And the presentation phase is more concise—a one-bar basic idea, literally repeated. A plausible continuation phase begins in measure 3 with motivic acceleration in an upward sequence. Although the sequence merely arpeggiates tonic harmony, it serves as an anacrusis to a downbeat arrival on a more stable, root position tonic in measure 4. Through elision with that downbeat arrival, a lyrical theme "takes flight," and just as in Op. 10, no. 2, the theme is marked by contrasts in texture (melody and Alberti-bass accompaniment), topic (singing style), and tessitura (beginning an octave higher).

Displacement of the expected sentence schema also occurs, but in Op. 22 the new idea shifts the underlying four-bar hypermeter as well. The fourth measure was beat 4 of the original four-bar hypermeasure, but here it is reinterpreted as the first measure of a new four-bar hypermeasure. The lyrical theme is also interpretable as an interpolation within the continuation phase of an implied sentence structure. Another elision at the downbeat of measure 8 launches the closural phase of this expanded sentence, marked by a return of the opening motive. The lyrical theme emerging in measure 4 is further distinguished by an internal expansion to five measures, achieved by expressively prolonging the melody's initial B♭ in measure 4.

If we compare the theme to the main theme of Op. 10, no. 2, Op. 22's lyrical flight begins *from* a climax; the lyrical continuation is like a huge exhalation that descends in an expanded sigh through two octaves. Robert Schumann opens his Fantasy, op. 17, with a similarly expansive sigh, as if beginning *in medias res.* Thus, Beethoven is anticipating the kind of freedom that will become a hallmark of Romantic stagings of subjectivity already in the opening of works.

Furthermore, the first theme of Op. 22 presents a sense of impending motivic will that leads to a breakthrough in measure 4, by contrast to the sudden shift of consciousness that occurs in measure 5 of the first theme from Op. 10, no. 2. The breakthrough in measure 4 is also an expressive climax, prolonging the initial B♭ as though to reflect on its miraculous emergence. A sense of transcendent awe spills over the next measures, echoing in (self-reflective) ecstasy before a dutiful, motivic cadential action (with the continuation-phase energy of m. 3) marks a sudden reascent to a half cadence. The open cadence serves as a dramatic moment of self-reflection as if catching one's breath: the rhetorical double-octave leap on F serves as both summary and punctuation of the registral space previously traversed by the theme.

In these two examples of staged shifts to a deeper subjectivity, the listener is led on a roller-coaster ride of composed spontaneity and lyrical release. Emotionally, there is a sense of epiphany in both of these interpolated, lyrical effusions. And they are not isolated examples. Compare the first movements of Beethoven's

Example 5.2. Beethoven, Piano Sonata in B♭ Major, op. 22, first movement, main theme (mm. 1–11²).

String Quartet in A Major, op. 18, no. 5, and his Piano Trio in D Major, op. 70, no. 1—noting how the opening theme in each work stages a second, more lyrical opening after the first in radically different ways, but in each case miming a subjective freedom that imaginatively constructs an alternate reality for itself. Or consider the reverse: the opening of Beethoven's Piano Sonata in F♯ Major, op. 78, stages a transcendent (if conventionally based) pastoral "sunrise" that is immediately followed by a shift to a lower level—a more workaday register of the pastoral. Yet that lower level is now illuminated by the transformative light of the introduction into a tropologically enriched view of work as vocation, as in my suggestion of a "georgic" pastoral topic for that theme (Hatten 1994, 83). These are deeply imaginative subjectivities for which the composer has provided a map, if not a fixed guidebook.

But subjectivity is available, as I have previously suggested, already in our engagements with earlier music—whether or not it stages signs of interiority by rhetorical shifts, breaks, or pauses. As part of the expressive inheritance of both madrigal and monody, however, rhetorical shifts continue to play a role—for example, in Bach's rhetorical silences and C. P. E. Bach's bizarre harmonic shifts. Such sudden swerves help define, along with the energy and pacing of comic opera, the Classical style itself (as Rosen has observed [1972, 96]). Just as importantly, the listener brings to the Beethoven examples something that is not there in the music—namely, a personal, referential grounding in experience that can transform these moments of virtual-subjective freedom, transcendence, or escape (choose your metaphor) into shared expressions of emotions or feeling states that have existential meaning as actualized through the life of the listener. I return to these issues in the next chapter, where I focus on virtual subjective emotion.

Back to Bach: Sinfonia in E Minor, BWV 793

In documenting the strategies that enable listeners to hear multiple contrapuntal lines as part of a larger *melos*, I have noted Bach's use of countersubjects derived from his subject either by use of the same motivic material, or contrapuntally by paralleling in thirds, sixths, or tenths (see chap. 4). This agentially motivated counterpoint, as I have dubbed it, may now be understood as a subjectivity-staging counterpoint in that the singular agent is increasingly conceived, in emergent fashion, as an ongoing subjectivity—as the multiple woven strands of consciousness experienced by a single individual. Bach's Sinfonia in E Minor may be interpreted as just such an inner drama reflecting the (moral) emotional growth experienced by a singular subjectivity. It achieves that development through the remarkable deployment of a few basic oppositions—register, mode, contrary motion and inversion, and rhetorical gesture.

Consider the use of a rhetorical break near the end of this sinfonia (see example 4.10[c]). Bach breaks off his impassioned development of the subject at measure 37 on a rhetorically anguished vii^{o7}. The subject returns in E minor with an implied stretto (the prototype for all derived counterpoints in this sinfonia). But the tonal return does not suffice to fully resolve the tensions of the diminished seventh that was left hanging. Indeed, the music eventually leads back to vii^{o7} in measure 42, now an octave higher and lower in the two hands, for another moment of rhetorical crisis. This time, the diminished-seventh chord is treated to a more thematically engaged attempt at resolution; the subject is contorted in its agonizing accommodation of tragedy before a positively resigned acceptance of the faith implied by the relative perfection of a Picardy-third close (or, if one elects to ignore the Picardy third, a more uncompromisingly tragic finish).[46] The dissonantly framed return of the subject thus undermines the resolutional tonic gravity of E minor and creates conditions for a far more complex subjectivity, perhaps one that cannot find surcease from an existential anguish. But the pain is not simply enhanced by dissonance or extremes of dynamics or register that work on the nerves; rather, it is exacerbated by the existential force of a deeper virtual subjectivity that appears to be struggling with a profoundly tragic situation.

A Singular Subjectivity from Virtual-Fictional Characters: "Am Leuchtenden Sommermorgen" from Schumann's *Dichterliebe*

The interactions between a willingly engaged listener and a carefully crafted musical work may range from the stereotypical (e.g., a generic hero achieving victory) to the emergence of a multidimensional, richly textured human subjectivity. When various virtual agencies are at play in a song (e.g., Schubert's "Erlkönig"; see Cone 1974, 1–19), we may want to keep the actorial roles distinct (and their levels: e.g., virtual narrator, virtual-fictional father and son, virtual-fictional-imaginary Erlking). Indeed, Schubert marks these roles registrally and topically for the singer, who can further project them through varying vocal inflections. But at other times, different apparent agencies may be interpreted through the lens of a single subjectivity—engaged by the listener through personal identification with a protagonist and intersubjective evaluation of other agents in their actorial roles (e.g., helper, antagonist), leading to a comprehensive understanding of these different agencies as various voices in dialogue within an overarching virtual consciousness.[47]

Consider "Am leuchtenden Sommermorgen" (On a shining summer morning) no. 12 from Schumann's *Dichterliebe* cycle, which is to some degree constrained in its staging of virtual agency by Heinrich Heine's poetic text (no. 15 from his collection *Buch der Lieder*, provided there with the indication "Lyrisches Intermezzo"). The poem has a clear fictional protagonist (a virtual actor), the spurned lover, who is walking through a flowering garden when the flowers appear to whisper and speak, scolding him for being mean to their sister (his beloved) and then rebuking him as a sad, pale man. The poem alone warrants a rich psychological interpretation: we are presented with a protagonist who is narrating his own experience of an encounter with personified flowers that speak as collective agents in defense of his beloved. We move deeper into subjectivity when we infer that the protagonist has "envoiced" the flowers with his own words and is thereby enacting a stinging self-rebuke. The power of this self-rebuke is enhanced by his abject recognition that, despite feeling betrayed by his lover, he still loves her enough to consider her undeserving of his complaints. Thus, the many agential voices and the three implied actorial roles (the man, the speaking flowers, and the spoken-of "flower-woman") are all interiorized as parts of a singular subjectivity. The flowers are personified and ventriloquistically envoiced in the troubled consciousness of a lover who is psychically split—one side feeling a justified grievance, the other an overpowering love that would somehow defend even the beloved's cruel actions

Example 5.3. (*Continued*)

Example 5.3. Schumann, "Am leuchtenden Sommermorgen" (Heine), *Dichterliebe*, op. 48, no. 12.

toward him. The fusion of these opposing feelings lends the resulting trope its devastating emotional force.

How, then, does Schumann enhance this interpretation through music's resources of harmony, tonality, texture, and dynamics? First, he sets the scene for the magical realism of a garden where flowers may be imagined as speaking. The scene-setting effect is achieved when an arpeggiated Mm^7 sonority (initially heard as a potential V^7) is mystically (enharmonically) reinterpreted as a German augmented-sixth chord that tonally resolves as it texturally blossoms into an arrival $^6_4$. The arrival $^6_4$ is enhanced in its positive epiphany by a Picardy-third effect (example 5.3, mm. 1–2).[48] The reversal when enharmonic lowered-$\hat{3}$ is displaced by $\natural\hat{3}$ is what gives the aural effect of a magical glow, a *leuchtenden* effect perhaps suggested by the glistening dew of early morning.

This expressive reinterpretation is reversed when the narrator speaks of the flowers whispering and speaking (mm. 8–9). Now, the German augmented-sixth is respelled as a V^7 of B major, the Neapolitan region, mystically displaced (by a half step) from the "reality" of B♭ major. But this V^7 of B never resolves to a stable key, instead moving to a dominant-functioning BM^9 in measure 9, which then resolves deceptively to C in measure 10, as though VI in E minor. Instead of a triadic VI, however, the addition of a seventh gives the C chord a dominant function, spurring a (demystifying, since routine) circle-of-fifths sequence that moves through FMm^7 to the original tonic, B♭ major. Thus, the stable frame of B♭ encloses a "purple patch" of harmonically unpredictable freedom.

When the flowers eventually speak (m. 17), they enact a kind of indirect discourse (there are no quotation marks in the original poem, but a colon—see

m. 16—and subsequent verb forms clearly indicate Heine's intent). Schumann provides the magical context for the flowers' now direct discourse via an augmented dominant with minor seventh (the latter in the bass) in measure 16^2, and this colorful chord then resolves even more colorfully (i.e., enharmonically) to G major in measure 17. This new key is a magical chromatic third displaced from B♭, and it opens an analogous, once-removed psychological realm, one where flowers are more likely to find voice. The pained reaction of the envoicing subject is hinted by a sudden *pianissimo*, as though by hearing the whispering (rustling of leaves?) the protagonist were imagining, then actualizing, what his split psyche would have the flowers speak. His subconscious mind delivers a devastating rebuke to his conscious mind through their words. But it is his enduring love that enables the flowers to speak to his grief, and if he can imagine their voices as touched with pity ("you sad, pale man"), he can maintain the illusion of the flowers' innocence even in the face of their "sister's" betrayal of his love.

The flowers do not have the last word, however, since their speaking ends unresolved on 2̂. The ensuing eighth-note syncopation creates the textural effect of a rhythmically displaced, and octave-displaced, mystical "other" (suspended over a dominant pedal). From this bell-like reverberation, self-reflectively prolonging the open cadence on the dominant, a magical but self-assured stepwise melody emerges (still displaced rhythmically into its own imaginative sphere). Is this the voice of the beloved—her song? Compare song number 10, "Hör' ich das Liedchen klingen" (When I hear the little song [that once my beloved sang]), which anticipates the texture of number 12 with its own eighth-note rhythmic displacement of the melody, thereby temporally shifting the sounding of the beloved's song to the realm of memory. Thus, by this association, the postlude to number 12 can suggest a melody that is "heard" by the lyrical protagonist as a memory. Furthermore, the melody is interrupted twice by the frisson of a diminished-seventh chord—the sonority par excellence to convey stricken recognition on the part of a subjectivity that is forced to reckon with an overwhelmingly fresh and painful awareness of the beloved's flowerlike beauty, her unattainability, and his never-to-be-denied, never-requited love. We are leagues from mere desire; Schumann creates a psychologically more complex and multi-dimensional subjectivity.[49]

Thus, Schumann's musical setting not only confirms a sensitive reading of Heine's poem in terms of a single subjectivity incorporating multiple actorial roles but also provides what only music can offer—a sense of immediacy juxtaposed with a displacement from reality. In effect, Schumann's virtual music presents a virtual-fictional protagonist who, in turn, imagines a virtual-fictional-imagined world where flowers can speak but whose thoughts are his own, reflected back to him. "Am leuchtenden Sommermorgen" reveals that music can develop its own resources to achieve these kinds of worlds-within-worlds effects. Even when depending on a literary source to situate the drama, music can further develop the "feelingful thoughts" of a psychologically profound subjectivity.

Subjectivity and the Autobiographical: Schubert's String Quartet in G Major, D. 887

The first movement of Schubert's last quartet features a second theme (example 5.4a) with minimal melodic motion, a marked harmonic shift, and a consoling articulatory gesture.[50] This theme is subject to a series of variations and modulations that may strike the uninitiated listener (or unsympathetic critic) as overly prolonged. What expressive motivations might justify this theme's remarkable extension?[51] I argue that obsessive rumination and subjective reflection, interpretable from the music itself, is also affected by Schubert's awareness of his own impending death.

The theme launches with a rhetorical harmonic gesture that disrupts the flow of the tonal discourse at a point where the dramatic trajectory (of sonata form) has already been strongly articulated by a presumed medial caesura (see example 5.4b later in the chapter). Schubert's unexpected dominant for this caesura, V/B minor, is perhaps motivated by the opening of the quartet, which features a sudden shift of harmony from G major to G minor, foregrounded as a tragic motto.[52] The fateful quality of Schubert's dominant caesura arises from the minor mode that it anticipates. But Schubert undercuts the (un)expected key of B minor here with a rhetorical shift that involves not only the key (which swerves toward the "proper" dominant of D major) but also the topic, dynamics, texture, and even genre. As the theme begins (example 5.4a), an echo of F♯ major harmony melts into a softer V_3^4 in D major. The willed reversal of A♯ to A♮ and consequent shift in key suggests an attempt at amelioration of, if not escape from, the fateful V of B minor.[53]

This initial amelioration does not constitute the final dispensing with the dominant of B minor, however. Its hint of the tragic is recalled at the end of the first four-bar phrase (m. 68) as V of B minor continues to oscillate with the dominant seventh of D major (m. 69). The progressively variational and diminutional treatment of the theme (not shown) serves to saturate the texture and imply a state of plenitude as fulfillment. Any sense of bliss that we might experience from this texture, however, is undermined tonally by the recurring V of B minor (m. 129), which leads to another medial-caesura event in measure 140. This time, the half cadence is *pianissimo* instead of *fortissimo* and is quickly concentrated on unison pitch-class F♯. The F♯, however, moves deceptively to G, which is then quickly captured as the seventh of a V^7 of D (this time in root position), and the theme returns for its most elaborate variation thus far. The exposition finally ends in the conventionally expected dominant key, D major.

Any criticism of Schubert's length might take this theme as prime evidence, were it understood simply as an overindulgence in harmonic color and textural plenitude. But the rhetorical shift from V of B minor to V_3^4 of D is itself being thematized, and it takes just this much repetition for the deeper, symbolic significance of the shift to be fully absorbed. Although a variation of the theme appears in the chromatic-third-related key of B♭ major (mm. 110ff.), it is the internal harmonic shift in the theme that simulates mystical reflection. The otherwise overextended second thematic group is motivated more by the numinous,

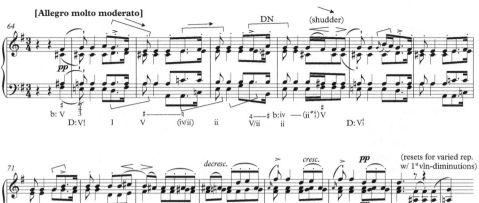

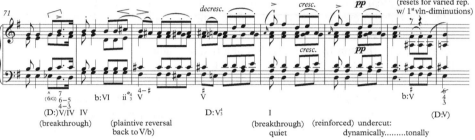

Example 5.4a. Schubert, String Quartet in G Major, D. 887, first movement, second theme (mm. 64–78¹ only), piano reduction.

internalizing resonance of this wondrous harmonic gesture than by the progressive tonal/formal discourse of sonata form.

Why, then, choose sonata form to present it? Certainly, Schubert had other forms at his disposal—various kinds of character pieces from *Moments musicaux* to *Impromptus*—but this quartet announces from the start the epic (hence serious and profound) character of its discourse, and the attempted amelioration of B minor in the second theme's prolonged interior reflection in D and B♭ major is further highlighted as a marked lyrical moment in an otherwise dramatic form.

Chia-Yi Wu (2010) notes another dimension in the quartet's allusion to operatic (and hence actorial) rhetoric in the continuation of the first movement's main theme as a solo voice with tremolo accompaniment. She also finds several intertextual references to Schubert's opera *Fierrabras*.[54] Thus, another means by which Schubert extends the expressive resonance of his late works is through blending, or troping, various genres.[55] The blend not only creates an integrative form, or higher dramatic vehicle, but offers a space where meditative depth can transfigure drama with a profoundly contemplative, subjective mode of reflection. This fusion of lyric, dramatic, and epic modes is influential for later nineteenth-century composers and justifies their use of sonata form for its epic associations, even when tonal motivations for the form may be attenuated.[56]

I turn now to a possible biographical motivation for Schubert's theme: his awareness that he was dying of syphilis. What is it about death that is most awful and awe-filled? Perhaps it is the sudden, irrevocable absence of life on

Earth—whether our own or that of a loved one. What might one choose to do when faced with imminent mortality? Try to delay it as long as possible, charm it with sweetness, or attempt to avoid thinking about it, even though one cannot help but obsess on the thought of death's proximity? The hyperextended second theme group appears to be obsessively flirting with the tragic and attempting to deny, perhaps by a form of wish fulfillment, an inevitable outcome.

Schubert ameliorates the tragic opening motto in the recapitulation first by reversing its original move from major to minor and then by taming the gesture of dotted-rhythmic, tragic-heroic response, turning instead toward quiet reassurance by means of even eighths and smooth legato articulation. Our knowledge of Schubert's own fate sensitizes us to his obsessive, varied repetitions of the second theme. Perhaps, as in measures 23 and following of Beethoven's Cavatina from Op. 130, the continued repetition of a theme might lead us to tears.[57] But this interpretation is also supported by the initial presentation of the theme, as a closer analysis of both its context and its content reveals.

As shown in example 5.4b, the transition (mm. 54–63) features an ascending fifth imitative sequence of the opening motto, and its abbreviated response with a long-range voice leading of the upper voice from G in measure 54 to F♯ in measure 58 for the modulation to B minor. After the medial caesura in measure 63, the second theme (example 5.4a) directly reverses the voice leading as F♯ is "led" to the seventh (G) of the dominant 4–3 in D in measure 65. But in the fourth measure of the theme (example 5.4a), a rhythmic shudder pulls us back as G collapses back to F♯ in the upper voice, harmonized by the fateful V of B minor. Within these four measures, the motto is recalled by the mutation of the dominant of D from A major to A minor in measure 66, and the transition is recalled by the series of ascending fifths leading from D through A to E (as marked by the brackets in the bass). Thus, both gesturally and harmonically, subjective interiorization is fully worked into the developing variational thread of the movement.

Perhaps the most telling detail, however, is that the rhythm of measure 65 is the same as that used in measures 51–53, where it celebrates the heroic closure of the first theme group in G major before the transition (see m. 53 example 5.4b). Might the second theme's positive spin toward D major be conceived as thematic transformation? Consider once more the minimal melodic motion in the second theme. Except for the double neighbor in measures 67 and 68, the melodic motion is completely stepwise. The symmetrical double neighbor occurs as part of a prolongation of the ii chord in D, which becomes iv of B minor. Also, the melodic descent through a minor third in measures 65 and 66 is symmetrically answered by an ascent through that same third in measures 66 and 67, as marked by brackets. Finally, the major-to-minor motto is symmetrically placed at the halfway mark in the first four measures of the theme. This uneasy alternation between up and down, major and minor, may suggest that Schubert is portraying a tentative balancing act, perhaps as an expression of a virtual agent's psychological attempts to forestall the fateful. With the articulated gestures (including the short-long figure discussed earlier) and their dancelike rhythm, one might

ascending circle of fifths sequence

Example 5.4b. Schubert, String Quartet in G Major, D. 887, first movement, transition (mm. 54–63).

interpret the passage as flirting not with death but with the thought of death. This suggests a subjectivity trying to reassure itself while attempting to skirt the unavoidable; but the inner protagonist is ultimately unable to break away from the thought of death, which constantly returns in the guise of the fateful dominant of B minor.

The next four measures of the second theme feature a brief amelioration of the tragic with the G–B embellishment in measure 69, and a new continuation breaks through by means of another G–B upward leap (m. 71)—heard now as a remarkably potent breakthrough against the background of continuous stepwise motion. This coincides with a brief but expressively effective tonicization of the more hopeful subdominant, G major. It arrives in measure 72 with a doubling that in Beethoven is associated with sweetness (two thirds and no fifths), analogous to a Picardy third, yet used in a major-mode movement.[58] But Schubert quickly pulls back with a palpably plangent sigh to his ongoing, tragic awareness of B minor. Thus, the theme continues to foster an uneasy sense of mixed emotions, capturing the listener in a fateful web of subjective reflection. Finally, the last phrase echoes the opening gesture in its second measure with energetic leaps of a fourth in measure 74 and then a sixth in measure 75 before quietly breaking free to a cadence in D major. The cadential breakthrough is first reinforced dynamically with the *crescendo* to the downbeat of measure 76 but then undercut as the *pianissimo* echo leading to measure 77 drains its strength. Schubert then relapses into the problematic V of B minor for a varied repetition of the theme. This time, a refraction of the theme appears in diminution in the first violin, which pleads even more persuasively, not against Death personified (as in the quartet movement based on the song "Death and the Maiden") but rather against a gnawing awareness of death, attempting once more to charm it away in a perfusion of wishful denial.

Have I made the case that this theme exemplifies wish fulfillment as avoidance, made achingly poignant by constant, obsessive reminders of a fate Schubert would want to avoid as long as possible? This interpretation may appear too autobiographical for some listeners. I offer it, then, as a form of poetic criticism in the sense that the verbal description is a way of capturing qualities in the piece rather than assuming the piece expresses what can be captured in a single verbal description.[59] Indeed, understood as a numinous symbol, the expressiveness of this theme refuses to be pinned down by a single set of signifieds, either as labels for its subtly mixed emotional resonance or as characterizations of its contextual role in a larger expressive trajectory. We might choose to engage subjectively with such passages in late Schubert, then, not as literal responses to death but (in more allegorical terms) as expressing the evanescence of that which is most beautiful, the vulnerability of that which is most sacred, or ultimately, the elusiveness of that which is most meaningful.

Schubert's choice of the Moor, Fierrabras, as a protagonist in his opera suggests significant parallels with Schubert's own life: an outsider offering aid (in Schubert's case the gift of music) to those whose lives must have increasingly appeared closed to him and yet for whom his actions might be construed as heroic. Then, more personally, the drama of his own impending death, his desperation to make his musical legacy measure up to the spiritual example of Beethoven, and his inevitable wish to escape may be understood as three further psychological motivations for the mysterious subjective alchemy that Schubert achieves in this late quartet.

Schubert not only heightens the inherited dramatic schemes of the Classical style in his late works. He also transfigures their intricate surfaces through extraordinary effects that transport the listener to more profound spiritual depths. If Schubert appears to be moving from traditional communicative signs to more ineffable symbols of interiority, we can nevertheless trace the rhetorical markers for these shifts and note their rarefied effects. But as the symbolic takes on mythic dimensions, its immediate meanings are revealed to each of us in ways that are highly personal and for which terms like "tragic" or "transcendent" can provide only the most general of labels. However, it is through these highly configured musical passages, embedded in the structure of a movement whose dramatic trajectory they richly enhance, that Schubert's late style touches us most directly and deeply.

Conclusion: Toward the Syntheses of Subjectivity

The virtual actants, agents, and actors examined in earlier chapters may also be understood as parts of a single, all-embracing subjectivity. Virtual subjectivity, as akin to a higher form of consciousness, emerges from the integration of musical energies, motions, identities, roles, *melos*, and a continuous musical discourse. By continuous, I do not mean that emergent feelings/thoughts are themselves necessarily unbroken—indeed, the discourse may well be undercut or fragmented and the dramatic trajectory may be frustratingly unfulfilled. Rather, these feelings/thoughts and their discourse(s) may be understood as ultimately cohering in the multifaceted, robust consciousness of a single (even singular) subject, one whose identity is sustained through musical means.

A virtual musical subjectivity interiorizes a dialogue between (or among) previously delineated actorial roles that may be in direct conflict with each other. It also interiorizes emotions and their continuous development. To complement my earlier emphasis on the staging of freedom, a virtual musical subjectivity may also imply the opposite—such as states of entrapment, emotions as akin to frozen grief, or dramas as inexorable tragedies portraying the subjectivity of a protagonist unable to escape or rise above the constraints of a virtual world (expressed most poignantly in Schubert's final song cycle, *Winterreise*).[60]

To be sure, the previous levels of agency (actants, agents, actors) also presuppose an active, engaged listener who can make the necessary inferences. What differs at the level of virtual subjectivity is the degree to which the listener comes to identify with the entire discourse and in turn is impelled to draw on her experience and capacity for growth in order to merge with the emergent meaning of a virtual subjectivity. The listener thereby provides human, existential significance to an expressive trajectory in the form of actual referents, groundings, points of connection, characters, and ultimately a coherent field of conscious imagination within which the virtual staging of musical life can be actualized (or, depending on your perspective, revirtualized) within a living, embodied, and imagining mind.

Whether or not music fully stages a complex virtual subjectivity, listeners may project their own subjectivity based on minimal cues or direction (as in the case of melodic contour). Recall the discussion of spiritual engagement presupposed by attuned listening to the chants of Hildegard of Bingen in the twelfth century. Clearly, human capacities (and needs or desires) for these kinds of subjective identifications go deep into human history.

What I would add at this point is a natural conclusion: that we as listeners are predisposed to engage with a kind of subjective identification whenever we listen to music—both by our human nature and by sedimented habits of listening entrained over the history of music. Listening in this way, we are immediately rewarded not only by the expansion of our own subjectivity as the music lends its temporal shaping to our subjective imagination, but also by the grounding in our own experience of all that music is capable of expressing. And through our capacity to experience personal growth along the lines of the music's discourse, our subjective engagement is further enhanced.

We may find sensibility in the Enlightenment era or interiority in the Romantic era as historically distinctive manifestations of subjectivity, but the staging of various kinds of virtual subjectivity begins much earlier, with clear evidence from at least the sixteenth century. And subjective engagement, by which I mean the capacity to identify with any of music's virtualized properties, may well have been present from the start.

Notes

1. Engagement with music, however, is a story that predates written history. Upper Paleolithic bone flutes (more than 42,000 years old) found in cave sites with paintings (as early as 32,000 years ago) provide evidence that early humans tied both music and art to rituals involving shamans (Neal 2015, 71–81). Indeed, a community's "music" may have been inseparable from its cosmogony, as evidenced by the 40,000-year tradition of the "songlines" in Aboriginal culture (Chatwin 1988). Music's spiritual agency would have been unquestioned in those times, although we cannot know just how it was experienced (e.g., whether it was focused in an individual shaman or diffused among the natural elements). When music began its long journey toward both pragmatic and aesthetic independence from its immersion in human cosmology (from collective work songs to individualized dances and from communal spiritual participation to individual skilled performances), those early ties to a spiritual wholeness were gradually loosened, although the potential for embodiment and spiritual engagement remained strong. With the Greeks we have evidence for the emergence of critical awareness, which is to say the emergence of an aesthetic capability for appreciation (as evidenced by Greek theorists' concern with *ethos*, or the ethical characteristic of given modes). Total identification with the music (still possible) would have rubbed shoulders with critical appreciation (and even critical questioning) of music's various properties and potential meanings.

2. An analogue is to be found in the history of emotions. As Barbara Rosenwein notes, what we might identify as compassion (though not at that time clearly conceptualized) may be understood as operative already in the pastoral practices prescribed by Pope Gregory the Great: "The process of consolation is that when we want to stop an afflicted person from grieving, we first try to empathize [*concordare*] with his sorrow by grieving" (*Ordo quippe consolationis est ut cum volumus afflictum quempiam a maerore suspendere, studeamus prius maerendo eius luctui concordare.*) ([591] 1979, 1:127, cited in Rosenwein 2006, 85; see also 2016, 320). The capacity for empathy may be included among those components of subjectivity that emerge early in human history, well before its conceptualization by philosophers (or attempts at explanation

by scientists, via "mirror neurons"). Michael Spitzer is working on a history of musical emotions along the lines of Rosenwein and other emotion historians.

3. Anicius Manlius Severinus Boethius (c. 475–77 to c. 524–26) was widely influential throughout the Medieval and Renaissance periods for his translations and commentaries on Aristotle's logic and Porphyry's *Categories, On Interpretation*, and *Isagoge* as well as textbooks on arithmetic and geometry modeled on the Greeks, texts on various branches of logic, and four *Theological Treatises* (*Opuscula sacra*) that approach problems of Christian doctrine through logic. His *De institutione musica* is one of the foundational texts in the history of music theory, but its quantitative approach to music is a far cry from my approach to virtual agency in music. Calvin M. Bower (who translated the treatise) perhaps best sums up the problem: "The values that the Boethian *musicus* applied in his judgments were *a priori* principles grounded in abstract thought, not principles grounded in experience of actual music" (2002, 147). Thus, I do not draw on Boethius's approach to music but rather examine *The Consolation of Philosophy* for what it (at times unwittingly) reveals about the experience of human subjectivity in the early sixth century.

John Marenbon notes that *The Consolation of Philosophy* "far exceeded" Boethius's other works in "popularity and importance." As he continues, "One measure of the extent and character of its readership is the translations, not merely into almost every medieval vernacular, but also into Greek and even Hebrew. Among the translators were two of the greatest vernacular writers of the whole epoch: Jean de Meun, who put the *Consolation* into Old French in the later thirteenth century, and Chaucer, who translated it into Middle English about a century later. As their involvement suggests, Boethius's dialogue was a text which popularized philosophy outside the universities, and its literary features, as well as its arguments, inspired imitations and creative adaptations, from Alain of Lille's *De planctu Naturae* ('Nature's Lament') to, more distantly, Dante's *Convivio* (*The Banquet*) and even Chaucer's *Troilus and Criseyde*. Philosophers and theologians, too, used the work; it was part of the school syllabus from the ninth to the twelfth centuries, and although Aristotle's treatises left no room for it in the university curriculum, it continued to be studied by students and teachers there. For example, [Thomas] Aquinas's account of the highest good in his *Summa Theologiae* IaIIe builds on the *Consolation,* and the definition of eternity given by Philosophy in Book V became the starting-point for almost every later medieval discussion of God and time" (2013, sec. 8, par. 4).

4. For the concept of abnegation and its musical structuring in Beethoven, see Hatten 1994, 20, 59–63, 218–19, and 281–86.

5. This passage is explored further in interlude II from the perspectives of three hypothetical listeners. The musical staging of nobility may also play host to an array of emotions not explicitly expressed by the work but drawn from listeners' own memories. They can then experience those personal emotions more intensely as "ennobled" within the context of a solemn or spiritually elevated virtual environment. See the discussion of Edward Elgar's "Nimrod" variation in chapter 6.

6. In summarizing Beethoven's staging of Romantic irony in his work, I have stated that "reflexivity extends the notion of Romantic irony as self-conscious awareness and commentary on the work" as achieved through "shifts in level of discourse" and Bakhtinian multiplicity of voices (*heteroglossia*). See Hatten 1994, 202, and Bakhtin (1935) 1981. Such reflexivity has a history in Western music that would be worth exploring more closely. Bach's "Echo" from the Overture in B Minor (*Clavier-Übung,*

Part II, BWV 1067), would qualify as an early example; see the analysis by Laurence Dreyfus (1996, 224–32), expanded in terms of topical troping in Hatten 2004, 69, and discussed in chapter 8.

7. More recently, Mauro Calcagno has expanded the kinds of subjectivity that may be recovered from late Renaissance madrigals and the operas of Monteverdi. He demonstrates the ways in which composers effectively staged Petrarch's "diffracted and polyphonic self" as a "dialogic subjectivity" in their works (2012, 85). I am grateful to Michael Spitzer for acquainting me with Calcagno's book.

8. It is worth quoting more fully McClary's impassioned defense of this approach, which I strongly support: "It is, of course, notoriously difficult . . . to rely on nonverbal media for historical data. Pitches and rhythms reside a long distance away from the apparently solid semiosis of language. Yet if music is to figure as anything other than a mere epiphenomenon . . . , then we must find approaches that will allow us to examine its meanings. Otherwise, we will continue simply to graft music onto an already-formulated narrative of historical developments; more important, we will fail to learn what music might have to teach us or to question seriously what may be incomplete accounts of the past. At the very least I want . . . to shake loose a version of early modern subjectivity too neatly packaged in recent studies and to encourage a process of historical revision that takes music as a point of departure" (2004, 7). In her study of seventeenth-century music, for which *Modal Subjectivities* served as a "prequel" (2012, 14), McClary amplifies this point: "I believe that musical scores qualify as crucial repositories of evidence for anyone seeking to understand the people who lived in another time and place. More concretely than verbal documents, music can grant us at least provisional access to a period's assumptions concerning temporality, affect, the body, the divine, sexuality, sociality, ethics, and selfhood" (5).

9. In an 1801 letter to his childhood friend Franz Gerhard Wegeler, Beethoven wrote, "I have often cursed my existence. *Plutarch taught me resignation*"(cited in Newman [1927] 1970, 63; emphasis Beethoven's).

10. Note Friedrich Schlegel's recognition of self-critical (and hence ironic) romanticism as present already in Cervantes and Shakespeare (Millán-Zaibert 2007, 173).

11. In the same treatise, Momigny goes so far as to arrange (for purposes of theoretical demonstration) the first movement of Mozart's String Quartet in D Minor, K. 421, presenting on ten staves the four string parts of the quartet, a text setting of the melody as an operatic aria (a lament by Dido, with his own French verse drawn from Virgil's *Aeneid*), and corresponding figured bass, harmonic, and melodic analytical reductions. Edward Klorman (2016, 52–70) extensively analyzes the unusual results, noting what it reveals about Momigny's understanding of implied agency in the quartet. Klorman has recorded his own performance of the movement; it is available, along with a complete copy of the score in Portable Document Format (PDF), on his book's dedicated website.

12. See Allanbrook 2014 for more on this "secular commedia" in late eighteenth-century music.

13. Hildegard's virtual agencies may have relied on the scaffolding of religious texts and her foray into fictionalizing on the scaffolding of medieval mystery plays (as in her *Ordo Virtutum*), but there is clear evidence of her music's own actantial energies affording an interpretation of virtual agency as well as subjectivity.

14. Other neurologists (Annoni et al. 2005) have suggested that mild strokes are implicated in sudden creative shifts in style by painters.

15. Newman 1985 is representative of a trend to interpret Hildegard's accomplishments from a feminist perspective.

16. The motivic sophistication of her chants (detailed in Gebuhr 2012, 90–103) supports the emergence of a musical discourse. Gebuhr also identifies a "signature motive" (78) that involves the marked use of two consecutive perfect leaps outlining an octave (e.g., A4–E5–A5). This motive sets the words *lorica vite* (breastplate of life) in Hildegard's sequence, *O ignis spiritus paracliti* (O fire of the comforting spirit), which describes the Holy Spirit that "will unite all bodily limbs" (79)—allegorically, healing the schism within the church.

17. For more on topical uses of dance types, see Ratner 1980, Allanbrook 1983, Zbikowski 2008, and Mirka 2014.

18. However, the lineage of a musical dialogue between individual and collective agencies may be traced back to the singing of responsorial psalms in Jewish synagogues, as adopted by the early Christian church. Alternating half-choruses (antiphonal psalmody) was introduced later.

19. See McClary 1986 and 1987 for more on this kind of "dialectic" in concertos by Bach and Mozart, respectively.

20. For more on Liszt's projection of virtuoso agency in both performance and composition, see Kramer 2002, 68–99, and chapter 8, note 2.

21. In chapter 4 I note several ways that composers can expand on this flexibility among leading voices as they participate integratively in creating a rich *melos*.

22. For more on sociability, see Sutcliffe 2013. For an approach to multiple agency (both implied and actual) in Mozart's chamber music, see Klorman 2016.

23. For more on the importance of sensibility for eighteenth-century music, including important influences on music from the sentimental novel, see Boisjoli 2018.

24. Berthold Hoeckner offers a more interpretive approach in *Programming the Absolute: Nineteenth-Century German Music and the Hermeneutics of the Moment* (2002). A more comprehensive historical account may be found in Mark Evan Bonds's *Absolute Music: The History of an Idea* (2014), which traces the history of absoluteness from Orpheus and Pythagoras through the early twentieth century. Gary Tomlinson's *A Million Years of Music: The Emergence of Human Modernity* (2015) goes still further in tracing what I would call the virtualizing aspect of absoluteness back to the very beginnings of what we would come to call music (see this book's postlude).

25. For a thorough music-theoretical updating and reinterpretation of Adorno's insights into late Beethoven, see Spitzer's *Music as Philosophy* (2006), where he develops the concept of "hearing as" from his earlier book, *Metaphor and Musical Thought* (2004), in a way that is deeply consonant with the approach to virtual agency and subjectivity proposed here. I do not pursue Adorno's (and Spitzer's) fascinating examination of negated subjectivity in music (see Spitzer 2006, 60).

26. Burnham (2009) also examines extremes of subjectivity from intimacy to impersonality in late Beethoven. Kristina Muxfeldt (2012) usefully explores subjectivity through interior worlds, memories, and fantasies as found in the music of Beethoven, Schubert, and Schumann.

27. His further interest (not pursued in my study) concerns music that "listens and reasons; listening in order to reason, to learn the (political) art of subjectivity" (Steinberg 2004, 9).

28. As Steinberg elaborates, "The subjectivity is of the music itself, which according to the same fundamental fiction [of music speaking in the first person] has the capacity of memory, a sense of past and future, and a language for their articulation" (2004, 9). He adds the following: "Rather than narrating . . . , [music] shares with its listeners a discovery and presentation of the self as a performative act," and "music's

self-consciousness resides in the fiction that the music listens—to itself, its past, its desires" (9).

29. See Bowie 2003 on subjectivity from the perspective of aesthetic theory from Immanuel Kant to Friedrich Nietzsche. Lawrence Kramer (1995) ventures a postmodern approach to Classical music; Klein (2015) takes a Lacanian approach to musical crises in subjectivity for nineteenth- and twentieth-century music (see the discussion later in this chapter).

30. See Foucault's (1997–99) critiques of asylums, clinics, prisons, and other authoritative institutions in works published from 1954–84.

31. See Mansfield 2000 for a helpful review.

32. A parallel may be found in the similarly vague but useful notion of well-being that is presupposed as a goal for right action in Greek *eudaimonistic* ethical theory. See Nussbaum 2001, 31–32, for a definition of emotions as *eudaimonistic* in their concern for a person's "flourishing" (as opposed to a more simplistic notion of "happiness"). I should note that my attempt to identify common-denominator components of subjectivity does not deny the robust subjectivity of those who experience various physical or intellectual disabilities even as their cognitive capacities and constructions of the world may differ. Licia Carlson emphasizes a similar flourishing in describing her experience as an undergraduate volunteer "in a classroom for children labeled 'multiply handicapped'" (2016, 41). She recalls a listening experience: "We not only were moved by the music but also moved with it in a shared temporal landscape, achieving a synchrony in our embodied responses that brought us together in ways that verbal communication could not." And she adds, significantly: "This was not a therapeutic endeavor with a set goal; rather than being directed at teaching, normalizing, or cultivating particular skills, this musical experience unfolded organically and was valuable and valued for its own sake" (41). I am interested in constructing a theory of virtual agency and subjectivity that can be used to help explain this kind of robust "musicking" (Small 1998). For important work in the burgeoning field of music and disability studies, see Lerner and Straus 2006, Straus 2011, and Howe, Jensen-Moulton, Lerner, and Straus 2016.

33. As Foucault argues, discourses of institutions constrain the very individuals whose identities they define: the insane, the sick, and the criminal. I do not find Foucault's institutional constraints sufficient to overpower the robust subjectivity I am proposing, although I concede that there are institutional forces that one must work hard to overcome. For example, pressures of academic promotion and tenure may negatively impact a scholar's creativity and willingness to take risks, but those pressures can be resisted.

34. Klein's reversal of the hierarchy suggested by Seth Monahan's (2013) theory of agency (which is discussed briefly in this book's prelude) is provocative, but I hope to frame the issue in a way that can help us avoid or at least mitigate the indeterminate and fractured subjectivity that is presumably governed by Lacan's Symbolic Order.

35. His literary masterpiece is, tellingly, a place where he addresses the consolation of philosophy, not its conundrums.

36. For an earlier application of Lacanian notions of subjectivity to music, see Schwarz 1997.

37. As Humboldt phrased it, "Language is quite peculiarly confronted by an unending and truly boundless domain, the essence of all that can be thought. It must therefore make infinite employment of finite means" ([1836] 1999, 91).

38. See Hatten 1994, 44–56, and 260–68, for elaboration of the type-token concept and its utility in explaining style growth and change.

39. A similar staging of virtual freedom can be found in opening themes by Haydn (String Quartet in B♭ Major, op. 50, no. 1, m. 6⁴) and Mozart (Piano Sonata in F Major, K. 332, m. 5). In these two examples, chosen to illustrate her analytical approach to the "comic surface," Allanbrook emphasizes radical shifts in topic as motivating expansions in phrase structure (2014, 122–23 and 111, respectively). Janet Schmalfeldt's exploration of the concept of "becoming" in Beethoven's themes is related to my concept of "emergence"; see Schmalfeldt 1995, 2011. For further discussion and examples of Beethoven's emergent themes, see Hatten 2017c. Daniel Chua's *Beethoven and Freedom* (2017) appeared too late to be incorporated into my conceptualizing of virtual freedom, but its extensive meditation on the topic, drawing on Adorno, is relevant to my own investigation here.

40. The phrase terminology here is taken from Caplin 1998 with one adaptation: I call the four-bar presentation unit a "phase" rather than a "phrase," since it does not contain a significant harmonic progression (William Caplin indeed notes that the presentation is usually a tonic expansion). I follow William Rothstein's terminology in considering a phrase as "a directed motion in time from one tonal entity to another" (1989, 5) that exhibits "*tonal* motion with beginning, middle, and end" (7; emphasis in original). By this criterion, the entire twelve-bar theme constitutes one phrase (a sentence with an internal expansion).

41. Another option for the Beethoven theme would be to place an authentic cadence in mm. 7–8 (instead of digressing to the subdominant), but a cadence there would have sounded premature with respect to the new material launched in m. 5 by ignoring its implications for further development.

42. Beethoven will enjoy several buffa-inspired dislocations in this movement, including a false dominant preparation (establishing V of A minor) before the sudden shift (a flight of free will) to a theme in the as yet unprepared key of C major. Later, a false recapitulation in D major "realizes its mistake" only after returning all twelve measures of the first theme; then, through harmonic sequence and motivic liquidation, the theme resets to F major for a definitive tonal return. But the theme's tonal return in the recapitulation begins at the fifth measure of the original, suggesting that this was the initiation that truly counted, both expressively and now structurally.

43. See, for example, the many references to Heinrich Koch and Johann Philipp Kirnberger in Rothstein's (1989) interpretations of phrase expansions.

44. Unfortunately, giving priority to continuity and coherence in explaining this theme might devalue the extraordinary effect of its extravagant departure, instead reducing it to a normative, hence deeper structure (as in some more naïve Schenkerian analyses). But greater depth is achieved expressively by the departure itself (heard, to be sure, against the backdrop of conventional might-have-beens). The departure, in effect, creates a deeper experience of virtual subjectivity by enacting emergent freedom. This is an insight not out of keeping with Schenker's own sense of Beethoven's *Phantasierung* (imaginative, creative, musical fantasizing), although it was not fully worked out in Schenker's more structural theory.

45. Because of the intertextual connection to the Haydn sonata, I do not hear any downbeat ambiguity in the opening of Beethoven's Op. 22; despite its tonic anacrusis, the Beethoven theme punctuates the downbeat with a strong octave entry in the left hand.

46. Stephen Rumph eloquently frames a third interpretive option for Bach (concerning the Picardy thirds that end the opening choruses of the *Mass in B Minor*

and the *St. Matthew Passion*): "The major cadence does not alleviate, let alone reverse, the profound pathos of these movements. Instead, the greater stability of the major triad signifies closure, stability, and finality, values that transcend the tragic/nontragic opposition" (2012, 100).

47. And all (or at least part of) the while, the listener is experiencing the work with reference to a critical subjectivity that discriminates, evaluates, and judges the properties and quality of a musical work's staging of subjectivity as higher consciousness, self-reflexively examining these processes in terms of the listener's human needs and interests.

48. Schumann visually mitigates this wonderful aural effect by respelling the German augmented-sixth as a spurious doubly augmented-sixth chord. Changing the "correct" scale degree of $\flat\hat{3}$ to an easier-to-read $\sharp\hat{2}$ implies a less-exotic embellishing chromaticism. Although this kind of embellishing chromaticism has its own pastoral associations, they are perhaps better reserved for the augmented dominants that appear later in the song.

49. For illuminating interpretations of such subjective depth appearing already in Schubert's *lieder*, see Kramer 1998.

50. The interpretation of the first movement in this section, focusing on the first part of the second theme, is drawn from a keynote address I gave for the international conference "Thanatos as Muse: Schubert and Concepts of Late Style," organized by Lorraine Byrne Bodley and Julian Horton at the National University of Ireland, Maynooth, Ireland, October 21–23, 2011, which was previously published as Robert S. Hatten, "Schubert's Alchemy: Transformative Surfaces, Transfiguring Depths," in *Schubert's Late Music: History, Theory, Style*, ed. Lorraine Byrne Bodley and Julian Horton (Cambridge: Cambridge University Press, 2016), 91–110. Anne Hyland (2016) offers a compelling formal analysis of the first movement's variation elements, focusing on their manipulation of temporality. An account of Schubert's own subjectivity as expressed in his works will appear in a groundbreaking biography by Byrne Bodley (forthcoming).

51. See Burnham 2005 for an account of Schubert's expressive motivations for repetitions and variations in this second theme that is complementary to mine. Burnham notes, for example, that the theme is tonally defamiliarized, producing "a different order of thought" that is "more inward" (2005, 32–33).

52. Beethoven used this harmonic effect (V/iii) in the G major slow movement of his Violin Concerto (mm. 3–4) for its antique, mystical character.

53. For an elaboration of such chromatic shifts as willed reversals and their interpretation as positive resignation or abnegation, see Hatten 1994, 59–63.

54. Compare the intertextual links between *Fierrabras* and the Piano Sonata in A Minor, D. 784, in Hatten 2004, 190–91.

55. For a preliminary discussion of the troping of topics and genres in the nineteenth century, see Hatten 2004, 71–89. Beethoven could have been the model for Schubert's generic troping: consider Beethoven's artful blending of recitative, arioso, and fugue in the finale of his Piano Sonata in A♭ Major, op. 110.

56. Or, as in the case of Chopin's Ballade in F Minor (see chap. 9), deliberately undercut for expressive reasons.

57. This is how Jean-Jacques Rousseau (1768) describes the *Romanze* in his dictionary entry on the genre (cited in Jander 1983, 162).

58. An extensive theoretical justification for interpreting major triads with doubled thirds in this way is given in Hatten 1994, 50–54.

59. Leon Plantinga explains Schumann's concept of poetic criticism in similar terms: "Thus the music does not denote or portray the program; something like the reverse is true: the program suggests and clarifies certain qualities of the music" (1967, 120).

60. For a compelling treatment of the theme of death in *Winterreise*, see Suurpää 2014.

6   Virtual Subjectivity and Aesthetically Warranted Emotions

How do listeners actually engage with virtual agency and subjectivity? In other words, how do they access and interact with those emotions that are staged by the composer as intensified agential expressions? The possibilities are endless. Consider the following account, which valorizes a listener's capacity to go far beyond what is presumed to be expressed by the work:

> The meaning of any beautiful created thing is, at least, as much in the soul of him who looks at it, as it was in his soul who wrought it. Nay, it is rather the beholder who lends to the beautiful thing its myriad meanings, and makes it marvelous for us, and sets it in some new relation to the age, so that it becomes a vital portion of our lives, and symbol of what we pray for, or perhaps of what, having prayed for, we fear that we may receive. The longer I study, Ernest, the more clearly I see that the beauty of the visible arts is, as the beauty of music, impressive primarily, and that it may be marred, and indeed often is so, by any excess of intellectual intention on the part of the artist. *For when the work is finished it has, as it were, an independent life of its own, and may deliver a message far other than that which was put into its lips to say.* Sometimes, when I listen to the overture to *Tannhäuser*, I seem indeed to see that comely knight treading delicately on the flower-strewn grass, and to hear the voice of Venus calling to him from the caverned hill. *But at other times it speaks to me of a thousand different things, of myself, it may be, and my own life, or of the lives of others whom one has loved and grown weary of loving, or of the passions that man has known, or of the passions that man has not known, and so has sought for.* (Wilde [1891] 1968, 1399–1400; my emphasis)

As Oscar Wilde rhapsodizes on his freely subjective listening experience, he reveals what might appear to be a naïve way in which music is heard and assimilated by the reflective mind into the personal concerns of a listener. But Wilde's ruminations also remind us that a listener may go beyond obvious programs and characters to hear a deeper subjectivity as triggered by the music's own structuring—even when it may appear to deny the presumed communicative intent of the composer. Where Wilde's imaginative account and my own speculative theory intersect is in the way he finds actual emotions accruing from a subjective personalizing of music's expressed emotions. From my view, that personalizing is often (but not always) achieved through identification with implied virtual agents, actors, and subjectivities. In this chapter I explore the interaction between emotion as expressed in music and emotion as felt by listeners, considering from this perspective how virtual subjectivity may be negotiated with the actual subjectivity of a listener. I begin my speculative quest with the range of emotions that one may feel in direct response to (i.e., in following the sequence of) those emotions virtually expressed by the music.[1]

Toward Aesthetically Warranted Emotions

In defending listeners' actual subjective engagement with virtual subjectivity in music, I have set aside various other uses of music that may be less engaged with its virtual staging and expression of human emotion. The following examples of typical significations are not pursued here:

a. Very general cultural associations (e.g., music as emblematic of civilization, or Beauty, or other general values). One can be moved by the fact of—the very presence of—music, without regard to its professed expressive content.
b. More specific personal associations triggered by "functional" or "occasional" music (e.g., patriotic tunes, wedding music).
c. Particular associations unique to an individual, perhaps by contiguity with a real-life event charged with emotion (e.g., "they're playing our song").
d. Physiological or involuntary responses to aspects of sound (e.g., the startled, charged response to a sudden, loud note).

Although emotions generated by music do not appear to be directly linked to physical survival, as in the evolution of basic emotions, some may be motivated by useful psychic needs, such as the release of repressed emotion, the integration of psychic conflicts, the enhancement of a sense of social community, and the support of a spiritual or existential quest for meaning.

In my argument for a listener's engagement or identification with virtual subjectivity, I focus primarily on what I call aesthetically warranted emotions—those felt emotions that are directly motivated by stylistically competent interactions with what I call composed expressive trajectories—those musical discourses that involve the intentionally conceived presentation, development, and interaction of expressive states.[2] My argument addresses five key concerns: (1) how we interpret expressed emotion in Western art music, (2) the role of prior emotional experience, (3) whether we actually need to experience real emotions while listening to have an engaged experience with what is being expressed, (4) whether those emotions need be congruent with expressed trajectories in the music, and (5) the complexity of aesthetically warranted emotions, hence the complexity of our cognitive identification and/or experiencing of them.

In the following analysis and interpretation of a Mozart sonata movement, I do *not* specify precise emotions the listener should be experiencing (within the broader expressive categories I present). The individual listener may actually experience a range of explicit emotions in "filling out" or reacting to the expressive intensities presented in a composed expressive trajectory, and it is not my task here to detail those individualized, actual emotions. Instead, my focus is on the detailed framework within which an unsituated but nevertheless very substantial emotional drama can take place. The resulting dramatic trajectory features the ongoing development of expressive intensities interpretable as emotions experienced by a virtual agent (or actor, or even subjectivity). While identifying with or reacting in some other way to the virtual emotions sparked by this expressive journey, a listener may indeed experience actual—and specific—emotions. But these may or may not correspond to the specificity of virtually expressed emotions, and in any case, they will be situated in a personal context that makes them existentially relevant to the listener's own life experience. In other words, moving from virtual to actual emotion involves a negotiation that will inevitably be individual for each listener, even among those listeners who are competently engaging with the work's style and its strategies, and even for one listener approaching the same work at different times.

The Role of Marked Musical Gestures and Stylistically Unmarked Alternatives in Reconstructing and Interpreting Composed Expressive Trajectories (How We Might Stylistically Interpret What's There to Be Experienced)

To assess the expressive power of composed expressive trajectories and the virtual emotions they imply, let us compare two Classical themes. The first is my version and the second the original opening to the slow movement in B♭ of Mozart's Piano Sonata in F Major, K. 533, composed in 1788. My version (example 6.1, lines *a* and *c*) roughly parallels the opening two phrases of the sonata, adhering to its initial contours, gestures, and motivic premises. Rather than offering a Schenkerian reduction, which can itself provide a valid means of highlighting some of the norms against which Mozart's expressive achievement may be assessed, I have instead chosen to compose a less highly marked and admittedly less artistic but still fully realized version of Mozart's flexible phrase and climax structure.[3]

An analytical interpretation of my version would note the following: after a somewhat resigned melodic drop in the second measure, a leap to C and an applied dominant (V^6 of V) climaxes on the downbeat of measure 3 followed by a slightly faster stepwise descent that releases onto an incomplete cadence on the tonic (with a graceful, galant cadential gesture). Imagine Mozart's having initially sketched in his mind this somewhat bland, if nevertheless stylistically plausible expressive trajectory and then deciding to enhance its potential for expressivity: line *b* of example 6.1 shows what he actually composed. The melodic drop in the second measure (marked with an asterisk as an expressive crux) is now surprisingly dissonant (a diminished fifth), and it is harmonized with a markedly dissonant chord (vii$^{\circ 6}_5$ of V instead of my milder ii^6 and V^6/V). Mozart's borrowing of the lowered sixth, D♭, from the parallel minor, enhances the "darkness" of this

Example 6.1. Mozart, Piano Sonata in F, K. 533, second movement, main theme.
Line *a* shows measures 1–4, recomposed and simplified (expressive dissonance and
embellishments removed but relative melodic contour and length retained). Line *b*
shows measures 1–4 as composed by Mozart, with expressive dissonance and climactic
recovery marked by asterisks. Line *c* shows measures 4³–10², recomposed from measure
8 with an earlier climax (asterisk). Line *d* shows measures 4³–10² as composed by
Mozart, featuring a later climax (asterisk).

marked moment, which is, however, quickly ameliorated by a melodic leap up
to C (marked with a second asterisk as an expressive climax). This note anticipates a restoration to the dominant, which arrives in measure 3, just as in my version. Mozart's expressive effect, however, is much more strongly foregrounded by
means of the dissonant-to-consonant harmonic contrast from measures 2 and
3 as well as by three interrelated expressive embellishments: (1) the melodic C is

treated as an anticipation (highlighting as well as helping to expand an expressive climax), (2) the subsequent C (on the downbeat of m. 3) is ornamented with a turn figure (a typical expressive marker for Mozart), and (3) the tenor voice is delayed to create a 4–3 suspension (the latter topically associated with religious music, hence a detail that adds to the spiritual resonance of the climax). These various details are integrated to create a gesture whose emergent meaning I interpret as akin to suddenly experiencing an enrapturing insight. The spaciousness created by these three expressive figures opens up a corresponding temporal space for interiorizing reflection.[4]

The marvelous, if brief, suspension of the temporal flow is then compensated by a sudden and precipitous descent in sixteenths (twice as fast as in my more normative version). The emergent effect of this faster, descending gesture in the context of the larger expressive trajectory is, for me, a kind of thrilling inward reverberation of the climax, as though the relief from the dysphoric disturbance in measure 2 was not only spiritually insightful but too intense to be prolonged.[5] The trill on the cadence further shudders and tucks into its delayed resolution rather than energetically achieving a cadence as affirmation of arrival with metric closure on a downbeat.

I have just presented an analysis of Mozart's initial thematic phrase that supports a range of aesthetically warranted and at times cognitively complex virtual emotions that one might actually coexperience when listening to the opening four measures. Against the background of my more trivial version, which is at least stylistically competent and thus capable of generating some emotion, one can begin to appreciate the much greater artistic richness of Mozart's four-bar composed expressive trajectory. This expansion, I would emphasize, does not simply achieve greater expressive intensity; it further dramatizes that expressive intensity as part of a more complex, interiorizing subjectivity.

How might one experience this theme in terms of the various agential levels introduced thus far? Given its importance thematically for the entire movement, the initial motive is rather unmarked—merely a neighbor-note figure. Thus, as an actant it conforms to virtual-environmental musical forces (initially, gravity motivates its descent, but then magnetism motivates the recapture of A by B♭).[6] The accompaniment may suggest greater agential energy by countering gravity in a stepwise ascent. Parallel thirds hint at pastoral simplicity and hence a contented mood for a conjectured virtual human agent. But the catastrophic drop by a tritone in measure 2 to a diminished-seventh sonority is a surprising rhetorical gesture. This sudden jolt inaugurates drama in its sharp interaction with what was just heard. The unexpected dissonant drop is not a gesture that can be explained with reference to gravity alone. Nor might we plausibly imagine a virtual agent willing such an untoward event. The very extremity of the shift suggests an encounter with an external agency. And that more negative, external agency (whether imagined as Fate or Chance) has made an impact on the virtual agent's course in a way that demands a dialogical, actorial response by a determined protagonist. The response is immediately forthcoming on the third beat of measure 2, and it is remarkably positive—even heroic in its context: considerable energy is implied by the leap back upward, past B♭ to C (a note that might have been a plausible continuation from B♭, had the dissonant drop not intervened). And C is celebrated with a turn figure that, complemented by the 4–3 suspension in the alto, supports an interpretation of spiritual resilience in the face of adversity. After apparently reveling in this expansive response, the virtual agent appears to react to this temporal delay by suddenly attempting to "catch up," as marked by a sudden rhythmic acceleration in the stepwise descent that enables the theme to close in four measures with an incomplete authentic cadence. This descent, when interpreted as an expressive gesture motivated by the ongoing drama, may also suggest a shiver of awed acceptance, further marking the preceding shift to a more positive realm as spiritually significant—and also enhancing our understanding of the virtual agent/actor in terms of its more profound inner life: its virtual subjectivity.

Notice how in a mere four measures we have moved from inferences of actants to a potential human agent to the actorial roles of two agents—protagonist and antagonist in a drama of conflict and willed overcoming—and finally to the interiorizing and allegorizing of this highly expressive drama in terms of a spiritually profound subjectivity; and we have traced a moral emotion, willed resistance to an antagonizing intrusion, into a spiritualized emotion, awed acceptance of a self-generated, positive insight.

It may appear that I am somewhat artificially reconstructing the progressive sequence of a music-cognitive ontogeny in order to recapitulate a style-historical phylogeny.[7] But listeners who have been entrained to hear purely instrumental music in terms of subjectivity—from Bach to Brahms and beyond—may instead experience virtual subjectivity as a listening stance from the start and then progressively fill it in with the kinds of humanly expressive and dramatically actorial interactions that I have detailed in my analysis. And whereas one listener may experience emotional expression before inferring virtual agency, another may initially interpret an unfolding emotional experience through a presupposed virtual agency. In any case, the path to musical understanding need not be the same for every listener.

The next six measures of the theme feature an actual phrase expansion leading to a delayed climax (marked by an asterisk in line *d* of example 6.1) followed by a half cadence as Mozart keeps the tension mounting through an extended sequence. Note that my recomposition (line *c* of example 6.1) duplicates the first three measures but preserves the phrase expansion to six bars by providing a more normative, earlier, and far less exciting climax (also marked by an asterisk) as well as a more closural resolution to a perfect cadence. My composed alternative clearly undercuts the expressive force of Mozart's dramatic ascent, which builds through an extended sequence of implied two-note sighs to its ultimate climax on C in measure 9 (perhaps thereby echoing, an octave higher, the climactic C in m. 3).

Several presuppositions of this analysis are worth emphasizing. Implied by my interpretation of the compositional process is the degree to which a concern for expressive intensification motivates the composer's choice of unusual or marked events on the surface.[8] Contemporaneous theorists emphasized the importance of such marked dissonant moments, as J. J. Quantz illustrates in a famous extended example from his treatise ([1752] 1966, 255–59), where he provides increasingly more dissonant harmonies with increasingly more intense dynamics.[9] One can find a more literal use of dynamics in the interpretive response to marked tonal moments of Nathan Broder's revised edition of the sonata as added to the score of the exposition (see example 6.2 later in the chapter; Mozart 1960). Significantly, Mozart did not provide any dynamic markings for this exposition.[10]

Also implied by my analysis is my commitment, as both analyst and performer, to the deep expressive import of those events that in purely structural analyses are too often quickly bracketed off—for example, by interpretations that unwittingly depreciate nonharmonic tones as mere ornaments or diminutions elaborating a more fundamental structure. Instead, the analysis gives full weight to what I have described as "the irreducible significance of the surface" (Hatten 1994, 160, 278).[11]

Finally, the richness of an emotional encounter with the Mozart theme is presumed to depend on a rather complex cognition of expressive meaning, drawing on considerable stylistic competency—even though that rich response may appear to be immediate.[12] Competency in style, which includes the type level of expressive meaning, is at the same time (1) learned or entrained, (2) aesthetic or artistic, and (3) historically (and theoretically) reconstructed. Each of these presuppositions, I have long argued, is fundamental for stylistically competent musical cognition (Hatten 1989; 1994, 272–74). If one must first learn a historically appropriate, aesthetically flexible, and artistic mode of expression, one cannot factor out such variables in psychological tests and still hope to capture human cognitive capacities for sophisticated musical experience. Fortunately, music psychology has moved well beyond such naïve considerations.

Though dependent on our biological and cultural knowledge of emotional experience, which I consider in the next section, the expressive states and correlative emotions that I have interpreted here are nonetheless based on or in some sense grounded in an artifice. They exist because of an aesthetic contract in which we play, or "make-believe" as Kendall Walton (1990) emphasizes in his theory of art—not unlike how we simulate a reality when reading fiction. As evidence of the particularly aesthetic grounding of these musical emotions, consider what would happen if someone yelled "Fire!" in the middle of a performance in a concert hall. The aesthetically warranted, virtual emotions in progress would suddenly be displaced by an actual emotion grounded in more immediate, survival-oriented reality. Nevertheless, as philosophers from Plato and Aristotle to the present have attested, music can lead listeners to very real emotional experiences and even catharsis.[13] Aesthetically warranted emotions arise from this conspiracy of fictive play that we share with the composer, even if we fail to fully share his or her expressive conception of the work.

The Affordance of Prior Emotional Experience for an Individual's
Complete Cognitive Understanding of Composed Expressive
Trajectories (How Personal Experience Helps Us Gauge the
Expressive Significance of What's There)

Here I simply want to underscore what may appear obvious: that our ability to have the kinds of deeper emotional experiences implied by the Mozart theme depends heavily on our having had similar emotions in real-life contexts, such that some kind of transference takes place—however we might argue about the mechanics of that transfer. The affordance of having had prior experience of, for example, sudden shifts to despair or to rapture would appear critical to our interpretation of musical cues for similar shifts. And our evolutionarily enhanced abilities to glean affective significance from gestures—defined as energetic shaping through time regardless of sensory modality—is readily adapted to respond to such energetic shapes as music presents (Hatten 2004, 109). The exquisite shaping of energetic structures in music may also help deepen the range of what we may experience in life, as Jenefer Robinson has also suggested (2005, 267). And as Nelson Goodman argues throughout *Ways of Worldmaking* (1978), the arts create meaning as well as recreate it. Nevertheless, to experience the reality and depth of emotions triggered by music, we must first have experienced some of those emotions elsewhere. Our familiarity with various tokens of an emotional type gives us yet another competency, that of emotional experience, which we can bring to bear on our stylistic competency to help us recognize or come to know for the first time those familiar and unfamiliar emotional states that a musical work expresses.

The nineteenth-century philosopher and psychologist William James, in his fascinating lectures on the varieties of religious experience, touches on this same point when emphasizing the importance of often ineffable but nonetheless real experiences and their essential role in aesthetic experience:[14]

> Lyric poetry and music are alive and significant only in proportion as they fetch these *vague vistas of a life continuous with our own*, beckoning and inviting, yet ever eluding our pursuit. We are alive or dead to the eternal inner message of the arts according as we have kept or lost this mystical susceptibility. (James [1902] 1958, 295; my emphasis)

Whether One Actually Needs to Experience Aesthetically Warranted
Emotions to Cognitively Understand and Appreciate Composed
Expressive Trajectories (How We Might Engage with What's There)

If James suggests that only our mystical susceptibility enables us to engage fully with music, then it might appear that we have had an impoverished encounter if we do not actually experience the emotions that correlate with expressed states and trajectories such as one might claim for the Mozart example. But that would be a fallacy, akin to the oft-cited "expressive fallacy" in which one assumes composers are actually feeling the emotions that they are composing as expressive states into a musical work. As a sometime composer, more frequent performer, and most frequent listener, I can report that in each of these roles I have at times been completely and deeply engaged by the emotions spawned by my cognitive appreciation of expressive states. Nevertheless, when listening to music I am also frequently cognitively engaged without overt emotional symptoms while being no less committed to the expressive force of the music. For example, I can be completely engaged with a complex movement of a Beethoven string quartet, following its trajectories in minute detail (as enhanced by previous study of the work), without actually experiencing its expressed emotional states. Granted, sophisticated tests could easily find evidence of latent emotional response in me during such engaged listening, but those responses might as easily correlate with emotions resulting from any kind of satisfying engagement in cognitive activity, not necessarily with those emotions interpretable as being directly correlated with expressed emotional states in the music.[15]

Beyond this necessary commitment to and engagement with expressive meaning as a listener—whether experiencing an actual emotion or appreciating within a more reflective, imaginative, aesthetic consciousness—as a performer (or composer) I also highly value the heuristic process of embodying musical gestures as a reliable source of information on their emotional valence. Thus, when learning a work (or when playing the Mozart theme during a lecture), I may attempt to embody (or didactically exaggerate) the energetic shapes I am attempting to interpret—constrained, of course, by stylistic and work-specific contexts. François Delsarte (1811–71), noted teacher of expressive declamation and gesture for singers, discovered that when one assumes the gestures and postures associated with given emotions, one may begin to feel those emotions as a consequence (Delsarte 1884). Thus, if a musical gesture correlates with grief, and one plays it with what one understands of grief (slowly, heavily, as though burdened), one may not only project but actually feel the expressed grief of the gesture. Australian music psychologist and pianist Manfred Clynes found an interesting effect emerging from his tests for "sentic shapes" in that respondents often reported a greater sense of emotional well-being after going through the 150 finger presses for each of the emotional types that he was attempting to measure and generalize (1977, 104–39). Perhaps the "exercising" of a given emotion gave expression to a human subject's repressed psychological conflicts, and their energetic build-up was suitably released, or eased, by such facilitated emotional experiencing.

Full experiencing of an emotion such as grief can be debilitating for a performer, and thus it is a luxury that typically only listeners may thoroughly indulge. I have twice performed the slow movement of Beethoven's *Hammerklavier* Piano Sonata, op. 106, for memorial services, allowing myself to participate, at least to some degree, in the emotions expressed by its tragic to transcendent expressive genre.[16] By the end of this movement, which lasts more than a quarter of an hour, I was completely drained each time. Had this been a concert performance of the entire sonata, I would not have had the physical or emotional resources to tackle the finale with its technically challenging double fugue. In turn, listeners cannot always afford to lose themselves in complete emotional identi-fication with a work's expressed states—for example, if listening while engaged in a demanding task such as driving. But there are those moments that catch us unawares, when we are overcome with emotions beyond our aesthetic intentions. To these states of presumed musical "possession" (which may reflect the trigger-ing and release of a listener's subconsciously repressed feelings) music owes its reputation for mystical powers.[17]

Nevertheless, actors as well as performers and sophisticated listeners can con-centrate their energies on the cognitive appreciation of and engagement with composed expressive trajectories without necessarily experiencing their implied or expressed emotional states. Such abstracted—or better, distilled—experience is a possible consequence of aesthetic distance. An absence of "actual" emotion would only be judged as sterile if there were no commitment to a continual en-gagement with expressive states in music.

Whether Emotional Engagement Need Always Be Congruent with, or Isomorphically Constrained by, Composed Expressive Trajectories to Qualify as Aesthetically Warranted Emotions (How We Might Develop or Go beyond What's There)

Having emphasized a commitment to cognitively appreciating, if not overtly experiencing, the emotions associated with composed expressive trajectories, I want to shift ground and explore the opposite side of the equation. What if our emotions go beyond that which is warranted by the structures we can analyze but nevertheless remain within a universe warranted by the prevail-ing aesthetic? Must one always traverse the musical landscape in lock-step with the temporal sequence of all its details, as in the "musical melisma" of Aaron Ridley's (1995) near-gestural formulation of melody and harmony or in my conception of *melos* from chapter 4? Consider Meyer's (1956) original theory of emotion as frustrated expectation, and imagine that one received an emotional charge every time a (statistically relevant) expectation was frus-trated. One would be a nervous wreck before the end of a movement. What is more likely is that we process such denials and deferrals more holistically, or holarchically, to use Arthur Koestler's (1969) helpful image.[18] Although the emotions that emerge from such complex processing will share important fea-tures and even marked turning points (such as the dissonant chord in bar 2 of Mozart's opening phrase or the reversal of melodic direction leading to its rap-turous climax in bar 3), they will not likely replicate a myriad of cross-currents that are constantly impinging on the flow. Instead, there may come moments when our cognitive evaluation of detail is sufficient for our minds to float free and experience an emergent emotion, one that is warranted by a composed expressive trajectory but that does not reproduce its temporal sequence or pacing.

Such moments may be triggered by what I call "rhetorical gestures," which I define as those more highly marked events that break the unmarked flow of the

Example 6.2. Mozart, Piano Sonata in F, K. 533, second movement, complete
exposition (showing editorial dynamics and bracketed slurs as found in the
Broder revised edition of 1960).

discourse (Hatten 2004, 135). However, the number of striking events that may
be accommodated into what one might consider the unmarked flow of a musical
discourse depends on the musical style as well as the sophistication of the listener. It may even depend on the work. Return to the Mozart example and compare the parallel construction of the first theme's modulating, compound period
beginning in measure 11 (example 6.2). Measures 11–18 correspond exactly to

measures 1–8. On second hearing, those events that were originally marked will lose some of their surface foregrounding of surprise and interest. To counter the absorption of thematically marked into unmarked in our ongoing experience of the music, Mozart further expands the second phrase, effecting a sequential modulation in bar 19 that intensifies the move to an even higher climactic pitch in bar 21.

In bar 33 we reach the essential expositional closure of this sonata-form movement.[19] How do we interpret what appears to be unmarked, closural material in measures 33–36? Here, for me, the dramatic significance of the material enhances its expressive content. When considered in isolation, the closing theme is charming but simple. However, coming as it does after a very intense and undercut climax in measures 28–33, this closing theme has an unusually poignant expressive power that emerges from its functional role in a higher drama, not from its independent or decontextualized structural capacity to provoke emotion. I return to this theme in the next section.

The Status of Aesthetically Warranted Emotions as Multileveled and Integrative, Synthetic and Emergent, and Varying in Intensity (How We Might Characterize the Rich Complexity of Aesthetically Warranted Emotions and Our Cognition of Them)

By this last point, I wish to counteract any possible misunderstanding arising from my use of the expression "unmarked flow." Although highly marked rhetorical gestures may well serve as major signposts for our understanding of a discourse and the form of a movement's expressive genre, as competent listeners we are engaged in fully processing the expressive richness of every detail we can possibly grasp. We do not wait to be prodded into action. But this continuous processing, in order to be temporally efficient, requires something akin to cognitive chunking. Adapting the information-theory concept of chunking (Miller 1956), I propose a series of emergent bundles in which the mind gathers up and synthesizes the complexities of musical events. What counts as a bundle? Here, gestalt theory meets music theory, as Meyer and others have demonstrated.[20] The motive is one such meaningful gestalt (see Schoenberg [1934, 1936] 2006). Perhaps more compelling, however, is the musical gesture, which, as I have theorized (2004, 101–2), combines the power of both imagistic and temporal gestalts in a richly synthetic perception. In this sense prototypical musical gestures are like those basic categories studied by cognitive theorists, as Lawrence Zbikowski (2002) has theorized for musical motives.

In the Mozart example, the $\frac{3}{4}$ meter might also suggest one cognitive aid to bundled processing: the creation of consistent groupings in measure-length units. But some of the expressive gestures I have analyzed do not align with the metric boundary, such as the melodic drop between bars 1 and 2 and the melodic reversal on the last beat of bar 2, both of which occur in my own version as well as in Mozart's original. Nevertheless, the expressive force of these gestures is understood partly by the ways in which they suggest an embodied (human) agency wilfully expressing itself within the virtual environment established by a consistent meter. As Larson (1994, 2012) suggests and I further elaborate in chapter 2, this notion of a virtual environment within which one pays off debts to various forces, such as implied gravity, provides the trace of a virtual agency with which we can identify. When we engage with a work's implied subjectivity, we have yet another means of experiencing its emotional trajectory.

With agency in music, there is much that may appear indeterminate. When do multiple actants suggest a single agent versus interacting agents? When does a musical event become willed or acted by an actor, as opposed to forced on or experienced by that actor? Eero Tarasti (1994) explores these questions through his application of Greimassian modalities to music. Robinson (2005, 259), drawing on the works Edward T. Cone (1974) and Bruce Vermazen (1986), makes a compelling case for hearing, or listening through, a persona in her theory of expression for Romantic music. But Stephen Davies (1997) argues that music is too indeterminate to claim that our hearing a persona in a musical work is necessary to our full understanding of its musical expression. I support Robinson's carefully nuanced position while recognizing various stages of virtual agency. And I agree with Ridley (2007) that (with respect to hearing a persona, in his case) agency must be argued on a case-by-case basis. Given a virtual emotion as expressed (not merely represented) by an implied virtual agent, one may more readily distinguish between (1) the actual emotion a listener may coexperience (rather than merely recognize) in tandem with that expressed by an implied virtual agent and (2) the actual emotion a listener may experience in reaction to that virtual agent.[21]

Returning to the Mozart exposition, the initially rather unmarked closing theme (mm. 33ff.) is nevertheless expressively enhanced by its place in the dramatic trajectory. Just as the first theme recovers from its dissonant drop by a sudden leap upward, the second theme recovers from its dissonant imbroglio by a sudden (perhaps too sudden) restoration of pure consonance in measures 31 and 32. The closing theme, though expressively unmarked by itself, suggests a virtual agent who is basking in a feeling of relieved contentment, having apparently mastered the threatening tragic drift of the second theme. An otherwise naïve theme is thus strategically marked by its position in an unfolding drama, and we may identify with a virtual actor as protagonist here, coexperiencing its sense of heightened relief.

My actual emotion in hearing or playing this theme goes further when I recognize, from a more critical position, the "too easily" gained relief and suspect that the virtual protagonist is in denial. From this perspective I am now reacting to the plight of that virtual agent/actor, who has repressed a tragic dread by means of a sudden turn to major in measures 31 and 32. At this point, my emotion is not the virtual actor's relieved contentment but rather an intense feeling of poignant compassion, since I recognize the unresolved tensions underlying an attempted repression and thereby experience the vulnerability of an initially euphoric theme. This is a powerful effect akin to dramatic irony, in which the audience knows more than the character knows. With a theory of virtual agency, the effect of dramatic irony becomes possible to experience even in purely instrumental music. Through this awareness, we feel a different emotion from that experienced by the virtual actor in the music, and yet that different emotion is aesthetically warranted by the composed expressive trajectory. To the extent that we empathize, not merely sympathize, with the virtual protagonist (perhaps by recognizing times in which we, too, have tried to repress or deny a too-powerful emotion), we can interiorize—and share—a virtual subjectivity that we have helped to flesh out. If, in our response to the characters in a Chekhov play (as noted in interlude I), we are enjoined to fill out the content of a deeper subjectivity that is only implied by a character's distracted words and silences (dramatically placed), so in our response to the Mozart slow movement we may also be impelled to fill out the deeper psychological implications of the surface drama—as cued here by Mozart's "too easy" feint at resolution.[22]

Mozart provides further evidence to support this interpretation; the naïvely contented closing theme encounters, in successive measures, increasingly intense reminders of that which was repressed. First, there is a marked rhetorical gesture in measure 35: the leap from E♮ up to B♭. This deflection may well have been motivated by the deflection from B♭ down to E♮ in measures 1 and 2 of the opening theme, understood here as a questioning inversion (subjected to key and scale-degree variation). In measure 38 Mozart accelerates the temporal pace by repeating measure 37 but intensifying the leap by the use of D♭, and the modal mixture recalls the dark moment in measure 2. Measure 39 attempts to ameliorate the D♭ by reinterpreting it as part of a V$^6_5$ to A♭ major (the relative major of an implied F minor). But measure 40 wrenches back from A♭ by means of G♭ and a Neapolitan-sixth chord that resolves to a cadential $^6_4$ in F minor in measure 41. Fully minor-mode mixture is then reversed, leading spectacularly to the expected closural key of F major by means of a vocal portamento implied by the leap from F to high A. Note that the arialike portamento leap both restores consonance and avoids the perfect closural cadence implied by the harmony. By analogy with the rhetorical arrival $^6_4$ (Hatten 1994, 15), this "arrival $^5_3$" rhetorically marks a breakthrough moment of positive insight in the unfolding expressive drama.[23] The initially unmarked closing melody has increasingly demonstrated individuality through its questioning leaps, enhanced by a topical transformation from simple conventional closing material through *empfindsamer* sighs to an arialike climactic breakthrough. Galant decorum is then restored with the long-deferred cadence.

The exposition of this movement features continuous motivic unfolding, an early example of the process Schoenberg calls "developing variation" (Frisch 1984, 1–2). The technique is most obvious in the second theme's motto-like development (mm. 23–27) of the opening four notes of the first theme. Mozart varies the interval of the melodic drop and dialogically echoes it in a diminutional cascade that embeds other intervallic leaps (d4 and P4 as well as d5), leading to a hocketing imitation of the neighboring quarter notes in the following measure. Mozart's use of refractive counterpoint (recall chap. 4) here has the effect of enhancing a single motive by dramatizing its increasingly dissonant drops as echoed within the diminutional cascade (compare this texture with the opening of the development section, measures 47–48, where the motto drops by a diminished fourth). The intensifications in the second theme coalesce into tragic diminished-seventh and minor $^6_4$ harmonies before giving way, suddenly, to a reassuring F major in measure 31. Thus, the later emergence in measure 42 of brighter F major from darker harmonies is prefigured in the second theme area, and the closing moment will receive some of its emotional coloring from our memory of the second theme. Notably, the music is staging an emotional drama whose interiority depends on global memory as well as more local reflection or rumination. And the sonata form's structured hierarchy of temporal units can support such long-range feats of memory as enhanced by strategically thematized relationships.

For example, the weighty development section (mm. 47–72, not shown) begins by reengaging the opening motive, now in dialogue with the triplet figuration introduced in the closing section of the exposition (itself perhaps inspired by the accelerated sixteenth-note descent in m. 3). The second half of the development explores the sequential sixths and thirds from measures 5–10, further stretching their extended sequence in a way that appears to move beyond rational stylistic syntax.[24] In the recapitulation Mozart extraordinarily recalls and resolves the main theme as presented in the development by inserting a version of the development's dialogical treatment of the motive, now in place of the parallel phrase of the first theme's modulatory period. Measures 85 and 86 expand this interpolation with a wedgelike acquiescence to I⁶. What might have been mistaken for a varied treatment of the second theme area is then framed by the extended sequence that closed the original period, resolved down a fifth, for a medial caesura in B♭.

The second theme's treatment of the main theme, anticipated already in the first group, is marked in the recapitulation by textural inversion and a higher register. Although the tragic chords return, the effect is less somber. Indeed, the remainder of the exposition is registrally transposed up a fourth rather than down a fifth, emphasizing the lighter and brighter trajectory of a progressive emergence into unclouded B♭ major. A brief coda spins out the sixteenth-triplets as a means of undermining both register and mode. After a deceptive cadence, the descent restores the lower register, and one lone, widely separated diminished-seventh chord plaintively colors the final cadence with a last memory of the repressed tragedy of the movement.

This highly abbreviated interpretation of the remainder of the movement offers further illustration of how Mozart's play with formal expectations (implications) contributes to the overall trajectory of the movement—its expressive genre (Hatten 1994, 67–71), which in turn guides a stylistically competent expressive interpretation and, potentially, an aesthetically warranted emotional response. Note my use of the word "response" here, which hides a distinction that has enormous consequences for how we may choose to experience a musical work.[25] We may "respond" by identifying with an implied subjectivity, a protagonist-like agent that works its way through a kind of "pilgrim's progress" of experiences, or we may literally "respond" by reacting from the perspective of our own subjectivity to the plight of that projected protagonist, feeling some degree of empathy or sympathy for a character rather than identifying with that character—as Ridley (1995) and Robinson (2005) have also observed.[26] I would add that it is typically our choice whether we process musical expressivity in bundled fashion from the "inside" of the drama as engaged participant or from the "outside" as engaged spectator—although the drama of Mozart's closing theme suggests that a composer can create the conditions for a powerful merger of these two perspectives. And I would emphasize once more that we need not experience actual emotions ourselves, either as coparticipants or compassionate witnesses, even when we recognize those emotions to have been expressed in the trajectories composed into a work. Whether we do or not, a full experience of the work demands our commitment to its expressive meaning and our willingness to focus on that meaning as guide to our own, inevitably emergent experience.

Once-Removed Emotions: Edward Elgar's "Nimrod" Variation

I return now to the different kind of engagement envisaged by Wilde at the opening of this chapter. As he observes, "When the work is finished it has, as it were, an independent life of its own, and may deliver a message far other than that which was put into its lips to say." To be sure, the particular emotions that one feels and the degree to which one engages emotionally often depend on personal factors not predictable from the music alone. Within a realm of expressed grief or sadness, listeners are free to associate personal experiences that both situate and intensify their identification with grief or sadness. And a particular kind of reflective sadness may emerge from one's subjectivity when engaged with the emotions expressed by a musical work. This emotional response need not track an embodied virtual agent to distill a powerful essence.

However, it is always possible that powerful emotions may be evoked in a way that is nevertheless warranted, even when those emotions are not directly expressed by a musical work. Consider the celebrated Variation IX, "Nimrod," from Elgar's *Enigma Variations*, op. 36. One may, of course, follow its opening sigh motive through extensive sequencing and transformation (notably, expanding from a comforting descending third to a more plaintive descending seventh), but instead of pursuing this kind of close analysis, I want to step back and examine how a powerful emotion that appears only marginally linked to the expressive journey of an implied virtual agency can nevertheless emerge as significant.

Certainly, the spiritual, hymnlike topic supports other markers of nobility in this *Adagio* variation, such as its processional character.[27] But spirituality and nobility are not situated emotions in themselves; rather, they serve to elevate the significance of any deep emotion to a level of profundity.[28] Thus, listeners could be led to recollect those experiences that, on reflection, they find profound or profoundly moving. A listener's own emotional life is thereby nurtured, enhanced, and ennobled even as it surges through the climactic contours of the music. But the listener would be moved to tears as much by the recall of personal experiences as by anything "in" the music, whose role here may well be that of aggrandizing and ennobling emotions it need not directly embody. Another might experience tears of patriotic fervor (a generic emotion that the anthemlike music does indeed support, especially for British listeners), but one could also experience a wide range of positive and negative emotions—from fond nostalgia to poignant grief—and each of these would be felt more profoundly through engagement with the spiritual nobility expressed by Elgar's dignified hymn.[29]

Common to all these different emotions is the higher power of a listener's memory—as recollection but also as leading to deeper reflection on that which is inevitably lost, whether or not tragically, through the passing of time. The music thus enables recognition of the profound significance of whatever life experience one brings to the table. This is an important mode of experiencing music; indeed, even works that engage more directly with virtual agency and more markedly with a particular emotion may also be experienced in this reflective way.

But Isn't This Just Arousal?

The arousalist theory claims that musical events trigger particular responses in a kind of cause-and-effect relationship. This theory is often misconstrued or even mislabeled as "subjectivist." Lydia Goehr (2008, 8) helpfully contrasts this subjectivist account with Eduard Hanslick's more objectivist account of music's own movements. Certainly, one would want to preserve the invaluable subjective contribution in interpreting musical events, which is not captured by the basic cause-and-effect relationships proposed by arousal theory. In other words, we should attempt to describe what listeners contribute, in addition to their stylistic competency, in engaging subjectively with musical works. And that engagement, as we see in previous examples, goes far beyond the forms of subjectivism by which listeners associate hearing a work with an event in their lives and thereby endow the work with personal meanings.

Within the levels of virtual agency I have presented, virtual subjectivity emerges from the recognition of specific energies and dramatized contexts for the identity and development of agents as actors. How these particularized roles are relevant at higher levels of human experience will be different for each listener, and thus the "subjective" aspect of this kind of arousal has often been suspect in theories that purport to explain music's immanent meanings (with Hanslick as an early critic). Given music's presumed lack of reference, even virtual agency (conceived as a persona) has been subject to withering critique by philosophers such as Peter Kivy (2009).

But the subjective character of the listener's engagement is an indispensable component of artistic understanding, even when, as in Schumann's "Am leuchtenden Sommermorgen" (see chap. 5), actorial roles are spelled out. Our engagement with the artistic presentation and development of characters (whether in a play or virtual actors in music) depends not just on a distanced recognition of their features but on our ability to relate (and evaluate) that character's "character" with respect to real-life people with whom we are familiar, subjectively and/or intersubjectively. We may identify with aspects of characters that are like ourselves, or we may variously empathize with or feel sympathy for characters who recall others we have known, even though never in quite that way. In other words, we draw on our subjective awareness of our own selves and our intersubjective experience of a wide range of "others" in evaluating the plausibility and engaging emotionally with a variety of characters in a play or virtual actors in a musical work.[30]

The dialogical aspect of personhood suggests one reason why the virtual actorial level remains important for inferences of virtual subjectivity, even when we do not infer fictional characters. Actorial interaction (as dramatic conflict) fosters the means by which we create our sense of self out of dialogical negotiations with the positions of others in a way that enables us to find our center, carve out a niche, and fashion an identity. At the level of virtual subjectivity, those other virtual actors may be understood as allegorical stand-ins for internal others with whom we argue and interact in the processes of thinking and feeling. Empathy depends on this capacity to internalize virtual others.

Instrumental music's much-touted lack of referentiality, then, is rescued in part, as I have demonstrated, by the range of virtual agencies that it implies, but those agencies in nonprogrammatic music remain in need of filling out. For example, how do we fill out the staged subjectivity in the Beethoven piano sonata themes discussed in chapter 5? Presumably, we do so with a relevance to our lives that comes from engagement—an interaction that involves a listener's own contribution to the music. We relate virtual agencies (and their actions and expressed feelings or thoughts) to our own experience of similar agencies—whether personal (as in the case of identifying with) or social (as in cases of empathy beside or sympathy for). Such interaction does not simply "use" the music as a kind of virtual experiencing (like those who substitute virtual-reality games for life in the real world). A listener may indeed become entranced by subjective identifications with music that are so strong as to cause weeping or profound emotional reaction, but the same listener may also engage with the very same piece in a more distanced manner—appreciating, evaluating, and even critiquing the constructions of virtuality that she recognizes or is able to reconstruct. A listener may even alternate among these modes of engagement during a single listening experience of a work.

To say, then, that a work arouses a particular emotion, as implying a cause-and-effect relationship, is to leave out a significant way in which we as human listeners interact with it. One theoretical response has been to distinguish what the work expresses from those emotions it evokes. In that framework the listener either receives the emotion that is evoked or merely recognizes its existence as expressed in the work. I would caution against the implied transaction still lurking in these formulations and propose instead a more continuous interaction. In support of that continuity, I have argued that emotions are not simply represented or expressed as singular emotion packets; rather, we engage with the continuously unfolding development of a character or subject through its virtual emotional life (with implications for thinking, for moral awareness, and for psychological *Bildung* as the growth of an individual's character).[31] And that engagement, as Robinson (2005) reminds us, involves not only identifying with familiar characters but coming to understand new identities. As we continue to learn from their journeys, we develop our own subjective and intersubjective competencies. And as interactive listeners we elaborate a musical work's virtual subjectivity by referencing our own subjectivity, virtually anticipating a future, moving through a series of choices or reconsiderations, experiencing moments of epiphany, and reflecting on what has passed.

Notes

1. This chapter's discussion of the slow movement from Mozart's Piano Sonata in F Major, K. 533, is drawn in part from Robert S. Hatten, "Aesthetically Warranted Emotion and Composed Expressive Trajectories in Music," *Music Analysis* 29, no. 1–3 (2010): 83–101, as revised and focused here through the lens of virtual agency.

2. By "aesthetically warranted" I have attempted to employ as neutral a term as possible to indicate the importance and relevance of a historically reconstructed aesthetic perspective (and in my further analyses, a particular stylistic competency) in first interpreting those emotions expressed in a work. These expressed emotions are the motivation (not the prescription) for (not necessarily identical) emotions felt by a listener. I do not claim that aesthetically warranted emotions are somehow better or the only ones to be taken into account. Listeners are free to experience any emotions, and those responses are valid in their own right; indeed, psychological testing of listener reports tends to encounter an enormous range of reactions to musical samples. In my investigations in this chapter, however, I am more interested in exploring the kinds of emotions that may emerge from interactions with those emotions that can provisionally be reconstructed as having been expressed by some virtual agency in the music. I grant the speculative nature of this investigation, but it is not without its own kind of rigor, based on a body of stylistic, analytical, and hermeneutic scholarship.

3. In this sense, my version is akin to what Leonard B. Meyer, in his theorizing of music style, would consider to be "what might have happened given the constraints of the style and the particular context in which choice was made" (1989, 6). Thus, my version is stylistic, in a more normative sense, while also preserving many of the initial strategic decisions of this particular phrase, against which we can then measure the significance of further (expressively motivated) choices made by Mozart.

4. For more on reflection (as affective appraisal) in interpreting emotion as inspired by music, see Robinson 2005, 310–11.

5. Edward Lowinsky also remarks on the acceleration with which the four-bar phrase ends and finds it thematic for the movement: "The principle of acceleration is responsible for the rhythmic shape of every phrase" (1956, 180). Robert Levin directs his attention to the "harmonic audacity" of the movement as having "no parallel in any other Mozart solo keyboard work" (2003, 333).

6. Recall Steve Larson's musical forces as explained in chapter 2.

7. For a similar analogy based on biologist Ernst Haeckel's (1834–1919) outdated recapitulation theory, but from the perspective of style historical and evolutionary

justifications for Arnold Schoenberg's progressive innovations, see Taruskin 2005, 358–61.

8. As developed in Hatten 1994, markedness is the ranked value given to one term of an opposition by means of which it carves out a more distinct or specific realm of meaning. Marked oppositions typically take the form of X versus not-X, where X is some relevant feature distinguishing the marked term (e.g., unusual dissonance). Marked music-structural oppositions correlate with marked oppositions among cultural meanings, including, for our purposes here, emotional responses (and their intensity). Mozart's choices in this slow movement may be considered strategically marked events according to my adaptation of Meyer's distinction between stylistic rules and strategies (1989, 17–23; see also Hatten 1982). Composers' choices of marked events to enhance expressivity often depend on their salience (foregrounding as perceptually "marked"), which is often due to their undercutting or deferral of stylistic expectations (Meyer 1956), or implications, in Meyer's later formulation (1973, 110–13). My perspective on unusual, marked events as employed to enhance expressive meaning goes counter to John Sloboda's general suggestion that music's "cue-impoverishment" and ambiguity engender "profound and semi-mystical experiences" (1999, 226). While this may be the case at times, listeners to Mozart may also experience profound emotions that are, in fact, cued by such marked moments—however ambiguous they may first appear to be. However, as I argue under my fourth point in a later section, individuals may also experience emotions that go beyond these anchoring cues in ways that could still be considered "aesthetically warranted" in my sense, if such expansions can be understood as inspired and guided by corresponding "composed expressive trajectories." In any case, such emergent emotions need not be mystically diffuse.

9. As noted by Evan Jones, Quantz's use of dynamics is clearly theoretical in distinguishing various classes of dissonant harmonies, and thus they are not prescriptive for performance, although the dynamic markings "reaffirm the traditional association between dynamics and dissonance in the context of the hierarchy of harmonic stability that [Quantz] advances" (2003, 3).

10. Levin notes that this "peculiar feature" of Mozart's later, more individual style is also found "in the slow movements to the Sonatas in C K. 545, in B♭ K. 570, in D K. 576, and in nonkeyboard works as well" (2003, 334). By contrast, the Adagio in B Minor, K. 540, is filled with *empfindsamer*-inspired extreme oppositions among dynamic markings. I would add that while the marked events in the slow movement of K. 533 require foregrounding, dynamics are but one of a performer's means. Subtleties of timing (placement), articulation (accent and duration), touch, and pedaling may also contribute to the foregrounding of these events. I would also note cases where Broder's dynamics appear counterintuitive—for example, the second theme in mm. 23–27, where I would foreground the left hand's motto (drawn from the primary theme) and play the right hand's diminutions of the motto more softly, as a kind of reverberant reflection.

11. Wye Jamison Allanbrook shares this concern in her theorizing of the comic surface in Mozart's (and Haydn's) mimetic play with topics but without presuming a single persona or dialogue between agents (2014, 117; see also note 17 in chap. 4). Naomi Cumming's framing of the issue of "depth" for her combined gestural and voice-leading interpretation of the *Adagio* movement from Bach's Sonata in G Minor for Solo Violin (BWV 1001) features agency as means of mediating between levels: "Depth is neither in the 'background' nor in the 'foreground.' It is not in any kind of sign taken alone. It is in the unfolding of a complex musical 'persona,' who must negotiate conflicts of agency, and deflections of purpose, while moving towards some goal" (2000, 239).

12. I have defined "stylistic competency" as "the internalized (possibly tacit) cognitive ability of a listener to understand and apply stylistic principles, constraints, types, correlations, and strategies of interpretation to the understanding of musical works in that style. More than a lexicon of types or a set of rules" (Hatten 1994, 288). So-called rules are in effect regularities that reflect "typicality in the style, not to be confused with a prescription for behavior by either composer or listener, other than as a habit of correlation or stylistic interpretation" (293). Judith Becker (2001) recognizes some of these same characteristics in the related, if larger concept of a "culture," especially in her application of Pierre Bourdieu's (1977, 72) concept of "habitus," defined as "principles of the generation and structuring of practices and representations which can be objectively 'regulated' and 'regular' without in any way being the product of obedience to rules" (cited in Becker 2001, 137). Becker conceives of a "habitus of listening" that is "tacit, unexamined, [and] seemingly completely 'natural'" (138). She uses moves to a socially interactive concept of listening habitus to address intersubjective ("supra-individual") levels of emotional response as distinguished from those unique to the experience of each individual: "While it is the individual who experiences the emotion, it is the group and its domain of coordinations that triggers the emotion" (153). Although this is clearly the case in many cultures, style alone is sufficient (without group interaction in the listening process) to coordinate an individual's responses to aesthetically warranted emotions in much Western music. Nevertheless, artistic styles (especially historical ones) cannot effectively guide listening unless they have been inculcated through a process of learning or entrainment through extensive listening.

13. Catharsis is best understood as clarification rather than purging of the emotions. "[Martha] Nussbaum (1986) has shown that the central meaning of catharsis (and related words e.g., 'kathairo,' 'katharos'), common before Aristotle, used frequently by Plato and Aristotle, and continuing after Aristotle's time, was that of clearing up or clarification, including the cognitive meaning of understanding clearly and without obstacles. The spiritual term 'purification' is a derivation, indicating an absence of obscuring blemish. The medical one, 'purgation,' is also secondary, indicating freeing the body from internal obstructions" (Oatley and Gholamain 1997, 267). Further, "Nussbaum [1986, 391] argues that catharsis in the theatre was a cognitive process: 'The function of tragedy is to accomplish, through pity and fear, a clarification (or illumination) concerning experiences of the pitiable and fearful kind'" (cited in Oatley and Gholamain 1997, 267).

14. Compare the quotation from Wilde that opens this chapter.

15. This is one problem I foresee in music psychologist Klaus Scherer's "aesthetic emotion" (2004, 241) classification: that it may confuse what I have been interpreting as the coexperiencing of emotionally compelling trajectories with another valuable emotional experience, one that might also be aesthetically warranted in many cases but one that is radically different in kind—namely, the aesthetic appreciation of the work's achievement, ranging from its craftsmanship to its general effect.

16. See Hatten 1994, 9–28, for a close interpretation of this movement's composed expressive trajectory.

17. The quintessential Romantic literary expression of music's mystical powers is found in Heinrich von Kleist's "St. Cecilia or The Power of Music" ([1810] 1978, 217–30).

18. Basically, a holarchy is a hierarchy of wholes, each of which can be closed at one level but open from the perspective of higher levels. Narmour (1977) introduced Koestler's concept to music theory; he argues, analogously, that a given musical event may be both closed (with respect to realized implications) and open (with respect to unrealized implications).

19. In their sonata theory, James Hepokoski and Warren Darcy apply the term "essential expositional closure" to the perfect authentic cadence that closes the secondary theme zone and demarcates the beginning of the closural zone in the exposition (2006, 17–18).

20. Among other important "gestalts" for the Classical style, one might include (1) phrase types, as theorized by William Caplin (1998); (2) compositional modules, as taught in the eighteenth century and subsequently theorized as schemata by Robert Gjerdingen (2007); and (3) topics, as theorized by Leonard Ratner (1980), Allanbrook (1983), Kofi Agawu (1991), and Hatten (1994, 2004, 2014b).

21. Recall the discussion in chapter 1.

22. I offer a similar account of repression that ultimately fails in my interpretation of the exposition from Schubert's Piano Sonata in A Minor, D. 784 (Hatten 2004, 187–92), as summarized in chapter 4.

23. In the arrival $^6_4$, "the point of arrival has an expressive connotation of transcendent resolution, as opposed to mere syntactic resolution" (Hatten 1994, 15), and it often involves a modal shift from lowered-$\hat{3}$ to raised-$\hat{3}$, which adds the positive effect of a Picardy third. William Kinderman describes the high A as "a ray of light emerging out of the darkness of the minor" and notes that this A "becomes the starting point for the chain of sequences that initiate the forceful development" (2006, 64).

24. Levin calls attention to "the relentless grating of the parallel thirds in the development—that catapults the piece over the precipice in a moment of breathtaking awe" in his apt characterization of this remarkable passage (2003, 333). Mozart's syntactically obscure progression features an underlying intervallic scaffolding, its sequential unfolding, and a clearly refractive counterpoint that integrates the voices into a coherent *melos* with singular force (see chap. 4 for these concepts).

25. Indeed, David Huron (2006, 7–15) distinguishes five response systems to expectations, which he then applies to the expectations experienced in listening (stylistically) to music: imagination, tension, prediction, reaction, and appraisal. Each of these can lead to specific emotional reactions, the first two before an expected event and the last three after.

26. Earlier adaptations of empathy (as *Einfühlung*) underlie the theories of Ernst Kurth (1886–1946) and Arnold Schering (1887–1941), as Lee Rothfarb (2002, 946) notes. However, in their theories empathy is more akin to a general principle underlying our capacity to understand and enjoy music as opposed to a concept developed with reference to a coherent theory of agency.

27. In a compelling lecture on nobility as a familiar theme type in Elgar, Ellsworth Peterson (2017) observes that Elgar included the indication "nobilmente" for this variation, but only later, in his piano reduction.

28. Consider, by analogy, Blake Howe's insightful analysis of the schemalike structure of obsession as represented in music by a musical space or topos (2016, 219) divided into sharply contrastive gestural fields: one features "diverse and varied melodic ideas" while the other "reiterates one note or a small group of notes" (222). Obsession is pathological in the cultural models that Howe surveys, but the obsessive topos, while also typically dysphoric, does not have just one emotional signifier. Rather, it can be used to frame a number of emotions ranging from anger to guilt or shame. It may even suggest a repressed emotion, as in Howe's example from act II of Christoph Willibald Gluck's opera *Iphigénie en Tauride*, when "an A repeated by the violas in a rhythmically distinct pattern suggests a repressed thought" that would appear to undercut Orestes's emotional appraisal when he sings "le calme entre dans mon coeur" (calmness enters my

heart) (237). Like nobility, obsession is not an emotion, but both are complex dramatic frameworks that music can stage, such that listeners are able to gauge further expressed emotion from the musical context and have unique emotional responses by situating these expressed emotions in terms of their own life experience.

29. For the film *Dunkirk* (2017), composer Hans Zimmer adapts an extremely slowed-down version of this variation to (perhaps subliminally) achieve a profound emotional effect, from the perspective of the British naval officer played by Kenneth Branagh, when he sees the arrival of countless fishing and pleasure boats that would save most of the stranded allied army on the beaches of Dunkirk. The emotional effect draws on the near iconic status of the movement, but the music can work its magic even on listeners not familiar with the music's acquired patriotic meanings, because of the general expressive character of a hymnlike theme that can support a complex of emotions, such as those associated with this highly dramatic moment of deliverance.

30. See also Palfy 2015 on the role of intersubjectivity in agential interpretation.

31. My proposal of bundled cognition allows a listener just such moments of freedom from the ongoing cognitive labor of processing, thereby enabling the listener to integrate what has been heard into a continuous emotional development, as well as relate it to emotions that may arise in response to that development—in particular, those emotions that reflect the contribution of the listener's own subjectivity.

7   Staging Virtual Narrative Agency

As we have seen, a fundamental feature of subjectivity is the capacity to self-reflect—to examine one's situation, to reflect on one's actions, and to internally critique or comment on one's state or behavior. As listeners to music, we can and often do take stock of those virtual actions and expressions we've heard, summarizing their significance for both virtual and actual subjectivities. This continuous process begins with our capacity to move cognitively and emotionally beyond a lock-step identification with the ongoing expressive *melos* to assimilate and integrate what we've heard—from the lowest levels of gestures and phrase units through "hierarchies of closure" (Meyer 1973) and dramatic trajectories of expressive genres (Hatten 1994). In addition to these formal articulations and dramatic contours, various rhetorical gestures provide opportunities for reflection (via rests and fermatas) or reappraisal (via unexpected disruptions) of the ongoing musical discourse. Further evidence for critical perspectivizing is found in our capacity to feel sympathy ("feeling for") a virtual agent in music. Sympathy is an emotion that is not at the same level as the virtual agent (identification's "feeling with" or close empathy's "feeling beside"); rather, it reflects a higher awareness that recognizes our critical separateness even as we continue to engage with a virtual agent, actor, or subjectivity.

In this chapter I explore how similar perspectives may be staged within a musical work, perhaps even enacted by a virtual agent, resulting in what I call narrative agency. Distancing is required for a narrative agent to appear to comment or reflect on, or provide clear reactions to, the discourse. In addition to various musical cues that suggest the capacity of a musical discourse to reflect on itself, a composer may more directly assume a narrative role by reordering the implied sequence of musical events or by manipulating our emotional responses to virtual agents (e.g., characters in an opera).

This chapter's focus on narrative agency recognizes an important distinction between drama (enacting) and narrative (presenting). The distinction is often blurred for music, where virtual agencies may enact a dramatic trajectory that also appears to have been presented by (hence, in some sense narrated by) a composer. But we will see how more specific kinds of narrative agency may also be staged in the music, and how narrative agency may even be enacted.[1]

Shifts in Level of Discourse

In my speculations on narrativity with respect to musical expressive meaning and gesture (Hatten 1991, 1994, 2004), I have noted that a principal marker for narrative agency is a "shift in level of discourse," which may be implied through a striking contrast in texture, register, dynamics, key, harmony, theme, or topic. Such striking contrasts are often launched by "rhetorical gestures," defined as those that break the unmarked flow of the discourse (Hatten 2004, 136). Striking shifts often mark locations where a virtual subjectivity may be enhanced by the capacity to react to its own discourse by commenting on or even critically rejecting it. Although breaks in discursive continuity may be interpreted as mere exclamations or emotive outbursts, they are potential cues for the projection of another level of discourse—one that offers a higher perspective or commentary on preceding events.[2]

One cue often found in Beethoven is what I call the recitative chord—a sudden major $\frac{6}{3}$ sonority that functions like the V^6 with which operatic recitatives begin, or by means of which they shift to a new key (abruptly rather than by smooth modulation), thereby marking a new idea or train of thought in an ongoing dialogue. Having acquired this association, a major $\frac{6}{3}$ chord can then be topically imported in a way that triggers a similar association in a purely instrumental context. I have explored several such examples in Beethoven, from the opening of Op. 31, no. 2, to the shift in measure 17 of the third movement from Op. 130.[3] Franz Schubert employs the recitative $\frac{6}{3}$ in the coda of the finale of his Piano Sonata in A Major, D. 959, and marks it further as an irregular resolution of a German augmented-sixth chord, producing the effect of an arrival $\frac{6}{4}$ achieved as an arrival $\frac{6}{3}$. Brahms, with his abrupt move to a B♭$\frac{6}{3}$ in the opening of his first piano concerto, creates an intertextual allusion to the annunciatory force of the climactic $\frac{6}{3}$ at the recapitulation from the first movement of Beethoven's Ninth Symphony.

Some narrative-agential effects are so extreme that they appear to originate from a compositional intention to intervene critically, even to the point of dismissing the entire preceding discourse of a work. Rey Longyear's (1970) interpretation of Romantic irony in the surprise addendum (*after* the coda) to the finale of Beethoven's String Quartet in F Minor, op. 95, is an apt interpretation of this extreme shift. The music abruptly departs from the Picardy third marking the close of the finale's coda. This unpredictable shift to the *buffa* topic undercuts the previously tragic discourse with a frenzied hilarity that is completely unprepared. Longyear, drawing on Jean Paul Richter's "annihilating laughter," considers this passage as exemplifying Romantic irony through a similar annihilation of, in this case, the prevailing seriousness of the quartet. Romantic irony implies a higher level of intentionality, and the "laughter" may well be more desperate than joyous, reflecting a virtual subjectivity that is attempting to rise above suffering by dismissing its power.[4]

In chapter 4 I demonstrate how a musical discourse draws together disparate voices or textures, integrating them into a continuous, coherent, and persuasive *melos.* I show how techniques such as developing variation (an unfolding, evolving thematic discourse) and refractive counterpoint (a thematically derived counterpoint that implies a single agency) support the interpretation of a musical discourse. The expressive "argument" of a musical work is grounded in this primary discursive level, with its actorial roles of protagonist and antagonist (or principal internal and external agents). Given the dramatic trajectory that this implies and the analogy of such drama with the stories of fiction (hence, implying narrative in this general sense), one might take a cue from film theory and refer to this unmarked level of discourse as the diegesis—where the main "story" takes place, in a fictive world with actorial agents. Just as in film, nondiegetic elements would be those that occur outside this primary discursive level, and as in the case of nondiegetic film music, they may also serve various narrative roles in framing, commenting on, or in some way providing a meta-level perspective on the events in the diegesis.

Note that by this analogy one need not insist on a past tense for purely musical narrative. In fact, as I have argued elsewhere (Hatten 1997), even literary narrative does not require a past tense; rather, the apparent past tense is actually the "epic preterite" that serves as a cue marking the discourse as a narrative.[5] One of the most primitive markers of that special discourse we call narrative fiction is framing (as in "once upon a time"). And music is eminently capable of providing such simple frames. A clear example (Hatten 1997, 628) is found in Schumann's "Fabel" from the *Phantasiestücke*, op. 12, which stages a narrative voice with a slow, once-upon-a-time phrase before departing in a fast scherzo of activity. The slow frame returns in the middle as well as at the end, setting apart the faster music as the tale that is being told and reflecting on it from outside its frenetic "present" action. The slow introduction to Felix Mendelssohn's Overture for *A Midsummer Night's Dream* exhibits a similar framing function. More subtly than the Schumann frame, however, Mendelssohn's slow introduction not only serves as the invocation of a magical world (which will be launched by the fairy music of the *Allegro*) but also suggests moving backward in time to that magical fantasy world by means of another marked cue: a harmonic retrogression from V to IV (Hatten 1997, 629).

Other framing techniques include the use of topical cues such as the bardic (Dickensheets 2003). This cue typically involves arpeggiation, evocative of an ancient bardic harp, as in Mendelssohn's *Song without Words*, op. 30, no. 3, which uses opening and closing arpeggiation to frame the central men's choir topic.[6] The bardic topic also marks the arpeggiated opening of Chopin's Ballade in G Minor. Combined with a recitative chord (here, the Neapolitan in $^6_4$ position), the ballad's opening conjures up the recitative-like "telling" of a bard. The bardic topic may also be suggested by a quasi-recitative texture with heavy octave doubling of the melody. Two examples from Schumann are the "Im Legendenton" (In the style of a legend) episode from the *Fantasy*, op. 17, and the eleventh dance in the *Davidsbündlertänze* (Dances of the League of David), op. 6.

Although framing may provide a historicized or fantastic setting—setting a mood for or perspective toward the subsequent "story"—it is a relatively primitive narrative technique that often lacks greater consequence for the expressive drama of the diegesis. By contrast, the kinds of rhetorical gestures that signal a higher level of discourse are often more consequential for a progressive discourse, and their frequent use encourages the listener to integrate the different levels of discourse into a singular, more complex subjectivity. The *locus classicus* for this integrative subjectivity is the slow movement of Beethoven's Piano Sonata in B♭ Major (*Hammerklavier*), where such shifts constantly threaten to break up the continuity of the presumed primary discourse. Listening to Artur Schnabel's performance of this movement, one notes a considerable smoothing over of this jagged discourse, and while the performance succeeds in creating a Romantic sense continuity with its soaring melodic arches, it loses an essential part of what constitutes the unique *melos* of the movement. That *melos* suggests an anguished subjectivity that is constantly torn or distracted by sudden undercuttings, miming moments of uncertainty, despair, or hope (visionary transcendence).[7] Thus, a self-generating narrative enacts the drama of a singular subjectivity, which inverts the notion that a drama exists prior to its narratizing (or a story prior to its discourse).

The Self-Narratizing Virtual Agent

The self-narratizing virtual agent may be found in an example first discussed by Cone (1974) and further theorized by Ian Gerg (2015) as the "virtual observing agent," illustrated by the actorial role of Harold in Hector Berlioz's *Harold in Italy*. Although Harold is a protagonist, his role is that of an observer—perhaps even an exile, as in Lord Byron's semiautobiographical poem, *Childe Harold's Pilgrimage*—whose access to life is primarily through empathetic projection into the lives of others. Harold is identified as a virtual agent in the music by means of his association with the solo viola and its signature theme, although this identification is fluid.[8] In the second movement (example 7.1), where Harold encounters pilgrims, their singing procession is enacted through what Constantine Floros (1980, 160–66, 178–79) has identified and I have labeled as a new Romantic topic, emerging from the troping of two topics: the layering of a march topic (typically represented by pizzicato bass; either a walking bass, as here, or a tonic-dominant alternation) and a chorale-prelude topic (typically represented by a chorale or chorale tune, here the *canto*, separated out into individual phrases, each ending on a fermata).[9] This "pilgrims' processional" topic, as I call it, constitutes the diegesis of the pilgrims—virtual actors who are fictively singing as they march. Since Harold is observing the pilgrims, he is clearly part of the fictive diegesis, although his presence (marked by his signature theme) would not necessarily be seen (heard) by the pilgrims in their narrower diegesis. Harold's observational role is akin to a narrative one: his impressions suggest a level of evaluative distance.[10]

To what extent does Berlioz's virtual Harold comment on or critique the pilgrims' procession in his fictional world? In a discussion with Gerg, I noted that "Harold" appears to empathetically coparticipate by "singing along" and perhaps

Example 7.1. Berlioz, *Harold in Italy*, op. 16, "Marche des pélerins" (mm. 64–75). Harold's theme is on the top staff and the pilgrim's processional on the lower three staves, with the chorale melody (Canto) shifting in measure 72 from second violins to cellos, bassoons, and pizzicato basses.

marching alongside the pilgrims, since his signature theme is woven into the texture of the pilgrims' chorale (see example 7.1). But Gerg (2015) goes further by noting a later, delayed entrance featuring both grouping and displacement metrical dissonances between the chorale and the signature theme. The greater emotive distance that results is perhaps more representative of sympathetic engagement by the virtual-fictional Harold—or possibly a more critically distanced empathy. We might also speculate that Harold functions as a persona, not only poetically for Byron but musically for Berlioz. Indeed, Berlioz may well be capturing something of his own experience, since he also hiked through the Abruzzi hills during his Prix de Rome stay. But that would lead to another realm of interpretation, one that assumes Berlioz is simply writing a psychodrama of his own life (recall the discussion in chap. 6 of Schubert's own autobiographical motivations for the String Quartet in G). Instead, Berlioz is perhaps best understood as conjuring a distinct virtual agent in Harold—drawing on his own experience but not assuming the kind of personal identification that the term "persona" tends to imply.[11]

Another kind of narrative agency, however, provides clearer evidence of more direct manipulation by the composer—not through a persona but through a politically tinged consciousness. Since this example offers an instructive contrast with respect to the narrative agency that is staged (as a fictive narrator) in its literary source, I treat it at greater length.

Dmitri Shostakovich's Narrative Agency in *Lady Macbeth of the Mtsensk District* (1932)

Opera may be understood to comprise, in its dramatic trajectory, some form of transvaluation that could be understood under the rubric of narrative. What I want to examine, however, is how a given opera may exhibit narrative agency in less obvious ways than the staging of a narrator—as in Ned Rorem's operatic setting of Thornton Wilder's play *Our Town* or the narration by one of the operatic characters of past events as found in Brangäne's and Isolde's narratives in Wagner's *Tristan und Isolde*. Shostakovich's opera is based on a literary work with a staged narrator, but the composer dispenses with that narrator in his operatic version. How, then, is narrative agency achieved? I turn first to the literary source.[12]

Published in 1865, Nikolai Leskov's ([1865] 2003) realist novella, *Lady Macbeth of Mtsensk*, begins with a reassuring narrator who calmly and clinically reports a chilling history from the hinterlands. As Caryl Emerson perceptively notes,

> [Leskov] weaves these events skillfully, even lyrically, into a rich and placid folk narrative where sensuous imagery and strategically placed folksayings accompany the most brutal acts. To further complicate the literary genre, Leskov, apparently influenced by real-life prototypes, chose to present this curiously aestheticized tale as a "sketch" for notes to a court case. (1989, 61)

The story is indeed brutal. Katerina, a bored and unfulfilled housewife, succumbs to her passion for Sergei, a virile serf working in her merchant husband's compound. Her father-in-law discovers Sergei leaving Katerina's house and beats him. Katerina then murders her father-in-law (whose suspicions have fueled his own lust) by feeding him a dish of poisoned mushrooms. Katerina then enlists Sergei's help to murder her husband when he returns.

The inexorable sequence of horrific events echoes the larger dramatic arc of Shakespeare's *Macbeth*. The two lovers succeed at first but are ultimately caught and sent to Siberia. The wheel of fortune bears down most heavily on Katerina when her love is ultimately betrayed by Sergei. In a final act of animalistic violence, she seizes Sergei's lover, Sonetka, and plunges with her from a ferry barge, pulling Sonetka under the water in a shocking murder-suicide.

Shostakovich's opera dramatizes the salient events of the novella but dispenses with a literal narrator. Instead, narrative agency is staged musically in at least two other ways.[13] The first is purely instrumental: the orchestra functions like a Greek chorus, stepping outside the drama to deliver the powerful emotional reaction calculated by the composer. As in Alban Berg's *Wozzeck*, where a symphonic interlude before the final scene channels an emotional catharsis through its tragic commentary on Wozzeck's and Marie's deaths, Shostakovich employs symphonic interludes to trigger his desired emotional reactions to preceding events.

The second means of achieving narrative agency is by using contrasting musical styles for the characters, thereby manipulating our response toward them. Unlike Leskov's narrator, Shostakovich's musical commentary is far from dispassionate: he builds sympathy for Katerina while undermining the other characters through irony and parody.[14] Shostakovich exhibits his own music-narratizing power by transforming Katerina from a monster driven by animal passions in Leskov's tale to, as Shostakovich interprets her, a representative victim of heartless bourgeois capitalism who is also trapped in a loveless marriage. As he states in a 1932 article for *Sovetskoye iskusstvo* (Soviet art), his opera is "a most truthful and tragic portrait of the fate of a talented, clever, and exceptional woman perishing in the nightmarish conditions of prerevolutionary Russia" (cited in Fay 2000, 69). Two years later, Shostakovich (1934, 8) further reveals the ideological twist he has given to Leskov's Katerina, claiming that (in his operatic version) Katerina's "crimes are a protest against the tenor of the life she is forced to live, against the dark and suffocating atmosphere of the merchant class in the last century" (cited in Taruskin 1997, 501). As Taruskin wryly observes, "[Shostakovich] has undertaken to turn Leskov's naturalistic horror tale into a high-minded realist tract" (1997, 500). Although we are not likely to condone or excuse Katerina's ruthless murders even from the perspective of such a sociological interpretation, we are able to more closely empathize or at least sympathize with Katerina. As she becomes a more human protagonist, we may even begin to identify with her emotionally—not unlike our identification with Salome through Richard Strauss's empathetic musical portrayal of her love in her final aria sung to the head of John the Baptist.[15] An unintended consequence of Shostakovich's approach (as with Strauss's), is that Katerina's monstrous behavior becomes even more horrific when juxtaposed with our compassion for her plight.[16]

After the famous passacaglia interlude in which Shostakovich manipulates our emotional reaction to Katerina's murder of her father-in-law, Katerina begins act 2 with music in which she expresses her sincere love for Sergei and her vision for the future. This excerpt ends with a Romantic climax, including a Wagnerian appoggiatura over the cadence. Given her father-in-law's brutal and lustful behavior, we might at first find justification for Katerina's actions, especially since the music maintains Shostakovich's idealization of her character. When Sergei sings, however, we gather that his motivation is one of self-interest: he desires social status, which he can only achieve if Katerina marries him. The orchestra gradually parodies his desire, in contrast to Katerina's presumably more authentic love.

Shostakovich then introduces a scene reminiscent of Mozart's *Don Giovanni*. Katerina hallucinates seeing the ghost of her father-in-law, who has come to accuse her of murdering him. This scene's tragic undertone is mixed with her fear and guilt for what she is still able to recognize as criminal behavior. But the resulting trope, or blend, of the ghost's parodized music and Katerina's fearful/guilty music tends more toward the grotesque than the tragic. A similar trope occurs with the arrival of Katerina's weak husband, Zinovij, ironically heralded by a heroic fanfare. His ensuing argument with Katerina combines serious issues with comic elements, once again resulting in the grotesque. After the lovers strangle Zinovij, Sergei must bury him in the cellar, which he mimes to a grotesque march topic in the bassoon. Katerina then makes love to Sergei and pronounces that he is her husband now.

Shostakovich's narratizing may strike the listener as too didactic: he often "tells" us by the music how we are meant to feel rather than allowing our feelings to emerge from the drama itself (a weakness often encountered in film music as well). His narratizing can also misfire, with the consequence that we lose track of Katerina's more noble motivations in the face of her reprehensible behavior.

In the last scene, Shostakovich elevates his satiric tragedy to the epic mode, marked by a communal lament by the prisoners who are being marched under guard to Siberia. The music here is framed by a minor triad, emblematic of stark tragedy. Contemporaneous audiences would not have missed the allegory of a group of convicted criminals standing for an entire nation's repression under Joseph Stalin. Shostakovich's addition to his literary source briefly enlarges the genre from grotesque tragedy to political epic and further foregrounds his own narrative agency in transforming Leskov's novella.

Another narratizing strategy involves the juxtaposition of parody with bitter betrayal as Shostakovich refocuses on Katerina's personal tragedy. Here, an extremely powerful tragic climax marks Shostakovich's sympathy for Katerina as a victim—one who has been driven beyond reason to her final act of vengeance.[17] The female convicts mock Katerina's discomfort when she realizes that Sergei has betrayed her with Sonetka. Sergei has given his new mistress the same stockings Katerina had given Sergei to keep him warm. The convicts' parodic exchanges reach their climax on a minor triad (again, as a tragic emblem). Katerina's ensuing aria begins conventionally by expressing her devastation at betrayal by the man she had considered her true love. But it also reveals her demented resolve to wreak vengeance. The imagery of the lake with its deep, black water may be meant to imply a late recognition of the depth of her sins; however, there is no atonement sought or found for Katerina. Thus, the social dimension of her tragedy looms even more oppressively as we begin to anticipate her inexorable path to death.

To summarize, Shostakovich reveals a heavy narratizing hand by adding (and subtracting) scenes not found in the original source, by commenting on events through interludes, and, most directly, by clothing his characters and their actions in musical styles that manipulate his audience's responses. These strategies reveal the narrative agency of the actual composer—an agency that differs considerably from the role performed by the fictional narrator in Leskov's tale. As Emerson aptly summarizes,

> The orchestra is always on Katerina's side, functioning as the narrator and conscience of the tale, lending its intonation—in particular the famous symphonic passacaglia between Acts IV and V—to render the heroine's acts of violence pathetic and defensible. The characters surrounding her remain . . . one-dimensional, either trivial or evil. Their words match their deeds, and both match their music, which is dissonant and grotesque in the service of what the Russians call *razoblachenie*, an exposure of moral corruption. When the others do become lyrical, melodious or romantic, it is a sign of their insincerity—and strident interruptions from the orchestra punctuate that fact. (1989, 69)

Narrative Agency and Narrative Archetypes

Up to this point I have concentrated on narrative agency as comprising a narrator-like agency, noting the ways in which composers can stage narrative effects akin to those we associate with narrativity in other media, from literary fiction to film. I return to Byron Almén's theory of musical narrative (introduced in chap. 4), in part because it dispenses with literary-inspired narrators or analogues with other media to promote a more independently musical approach to narrativity. For Almén, musical narrative occurs whenever there is a transvaluation based on the outcome of a conflict. This transvaluation occurs in the marked relationship between two competing agencies (if one can extend agency to cover the broader institutional agency of a given "order"). In this section I explore how our choice in identifying with one virtual agency over another can determine which of Almén's narrative archetypes we will experience: tragic, comic, romantic, or ironic.[18]

Almén's (2008) theory of musical narrative is drawn from Liszka's (1989) semiotic theory of myth.[19] Almén similarly addresses dramatic conflict as arising when an initial order, understood as a hierarchy of values, is threatened by some kind of transgression. The transgressive element either successfully overthrows the order—in effect reversing or upsetting the hierarchy of values—or fails to do so. Not just two but four possible narrative outcomes (transvaluations) are possible, depending on whether we identify more closely (and positively) with the initial order or with its attempted transgression. As table 7.1 shows, the plus (+) value indicates the positive perspective we as listeners assume as we identify with (the agency implied by) a given order or a given transgression and as we interpret the expressive trajectory of the work through that lens.

Almén maps four possible narrative outcomes onto Frye's four literary modes—Romance, Tragedy, Comedy, and Irony—as archetypal narratives (see the first column of table 7.1). I provide a typical exemplification of each archetype

Table 7.1. Byron Almén's archetypal narrative trajectories understood in terms of listener identification with either a positively valued order or its transgression

Frye's modes	Order	Transgression	Possible outcomes
Romance (e.g., pastoral)	+ (valued state) (e.g., clear weather, calm)	− (negative intrusion) (e.g., storm [passes away])	Victory of + order (e.g., restoration of clear/calm)
Tragedy (e.g., heroic)	− (negative state) (e.g., oppressive society)	+ (valued intrusion) (e.g., hero [dies])	Victory of − order (e.g., oppressive society persists)
Comedy (e.g., *Figaro*)	− (negative state) (e.g., Count's power [overturned])	+ (valued intrusion) (e.g., Figaro [undermines Count])	Victory of + transgressor (e.g., change of society)
Irony	+ (valued state) (e.g., illusions/ innocence)	− (negative intrusion) (e.g., reality/ experience)	Victory of − transgressor (e.g., rueful regret)
Tragic irony (Schoenberg, Op. 19, no. 4)	+ Tonality	− Disruptive atonality	Psychic disintegration

in parentheses, ranging from Nature (calm vs. storm) to human society (oppressive order vs. heroic transgression), and from particular characters representing these functions (Count Almaviva vs. Figaro) to inner states that may be experienced within a single subjectivity (illusion vs. reality). These are not the only possible realizations of these functions but rather a sampling suggestive of the range of agential interpretations that may be inferred by a musical work's narrative conflict. Furthermore, as Almén demonstrates, each of these four narrative types may be combined into various blends, such as tragic irony (see the last row of table 7.1).

These various agential characterizations help clarify how our identification with either a preexisting order or its transgression determines the kind of narrative we experience. For example, our identification with Figaro (as clearly channeled by Mozart and his librettist, Lorenzo Da Ponte) is what makes *The Marriage of Figaro* a comic narrative. Were a given listener to instead identify with the Count and approve of the society that he represents, then Figaro's success would make the narrative an ironic one for that listener.[20] The same event occurs—the Count's authority is ultimately overturned by Figaro—but the listener's opposite valuation now radically changes its narrative interpretation.

This is helpful to keep in mind when we consider Almén's (2008, 139–61) narrative interpretation of the first movement of Schubert's Piano Sonata in B♭ Major, D. 960. The work opens with a theme (example 7.2) that is already a blend, or trope, of several topics: a singing-style melody-and-accompaniment texture is melded with a hymnlike texture, and the pedal and slow harmonic rhythm characterizing the pastoral is inflected in measure 5 with a noble/heroic elevational $^6_4$ on IV, intertextually akin to the opening of Beethoven's "Archduke"

Example 7.2. Schubert, Piano Sonata in B♭ Major, D. 960, first movement, main theme (mm. 1–9[1] only).

Piano Trio, op. 97—also in B♭ major, with similar texture and melodic rhythm (142). The initial order or hierarchy is thus positively valenced—spiritually serene and noble—and would likely be interpreted by a listener as positive. Even with that assessment, however, a listener can experience either a Romantic or an Ironic narrative, depending on whether she interprets the positive order as being restored by the end of the movement (Romance) or irreversibly undermined (Irony).

But how should one interpret the low G♭–F trill appearing as a marked disturbance at the end of each phrase? In Almén's "psychodynamic" interpretation, conflict within the isotopy (narrative unit) constituted by the entire theme may be understood as psychic conflict within a single agent (in the actorial role of protagonist); thus, the oppositional trill may be interpreted as a "character flaw" in that agent (2008, 143). Almén's positive identification with the agent marks it as a positive transgressor attempting to overcome a negatively valued order (a hierarchy in which positive, pastoral values have been undercut by the trill and its later dissonant consequences). The ultimate failure of the valued theme, as heroic agent, to overcome the reversed hierarchy of value (relative to the hero's interest) makes this a tragic narrative for a listener who has made those initial commitments.

Rather than internalizing the conflict (in effect hearing actorial conflict as part of a larger, singular subjectivity), one may also construe the opening theme as implying a positive order. In this interpretation a pastoral/heroic realm is threatened by the transgressive intrusion of the low trill (considered here as a separate agent—an actorial antagonist, perhaps interpretable as tragic Fate). The return of the low trill at the end of the movement would then suggest an overturning of the initial positive order, and the relevant narrative archetype would be Irony. Compare the example of Irony in table 7.1, whereby an initial state (pastoral/spiritual/heroic, interpretable as serene nobility) is undermined as illusory in the face of harsh experience (the grim reality invoked by the low trill), and untroubled noble serenity is never fully regained.

Thus, even if two listeners share a positive topical association with the opening theme and a negative valuation of the low trill, they can still experience different narrative outcomes if one listener identifies the initial pastoral music with a positive order under threat, and another listener interprets the theme as a positive transgression (by a hero attempting to fulfill his or her potential) of an implied negative order.

Let me be clear that these alternative views in no way invalidate Almén's theoretical model, which accurately accounts for the particular narrative type experienced under each listener's interpretation. Rather, it suggests that initial agential identification and valuation is a crucial choice in defining how one interprets a narrative—in effect, how one interprets a narrative conflict.

Consider a second example analyzed by Almén, Schoenberg's *Sechs Kleine Klavierstücke*, op. 19, no. 4 (example 7.3). Almén convincingly hears the near-diatonic opening melody with its carefree rhythm as suggesting a positive initial order that, beginning with the punctuating dissonant chords, is disrupted and completely overwhelmed by transgression. By hearing and identifying with the positive initial order, we would experience Irony as our narrative mode. Arnold Whittall, however, critiques Almén's interpretation, rejecting the negative characterization of atonality undercutting tonality as counter to his own appreciation of the work, which he experiences "as exuberantly witty, ebulliently engaged in a playful boisterous spirit with its post-tonal discourse of dialogue between forcefulness and delicacy, and perhaps even consciously aimed to show that expressionism need not be all gloom and doom" (2013, 91–92). Whittall recognizes (as Almén's theory indeed predicts) that his interpretation would fall "into the orbit of the comic narrative archetype" based on his citing of Almén's criteria: "the successful overthrowing of the old order" and "a problematic initial hierarchy . . . transvalued in favor of transgressive elements" (Almén 2008, 74). Along the lines I have been developing, this would be true if Whittall heard the more tonal opening as cueing a negatively valued, older order that is wittily overthrown by more positively valued, transgressive atonal elements. But Whittall argues that even this interpretation fails to capture his own experience, since it "miss[es] the point of the music's sharply pointed ambivalence: the ways its modernist tendency to suspend tonality requires the 'old order' to remain in view not as something 'problematic' but as a still relevant counter-pole" (2013, 92). For Whittall, then, the outcome is not a simple victory of one over the other; rather, Schoenberg "reinforces the ambivalence rather than resolving it" (92).

Note that Whittall and Almén both identify the opening quasi-tonal music as an initial order and the atonal disruptions as transgressive of that order. The difference is in their opposing valuation and, I would add, agential identification with one or the other. For Almén, the initial order (quasi-tonal) is positively valued; for Whittall, the transgressive elements (atonal and topical) are more

Example 7.3. Schoenberg, *Sechs Kleine Klavierstücke*, op. 19, no. 4. Used by permission of Belmont Music Publishers, Los Angeles.

positively valued. One might note that Whittall ultimately opts out of a narrative outcome along the basic archetypes in table 7.1, but his proposed "ambivalence" still counts as an outcome, and one in which the initial "tonal" order has been defeated or fails to be restored, whether or not the topical and atonal transgressions fully establish a competing order in its place.

I find merits in each interpretation, and I can hear the piece convincingly in any of these ways. What is important to recognize is that Almén's theory can account for each listener's interpretive commitments to the extent that they involve an opposing positive valuation of the initial order (as in Almén's hearing), a negative valuation (as in Whittall's first alternative), or even an ambivalent valuation (as in Whittall's second alternative).

In my interpretation of Almén's theory, I have thus far only hinted at how, and at what levels, agential identifications are made. In discussing the Schubert theme disrupted by the low trill, Almén notes that we can interpret this musical event in terms of "psychodynamic, historical, or interpersonal situations that have a parallel or similar shape," since "rules in a musical system mirror those in human psychology and society" (2008, 45). Drawing on Eero Tarasti's (1994) Greimassian-based theory with its discursive categories and arenas of spatiality, temporality, and actoriality, Almén nevertheless emphasizes that a musical agent need not be a literal actor (Almén 2008, 55–56, 59). Narrative conflict may be generated by either spatially marked oppositions (most obviously through the more literal spatiality of opposing pitch registers but also through the familiar analogue of close vs. distant keys) or temporally marked oppositions (most obviously in rhythm and meter but also in memory or expectation) as well as the more familiar actorially marked oppositions through which we infer themes as actors—for example, protagonist versus antagonist.

How do musical elements coalesce into the larger discursive categories of an order and a transgressor? Perhaps through synecdoche, the metonymy of "part for whole," by means of which we can identify an agent with the order it represents. My "comic" example in table 7.1, from the *Marriage of Figaro*, has the Count standing for his oppressive regime by synecdoche. Figaro serves as the transgressor, who succeeds in overthrowing at least one aspect of that regime—the one that matters most to him—the Count's "right of first night" with Figaro's bride.

But how might we understand agency at this level in purely instrumental music? Assuming that we can agree with the identification of various actants or agents, what is it that guides our next level of interpretation into the agential force of an order and a transgression that will command either our allegiance or distrust? In Romantic works we typically experience a kind of subjective identification with a protagonist in which various actants represent sides of the protagonist's character (as in the "tragic flaw" mentioned earlier). Thus, what Almén calls a psychodynamic interpretation often emerges in works of the nineteenth century. This is akin to what Márta Grabócz, inspired by Mahler's programs, terms an "internal [narrative] program" (2008, 36), and it involves our emotional identification with a protagonist—or with what philosophers such as Jenefer Robinson (2005) more broadly term a persona. But even if we commit to that interpretation early on, why do some contrasting actants resist incorporation into a protagonist—as, for example, component parts of his psyche—and instead take on a more oppositional agential role, as antagonist to a protagonist? In the finale of Mahler's Sixth Symphony, the hammer blows can only plausibly come from some antagonistic agency, whether personified as an opposing character or objectified as Fate. Here, the Greimassian analyses of Grabócz and Tarasti are compelling, with agency distributed among diverse functional roles in a narrative: for example, sender, object, receiver, helper, and opponent.[21] Various sequential, and hence narrative, paths between vertices of the Greimassian "semiotic square" may then enact various kinds of transformations, if not transvaluations, of A. J. Greimas's nuanced varieties of conflict (e.g., contrary or contradictory).

Grabócz presents Anne Hénault's (1979, 143–44) definition of narrative in this Greimassian sense:

> One can say that narrativity occurs when a text describes, on the one hand,
> a state of departure in the form of a relationship of possession or dispossession
> of a valorized object, and, on the other hand, an act or a series of acts producing
> a new state, exactly the inverse of the state of departure. (Cited in Grabócz
> 2008, 23)

Conclusion

A theory of virtual agency can provide clues to understanding the many ways it is possible to stage narrative agency in music. Composers stage virtual narrative agency by enacting the functions of framing or rhetorically breaking the discourse to comment or reflect on it from the outside. Composers may also situate narrative agency as a virtual actor (as in the case of Berlioz's Harold) through whose eyes and ears we are presented with the action of other agents. By observing and either identifying with or critically reflecting on the actions of other virtual actors in the same diagetic space, such a "virtual observing agent" (Gerg 2015) can exhibit some of the functions attributable to a narrative agency (e.g., point of view or empathetic distance). And finally, composers may assume narrative agency more directly, by modalizing musical events (through parody, for example) and manipulating listeners' emotional responses in a way that supports ideological or critical interventions into a fictive story (as in the case of Shostakovich's opera).

Yet another possibility is that listeners may choose to value one or the other of two conflicting processes or characters (which Almén, following Liszka, identifies as an order and a transgressor) and, by identifying with their chosen agency, create a plausible narrative based on the outcome of the conflict. Thus, listeners may exert their own agency in choosing among possible narrative interpretations. In the case where a composer may not have offered an unambiguous outcome (as in the Schubert example) or clearly directed the listener to identify positively with one of two competing agencies (as in the Schoenberg example), the listener is free to navigate among plausible options in ways that may lead to quite different narrative constructs.

Notes

1. Current approaches to narrative in music (e.g., Almén 2008) discount the need for a narrator to cue narrativity, instead focusing on a dramatic shift (e.g., transvaluation) from one state to another, as will be discussed in the next section.

2. Andrew Davis (2017) traces such fractures in the piano sonatas of Chopin, Schumann, and Brahms as a narrative technique marking both a shift in temporality and a move from outer to inner thoughts of an agent (akin to the interiorizing of subjectivity discussed earlier). Matthew McDonald (2014) explores even more extravagant shifts of temporality in the music of Charles Ives.

3. For several of the examples mentioned in this paragraph, see Hatten 1994, 175–76, 183–84. Janet Schmalfeldt (1995) also notes the recitative-chord effect in the opening of Beethoven's Op. 31, no. 2.

4. Another, more psychoanalytic interpretation may be the attempt to brush aside what might be perceived as too intimate a disclosure (Hatten 2009b). Evidence for this possible motivation comes from Beethoven's behavior when he was playing for a small audience in a salon. Apparently, he was improvising an adagio, looked up and saw the emotional reaction of his audience, and dashed out of the room, calling them all fools. What is interesting is Beethoven's abrupt shift from virtual to actual emotional worlds in this admittedly anecdotal report.

5. Käte Hamburger ([1957] 1973, 64–81) labels the "past tense" as used in narrative the "epic preterite," noting that "the preterite loses its grammatical function of designating what is past" (66). If the virtual present as narrated requires a past tense, the past perfect tense is employed. The present tense may also be used to narrate, especially if the expressive intent is to create a greater sense of immediacy. Thus, even literary narrative does not require a past tense. For music, narrative agency is cued not by an analogue of linguistic tense but by a shift to another (fictive) level of discourse through such devices as framing and distancing (Hatten 1997, 628–29).

6. Edward Cone (1968, 22) mentions this piece as a typical example of framing. Richard Littlefield (1996) discusses still other kinds of frames, extending the notion to include the silence surrounding the performance of a work.

7. See Hatten 1994, 9–28, for further interpretation of this movement.

8. As Cone notes (1974, 91, 93), the theme may appear in other instruments; indeed, Harold's expressive field involves more of the orchestra than the viola alone, whether or not we conceive of the orchestral harmonies in my sense as nondiegetic.

9. As Floros observes, this style type may be used both literally (as in Wagner's *Tannhäuser*) and allusively (as in the second movement of Brahms's Third Symphony). As I have noted (Hatten 2001), the pilgrim's processional topic is found in both the second and fourth movements of Bruckner's Fourth Symphony (with different themes, but the same key of C minor and the same topical form), thereby suggesting a fictive agency (one that may well be autobiographically inspired) enacting a "pilgrim's progress" of faith. This progress is dramatized as a difficult passage through the world beset with spiritual trials but culminating in a transfiguring, salvational ending.

10. Of course, the composer staging these two levels may be considered the ultimate narrator of this scene. Cone, however, argues against "any attempt at objective narration" by Berlioz, since "every composition reports a subjective experience" of, in this case, "an unspecified musical persona" (1974, 93). For Cone, Harold is "always an observer . . . rather than an actual participant in the form of the movement" (92). I discuss later how Gerg (2015) develops this insight as a "virtual observing agent" and consider its consequences for understanding the extent of Harold's "observation" of the pilgrims.

11. This is one reason that I have not focused my theory of virtual agency on a persona.

12. The interpretation in this section is drawn from my paper for the 2013 meeting of the Semiotic Society of America. My interpretation closely parallels that of Caryl Emerson (1989), as can be seen from the extensive citations.

13. This is also noted by Emerson (1989).

14. Richard Taruskin (1997, 498–510) goes still further in exploring the "inhuman" representation of everyone but Katerina. He concludes that the positive treatment of Katerina is ultimately unethical given her monstrous actions.

15. Audience responses will be influenced not only by Strauss's glowing love music but by potentially negative visual elements in any given production, which may redirect our attention more strongly toward a revulsion that, I would argue, Strauss saves until after the triumphant cadence in C♯ major. At that point, a conventional plagal extension is undermined by a gruesomely dissonant chord that both marks a shockingly grotesque return to reality and anticipates Herod's disgust, reflected in his peremptory order, "Kill that woman." For further theoretical elaboration of the grotesque in music, see Sheinberg 2000, Uno Everett 2009, Hatten 2012c, and Johnston 2014; Hatten and Johnston both examine the *Salome* example.

16. Shostakovich omits the novella's account of Katerina murdering her husband's child, but that is not enough to justify his—or our—sympathy for her actions, even though Shostakovich's music for Katerina's reflections can very well elicit sympathy for and even identification with her feelings as somehow divorced from our ethical appraisal of her actions.

17. This is not unlike what Berg achieves with the character of Wozzeck, whose final humiliation in suffering the mockery and brutality of a commanding officer who has slept with his love, Marie, is marked by a dramatic recognition at the close of act 2. Pushed beyond reason, Wozzeck will resort to desperate measures.

18. These four narrative archetypes are drawn from Northrop Frye's influential *Anatomy of Criticism* (1957), as adapted by James Jakób Liszka (1989).

19. I provide a brief sketch of the theory at the beginning of chapter 4.

20. Typically, a composer will tilt interpretation strongly toward one narrative reading, although not always as overwhelmingly as we see in the case of Shostakovich.

21. Tarasti also interprets a "valorized object" as a certain sought-after emotional state in a Romantic protagonist.

8 Performing Agency

A performer's agency not only actualizes the sounds but also embodies the virtual agencies implied by a musical work.[1] When virtual agency seems indeterminate or when there are multiple possible agencies, a performer's choices guide a listener's interpretation in constructing agency or in selecting a central agency among competing ones. Thus, through an actual body's energies the virtual work (the notated score and the tradition of interpretations that help shape it as a work) is realized as a sounding discourse. In the nineteenth century, the performer-virtuoso (Niccolò Paganini, Franz Liszt) appeared to fully inhabit every level of virtual agency—technically projecting actantial energies, embodying their human character, enacting fictive actorial (and narrative) role(s), and ultimately revealing a personalized subjectivity.[2] Whenever the music was also the performer's own composition, the illusion of identity between actual and virtual agency could well have seemed complete for many listeners.[3]

However, no single performance ultimately "realizes" a musical work. Rather, the concept of the musical work is a placeholder for the ongoing network of interpretations by theorists and historians, listeners, performers, sound engineers, and critics—all of which lead to constantly shifting conceptions of that work for various individuals and communities. Whenever we participate in an interpretation, typically through listening to a performance, we can enhance our own creative understanding by selecting among the cultural offerings of a work's reception history. These include the current reconstruction of its style and strategies, the potential acoustical resources of its performance manifestation, and even the potential degree of identification we may choose to have with the work in order to form our own, ever-evolving interpretive concept.

In this sense of the work, performers are not merely conduits through which a preconceived set of notational instructions is more or less accurately transmitted but creative interpreters who bring to bear their stylistic competency and their selection from the vast constellation of sounds and meanings attributable to a work. And those meanings do not stop with already established correlations between structure and sense; they continue to grow and expand through interactions with interpreters, further refining the correlations of a style and extending interpretations all the way to those shared subjectivities by which we not only situate but make personally significant its potential meanings.

Ideally, a performer can fluently embody the movements that correspond to those virtual gestures implied by the notes. Unfortunately, performers may at times appear physically disconnected from the gestural flow and continuity of the discourse. Alexandra Pierce (2007) has devoted her career to helping student performers explore more direct connections between gesture and interpretation. Taking a Schenkerian perspective, she interprets rather sophisticated hierarchies of movement, primarily through the body's heuristic experience of discovery rather than through an imposed or prescriptive analysis. Having taught her approach, I can attest to the immediate improvement achieved by performers who quickly discover, and embody to their delight, the lilt of a given meter, the just-so location of a climax for a phrase, or the satisfying timing of juncture between phrases. Of course, there are infinite ways to achieve such embodied connection to the music. And the visual impression of a performer is not always the best evidence of that embodied engagement, which may be reflected more convincingly in the resulting sound than in the visualized body. As noted in one of the sample cases presented in chapter 1, a performer may appear absolutely still, maintaining an upright position in head and torso, and still channel a virtual agency through highly refined movements that create natural-sounding phrases. Such renunciation of freer gestures may be a performer's conscious strategy to bypass crude visual embodiment and encourage a more transparent sense of engagement with the deeper virtual subjectivity developed by the work. In this sense an interiorizing of gesture may suggest a comparable interiorizing of meaning. Indeed, the spiritualizing that this subtle channeling encourages (where a virtual agency is manifested more as an imagined subjective consciousness than as an embodied human agent) has been a marked aesthetic preference by some performers in the twentieth century (e.g., Josef Hoffmann and the later Artur Rubinstein), as opposed to the more visceral, powerful, and visible gestures of other pianists (e.g., Rudolph Serkin or, more recently, Lang Lang).[4]

Fittingly, a less-embodied mode of performance may convey objectivity or critical distance, as in the case of severely formalist or abstract avant-garde music. And the embodiment of electronic music remains virtual when the "performer" is a machine or a computer. Arnie Cox refers to works such as Karl-heinz Stockhausen's *Studie II* as "post-corporeal" music (2016, 200). On the other hand, performers of severely formalist music may also default to exaggerated gestures (as in the Kontarsky brothers' performance of Pierre Boulez's *Structures*) in the absence of those clearly specified by the score. Their actualizing (and even creative reconstruction) of less humanly conceived musical gestures lends the music a more performative virtual agency that is at least virtually human and can sound (in some cases) humanly intentional. Integral-serial experiments such as *Structures* tend to create "structures" sui generis, lacking style-grounded and affectively motivated correlations. Thus, enlivening them with such gestures is one way of making the music sound more vital, especially when listeners are not likely to hear the "structures" as intellectually conceived.

To the degree that integral-serial music forgoes tonality and meter, along with their more robust implications of virtual environment and implicative energies, a composer may compensate by emphasizing motivic or thematic developing variation, which helps support a more continuous virtual-agential identity throughout a musical discourse. Even in the absence of such cues, however, we can still hear a virtual environment as created by our ingrained sense of up and down (registrally and rhythmically) or near and far (dynamically), and these low-level inferences may be sufficient to sustain the projection of humanlike gestures. Ironically, the dynamic gestures of the Kontarsky brothers may nevertheless be interpreted as abstract by a listener whenever the gestural embodiment lacks clear motivic continuity. Such chains of humanized gestures may instead be heard by listeners as energetic manifestations of a disembodied consciousness, sparking its thoughts in a realm of pure intellection that is strikingly absent of intentionality and hence teleology. This may well be an equally powerful aesthetic achievement.

An outwardly similar extreme of performing embodiment (for which Lang Lang has at times been unjustly criticized) is one in which the performer clearly exhibits in his body the effort in achieving—but also the ease in mastering—superhumanly difficult music. Such a performing style may risk directing more attention to the performer's agency than the virtual agency of the music. But it may also lead to the imaginative manifestation of a superhuman virtual subjectivity, and that may appeal to many listeners. More conventionally, a performer who mirrors the gestures of the music through dynamic bodily sways (e.g., violinist Joshua Bell) can appear genuinely caught up in the music in a way that authentically communicates to certain listeners its phrasing and expression.

A performer may also choose to embody in extreme fashion the communicative interaction among players in an ensemble (e.g., Menahem Pressler with the Beaux Arts Trio), thereby directing both ensemble precision and the expressive coordination of exchanges that are so vital to the musical discourse of any ensemble. These directing gestures may also help cue the audience to significant expressive junctures in the music, much as a conductor might emphasize such cues with gestural underlining.

However, a performer's attempts to point out every significant event in the music by foregrounding it through dynamics or temporal placing can lead to a depressingly didactic mode of communication in which the performer's agency, pedantically that of a teacher, intrudes on the virtual agency being manifested.[5] I occasionally warn my students of this danger after I have didactically illustrated specific analytical points at the piano in this crude fashion; sometimes I replay an excerpt as I might actually perform it, to restore those more subtle nuances that can best reveal or enhance the music's expressive freedom from fixed interpretations.

Leech-Wilkinson notes Alfred Cortot's contrary tendency in lengthening not the notes that are "harmonic or melodic cruxes or key points of compositional structure" but rather those that are "signposts or pointers towards significant structural moments that are about to be reached" (2013, 48). He cites a tradition passed down through Cortot's students to this effect:

> Where a note of a phrase needs to be prolonged in order to give emotional
> significance to the moment it will usually be found that the anacrusis is the most

desirable note to prolong. By holding the commencement of a phrase[,] a sense of emotional stress, of trying to move through a resistance, can be added. (cited in Leech-Wilkinson 2013, 49)

The questions of performance practice as they bear on the performer's quest for suitable nuances (e.g., degrees of vibrato, portamento, and rubato; or when and how to perform legato, portato, nonlegato, and staccato) are wide-ranging, and I address several of them elsewhere (see Hatten 2004, chap. 7; 2009a; 2010c; 2014a). The burgeoning field of performance and analysis (and their interpretive or performative interactions) offers still further insights into the subtle relationships between theorists' and performers' modes of interpretation (Hatten 2010c) and their mutual performativity (Cook 1999, 2003, 2005). I draw from these discussions as they have bearing on how performers, as interpreters, direct (or directly influence) the interpretation of listeners with respect to those virtual agencies as implied by the music: from the manifestation of actantial energies; to the endowment of characteristic (human) agency through embodiment, identity, and expression (actions, reactions, emotions); to the interaction of actorial roles in dramatic or narrative trajectories; and ultimately to the merger of actorial roles and staged narrative commentary as parts of a higher subjectivity.

To be clear, I do not presuppose (or recommend) complete control by performers over listener's interpretations. As a listener to another's performance, I bring my own ideas about the work and often bypass that performer's interpretation by "listening" to my own interpretation of virtual agency despite often contradictory manipulations by the performer of volume, pacing, articulation, pedaling, and the like. The manifested sounds made by the performer will affect my "hearing" insofar as I track in real time the sequence of notes of that performance, but I may nevertheless concentrate my "listening" toward my own interpretation of virtual agency as implied by the music. This maneuver is not uncommon for audiences, as those who have attended poor student recitals can attest.[6]

As a theorist who is also a performer, I am particularly interested in ways that my theories not only reflect my intuitions as a performer but also help me articulate those intuitions, and by deeper reflection, develop them further.[7] This position is not unchallenged. Carolyn Abbate (2004) urges us to respect the "drastic" spontaneities of performances and avoid being distracted by the "gnostic" over-intellectualizing of theorists and musicologists (even when the focus of theorizing is hermeneutic rather than strictly structural or formalist). Her point is well taken: overintellectualizing can indeed distract from the body's natural athletic flow, as argued by authors of sports books whose titles fit the template, "Zen and the Art of X." But imaginative interpretation of the source of the force can easily be integrated into the heuristics of preparing a performance interpretation prior to the act of performing. Indeed, such intellection is germane to establishing the practiced movements that precede performance; they allow one to enjoy a more drastic engagement in the moment without worrying about a drastic disaster. Just as an actor or dancer must prepare exhaustively with clearly intentional vocal intonations or bodily movements to achieve the appearance of unstrained freedom in performance, so must the musician prepare intentionally to achieve the verisimilitude of dramatic virtual agency. Thus, I would recommend not neglecting *any* relevant source of meaning (however "gnostic") or approach to interpretation (however intellectual) in that preparation.

The following examples demonstrate how an understanding of virtual agency can affect performance decisions as well as how the careful interpretation of notation within a stylistic context can lead to performances that suggest particular agential interpretations. In this heuristic give-and-take, performers and theorists contribute equally to interpretation, and the boundary between these roles can be quite permeable.

Performing Agency in Beethoven

The finale of Beethoven's Piano Sonata in D Minor, op. 31, no. 2 (*Tempest*), is a perpetual-motion movement that combines continuous sixteenths and the minor mode (example 8.1[a]).[8] Its sonata form modulates to the minor dominant rather than the relative major, serving to sustain an expressive effect of obsessive tragedy. How might we hear virtual agency in this movement? An obvious answer, well-supported stylistically, would be that a virtual agent/actor/protagonist's consciousness is struggling with a tragic contingency, and the movement enacts the protagonist's efforts to break through (or break free of) this condition. Certainly, if one follows Carl Czerny's ([1839] 1970, 44) pedaling, which sustains through each measure and changes on the downbeat, one could indeed embody the constant surging of the music and effectively realize an interpretation of agential struggle.

But there is another agency dialogically lurking in the music, and Beethoven provides notational clues for its realization that suggest a warranted alternative to Czerny's unsubtle pedaling markings.[9] Note the careful tie in the tenor of the pitch A and the separate sixteenth flag on the initial D in the bass. These niceties are meaningless if one uses a full pedal through each measure. Instead, they cue the performer to release the bass and use what Heinrich Schenker ([c. 1911] 2000) called "hand pedal" to sustain the A without use of the damper pedal (or with the merest touch of pedal, applied only after the bass has been released). The syncopated, sustained A is now strongly marked for the listener through both dynamic and agogic accents, and it is further foregrounded by repetition (it occurs in each of the first eight measures, four on tonic followed by four on dominant-seventh harmony).

This inner pedal on $\hat{5}$ has a stylistic lineage: in opera it suggests the fateful (e.g., Mozart's *Don Giovanni* or Verdi's *Il forza del destino*), often in association with the lowered-$\hat{6}$ in minor (for the *Tempest* finale, see the motivic emphasis on lowered-$\hat{6}$ to 5 in mm. 43ff. in A minor, example 8.1[b]). Thus, playing the opening bars without a blurring pedal can help bring out the intensity of this fatefulness, endowing it from the start with a vital actorial role. Using this agential motivation to achieve a more nuanced performance not only respects the notated score but can help establish a dialogical opposition between a virtual antagonist (e.g., Fate) and a virtual protagonist struggling to escape.

Example 8.1. Beethoven, Piano Sonata in D Minor, op. 31, no. 2, third movement (finale). (a) First theme (mm. 1–8 only). (b) Second theme (mm. 43–45 only). (c) Expressive climax in the development (mm. 169–173). (d) Expressive climax in the coda (mm. 350–358).

Indeed, the pitch A plays a thematized role in the dramatic trajectory, as witnessed by the climactic struggle in measures 169–73 of the development section (example 8.1[c]). Here, the syncopated A is echoed two octaves higher, on another location relative to the beat. Although G♯ grapples with A in these four bars, its ♯$\hat{4}$ functional urge (as magnetism) is insufficient to push A toward a definitive cadential resolution to D, and the resulting collapse requires another retransition to prepare for the recapitulation. The fatefully foregrounded A returns, horrifically, in measures 350–58 of the extended coda, where the doubled A is uncontested by G♯ and thus sounds inexorable in its fateful power (example 8.1[d]). Even the presumably last heroic efforts of the protagonist to protest—with leaps to high A, then high D, then ultimately climaxing on the high F (at the extreme of Beethoven's keyboard)—are all doomed to collapse chromatically. The movement ends not with a bang but a whimper, suggesting the ultimate expiration of a tormented spirit into the depths.[10]

Motivation for this kind of agential interpretation may be found in the first and second movements as well. In referencing the first movement in chapter 1 (see example 1.2), I note the main theme's cross-hand alternation of low, loud, triadic arpeggiation and high, soft, chromatic turn figure as a dialogue between fateful and pleading virtual agents. One could further characterize this agential opposition in performance with a contrast in touch—for example, harsh accentuation for the arpeggiation and tender legato for the turn figure. But another, even richer dialogical interaction is introduced at the very opening of the movement, between the mystical chord of nature—arpeggiating upward from the recitative chord (major $^6_3$) in a trope of profound expectancy—and the furious energy of a tragic virtual actor, whose initial energy soon subsides into a moment of reflection with a turn figure ruminating over a sustained chord. This dramatic arc, filled with pent-up energy and impending thought, gives evidence of another agential role (or virtual environment)—that of the mystical realm of spiritualized Nature cued by the arpeggiated chord of nature. If Nature in effect "calls forth" (by the recitative topic) the tragic human struggle, that struggle is in turn enhanced by the grandeur of its source. Furthermore, the agitated passage moves to the dominant for its own subjectivizing moment of reflection (embodied in the self-reflective contour of the turn figure and the reflective pause of the fermata).

The clues for a subsequent interpretation of opposing actorial agents as parts of a conflicted but singular subjectivity are thus already presented by this opening scenario, which encapsulates struggle within the domain of a vast interiority. Mystically sounded by the chord of nature and given annunciatory power through the recitative $^6_4$ chord, the opening arpeggiation summons the discourse of a deeply tragic subjectivity. The implication of the recitative chord as a musical topic is effectively realized in the later appearance of two actual recitatives just after the beginning of the recapitulation (mm. 144–48 and mm. 155–58), where they mark a narrative agential intervention, interpretable as profound reflection. And as the mystical here fuses (tropes) with the protagonist's tragic reflection, agential roles (internal, external, and narrative) are explicitly melded, further deepening the movement's projection of virtual subjectivity.

The second recitative is disrupted by a sudden enharmonic modulation (a rhetorical gesture enhanced by extreme textural and dynamic contrast) that marks a shocking return to F# minor, the point of furthest remove of the development section. This moment exacerbates the tragic implications of a problematized subjectivity. Again, there is no breakthrough to victory in the remainder of the movement but rather an ultimate collapse into the rumbling depths of the low register—an outcome of deep despondency, if not death.

The second movement might appear as a moment of relief, but B♭ major turns out to be inflected with funereal topics (most strikingly, the drum rolls and hymnlike horn cortège in mm. 17ff.). This memorializing includes recollections of the tragic, via diminished sevenths and reverberant arpeggiated descents that surround the return of the opening theme with an *ombra* topical veil. Thus, despite the noble dignity of this memorial ceremony (dotted rhythms and sarabande meter), the movement offers cold comfort. The final sounding of a low B♭ is perhaps heard as a tragic knell.

Thus, from the perspective of the dramatic narrative suggested by the first two movements, the finale might be allegorized (overprogrammatically) as representing the torments of a soul in Hell, with Fate taking on the uncanny association of a demonic force. From this perspective, one could interpret demonic agency as the focal protagonist with the human soul as its weakened adversary, doomed to failure. Note that in both this interpretation and the original one that centered on the struggling human protagonist, the narrative archetype would remain tragic for the listener, who would not be inclined to "value" the negative order of Hell and would instead tend to identify with the soul in its struggle against that order (recall the discussion of narrative archetypes in chap. 7). But understanding this demonic force as the more central agential force might lead a performer to reconsider, for example, the agential source of the triple octave arpeggiations of C major in measures 35–38. Since this emblematic fanfare is in the major mode, it may readily suggest a human protagonist's heroic struggle against a fateful, demonic force; however, it may also be emblematic of the power of that demonic force itself.[11]

Furthermore, if the insistent, metrically dissonant $\hat{6}$–$\hat{5}$ irritations of the second theme (mm. 43ff.) are emblematic of a death-grip struggle, who is it that gets the best of this conflict when the hemiola exits onto a syncopated F and the melody marches down, apparently triumphantly? Might we hear the demonic force already beginning to overwhelm the soul? Speculations of this sort, while perhaps unanswerable definitively, can lead to agential enhancements in performing this conflict. The heightened sense of a performer's commitment to embodying these virtual forces, regardless of which agency is being imagined for each musical idea, can only make the tragic obsessiveness of the music that much more existentially vital and thereby support the shared subjectivity a listener is encouraged to bring to an encounter with the music. This fictional plot can enhance the sense of dramatic continuity in a work that, if played mechanically (metronomically, as in a minimalist parody, or dutifully, by pedaling the harmonies rather than bringing out the accented syncopations), would quickly dull the imagination. By carefully managing dynamics and touch and respecting the *subito pianos* and other undercuttings of potential triumph by a demonic force, the performer can maintain the intensity of a drama that is absolutely unrelenting in the pressure of its continually varied, not just continuous, sixteenth notes.

Performative Agency as Narrative Agency

In my book on musical gesture (Hatten 2004, 230–31), I offer an example of performative agency in choosing between two different engagements with the rhetorical gesture of a "wrong note" in the first movement of Beethoven's Piano Sonata in C Major, op. 53 ("Waldstein"). The passage (example 8.2) occurs when the first theme in the recapitulation veers to A♭ instead of G at the end of its initial thirteen-bar sentence; the wrong note sparks a brief, speculative parenthesis that touches on both D♭ and E♭ major before a flurry of harmonic activity restores C major for the counterstatement. A performer can agentially inflect this surprising passage in at least three ways: (1) by embodying the surprise of a virtual agent experiencing the A♭ as something terribly amiss, thereby registering the shock the listener will also experience when the implied arrival on G is displaced by A♭ (perhaps implying an external agency); (2) by embodying the agency of a narrative agent, akin to a magician who is in complete control and has willed the evasion that so shocks the virtual agent and the listener; and (3) by attempting to embody both virtual and narrative agents as parts of a singular, more powerful subjectivity, projecting the sudden swerve as the inevitable result of subconscious forces that had suddenly emerged into the light of consciousness—like an "aha!" moment of recognition that simultaneously suggests "what if?"

By choosing the first option, the performer remains in the diegesis inhabited by the virtual agent, embodying that agent's plausible reactions. By choosing the second option, the performer takes on the narrative agency implied by such a rhetorical gesture. By taking on the challenge of the third option, the performer may be able to project a supersubjective level in which such subjective turns are representative of sudden moments of insight. The performer who chooses to embody virtual agency (first option) can maximize the rhetorical effect of surprise and disorientation. Choosing to embody narrative agency (second option), a performer can create the effect of a controlling narrative agent, one who is creating "in the moment." Choosing to embody a more interiorized merger of virtual agent and narrative agent (third option), the performer can enhance the sense of subjectivity by which all such shifts are interpretable as the workings of a higher consciousness, whether or not one is consciously able to predict them.[12]

Performing Virtual Narrativity

In an article on performing expressive closure (Hatten 2014a), I note how Chopin's Prélude in A Minor, op. 28, no. 2, presents several potential closures and how it is possible for a performer to project each of these, as guided by a dramatic trajectory within a narrative frame.[13] The prelude is fascinating from an agential

Example 8.2. Beethoven, Piano Sonata in C Major, op. 53, first movement (mm. 166–174[1]), featuring rhetorical swerves in the recapitulation of the first theme at measures 168 and 170.

perspective in that the funereal cortège and lament with which the work begins are presumably experienced in the fictive diegesis by a living virtual actor witnessing the funeral of another virtual actor who has died. As example 8.3 shows, the cart-wheel ostinato breaks off in measure 17, creating an abyss of existential recognition (perhaps the virtual actor experiences death vicariously at this moment). The lament motive then dissipates in measures 17 and 18 in a closure akin to the expiration type of closure noted earlier at the end of the first movement of the *Tempest*. A muffled echo of the cart's wheels in measures 18 and 19 (blurred with the only pedal marking in the work) suggests that the cart is also departing into the distance or, more poetically, that the memory of the oppressive sound is reverberating in the mind of the virtual agent. But a final echo of the lament melody in measures 20 and 21 leads to an unusual harmonization of $\hat{2}$ in A minor: the root position dominant (E) is tonicized by its own (applied) root position dominant on B with such a strongly projected texture that one might hear it as miming a final cadence (for which the implied 4–3 suspension in m. 21 in the right hand would provide appropriate closural dignity). But that illusion is quickly dispelled by a darker, arpeggiated V^7 that resolves to A minor in measures 22[3]–23.

The first harmonic cadence (mm. 21–22) gives the effect of a positive ending in E major, like a moral consolation from outside the diegesis—hence, suggestive of a narrative agency. Its positive consolation is supported by the topically religioso association of the 4–3 suspension and the illusion of a Picardy third if the E-major chord is heard as a closural tonic. The undercutting of that positive consolation by the second cadence (mm. 22–23), a completely tragic V^7–i in A minor, suggests yet another shift in level of discourse. This second shift might then

Example 8.3. Chopin, Prélude in A Minor, op. 28, no. 2 (mm. 14–23, end).

suggest a divided narrative agent, one who recognizes the futility of consolation in the face of implacable death. Alternatively, it might suggest an emergent subjectivity on the part of a virtual actor who embraces both closures: having experienced unsatisfying consolation with the first cadence, the virtual actor rejects that consolation with the second.

While this subtle degree of agential delineation may not be possible to project in performance, the musical clues for contrasting agential closures are unmistakable. The two framing cadences, with their shifts in level of discourse, may be interpreted in terms of one (or two) virtual narrators, as part of a larger subjectivity, or both. I suggest (and illustrate in performance, as available online through a web link in Hatten 2014a) how one might project these agencies in performance. I also discuss how one editor (Rafael Joseffy) breaks Chopin's single slur over both harmonic cadences as offering evidence of his performing interpretation along the lines of two narrative agencies. Chopin's ultimate decision to provide an unbroken slur may perhaps reveal that these two highly contrasting closures are to be merged into the continuity of a single subjectivity that experiences the first as dramatically rejected by the inexorably tragic closure of the second.

A second excerpt (Hatten 2014a) is drawn from the multiple closures that round off the set of eighteen dances in Schumann's *Davidsbündlertänze*, op. 6. These include (1) an embedded return of the second waltz in the seventeenth waltz that leads to a substantial, dramatic coda; (2) an appended dance that parallels, in C major, the key in which the first half had closed (at the midpoint, the ninth waltz); and (3) the rounded-binary form of that final dance, which begins *in medias res* and moves beyond its implied formal completion to launch an

Example 8.4. Schumann, *Davidsbundlertänze*, op. 6, no. 18 (final dance).

expansive coda. The agencies marked by Schumann (recall chap. 4)—the passionate Florestan, whose own coda in B minor ends the seventeenth number, and the dreamy Eusebius, whose tentative waltz opens the eighteenth number—are easily recognized and just as easily projected in performance through their characteristic gestural dynamics and tempos. Since Schumann conceived of Florestan and Eusebius as two sides of his personality, we are already cued to a level of subjectivity in the embracing of these two actorial roles as parts of a larger, singular consciousness. The return of the second waltz, a cyclical marker of closure, is also easily assimilated as part of the reflective memory by which a rich subjectivity can be staged in music. Florestan's emphatic coda to number seventeen is a dramatic and virtuosic acceleration to a tragic cadence with its own plagal extension. But Eusebius, as noted in a telling programmatic addition to the first edition score, adds a final dance that reflects his experience of emotional "overflow" (a more literal translation of *Überfluss*). And this manipulation of closure for the set (we had already "finished" with a cyclic return and extensive coda in the previous dance) marks one of the functions of narrative agency. Schumann (Eusebius) thereby eludes the conventional, internal frame of the cycle by proposing an addendum (example 8.4).[14] The addendum slips in, as the final B-minor chord of number 17 dies away, on a bichord (V^7 over tonic in C major), which will become a style type for Schumann.[15] The bichordal sonority of V^7 over tonic drone suggests a kind of pastoral floating whose origin in the galant appoggiatura cadence may also imply the "suspension" of impending positive closure.

When the halting waltz begins to transcend its formal boundary (exceeding the completed return of its implied rounded binary form in mm. 19–26), an unmistakable emotional windup leads to a cathartic epiphany. This climactic "overflow" is realized in two arcs—measures 27–34 and measures 35–41—before spilling over via inner voices in reverberant waves of emotion (mm. 41ff.). The reverberations spin out amid the tolling of two sets of twelve "midnight bells" on C, traditional signals for the end of a ball and loosely hinting at the "masked ball" climax of Jean Paul Richter's novel *Flegeljahre*.[16]

I have proposed and demonstrated in performance (see Hatten 2014a) how a performer might highlight the evasions of closure with respect to both rounded-binary form and the cycle as a whole, leading to an expressive epiphany. Florestan and Eusebius have become allegorical, at this point, for a listener's own negotiation with the work's virtual subjectivity. Even though they continue to play their role in the programmatic actorial level of characters (along the lines of Walt and Vult in *Flegeljahre*), Florestan and Eusebius are increasingly understood as two sides of a singular subjectivity.

A Performer's Prerogative: Performing Agency through Cadenzas and Embellishments

One of the most obvious means by which an actual performer can insert her actual agency into a composition (thereby creating another quasi-narrative virtual agent) is through an improvisatory cadenza. Cadenzas were expected

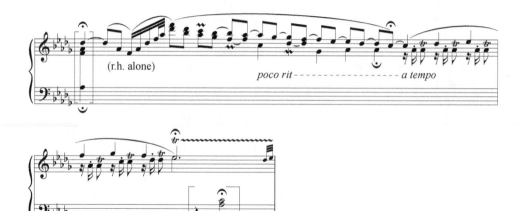

Example 8.5. Hatten, composed improvisatory elaboration of a fermata in Haydn, Piano Sonata in A♭ Major, Hob. XVI/46 (C. Landon 31), second movement (m. 77, expanded).

not only in movements of a concerto but often in operatic arias and sonata slow movements or rondo-finales. The freedom that a cadenza offers to a performer comes with the potential for abuse. The performer might hijack the direction or disrupt the coherence of a carefully conceived dramatic trajectory. Such abuses likely led composers (notably Beethoven) to notate their improvisatory-style cadenzas, thereby usurping the performer's prerogative. Beethoven, in a decision that reveals both empathy and ego, also wrote cadenzas for those Mozart concertos he performed (and perhaps sought to appropriate in this way).

I address the issue of agency in the performance of cadenzas with my (written-out) improvisatory-style elaboration (example 8.5) of the final fermata in the second movement of Haydn's Piano Sonata in A♭ Major, Hob. XVI/46 (C. Landon no. 31). In this cadenza I have tried to respect the virtual agencies of the composer by not imposing new material; instead, I have crafted an improvisational treatment of the composer's own ideas. The main idea is drawn from a passage (mm. 13–17) in which a single *melos* is enhanced by refractive counterpoint. In my elaboration I emphasize the implied merger of voices into a singular agency by playing an echo of this theme in a single hand (just as Haydn specifies playing the opening counterpoint of the movement in a single hand, although the opposite one). I also allow the counterpoint to emerge and then, in contrary motion, to merge into a single voice for the cadential trill. Thus, my "contribution" respects Haydn's musical material with decorum and restraint while offering something new that respects the function of a cadenza as a relatively free commentary. I only minimally adhere to another expectation of a cadenza, in which one distinguishes between virtual agent and actual performer to highlight the creative contribution and distinctive personality of the performer.

In responding to the challenge of a cadenza, the performer adopts the roles of both composer (whether by improvising or writing out an improvisatory cadenza in advance) and performer (whether by projecting one's own personality or attempting to simulate the general style and strategies of the composer).[17] My choice here (certainly not the only valid one) was to write out a simulated improvisation that draws from but does not exceed the thematic substance and strategies of the work. In an actual performance, I might further simulate free improvisation by taking extra liberties with time—suggesting the extratemporality of the cadenza as formal interpolation. I certainly recognize my own involvement as a performative agent, since my body is the site through which all the nuances of sound are being manifested. However, my cadenza is conceived not so much as a shift to project my own (distinctive) agency as a performer but rather as a (still personal) projection of a virtual narrative agent, developed within the constraints of the work and commenting or reflecting on the discourse by further realizing its compositional potential. Although I provide a touch of my own creativity in playing with the composer's thematic world, I would be pleased if a listener were unaware of any extra compositional effort on my part. My cadenza nevertheless allows me to share (as listener, performer, and composer) in the construction of virtual subjectivity as implied by the work.

The enhancement through elaboration and ornamentation of a reprise, as in a *da capo* aria, is another way in which a performer can augment the emotion that attends a return of the original theme. A composer's written-out elaborations may be in the form of diminutions (as in variations) that create a more saturated texture and hence correlate with a sense of "plenitude" (Hatten 2004, 43–52).[18] When the performer has the option to elaborate a thematic return, both diminutions and embellishments may be added to increase the textural density in a way that literally fills the musical space. By analogy, textural saturation creates a sense of fulfillment with respect to the particularized emotion(s) or expressive content of the theme. Such elaboration can also intensify any dynamic climaxes in the theme and thereby add urgency.

In my elaboration of the return of the main theme from the slow movement of Mozart's Piano Sonata in A Minor, K. 310, I venture greater freedom than in my discreet cadenza for the Haydn slow movement. Although the movement is in sonata form, both the main theme and its embellished continuation from measure 8 (shown in example 8.6[a]) clearly evoke an aria topic and warrant a further *da capo* embellishment of the recapitulatory return. Example 8.6(b) shows my elaboration of the excerpt from measure 8, which takes its cue for greater freedom from Mozart's own diminutional development. Here, I project my performative agency more extravagantly, with the aim of both expanding and intensifying the expressive effect of Mozart's coloratura-like continuation.

These forms of elaboration differ from the ornamentation that a performer of Baroque music had stylistic license to add, which was often limited to accentuating or sonically prolonging a significant musical event that would otherwise decay too quickly on a harpsichord. Sometimes, ornaments are part of a composer's strategic design for a motive, such that they become thematic nuances

Example 8.6. Mozart, Piano Sonata in A Minor, K. 310, second movement.
(a) Mozart's notated embellishment of the counterstatement in the exposition (mm. 8–14²). (b) Hatten, composed improvisatory elaboration of the counterstatement in the recapitulation (mm. 61–65¹).

inseparable from the identity of the musical idea. For example, the second subject, introduced at the end of measure 20, of Bach's Fugue in F♯ Minor, WTC II, BWV 883, features an inverted mordent in some manuscript sources (example 8.7).[19] But should the performer continue to play the ornament every time the short subject enters, perhaps risking an overly didactic emphasis on the subject? Or might cutting the ornament in later entrances allow the subject to weave more seamlessly into the *Fortspinnung* following its brief exposition, as a more integrated *melos* in three imitative voices?[20]

In an era before public concerts led to the evolution of a specialized performer, performers were routinely composers who also improvised. C. P. E. Bach's chapter on how to improvise a fantasy ([1762] 1949, 430–45) only hints at the richness of a performer's real-time improvisatory imagination (consider J. S. Bach's spontaneous improvisation of a three-voice fugue based on a difficult subject provided by Frederick the Great). But with Emanuel Bach we have a strong case of a performer channeling his own subjectivity through an expressive vehicle akin to a Shakespearean soliloquy (as in his *Hamlet* Fantasy). Charles Burney's observation that "drops of effervescence distilled from his countenance" during Emanuel Bach's performance suggest just how strongly this directly embodied expression of subjective interiority could be projected, even in an era of sensibility (1773, 270).[21]

Performing Emergent Agency

I want to return to Bach's Prelude in E♭ Minor, WTC I, BWV 853, analyzed in detail in chapter 3, to consider those opportunities where a performer can foreground a virtual agency that might otherwise go unnoticed. One case (see example 3.1) involves the climactic cadence following the surprise Neapolitan in measure 26 that marks a shift to a more direct, recitative kind of discourse—the kind of discourse found in fantasies. Certainly, most performers on the piano would mark the surprise Neapolitan sonority with dynamic foregrounding and similarly reinforce the subsequent V_2^4 chord, treating these sonorities texturally as cueing a dramatic recitative in the melody. But when the conventional cadential $_4^6$ chord appears, the performer following the interpretation given in chapter 3 would emphasize its equally surprising appearance (since it disrupts the V_2^4's implied resolution to i^6) and, perhaps with a stern tone in the piano, suggest an equally stern antagonist, undercutting with tragic vehemence the hopefully striving but hopelessly abandoned protagonist enacted by the upper line. This agential performance (in which the previously backgrounded accompaniment is foregrounded in the role of an implacable, perhaps fateful agency) lends the upper voice's 7–6 suspension (m. 29) an almost unbearably tragic quality, as though it were pleading against tragic closure (mercifully deferred by the deceptive move to iv^6). But the collective, fateful agency of the cadential $_4^6$ soon returns (m. 36), undercutting an angst-laden $vii^{\circ 7}$ that had intensified through registral expansion in measures 32–35. The external agency of the cadential $_4^6$ here overpowers the protagonist's resistance. After the cadence (which is again mercifully

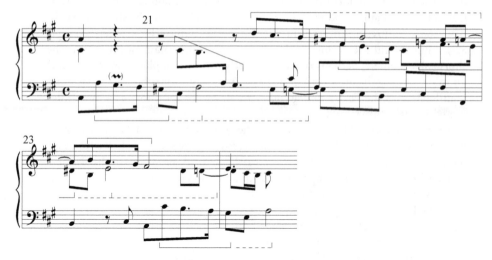

Example 8.7. Bach, Fugue in F♯ Minor, WTC II, BWV 883, exposition of the second subject (mm. 20³–24²), with optional inverted mordent shown in measure 20⁴.

ameliorated, this time by a V⁷/iv harmonization of the outer-voice closure to $\hat{1}$), the accompaniment subsides into a more neutral role, enhancing the environment of grief without projecting as significant an actorial role in the drama.

Returning to the opening of the prelude, we can now sense the potential of the increasingly monumental repeated chords, within a dignified sarabande $\frac{3}{4}$ meter, to constitute a virtual environment of grief, one that is distinctive for this movement. These chords contribute to the musical architecture the way massive repeating columns in some great, dark cathedral contribute to an atmosphere of portentous gloom. The performer may decide to give these chords a character of solemn weightiness from the start, perhaps enhanced by a brusque, even impersonal arpeggiation (as I would suggest for the arpeggiated cadential $\frac{6}{4}$ in m. 28), as opposed to a more lyrically gentle, ruminative strumming of the bardic harp or lute (as suggested by the arpeggiated markings first introduced at the end of m. 4 with the ameliorative turn to G♭ major).

Performing Oppositional Agencies

Bach's implicit cues for an emerging oppositional agency in the Prelude in E♭ Minor may be contrasted with the concerto genre's explicit cues for opposition between agential forces (whether concertino vs. ripieno, or soloist vs. tutti). As Susan McClary (1987) has elaborated, even where individual and communal roles appear defined in advance, Bach may allow an background instrument to be unexpectedly foregrounded, as in the harpsichord's shift from discreet continuo accompaniment to an animated, virtuosic projection of individual agency in its

Example 8.8. Bach, "Echo" from Overture in the French Style in B Minor, *Clavier-Übung*, Part II, BWV 831 (mm. 1–6).

cadenza to the first movement of the Brandenburg Concerto No. 5 in D Major, BWV 1050. McClary extravagantly interprets this unexpected cadenza as an "overthrow" or "hijacking of the piece" (1987, 28). However we may choose to allegorize Bach's meaning, his notation provides undeniable evidence of an emergent agency as the harpsichord takes on a more actorial role in the expressive trajectory of the movement.

Bach must have been fond of this kind of virtual agential play, and the "Echo" from the French Overture in B Minor (*Clavier-Übung*, Part II, BWV 831) offers compelling tropological evidence (example 8.8). Elsewhere (Hatten 2004, 69–70), I interpret four levels of troping between concerto and dance genres, drawing on Laurence Dreyfus's (1996, 224–32) own analysis of this movement. Here, I want to speculate on Bach's tropological play with the very means by which the Baroque concerto preserves virtual agential identity in a dialogical genre. The opposition of forces is typically reinforced by oppositions in dynamics, textural density, and at times, register. Individual agency (whether expressed through an individual instrument or a small ensemble of instruments) is generally less loud, dense, or registrally deep than the collective agency of the orchestra. However, by taking one of these cues, dynamics, and thematizing it as oppositional within the solo's statement (mm. 5–6) as well as within the collective ritornellos, Bach begins to undermine the boundaries by which his two virtual-actorial roles can maintain their consistent identities.

The performer, however, has the option of promoting a sense of discursive continuity across the discontinuities of sound, thereby embracing the various contrasts as complex nuances within an overarching subjectivity. The immediate echo-effects (whether of the same idea or of a dialogically contrasting response) are markers for distance, both spatial and temporal. To the extent that temporal distance implies memory or reflection, these echoes may in turn suggest self-reflectivity—and hence virtual subjectivity. Thus, a multidimensional subjectivity emerges that can encompass not merely the dialogue between individual and collective agencies but a degree of reflectivity in their interaction. The title "Echo" is a playful understatement with respect to all that is being "echoed" at various levels in the movement.

Performing Self-Reflective Agency

Reverberent echoes may also be heard in Bach's Fugue in D Major, WTC II. The fugue is dynamically unmarked, but its fluctuations in register and textural density approximate dynamic effects. Prototypical refractive counterpoint is omnipresent—the head and/or tail of the subject is heard in every measure, with overlapping imitation of the tail fragment comprising the episodes. Thus, self-reflective thematic discourse is in play from the start. But Bach exceeds mere echo and achieves a plenitude of reverberant self-reflectivity, if you will, in his tightly overlapping strettos, which mark points of textural culmination and expressive climax (*Steigerung*) in the last part of the fugue (example 8.9[a]). The thematic reverberation obscures, due to the repeated-note opening of the subject head, a separation into individual voices and instead further supports the merger of refractive counterpoint into a singular subjectivity. A performer cannot help but project this effect by simply playing the notes, but sensitive use of the pedal can further heighten the sense of merging that suffuses these stretto passages.

The reverberant suffusion and plenitude of a stretto need not be reserved as a culminating effect in a fugue. Bach topically imports this effect in the Prélude that opens his English Suite No. 3 in G Minor (example 8.9[b]). The textural crescendo in measures 1–7 takes similar advantage of a descending-third motive (though not as consistently as Brahms does in Op. 119, no. 1; see example 4.18) to splay four voices into registrally expanding alternations of tonic and dominant. Here, the implied stretto far exceeds four entries in its echoing *melos*, a preluding intonation that congeals into a harmonic accompaniment for the emergent sixteenth-note melody in the soprano.

Performing Subjectivity in a Dialogical Genre

Mozart's invention of the piano quartet as a fully dialogical genre extends Bach's agential play. The opposition of piano and strings (violin, viola, cello) in the Piano Quartet in G Minor, K. 478, is an obvious agential inheritance from the concerto—but here, more democratically, either body may take the lead with principal thematic material, or they may dialogue equally, exchanging variants of the same thematic material. But the imitative treatment of the strings, adapted to ritornello-like segments, is an agentially motivated textural intensification that individuates energetic agency within the realm of a larger collective agency—and again, provides warrant for interpretation of a complex, multilayered subjectivity. Dean Sutcliffe "highlights the textural medium itself as motivation for Mozart's numerous imitative sequences in the chamber music with piano from 1784 to 1786 (notably the Piano and Wind Quintet and

Example 8.9. Examples of reverberant stretto in Bach. (a) Culminating stretto in the Fugue in D Major, WTC II, BWV 874 (mm. 44–46). (b) Stretto as opening textural crescendo in the Prélude from the English Suite No. 3 in G Minor, BWV 808 (mm. 1–7).

the two piano quartets), in which the learned style is employed to individuate instrumental agencies and promote 'social flexibility'" (2003b, 64; see also Hatten 2012b, 182). What Mozart's texture engenders is, indeed, the flexibility with which any instrument can emerge as a leading agency or submerge into a more collective or backgrounded agency. The listener's inability to maintain virtual agential identification with just one instrument is strong evidence that a virtual actor need not be equivalent to an instrument or group of instruments.[22] Instead, the musical discourse itself suggests, at the actorial level, a virtual theater, and at the next level, an emergent subjectivity.

Conclusion: Choosing a Performative Stance

We have seen that the performer may easily project more than one agential role, as in solo piano works, and more than one performer may project a single agential role, as often occurs in chamber music (recall chap. 4). But there is also a subtle interaction between the performer's actual body and a work's expression of virtual agency. The performer may inject actual agency into the work, either enhancing or deflecting attention from the implied virtual agencies, or the performer may attempt to remain "invisible," as a transparent source— merely a transducer of the virtual energies implied by the work. The performer committed to virtual agency in music will likely adopt, as a performative stance, some position between the following two extremes.

1. As a foregrounded body that not only manifests embodied virtual agencies but also
   a. visually complements those agential energies with extra gestures and energies that draw attention to the performer's body
   b. projects the performer's own personal agency in terms of ownership of an embodied virtual agency, drawing attention to the performer's distinct personality
   c. creates an empathetic narrative agency external to the diegesis, controlling, in effect, the musical discourse by commenting on it
   d. directs listeners' attention (over)didactically to virtual agencies—either teaching or forcibly imposing one's interpretation on a listener
2. As a transparent "transducer" that not only realizes in sound a range of potential virtual agencies but also
   a. uses only those gestures required to convey virtual agential energies without drawing undue attention to its actual body
   b. does not inject its own personality but energetically projects virtually emergent agencies or actorial roles
   c. dispassionately embodies virtual narrative agencies
   d. modulates virtual subjectivity between active and reflective perspectives while maintaining a degree of distance

Obviously, neither the overly self-projecting nor the overly self-effacing stance is entirely desirable. For the performer, accurately gauging where audiences are most comfortable with performers along a continuum between these extremes can be crucial to professional success. For a performer who plays privately, there is no need to project; for a performer who plays in a large hall, projection is an unavoidable issue. Clearly, the ideal stance for any given performer depends on all the circumstances of the envisioned performance.

The performer ultimately fills simultaneous roles: as interpreter, self-critical listener, and even, at times, composer (when composing/improvising a cadenza, elaborating a return, adding ornaments, or participating in an aleatory work). The virtualizing imagination of the performer thus mediates between the presumed work and its listeners. And the performer's engagement with virtual agency, like the listener's, is grounded in life experience, with the potential to experience growth. However, the performer should not be viewed as an all-powerful gatekeeper who determines a listener's interpretation. Once sounds are set free, the listener is also free to negotiate distinctive paths through the virtual world of the work, perhaps rejecting or simply ignoring the performer's realization—especially in the case of a listener who already knows the work and can thus listen "beyond" the performer's manifestations to an identification of virtual agencies and their characterizations that may have eluded the performer.

A performer may bring to life the energies of virtual agencies, conveying roles and subjectivities with such human warmth and emotion as to fully embody those agencies, perhaps captivating the listener with a sense of profound empathy. To the extent this happens, the artistry of the performer, fused with humanity, is equivalent to that of the composer, whose work the performer so compellingly brings to life. It is through an artistic performer's embodied insights that listeners can learn to enlarge their own imaginative capacities, comprehending the significance of music's virtual worlds and emotions for their own lives.

Notes

1. By "the work" I include its notated forms (autographs and editions), its relevant style(s), its historical performance practice and ongoing reception history, and even contexts of its performance—not all of which will necessarily be digested by a performer, who in any case must make interpretive decisions about details that are not, and cannot be, fully specified. A balanced account of the issues surrounding the ontology of the musical work and its "authentic" performances is found in Davies 1991.

2. Lawrence Kramer (2002, 68–99) expands on the virtuoso's performative gestures in an extensive essay on Liszt. As Kramer notes, the "virtuoso self [Liszt] performs . . . is not ultimately defined by either technical genius or expressive depth, but by an incandescent power to act as a surrogate for the social transformation of the audience" (87). Kramer identifies a "bipolar narrative of furor and sentiment typical of Liszt's virtuoso performances" (96) as staged by Liszt through the compositional form of his Piano Sonata in B Minor, claiming "the virtuoso that the sonata constructs as its ideal executant . . . models, embodies, and in a sense suffers the 'deepest,' most 'authentic' dimensions of the audience's subjectivity" (96).

3. The shamanlike power of these performers, attested by contemporaneous reports, offers a distant parallel to the effect we might imagine from images of Paleolithic-era cave paintings, where buffalo shamans sounded their transcendent music through bone flutes magnified by the resonance of cave chambers (see Neal 2015). Such prehistoric embodiments may have ritually involved a deep identification with assumed spiritual beings or forces.

4. Daniel Leech-Wilkinson ties performance styles to historical trends, noting an expressive "inflation" from roughly 1900 to 1920 and a greater restraint following World War II (1945 on) (2009, 252). Among pianists, he notes that Rubinstein remarkably "changed his performance style after the war, cutting back on rubato to bring it into line with the new approach" (252). My own experience hearing and watching live performances by Serkin and Rubinstein in the 1970s was that Serkin's gestures were often violent, with his arm swiveling in a full arc to produce an accented chord, whereas Rubinstein appeared to use almost no excess motion and was practically immobile in his posture.

5. For more on the way didactic playing may undermine the (virtual) drama of a work, see Rothstein 1995.

6. Virtual listening (auralizing or audiating) need not require the performer's intervention at all, as when we silently read a score and hear it in our minds. This capacity, developed so extraordinarily in some composers, is what enabled Beethoven to virtually listen to his imagined musical ideas despite his increasingly degraded capacity to actually hear.

7. Janet Schmalfeldt (1985) dramatically projects this position as performer-analyst in a celebrated article where she "wears both hats."

8. This discussion of the *Tempest* sonata is drawn in part from Robert S. Hatten, "Interpreting the 'Tempest' through Topics, Gestures, and Agency," in *Beethoven's Tempest Sonata: Contexts of Analysis and Performance*, ed. Pieter Bergé, Jeroen D'hoe, and William E. Caplin (Leuven, Belgium: Peeters, 2009), 163–80.

9. The documentary evidence would appear hard to ignore, since Czerny studied all the piano sonatas personally with Beethoven. But Czerny's carelessness with respect to several outright errors in notating the theme from this movement may serve as a warning not to assume his recommended pedaling had Beethoven's approval.

10. A *locus classicus* for programmatic interpretation of this sort is Owen Jander's (1985) construal of the middle movement of Beethoven's Fourth Piano Concerto as not only a dramatic dialogue between individual piano and collective strings but programmatically a conflict between Orpheus and the Furies.

11. Consider the use of bright D major at the point of Don Giovanni's sudden descent into Hell; does this suggest the terrifying brightness of the flames? See also Treitler 1980, 195–96, and 1982, 165–66, on the "horrifying brightness" of the D major chord at the climactic recapitulation of the first movement of Beethoven's Ninth Symphony.

12. For another perspective on the performer as narrator, see Rink 1999. Rink exhaustively demonstrates how a performer can help construct a narrative in Liszt's "Vallée d'Obermann" from *Années de pélerinage: Suisse*.

13. The interpretations in this section are drawn from Robert S. Hatten, "Performing Expressive Closure in Structurally Open Contexts: Chopin's Prelude in A Minor and the Last Two Dances of Schumann's *Davidsbündlertänze*," *Music Theory Online* 20, no. 4 (2014), http://www.mtosmt.org/issues/mto.14.20.4/mto.14.20.4.hatten.html.

14. Recall Beethoven's addendum to his coda in the finale of Op. 95, which led Rey Longyear (1970) to his perceptive interpretation of Romantic irony.

15. It is also found in the opening of the sixth song of *Frauenliebe und Leben* and the opening of the postlude to the last song of *Dichterliebe*.

16. A translation of the penultimate chapter (63) of this novel, which presents the masked ball, is given by John Daverio (1997) in an appendix to his Schumann biography.

17. For more on these options, see Benson 2003. Nicholas Temperley (2009) examines ways in which performers such as Clara Schumann introduced piano works in her recitals by preluding: preparing the key and even at times anticipating the opening motive of a composition. I argue (in Hatten 2009b) that improvisatory passages notated in works of Robert Schumann and Chopin offer further evidence for a more fluid conception of the musical work and its boundaries in the nineteenth century, as opposed to the museum-work concept forwarded by Lydia Goehr (1992).

18. Two movements with multiple returns of the main theme (the G-major sonata-rondo finale of Beethoven's Cello Sonata in G Minor, op. 5, no. 2, and the sonata-without-development slow movement of the Piano Sonata in C Minor, op. 10, no. 1) offer striking examples of this strategy.

19. A useful comparison may be made with the fugal subject in the Toccata from Bach's Partita No. 6 in E Minor, BWV 830 (beginning in m. 27). All but one of the sources notate three inverted mordents on the first, third, and subsequent first beat of the subject; these are also given for the answer. With the third entry of the fugue, only one source includes the first two inverted mordents (perhaps due to greater technical difficulty, since the right hand here must accommodate not only the subject in the top voice but also some of the notes of the inner voice that the left hand cannot comfortably reach). In this case, however, the inverted mordents are desirable as markers of the temporally separated

entries. In the F♯ minor fugue, the intense overlapping of entries and fragments renders the continued use of inverted mordents as superfluous, since they are no longer thematically foregrounded.

20. My brackets in example 8.7 indicate the extended version of this second subject, which appears once in each of the voices in its most extended form. The stretto-like overlapping of the head of the subject serves to enhance the refractive counterpoint and saturated plenitude of the passage as a highly concentrated *melos*.

21. The relevant passages are quoted here. First, from Bach's private performance for Burney before dinner in Bach's home: "In the pathetic and slow movements, whenever he had a long note to express, he absolutely contrived to produce, from his instrument, a cry of sorrow and complaint, such as can only be effected upon the clavichord, and perhaps by himself" (Burney 1773, 270); second, after dinner, when he played continuously until 11:00 p.m.: "During this time, he grew so animated and *possessed*, that he not only played, but looked like one inspired. His eyes were fixed, his under lip fell, and drops of effervescence distilled from his countenance" (270; emphasis in original).

22. Edward Klorman (2016) emphasizes this point and elaborates it into a theory of "multiple agency" for Mozart's chamber music.

9 An Integrative Agential Interpretation of Chopin's Ballade in F Minor, Op. 52

Frédéric Chopin's last ballade has no explicit program, but as Michael Klein (2004) has demonstrated, its dramatic trajectory of keys, topics, and themes reveal an unmistakable narrative and expressive design. Here, I explore how virtual agential levels are activated, how they overlap in moving the listener toward engagement at various levels, and how they can reveal still more of the work's expressive meaning. My interpretation exemplifies how an agential approach can incorporate a range of analytical evidence—formal functions, genres, topics, tonal structure, rhythmic/metric structure, motivic structure, and the expressive implications of melody and harmony—leading to the narrative-dramatic emotional journey of a powerful subjectivity. I also incorporate my own agency as a performer of the work, at times providing suggestions for creating effective aural manifestations of virtual agency. In accounting for Chopin's expressively motivated formal processes, I emphasize the flexibility of an interpretive approach able to draw on multiple agential and structural perspectives. My aim is to illustrate how a theory of virtual agency can help us hear differently, thereby opening up fresh possibilities for expressive interpretation.

An initial problem for agential interpretation in the Ballade in F Minor is the apparently simple opposition between formal functions and their associated topics in the introduction (mm. 1–7) and the primary theme beginning in measure 8 (example 9.1). Meter ($^6_8$) and tonality (C major) immediately establish a virtual environment for inferring Steve Larson's musical force of gravity. The opening repeated octaves, however, suggest a rather diffuse source for the dynamically increasing energy. The left hand's tenor line is characterized by repetition, descent, and a "giving in" to virtual gravity—hence, it appears unmarked for human agency. The opening harmonic progression is also rather unmarked in its functional progress (T–S–D–T) and thus offers little evidence of independent harmonic agency. The reference to the subdominant (V^7/IV to IV) instead cues a contented pastoral topic evocative of Nature. The formal function of the opening, slipping into a texture and only hinting at a theme, suggests a kind of preluding— a Romantic *intonatione* that serves as a formal introduction by setting the key (the wrong one, as it happens).[1] An unusual feature of this introduction is its

Example 9.1. Chopin, Ballade in F Minor, op. 52 (mm. 1–12). Introduction (Intro) and beginning of the primary theme (P) are introduced by a break in texture at the end of measure 7.

incessant closure to tonic, perhaps implying a framing function.[2] Thus, potential narrative agency is suggested even without a clear virtual human agency being projected.

Giving in to virtual environmental forces implies an actantial source for the energy, and without clear evidence of individual human agency, a pastoral default might be to interpret this energy as the (virtual) action of, for example, the wind (perhaps acting on an Aeolian harp). However, it is possible to personify even such a diffuse force as the wind and thus to impute human agency.[3] Such personi-fication is musically motivated by dynamic swelling and appoggiaturas (rearticu-lated suspensions in mm. 2–3), typical musical features implying human gestural expression. Allegorizing the natural force implied by this topically pastoral in-troduction can also suggest a subjective level of deeper significance—Nature as freighted with parallel human meaning, as those once-removed Romantics, the Symbolists, would emphasize.

But the potential appears rather limited for this passage to suggest an actor in a larger dramatic trajectory.[4] The introduction instead appears to present a piece-specific background mood against which future thematic presentations may be understood as projecting more marked, distinctive emotions. The extensive ges-tural repetition and subsequent liquidation to a fermata in measure 7 provide suffi-cient time for deepening these impressions. The time for self-reflection afforded by this fermata further activates a subjective level of engagement.[5] Thus, even for this relatively unmarked introduction, we can infer several different levels of agency.

The destabilization of the tonic C in measure 8 results from the introduction of half steps on either side, invoking the voice-leading pattern of *le* and *fi* to *sol* and thereby transforming the fermata's reflection on C from tonic to dominant.[6] With the subsequent entrance of what we soon realize to be a primary theme in F minor, we encounter a much more gesturally individualized and thematically marked melody with a more direct emotional expression of human agency. Its twisting contour suggests a painful querying above the accompaniment's more normative waltzlike background.[7] Topically, melody and accompaniment may suggest differing agencies, but their foreground-background relationship grants dominance to the melodic topic. A performer can highlight melodic agential dominance by use of an individualizing rubato in the melody to project against the regular pacing of the accompaniment.[8] When heard together, the two vir-tual actants implied by melody and accompaniment create a discursive trope and merge into the unique expression of a singular *melos* expressed by a single vir-tual human agent. We may interpret the painful querying motive (labeled *a* in example 9.1) as further projecting a virtual actor (fictive protagonist) pondering a dysphoric feeling/thought within the melancholic mood of a *valse triste*. Sub-jectively, this inner querying receives immediate repetition (as parenthetically marked in mm. 9–10) that suggests obsessive rumination within a deeper con-sciousness. Having already activated a more generalized subjective response to the external mood of the introduction's actantial energies, we can now hear the internal actoriality of the waltz's dysphoric minor as supporting a more interior-ized discourse that characterizes a singular subjectivity.

Inferences are moving at lightning speed up and down various levels, which reflects something of the complex competency that we bring to our understanding of agency in music.[9] Another set of inferences is triggered when we hear the motivic relationships marked in example 9.1. The primary theme (P) is comprised of two motives, labeled *a* and *b*. Motive *a*, in tragic F minor, receives further "subjectivizing" by its immediate ruminative echo (in parentheses in mm. 9–10). Motive *b*, however, incorporates the repeated-note-with-stepwise-descent contour that recalls the introduction's motivic substance (see the tenor in m. 1 and soprano in m. 2). And motive *b* occurs right at the point where the primary theme shifts from F minor to A♭ major. The introduction is referenced here by motivic allusion (marked as motive *i*, for introduction), and its recall now seems calculated to perform an actorial role: specifically, helping move the dysphoric primary theme to the euphoric major mode. Strikingly, what we heard as merely actantial in the introduction's giving way to virtual gravity and unmarked harmonic progression, and only minimally agential in its humanlike dynamic swelling, we now understand in retrospect as having provided a foreshadowing of an important actorial role. Not only does this motivic cross-reference promote the coherence of a thematic discourse, but the particular location of the cross-reference is calculated to take advantage of the association of the *i* motive with the introduction's euphoric expressive character, supporting its role in moving the primary theme away from tragic obsession and toward a more peaceful acceptance in A♭ major. Given the potential narrative agency of the introduction (as frame), its motivic integration into the main thematic discourse also suggests a higher merger—as though the fictional protagonist were narrating his or her own story. And this further interiorizing of agential/actorial functions supports an increasingly profound subjectivity.

The sequential reflection of the *b* motive leads harmonically through D♭ major to a half cadence in B♭ minor (m. 18, example 9.2). The overall move from tonic to minor subdominant marks the tragic descent of the primary theme, which then unscrolls nearly literally above the prolonged V of B♭ minor. B♭ minor is ultimately subsumed as iv of F minor when a half cadence sets up the large-scale return of the theme in measure 23. This extensive, passive rumination on the theme over V/B♭ minor (mm. 19–22) threatens, by its literal anticipation, to undermine the active role of the theme on its tonal return in measure 23. Although Chopin does not provide any cautionary dynamics, I think the performer must recognize the potential confusion of actorial levels and do something to ameliorate it. From the perspective of my own agency as a performer,

> I suggest playing this mesmerizing prolongation of V/iv (from the second half of m. 18 to the downbeat of m. 22) as a parenthetical extension, emphasizing its plagal, codetta-like character by means of a veiled dynamic (perhaps with a coloristic use of *una corda*) and slightly blurred pedaling, clearing only with the cadential iv-V⁷ motion in m. 22. (Hatten 2010c, 59)

In recommending that the near-literal recurrence of the theme (over the prolonged half cadence in B♭ minor) be "sonically liquidated in a haze of slightly

Example 9.2. Chopin, Ballade in F Minor (mm. 18–23), featuring parenthetical section within the first theme group.

obsessive, lingering reflection" (Hatten 2010c, 59), I clarify its function in measure 18 not as a structural thematic return but as an interiorized reflection of the agential theme, whose actorial role is here submerged into the interiority of a Romantic subjectivity. This interpretation depends on a performer who can "perform agency," such that the reflective temporal perspective of the postcadential expansion may be interpreted as such by the listener.

In terms of large-scale form, the ballade draws from both sonata and variation genres without fully exemplifying either.[10] The F-minor first theme is subject to diminutional variations on subsequent returns. A putative second theme (example 9.3) does not appear in the expected relative major, A♭, or in the dominant key of C minor (the two conventional options for a sonata); instead, it surfaces in the highly unconventional major subdominant, B♭. But the theme's contrasting topic (a pastorale with siciliano rhythms and a hint of the barcarolle) affirms its positive, euphoric valence, as we might expect of a second theme in a minor-key sonata.[11] Like the introduction, the second theme appears to give in to gravity, suggesting euphoric contentment. This is expressed by a melodic descent through thirds (D–B♭–G) that ends with a sigh (reminiscent of the introduction) from G to F at the incomplete authentic cadence in measures 85 and 86. However, a more individualized (willful) virtual agency emerges in measures 86 and 87, where spontaneous, energetic leaps aspire upward, opening dynamically to a reflective expansion of the G–F gesture. If this G to F motion recalls the introduction's motive, it would be appropriate here, given the similarly euphoric character of the opening.

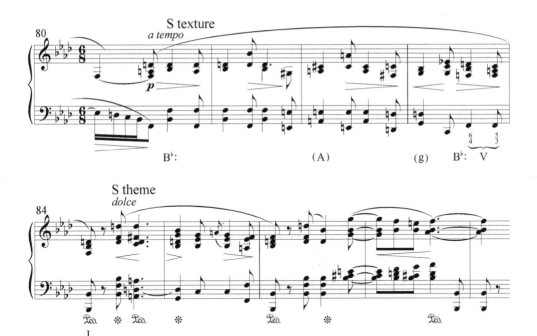

Example 9.3. Chopin, Ballade in F Minor (mm. 80–88¹), with arrival of the second theme (S) first as texture in measure 80, then leading to the (*dolce*) theme in measure 84.

Both primary and secondary themes are treated to quasi-developmental episodes, with the primary theme receiving two. In the fantasia-like episode following the initial presentation of the first theme (mm. 38ff.), the right hand reflects on the repeated-note opening of the introduction, but this time stepping more mysteriously—from G♭ major, past F, to F♭ major—and, through a sequence, to V⁷ of E♭/e♭ (a tonic that never arrives). At this point (m. 46), the reflective episode slips into what sounds like an elliptical return of the primary theme, *in medias res*, beginning with the *b* motive (the one that incorporates the introductory motivic fragment). This more explicit connection with the introduction is treated to circle-of-fifth harmonic sequencing and melodic expansion (the "alto" voice imitatively refracts the soprano in structural sixths and thirds (mm. 51–52). As an agential enhancement of the *melos*, the passage builds to what might have been a euphoric breakthrough, but its sequence overshoots the hoped-for positive goal—instead, leading to V⁷ of F minor (m. 53) for a return of the primary theme in measure 58.

The return of the theme features diminutional variation (example 9.4), as well as textural expansion of the melody by means of a refractive inner voice—in this case comprising an extended series of sixteenth-note sighs in scalar descents. These diminutions enhance the querying aspect of the theme with their urgent *pianti* (tears). Diminution is also a means of entering more deeply into the subjective core of an emotion and furthering its development. Here, the virtual

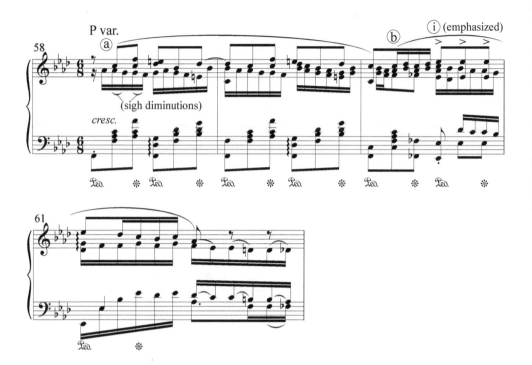

Example 9.4. Chopin, Ballade in F Minor, return of the P theme (mm. 58–61 only) with sixteenth-note sigh diminutions.

actor (and by extension, the virtual subjectivity) experiences emotional growth through suffering that is fully embraced (rather than simply queried).[12] The subsequent developmental episode is justifiably more dramatic, and its passionate expression of suffering leads to the most intense climax thus far. However, instead of breaking through to a heroically achieved resolution, the climax spills over and collapses, sinking into a euphoric B♭ major as a kind of escape (refer to example 9.3). A reverberant absorption of energy occurs in Chopin's initial sequential slippage down to A major and then G minor before cadencing in B♭ for the *dolce* emergence of the second theme's melody.[13]

The developmental episode following the second theme sounds more contrastive, as though the topical *tempesta* of the episode preceding the second theme were returning to negate the gentle relief of the second theme. G minor (m. 100) sequences to A minor (m. 104) but slips back to G minor (m. 108) for a sequence to A♭ major (m. 112), the conventional second key area for a minor-key sonata. In this key, the potential for a more lasting euphoric resolution is marked by pastoral parallel sixths and birdcall trills.

Rather than fully establishing another second theme, one that could retrospectively have cast the earlier second theme into an actorial role as transitional (perhaps invoking a three-key exposition), Chopin instead returns allusively to

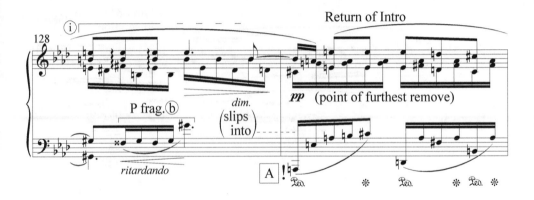

Example 9.5. Chopin, Ballade in F Minor (mm. 119–130), showing thematic integration and a heroic "breakthrough" climax in A♭ major (m. 125) dissolving to a "false" return of the introduction in A major (m. 129).

his first theme. Its two motives, *a* and *b* (example 9.5), are first developmentally integrated with each other contrapuntally (mm. 121ff.) and then climactically integrated with the melodic motive, *i*, from the introduction (m. 125)—a motive that was already integrated into motive *b* in the first theme. This further, explicit motivic integration not only gives the introduction greater actorial and (self-)narrative agency but helps (as before) inflect the first theme from a tragic to a more positive, and here, topically heroic affirmation—as though the expressive trajectory of the work might indeed move to triumph in A♭ major.[14]

The concept of *melos*, with its expanded melody and refractive counterpoint, is encountered here in spectacular fashion. In interpreting the expressive effect of the ballade as a meditative and melancholy dream, Rosen notes that

> the effect of a dream depends on the extraordinary skill of the transition [by which he means the integrative passage in mm. 121ff.], on the way Chopin brings us from one point to the other without allowing us to notice how each has been prepared. Part of the skill is the voice leading learned from a study of Bach: voices turn out to have thematic significance only as we realize that they have been there all the time, waiting with that potential for vital movement which is the essence of traditional counterpoint. (1995, 341)

Example 9.6. Chopin, Ballade in F Minor (mm. 135–147), featuring a stretto "retransition" to the recapitulation, arriving *in medias res* in B♭ minor (m. 146).

To this perceptive account, I would add that this is the climactic completion of a motivic/agential process that was in play from the very opening of the ballade, and although it occurs as a developmental integration, it is in the key of the relative major, a key that would conventionally constitute completion of a sonata exposition.

The immediate collapse into mystical A major, however, launches a literal recall of the introduction, as though marking a false recapitulation, and spawns a brief *Durchführung* ("leading through," referring to the keys in a development section) from this "point of furthest remove" through a ricercar-like stretto imitation of the first theme's tortured motive (example 9.6). The sequencing of this patch of stretto imitation enacts a series of quests for resolution, dramatized as *searching* (marked by the *a* motive) leading to apparent *finding* (marked by the *b* motive), and landing successively (but never definitively) on F major and A♭ major as potential euphoric resolutions. Each of these is undercut by ♭6, and the third sequence leads instead back to dysphoric B♭ minor. B♭ minor, recall, served as the key for a low point of rumination in the first theme's initial group (mm. 18–21). Now it provides a link, through motive *b*, into the recapitulation, where the primary theme in its original texture once more emerges *in medias res*.

The subsequent recapitulation is further truncated, setting up a return of the primary theme without an intervening episode. Not only is the primary theme on its return subject to variation, but it features topical transformation as well—as a *fantasia* with a diminutional melody. This is the most interiorized (dreamlike, lyrical) virtual subjectivity staged thus far.

The return to F minor has not launched a satisfactory sonata recapitulation, however, since the second theme will fail to resolve in either F major or minor. Instead, a brief developmental extension of the diminutional primary theme slips quietly into D♭ major and a return of the second theme as a kind of spiritual epiphany (example 9.7[a], mm. 169ff.). This return is soon aggrandized into a climactic apotheosis (example 9.7[b], mm. 177ff.) with the plenitude of texture suggesting more positive expressive fulfillment.[15] Sonata form serves as a regulative background for this projection of the ballade's implied drama. The second theme's two keys (B♭ and D♭ major) are expressively motivated as illusory, and they impart a sense of vulnerability to their positively oriented expressive topics.[16] Although filling a contrasting actorial role in the formal drama, the second theme also expresses one side of a singular subjectivity or consciousness. The second theme initially expresses serene consolation or reassurance (as a pastoral barcarolle in B♭ major) and then in the recapitulation, two types of transcendence (first as a quiet, interiorized epiphany and then as a heroic apotheosis in D♭ major), but neither can withstand the ultimately tragic trajectory of the expressive genre or fictional drama that is being enacted. These secondary keys (B♭ and D♭) are not so much dissonant as irrational from a Classical standpoint, and hence they are well chosen to underline the illusory status of their euphoric expressive fulfillment. They do not require any expressive or dramatic resolution, since their positive topics already represent a wish fulfillment on the part of the protagonist or virtual subjectivity; thus, they are emblematic of where and how

Example 9.7. Chopin, Ballade in F Minor, recapitulatory returns of the S theme. (a) D♭ major "epiphany" (mm. 169–171 only). (b) D♭ major "apotheosis" (mm. 177–180 only).

resolution of the conflict might have been resolved expressively and dramatically, if not tonally.[17]

The second theme is fated, however, to be undone by a tragic reversal. The horrific liquidation of D♭ into F minor underlines the ballade's ultimately tragic trajectory with a violence that is unprecedented (example 9.8, mm. 195–202). After an angry half cadence is disrupted by silence, we hear soft, bell-like reverberations of a V⁹ in F minor (mm. 203–10) as a spectral echo of the pastoral topic from which the second theme first emerged. The melodic contour is strikingly

Example 9.8. Chopin, Ballade in F Minor (mm. 195–212), featuring disintegration of the S theme (with spectral recall in mm. 203–210) and extreme dissolution of the P theme to launch the coda (mm. 211ff.).

similar to the opening of the second theme, thereby recalling its actorial role. But this moment's brief, reverberant, and reflective calm—further evidence of self-reflectivity on the part of a virtual subjectivity—only serves to enhance the "contrastive valence" of the tempestuous coda (mm. 211ff.) that suddenly disrupts that calm.[18] In the coda's ultimate diminution-as-tragic-dissolution, the first theme's contour is initially mangled in a chaotic whirlwind of agitation (m. 211). At this point, we might well revert to the actorial level, in which a fictive drama portrays tragic Fate overtaking the protagonist. Chopin's ending suggests a wilder version of the whirlwind close of the finale from Beethoven's Piano Sonata in F Minor (*Appassionata*), op. 57. The outcome is the same: an inexorably tragic ending that fails to resolve the desires of the protagonist. Tonal resolution to F minor is thus not a solution for the virtual agent but rather the final slamming shut of any hope for escape.

The distortion of the primary theme in measure 211 may also be interpreted as a psychic disintegration of the powerful subjectivity at the heart of the emotional journey in the ballade. As we identify with the protagonist of this tragedy, we also engage with its virtual subjectivity: a struggle between two opposing states within a larger consciousness. As listening interpreters, we can enlarge the significance of this passionate struggle by situating the expressive drama with respect to our own emotional lives. We may experience emotional growth if we come to understand the drama of the work's virtual subjectivity to have exceeded our prior experience. Or we may find that the ballade offers a deeper, more distinctive expression of what we may have sensed but never fully understood in quite this way.

Notes

1. The historical *intonatione* was "intended to establish the pitch and mode of a flowing vocal composition" in works by Andrea and Giovanni Gabrieli, but these intonations were often more virtuosic and toccata-like (Randel 1986, 402). I offer the analogy here because of the similar improvisatory character of Chopin's opening. Preluding to set up the key and character of a work was also common throughout the nineteenth century in piano recitals. For a fascinating study of the history of this form of improvisation and its consequences for our understanding of Chopin's preludes, see Temperley 2009.

2. Recall the framing examples discussed in chapter 7; harmonically, the tonic grounding of this frame is closest to the Mendelssohn *Song without Words* example.

3. I elaborate on the personification of Nature and machines in chapter 10.

4. Such a trajectory is proposed by the genre of the ballade—recall the bardic opening of Chopin's Ballade in G Minor discussed in chapter 7.

5. I should add that listeners are stylistically entrained to approach epic-scale Romantic works in terms of the projection of a heroic subjectivity, or at least a subjectivity whose emotional states are heroic in proportion. In my analysis, I demonstrate how Chopin stages that perspective. Beethoven's earlier contribution to the staging of heroic subjectivity is well documented by Scott Burnham (1995).

6. The schema *le-sol-fi-sol* as dominant-defining is theoretically articulated and historically documented by Vasili Byros (2012, 2014).

7. The $^6_8$ meter embeds two $^3_8$ waltz measures, creating the two-bar hypermeter characteristic of the waltz choreography (see McKee 2012, 94). However, Chopin offsets the hypermeter by beginning on the second of two $^3_8$ submeasures in measure 8, as marked by the opening theme's structural downbeat. For more on Chopin's play with hypermetric downbeats and expansions in this theme, see Hatten 2010c, 58–59.

8. The continuing performance tradition of this form of melodic rubato with consistently paced accompaniment is attested in Émile Jacques-Dalcroze's (1939, 188) account of his collaboration with the Belgian violinist Eugène Ysaÿe (1858–1931):

> In rubato melodic passages, he instructed me not to follow him meticulously in the accelerandos and ritenutos, if my part consisted of no more than a simple accompaniment. "It is I alone," he would say, "who can let myself follow the emotion suggested by the melody; you accompany me in strict time, because an accompaniment should always be in time. You represent order, and your duty is to counterbalance my fantasy. Do not worry, we shall always find each other, because when I accelerate for a few notes, I afterwards re-establish the equilibrium by slowing down the following notes, or by pausing for a moment on one of them." (cited in Cottrell 2012, 741)

9. I cannot imagine how one might design experimental or empirical tests to determine the sequence or simultaneity of these inferences, but that is not my task here. Instead, I am exploring the semiotic, stylistic competency presupposed by my interpretation of this work, both as a theorist and as a performer. I would defend the complexity of that competency against the simplification of overly basic cognitive or perceptual experiments. See interlude II for further discussion.

10. Drawing on James Hepokoski and Warren Darcy's helpful discussion of sonatas as dynamic and dialogic with respect to form as a process—"an intricate web of interrelated norms as an ongoing action in time" (2006, 10)—one might say that the ballade is "in dialogue" with sonata form.

11. Klein (2004) identifies the topic as a lullaby. Chopin's Second Ballade (op. 38) begins with an even clearer pastorale-barcarolle blend in F major. The use of B♭ major, a nonconventional second-theme key from the perspective of sonata form, is expressively motivated as a positive rejoinder to the tragic use of B♭ minor in the main theme group.

12. Recall the evidence of subjectivity in Boethius's recommendation to fully embrace pain as a means of fully comprehending and resolving it (chap. 5).

13. The effect is similar to Beethoven's sequential, subjective absorption of the extreme climax in E♭ major and subsequent collapse in the finale of Op. 111. As Charles Rosen notes, Beethoven's "diatonic circle of descending fifths . . . does not exist on a plane of real action, so that the long series of tiny harmonic movements that prolong this immense inner expansion serve only as a harmonic pulse and in no sense as a gesture" (1972, 447). I would add only that the unmarked sequencing can in fact serve an expressive purpose; it enacts an agential reaction to an extreme, harrowing emotional climax by absorbing the shock in stages. This is yet another means of staging virtual subjectivity.

14. The significance of this culminating heroic affirmation in A♭ major is curiously overlooked in Klein's (2004) narrative interpretation of this ballade. Instead, he gives priority to the waltz theme in parallel sixths that precedes this passage. Rosen (1995, 341) notes the importance of the introduction's repeated-note motive in this passage, and he considers what I have termed a climactic thematic integration as part of the ballade's development section (a section presumably launched in G minor right after the second theme in B♭ and subsuming the key of A♭ major). Although I interpret the passage

slightly differently, I recommend both authors' sensitive interpretations of the expressive effects achieved in this ballade.

15. The term "apotheosis" is Edward T. Cone's (1968, 85–86), and one of his examples is this very passage (also noted by Klein [2004]).

16. For a similar case in which a movement (granted, one with much clearer sonata outlines) features an illusory second theme key (and correspondingly vulnerable theme), compare the first movement of Franz Schubert's Piano Sonata in A Minor, D. 784 (discussed briefly in chap. 4; see also Hatten 2004, 187–95).

17. Recall Chopin's Prélude in A Minor, op. 28, no. 2, with its illusory, euphoric resolution on a Picardy third in E before the ultimately dysphoric tonal closure in A minor, as interpreted in chapter 8. It is also in this sense that the Neapolitan, G major, can function as a desired (and transcendently resolutional) key that is briefly envisioned and attained, but ultimately denied, in the coda of Beethoven's slow movement in F# minor from Op. 106.

18. For more on contrastive valence (a key concept in emotion theories) and its consequences for emotional responses to music, see Huron 2006, 21–25.

Interlude II: Hearing Agency: A Complex Cognitive Task

The preceding chapters demonstrate how a listener may infer agency at various levels in listening to works in diverse musical styles. Listeners also assume, more or less voluntarily, varying degrees of engagement when interpreting the implied agencies in a work, on a continuum from direct identification to close empathy to more removed sympathy (or lack of sympathy) to critical rejection and even to apathetic nonengagement. An empirical testing of my theory of virtual agency would have to negotiate among all these possible cognitive states. In addition, listeners may exhibit different levels of attending—the constantly shifting focus of actual listening, whose many tasks (conscious and unconscious) begin with the basic integration of what I call imagistic and temporal gestalts (see this book's prelude). The former captures the qualitative richness of an aural "image" (e.g., the timbre and quality of a harmonic simultaneity) and the latter, the continuous integration of an aural *melos* into an ongoing musical discourse.

I have theorized musical gesture as "significant energetic shaping of *sound through time*" (Hatten 2004, 95; emphasis in original), specifying the prototypical gesture as a relatively short gestalt that mimes human gesture and that maximizes imagistic and temporal gestalt capacities. The processing of gestures, however, already engages with more sophisticated style competencies, as I emphasize in interlude I. We initially understand gestures (both actantially and as implying virtual human agents) within the virtual environments of tonality and meter. In the case of post-tonal and/or ametric music, as we see in this interlude, virtual gravitational fields are roughly approximated through contoural movement (up and down) and rhythm (qualities of accentuation and articulation miming anacruses and downbeats). With tonal music, after quickly orienting ourselves tonally and realizing the scale-degree and harmonic functionality of thematic gestures (as motives) and topics (as expressive fields), we begin to match what we hear to familiar schemata (such as William Caplin's [1998] Classical phrase-structural patterns, Robert Gjerdingen's [2007] galant schemata, or my [Hatten 1994] expressive genres). Our (re)construction of a musical discourse (implying virtual actorial roles) responds to logical if unanticipated (creative) unfoldings (e.g., via developing variation) and surprising swerves (via rhetorical gestures that may imply shifts in level of discourse) to animate a dramatic trajectory that treats conflict as some kind of transvaluation within a narrative archetype (see Frye 1957; Liszka 1989; Almén 2008; chap. 7). As we coordinate our style-competent hypotheses (as implications), along with their realizations or deferrals, we also engage with increasingly larger formal schemas and negotiate various temporalities (e.g., in which distant returns may be understood as memories). The ultimate integration of all these levels of cognition contributes to our construction (or reconstruction) of a virtual subjectivity with all its dimensions of inner conflict, moral emotion, spiritual transcendence, and the like. And we engage with that virtual subjectivity through our own subjectivity—by reflecting on our own life experience and emotional understandings—thereby granting music its existential relevance for our lives.

It would be difficult to fit all these cognitive processes into an all-embracing description of what listeners do or even the order in which they do it. Recall, as well, my claims about subjectivity in chapters 5 and 6. Subjectivity may be emergent, but it is already engaged from the start as a warranted aesthetic perspective in many Western musical styles. Listeners throughout history have generally brought some kind of subjective engagement to their experience.

In attempting to tease out the modular competencies that contribute to this extraordinarily complex musical experience, cognitive theories of music face an enormous task. As I noted many years ago (Hatten 1989; see also 1994, 272–73), any experimental approach to music cognition must face three rather daunting obstacles: style competencies are historical (hence not immediately available but amenable to reconstruction, however biased), they are learned (hence not innate but subject to the potential biases of instruction), and they are creatively artistic (hence not predictable but subject to the potential biases of individual interpretive processes). Furthermore, composers' choices, even when they appear to be atypical, may not be stylistically anomalous but simply reflect a rarer, creative application of stylistic principles. Stylistic principles are not best conceived as prescriptive rules but rather as descriptive of regularities. Analogously, artistic interpretations may be rare or unusual but still aesthetically warranted. The lesson for scientists is that statistics can miss, or misconstrue, competent musical outcomes.

Thus, creating speculative theories of musical meaning and hermeneutic interpretations of musical meaning will continue to be important, even in the face of trends toward a more empirical musicology (see, e.g., Clarke and Cook 2004; Clarke 2005). Any empirical approach must stand or fall on its ability to help explain those semiotic capacities forwarded by more speculative theories of musical meaning. Speculative theories may appear arbitrary or unscientific, but to the degree that they capture intersubjectively shared practices of interpretation, they have validity for those communities of listeners.

Materialists may take what they will from the evidence I offer concerning virtual agency, and philosophers may continue to dispute to what extent such agency is "in" the music or relevant for its interpretation. I maintain that we have coadapted evolutionarily designed cognitive capabilities (e.g., the integration of imagistic and temporal gestalts, the tendency to construct some form of agency as a "source for the force," and the interpretation of energetic shapings through time

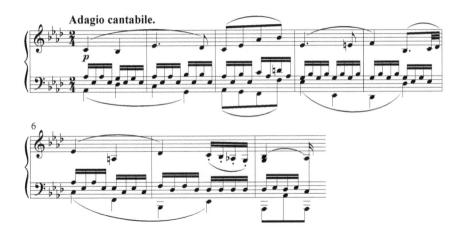

Example Int.2. Beethoven, Piano Sonata in C Minor, op. 13, second movement, first theme (mm. 1–8^2).

as affective) for extraordinarily flexible and subjectively compelling artistic ends. I claim that we can infer, or analogically glean, from the energetic, performative contours of any music's *melos* a kind of human (emotional) engagement. Furthermore, I argue that Western composers have artistically developed and shaped our predispositions to read gesture, agency, significant intention, and emotion into any form of energetic shaping. They have found compositional means of capturing and extending these predilections with respect to sound while staging still further subtleties that progressively turn music into a form of (virtual) consciousness. In turn, listeners have the capacity to experience various temporalities, engage in self-reflective awareness, and reflect on still other dimensions of a fully endowed human subjectivity.

As an example of the complexities of actual music cognition, I offer the following thought experiment in which three present-day listeners might approach the understanding of a familiar movement from a Beethoven piano sonata.[1] My thought experiment supposes three levels of attending (involving various musical competencies) among three very different listeners. I should emphasize that each listener has a richly expressive and meaningful experience of subjectivity, although clearly the third one best incorporates those competencies I explore in this book.

Example Int.2 presents the theme from the *Adagio cantabile* movement of Beethoven's Piano Sonata in C Minor, op. 13 (*Pathétique*). Our three hypothetical listeners focus on different musical features in creating their interpretations, as noted.

1. Concentrating on tempo, dynamics, texture, mode, contour, theme: This listener has a subjective emotional experience shaped by these primary dimensions of the music. She is moved without knowing why. She hears

a slow, soft, melody-and-accompaniment texture and perhaps follows the contours of the melody and its dynamics as they create a vague expressive melisma supporting the rise and fall of emotional intensity.[2] She recognizes the returns of the rondo theme and feels a sense of contentment when the final return is enfolded within a richer texture (while not explicitly recognizing the role of the diminutions in the accompaniment that suggest plenitude, or the form as a whole). She identifies what she hears as being expressed by the music, mapping the sequence and intensity of expressiveness onto her own emotional experience.

2. Including gesture, agency, topics, harmony, form: This musically trained listener recognizes gestures (e.g., the sudden shift upward in m. 2) as akin to specific human emotions, hence a human agency actively feeling and thoughtfully expressing itself within a topical field that recalls a hymn. He hears a nice give and take between the melody and the bass line that helps him track harmonic yieldings and yearnings in conjunction with the melodic contour. He recognizes the varying strengths of harmonic closure as defining aspects of the formal organization of the work and hears the episodes as transitional and developmental, respectively, creating a satisfying drama of tension and release. He imagines human agency as a central protagonist in a drama involving conflict and resolution, and hearing this conflict within the topical realm of a hymn suggests the spiritual interiorizing of that conflict and its reconciliation. He chooses to identify with that emerging (virtual) subjectivity and feels a great sense of poignancy in its expression of an emotional journey.

3. Adding further music-theoretical awareness (including intertextual knowledge) and deeper hermeneutic engagement: This more experienced listener engages with subjectivity at multiple levels and with greater detail. Her interpretation is informed by intertextual awareness of the theme's later "version," as transformed in the opening of the third movement from Beethoven's Ninth Symphony, *Adagio molto e cantabile*. She also hears the hermeneutic significance of the opening integration of the melody with bass and harmony: a yielding V_2^4–I^6 progression is troped with the melodic evasion of an implied (virtual gravitational) descent to $\hat{1}$, instead leaping from $\hat{2}$ to $\hat{5}$. This energetic countering of resigned harmonic acceptance leads her to an interpretation of hope in the face of resignation and a projection of energy that sounds noble, even spiritually heroic. Her sense of identification with a virtual agent's willful projection of hope extends to the arpeggiated (hence, by its association with fanfare, more conventionally heroic) ascent in the melody in measure 3. She feels, at least empathetically, the sense of that hopeful aspiration's loss of implicative momentum as the upward triadic arpeggiation loses force and manages only a weak step before sighing, as it were, in another acceptant move, this time enacted by the melodic drop to $\hat{5}$. She hears the striving upward chromatic passing tone at the end of measure 4 as enacting agential desire in the context

of this spiritual topical realm and feels the local tonal force of magnetism pulling up from raised $\hat{5}$ to $\hat{6}$ before once more dropping in acceptance. She interprets the sequence as transferring acceptance to a higher level. The (Schenkerian) descent of the (structural) upper line, moving down by step from F in measure 5 to closure on A♭ in measure 8, suggests a positively resigned acceptance—perhaps even a hint of abnegation that, intertextually, she is familiar with from her study of other works of Beethoven and their interpretation by scholars.[3]

I cut short the third scenario to observe that each of these listeners is affected by details at various levels of structure, and each attempts to integrate these details into a coherent experience. Each moves to a level of subjectivity rather quickly, whether or not they are critically aware of the reasons that might explain their interpretations. The agential energies that the third listener follows in such detail are arguably affordances that feed into the first listener's perception of the general contour or *melos* of the theme. The first listener may not hear (be aware of) the actantial motivations and virtual agential energies that lead to the emergence of complex moral emotions, such as resignation, hope, or abnegation, that affect the third listener. The first listener's sense of being moved may well be due to the integration of more holistic elements, including some of Leonard B. Meyer's (1989, 14–16) secondary parameters—tempo, dynamics, and texture— as well as the overarching major mode as it contrasts later with minor in the episodes. The first listener also relies more heavily on general energetic contours rather than an understanding of tonal syntax and other learned style competencies. Imaging of her brain while listening would likely indicate more activity in the holistic, emotional right brain, as opposed to activity in the more intellectual, syntactic left brain. More experienced musicians display a balance of right-left brain activity (see Peretz and Zatorre 2003). Strikingly, all three listeners report a richly subjective experience that shares basic similarities, but the second and third listeners might be understood to have "heard more" and experienced the music more comprehensively as a result.

Even in this oversimplified and highly speculative account, I do not assume a necessary cognitive sequence with respect to what a listener consciously understands herself to be hearing. Listening is messy—we grab on to whatever we can as we try to make a listening experience coherent, and many cues left by the composer may go unnoticed. I do not deny the greater value of stylistically competent listening in my own experience of coming to know this movement, yet I remember playing it as a teenager and feeling a close, overpowering subjective identification with certain ennobling spiritual emotions that I could not at that time fully articulate in language—and for which I had limited awareness of the causes or motivations.[4] Subjectivity is always present, and the impression of being one with the music (especially when the listener is also the performer) can be powerful regardless of one's ability to articulate either the effect or its reasons.

Notes

1. In speculatively accounting for three different listeners, I am inspired by Melanie Lowe's (2007, 78–98) virtuosic account of three fictional listening subjects. The difference is that her contemporaneous listeners to a Haydn symphony are historically constructed listening subjects whose ongoing interpretations are glossed with extensive documentary evidence relevant to their social standing, musical knowledge, and personal concerns. My account instead imagines three contemporary listeners with different semiotic competencies as theoretically constructed. And whereas Lowe features the polysemic interpretive range of Haydn's more public symphonic music, I differentiate three levels of interpretive depth in accessing virtual agency and subjectivity of Beethoven's more intimate *Adagio cantabile* movement.

2. For more on "musical melisma," see Ridley 1995.

3. For more on abnegation, see Hatten 1994.

4. Regarding ennobling emotions, recall the discussion of Elgar's "Nimrod" variation near the end of chapter 6.

10 Other Perspectives on Virtual Agency

In this final chapter I consider a number of fascinating issues bearing on agency: temporality; troping; intertextuality and meta-agency; the personification of Nature, machines, and unnatural others; and various psychoanalytical and psychological perspectives. Such concerns inevitably point toward the twentieth century, when music begins to confront us more directly with ethical dilemmas arising from the status of agents as subhuman or inhuman (Taruskin 1997). I address modernist distancing and estrangement techniques in works of Stravinsky that exhibit such extreme forms of agency and subjectivity, arguing for a more humane intent behind his apparently dehumanizing portrayals. Next, with an example from Schoenberg, I suggest how we might interpret virtual agency within a post-tonal virtual environment. In closing, I survey a few problematized twentieth-century agential narratives and some works where the conditions for inferring agency are highly degraded, noting how both musical narrativity and agency have been radically reconceived in the past century.[1]

Temporality

The concept of temporality in music goes beyond those aspects of musical time as measured by rhythm, meter, hypermeter, and tempo—or as shaped by gesture, phrasing, and rubato. Temporality refers more broadly to the experiencing of musical events as past, present, or future, as well as the aspectual relationship of events to each other on a virtual timeline.[2] As such, music's staging of temporality can deepen our sense of virtual subjectivity as a consciousness situated in time, reflecting on the past, anticipating the future, and understanding events in their temporal relationships to each other.

Among various stagings of temporality, those that suggest a perspective on the past include the various narrative frames discussed in chapter 7. Furthermore, the bardic topic that opens Chopin's Ballade in G Minor and frames Mendelssohn's *Song without Words*, op. 30, no. 3, alludes to the past by emulating a past style. And the retrogression from V to IV in the introduction to Mendelssohn's Overture to *A Midsummer Night's Dream* creates a temporal distancing as part of its narrative framing, preparing us for the magical world of enchantment that will be enacted by the fairy scherzo. The subsequent events presented in these works are thus interpretable under this double awareness: they frame enacted stories that are being "told" (presented from an outside perspective), and they invoke a time that is prior to the present of the frame. By invoking the past, a virtual narrative presupposes a virtual present (in literature, the present time of the virtual narrator) from which the temporality of the "story" may be perceived.[3]

A heavily doubled, folklike melody with recitative-like accompaniment—as in Schumann's *Davidsbündlertänze*, op. 6, no. 11, or the "Im Legendenton" section from the first movement of his *Fantasy*, op. 17—may also suggest an interpolation of the past into the unmarked present of virtual conscious experience (the experienced time of a virtual subjectivity). "Im Legendenton" transforms a theme presented earlier (from the transition), further suggesting the way virtual memory can reinterpret virtual events through a virtual agent's recollection.

The effect of thematic returns simulating virtual memory is a powerful expressive motivation for cyclical form. In Beethoven's landmark song cycle, *An die ferne Geliebte* (To the distant beloved), the recall of a quintessentially expressive theme mimes memory as reminiscence, but thematic recall may also be staged dramatically as a moment of insight or recognition that triggers some transformative action on the part of a virtual agent or subjectivity. For example, the transition to the finale of Beethoven's Piano Sonata in A Major, op. 101, stages a shift from tragic lament to heroic action, and it is marked by the mystical reappearance of the pastoral theme from the opening of the sonata (see Hatten 1994, 106–8). Such a return is especially effective because the pastoral topic has already been associated with reflection and interiority, and hence, it appropriately signals a deeper subjectivity through which we can interpret heroic action not as external but as internally allegorized.

The emotional effects of returns (experienced through the listener's own subjective engagement with a presumed virtual agent's subjectivity) can range from poignant nostalgia to a sense of being challenged by one's deepest being. The reencounter with a marked theme can galvanize a virtual agent, providing the impetus to find a new way through an impasse, or meet an existential issue with fresh awareness and renewed energy. In Op. 101 the protagonist takes a spiritually heroic perspective, as internalized by the troping of fanfare, learned, and pastoral topics. By contrast, in the finale of Op. 102, no. 1, after the return of the first movement's pastoral opening theme, the protagonist enacts a Romantic-ironic swerve, shifting to a *buffa* figure that appears to launch the finale by dismissing the previous discourse.[4]

Such shifts in temporal perspective need not be triggered by returns that suggest memories of the past. Perhaps the most audacious staging of virtual consciousness in the very act of imagining its own future is found in the transition to the finale of the *Hammerklavier*, where Beethoven "tries out" three successively more contrapuntal-imitative Baroque pastiches in anticipation of his energetic, positive, future-directed response to the tragic third movement.[5] The double fugue that emerges will eventually trope the heroic-extraverted first subject with a pastoral-reflective-interiorized second subject. The second subject is anticipated in the contour of a lyrical countersubject created for the retrograde of the first subject, which thereby interiorizes a speculative virtualizing of the future.

Of course, the gradual emergence of a theme from a slow introduction is not new with Beethoven: the first movement of Haydn's Symphony No. 92 (*Oxford*) stages thematic emergence as well. And it would become a standard mode of virtual consciousness in the nineteenth century through the continuously evolving process known as developing variation. Brahms would exploit this technique to extraordinary ends.[6] Wagner would also utilize the technique, in conjunction with thematic transformation, for a deeper mining of consciousness: the passionate unfolding of love from prolonged desire in search of fulfillment (*Tristan*) or the transcendent unfolding of grace from prolonged spiritual agony in search of forgiveness (*Parsifal*). The unfolding evolution of a musical idea through a musical discourse may in turn imply a virtual agent who can imagine a virtual future, "will" that future into the virtual present, and retrospectively reflect on it when it returns, recalling a virtual past. Indeed, the formal functions of introduction ("before the beginning") and coda ("after the end") even more strongly mark the "unique temporal character" that every formal unit in a sonata movement possesses (Caplin 2009, 25). The introduction is prospective, often marked harmonically by a prolongation of an expectant dominant, whereas the coda is retrospective, often marked harmonically by emphasis on the subdominant.[7]

Temporality is subjectivity's realm, as Henri Bergson ([1889] 1910) claimed. Music's capacities to stage temporality in turn enhance our interpretation and engagement with virtual subjectivity.[8]

Troping as Agential Merger

In chapter 4 I explore the troping of topics as one means by which implied virtual agencies could merge to form a larger agential identity. Troping of gestures, as well, can contribute to a richly characterized or subtly nuanced agential identity. An example of differing gestures merging as parts of a single agency is illustrated by the opening of Debussy's *Prélude*, "Des pas sur la neige" (Footsteps in the snow) (Book I, no. 6), in which the physical footsteps in the left hand and the dissociated psychological musings in the right hand are combined to present a very modern trope of frozen feeling and dissociated consciousness.[9] The two contrasting gestures may be heard as those of a single agent, that of the lonely wanderer. Debussy's emergent trope is perhaps anticipated by Schubert in the final song of *Winterreise*, where another wintry wanderer allegorizes, in terms of his own subjectivity, the hurdy-gurdy player's devastatingly empty music. In both works, a left-hand ostinato suggests the prevailing mood of hollow sadness, and fragile attempts by the melody to rise are frustrated. Debussy further estranges melody from accompaniment by his choice of scale-degree placement. Knowing both works, one might conjecture that Debussy is troping on Schubert, not by direct citation but rather by employing similar musical means to portray a frozen or dissociated repression. But Debussy's *Prélude* only presupposes a prior emotional devastation, whereas Schubert's cycle, as situated through the poetic texts of Wilhelm Müller, makes the protagonist's loss more explicit.

Although these gestural tropes imply a merger into a singular agency, there are also "tropes of discourse" (Hatten 1998, 197) emerging from a play of agencies that, instead of blending, dialogically interact in ways that engender irony or the comic. A trope of discourse may be understood as bringing together such oppositional agential forces at a higher level, as when virtual actors are understood as parts of a higher subjectivity. An example of this kind of play, involving both gesture and topic, is found in the development section of the finale from Beethoven's Sonata for Cello and Piano, op. 102, no. 1. In measure 77, the cello begins with an open-fifth drone emblematic of the pastoral. When the piano returns the main theme's four-note gesture in measure 79, it undercuts the cello, and the sudden *forte* on the final note also tropes the motive's original careless release, mocking its search for a closural downbeat. But this dynamic accent on a weak beat cannot substitute for a genuine metric accent as resolution. The negation (false accent) of a negation (weak release) is a trope that cannot fail to sound humorous, especially when the cello answers an eighth-note late, as though having lost its place.

The third time the cello attempts the serenity of the pastoral, the piano cooperates with a legato sequencing and imitation of the four-note motive played *pianissimo*, attempting to resolve the last note of the motive by means of a tenuto, understood as an agogic (durational) accent (m. 91). Imitation engenders another discursive trope, that between pastoral and learned styles. Although the learned style signals a traditional developmental working out, the fragmentation (ordinarily stylistically unmarked as typical of such passages) here becomes thematically marked by the troping of attempted solutions to the metrically displaced four-note motive. Having accented the last note on the piano, further extended by a straggling echo in the cello, and having sustained the last note with a tenuto, Beethoven now simply dispenses with it, lopping it off as he sequentially juxtaposes the first three notes in chains of "eighth + two sixteenths" (mm. 105–21). The recapitulation (mm. 122–24) fails to solve the problem, instead confusing it with textual accentuations from overlapping motivic entries (stretto) that further expose the weak-beat inadequacy of the fourth note. Only in the coda is the metric issue resolved, and only by another developmental technique that is motivated by the gestural premise of the movement. The augmentation of the motive (mm. 243 and 245 in the piano) twice resolves to the tonic on a downbeat, thereby allowing the movement to reconcile the motive's implied tonal and metric closures.[10]

The ongoing discourse premised by this "problem" has integrated, if not merged, the various actorial roles of gestures and topics as parts of a larger subjectivity that is staged as speculative and troped with comic wit and irony. Virtual subjectivity is staged through a process of thinking through (and acting out) a "problem" in search of an ultimate "solution" (no matter how improbable the problem and search may appear).

Intertextuality and Meta-Agency

As suggested by my interpretation of Debussy in light of Schubert, intertextual referencing can enhance virtual temporality by adding a historical layer.[11] Virtual consciousness of, for example, a profound, primal past (the Palestrina allusion in the slow movement of Beethoven's String Quartet in A Minor, op. 132) can interactively trope with the historical consciousness of an actual listener. And the evocation of the past may trigger other associations, perhaps with specific religious practices and beliefs or with a general sense of spirituality.

Intertextually enhanced agency plays a direct role in works that evoke a particular composer as an actually inspired (or fictionally inspired) virtual agent, as we see in chapter 4, with Schumann's evocation of the keyboard style of "Chopin" (and later, the violin style of "Paganini") in *Carnaval*. More recently, in works by composers as diverse as Mauricio Kagel and George Rochberg or Luciano Berio and George Crumb, we find quotations suggesting or programming historical composer-agents as virtualized actors in various dramas of subjective consciousness. Laura Tunbridge (2011) traces the association of Schumann with madness through specific quotations of his work that virtualize Schumann by metonymy or vocal commentary, as in R. Murray Schafer's *Adieu, Robert Schumann* (1978). Wolfgang Rihm uses a Schumann quote for a "dream vision" or hallucination by the title character of his opera *Jakob Lenz* (1978). The virtual subjectivity with which a listener engages is made more complex by these meta-agential allusions, which may be thematized as central (as in Schafer's piece) or evoked by "topical" importation (as in Rihm's opera), in the examples Tunbridge gives. The latter effect can be especially potent when enhanced by an exotic sonic medium, as when Crumb introduces a toy piano for a quotation of Bach's arrangement of "Bist du bei mir" (If you are with me, [I go with joy]) to create an uncanny sense of nostalgia in Crumb's *Ancient Voices of Children* (1970).[12]

In the later twentieth century, attempts to stage virtual consciousness appear increasingly postmodern, ranging from a barrage of quotations that suggests a perplexed and overwhelmed subjectivity, as in the third movement of Berio's *Sinfonia* (1968–69) to a cartoonlike sequence of stylistic or topical contrasts that projects subjectivity both artificially and self-consciously, miming the narrative style of a film noir, as in John Zorn's *Spillane* (1987).

Personification of Nature, Machines, and Unnatural Others

Although I agree with Peter Kivy's (1984) assessment that musical representation tends to imply expression,[13] I part company with him by claiming that we can and should infer a virtual agent as virtual expresser of virtual emotions. In music the "pathetic fallacy" is generally not a fallacy at all: we readily hear the turbulent waves in Mendelssohn's *Hebrides* Overture as emotional turbulence (as does Kivy to a degree). I would go further by claiming that this emotional turbulence belongs to some as yet unspecified virtual agent that we can interpret, by default, as part of the virtual subjectivity of the work. Thus, Nature matters to us as a reflection of our own qualities. This is a correlation aesthetically warranted throughout Western music history, and one that becomes increasingly important for musical styles ranging from Romanticism to Symbolism and Expressionism.

If Nature's movements were completely aligned with our own, then every character piece prompted by a scene in Nature would automatically be interpreted in terms of the actions of a virtual agency. However, Nature as conceptualized by artists is not typically teleological—and pastoral serenity in music can be more about "being" than "becoming." Storms have a beginning, a middle, and an end, however, and their temporality can readily be projected by music. A composer may impose teleology by introducing a storm as part of a programmatic trajectory (e.g., Beethoven's "Pastoral" Symphony, where an expanded "storm" introduction to the finale leads to a peasant dance celebrating the storm's passing) but also by aligning a storm's shifting intensities with those of a virtual agent/actor to allegorize a psychic drama.

Composers can represent animals as displaying qualities with which listeners might endow a protagonist or, eventually, a larger subjectivity. William Kinderman (2013, 205–9) interprets the swan in *Lohengrin* as a potent symbol (of purity) within what I view as the virtual subjectivity of that opera. He notes the swan's relationship to Elsa's "inward vision" and links her memory of a dream to the conjuring of Lohengrin's presence. Intertextually, the swan is musically referenced in *Parsifal*, where the *leitmotif* goes beyond its referential role to affect harmonic relationships as well.

Personification is not limited to Nature or its creatures. We can personify machines, endowing them with humanlike qualities based on their inherent properties (e.g., the power and goal-oriented trajectory of a train, exemplified by its engine, in Arthur Honegger's *Pacific 251* [1923]). One such early machine, the mechanical clock, inspired composers to write passages for which Leonard Ratner coined the topical label "clockwork" (1980, 391). Tamara Balter (2009) has described numerous examples in the string quartets of Haydn and Beethoven that suggest an "automaton" rather than a virtual human agent.[14] And Jacques Offenbach (in his opera *Tales of Hoffmann*) found amusing musical correspondences for the movements and quirks of that original automaton, Olympia, from E. T. A. Hoffmann's tale "The Sandman" ([1816] 1972). But even when agency is less than human, either an actorial role or an all-embracing subjectivity enables us to engage with automatons as parts of the trajectory of a virtual human consciousness. We have the capacity, by analogy or allegory (or both), to fit the nonhuman into a more human scheme of relationships and endow nonhuman energies with human motivations and goals.

Psychoanalytical and Psychological Perspectives

Some fictive agential narratives involve a *Doppelgänger*: an "other" (virtual external agent) who uncannily resembles the protagonist and hence threatens the protagonist's identity. Schubert's setting of Heinrich Heine's poem "Der Doppelgänger" is a celebrated example. Listeners who have read Heine and

Hoffmann would be inclined to interpret uncanny resemblance as a symptom of a deeper, repressed connection—as though the "other" could expose the split subjectivity of a singular individual. The imaginative projection of the other could also reflect a deeper pathology, perhaps not acknowledged by the protagonist.

In chapter 5 a different kind of split consciousness is featured in my interpretation of agency in Schumann's "Am leuchtenden Sommermorgen." In that song the virtual agent imaginatively projects a collective agency (the flowers, personified as the beloved's faithful female friends) that delivers a message of rebuke. Clearly, these virtual actorial roles can be understood as parts of a larger, divided subjectivity torn between two compelling emotional appraisals.

Such subjective splits can also be staged as madness in a virtual agent who is unable to balance their competing claims. Madness in an operatic character may be cued musically by incorporation of a unique, marked timbre (a glass harmonica in the mad scene from Donizetti's *Lucia di Lammermoor* and electronic music in the last act of Menotti's opera *Juana la Loca*). Inferring a similar psychic split can help explain one of Hanslick's conundrums with respect to expression in music: the use of major mode in the opening section of Orpheus's lament, "Che farò senza Euridice" (What will I do without Euridice?), from Gluck's *Orfeo ed Euridice*. As I have conjectured (Hatten 1994, 216), the powerful tropological effect of major instead of minor mode is psychologically justified if one considers Orpheus to be in shock and perhaps even denial, such that his music (emotional expression) has not caught up with his words (semantic acknowledgment). The split is devastatingly poignant, one of Gluck's greatest tropological achievements, if dramatically sung in this way (i.e., with a rigid posture and a somewhat fragile vocal delivery to signify extreme shock).

Wagner's interest in psychologically complex characters marked his entire operatic career. In his portrayal of Senta from *The Flying Dutchman*, as Katherine Syer (2009; 2014, 80–117) has carefully documented, Wagner worked progressively in designing his libretto and composing versions of the score to craft a character whose dreamlike states were integral to the drama (see also Abbate 1988). In a highly effective scene, Senta's boyfriend, Erik, recounts his own dream, but she listens to it as though she were dreaming it herself. Senta's Ballad features her account, interrupted at the point when she is overcome with emotion, at which point the orchestra falls silent as well. An *a capella* women's chorus continues the ballad and returns only when Senta regains sufficient composure to sing a coda. This simple device clarifies the role of the orchestra as sounding Senta's emotions and revealing her psychological condition. Typically, the orchestra enlarges the subjectivity of characters in an opera.

In *Porgy and Bess*, George Gershwin uses a similarly stark contrast to convey the opposition between the nuanced subjectivity of the inhabitants of Catfish Row and the white detective, policeman, and coroner who at various times enter their world like aliens. This social opposition is marked operatically by having the outsiders speak instead of sing, further exposing their lack of empathy.

Subhuman, Inhuman?

Richard Taruskin introduces the terms "subhuman" and "inhuman" in his characterization of works by Stravinsky and Shostakovich, respectively. Stravinsky's *Rite of Spring* is subjected to a withering ideological critique (1997, 378–88), ranging from the music's inhuman biologism (as inherent in its primitivism) to its presumed analogy with Nazi collectivism, and ultimately to its reflection of Stravinsky's anti-Semitism. Rather than identifying with the music's virtual subjectivity, then, a listener who recognizes these aspects might well experience a pronounced lack of sympathy toward Stravinsky's virtual actors, the society they imply, and even, from an ethical standpoint, the composer himself. Vaslav Nijinsky's choreography embodies the violent down bows of the famous *Rite* chord with the ensemble's collective lock-step stomping. And the *Rite*'s marked (and intentionally shocking) opposition to classical Russian ballet—where transcendent emotions are embodied in lifts, and swans on point appear to glide weightlessly across the stage—was certainly provocative for opening night audiences.[15] However, I resist this overly ideological interpretation of Stravinsky's intentions in creating his fictive world. Stravinsky exhibits a dispassionate but no less human sensibility for his virtual agents in their mythic and ritual enactments. Our shock at Stravinsky's primitivism is part of a deeply human, aesthetic encounter with a world that, although it may reveal insights into horrific political states, does not thereby endorse them.

Distancing and Estrangement

Distancing from too-easy agential inference and subjective engagement appears to be a key feature of many modernist works. But a composer may want to engage the listener even more deeply by this estrangement; indeed, since ironic allegories and myths demand a greater speculative effort, they may increase the listener's engagement. The listener is enjoined to probe a more profound (and often psychologically more acute) expression of human emotion and motivation.[16] Stravinsky's coherent if objectivist style had successfully achieved that aim even before the *Rite* delivered its body blows to humanist sensibilities. Already in *Petruschka* (a ballet so attractive to audiences that it successfully toured such backwaters as Fargo, North Dakota, shortly after its premiere in Paris in 1913), Stravinsky captures the despair of the outsider through his fairy-tale allegory of a near-human puppet. Petruschka is magically endowed not only with life but with its higher human emotions, unlike his decidedly less-human colleagues, the self-absorbed Ballerina and the animalistic Moor. Stravinsky implements a group of interactive musical techniques to substitute for traditional tonal/formal processes.[17] While not fully post-tonal, these techniques nevertheless create an entirely new virtual world. The "textural pedal" with which the work opens is comprised of ideas that repeat without progressing, merging into a collage that fills registral space for a period of time. By repetition or permutation of a limited diatonic collection with no clear beginning or end (often merely repeating a pitch indefinitely at the beginning or end), Stravinsky can create textural-pedal strata out of his folk-tune allusions. Familiar tonal melodies are thereby distanced from their teleological contexts, and their implicative momentum is degraded through repetition and denial of closure.

Contrapuntal separation of lines (as opposed to layers) is traditionally achieved by contrary motion, rhythmic give and take, smooth melodic lines versus functional leaps in the bass, motivic contrast, and the like. Traditional layering is achieved through the use of varied textures, contrasting timbral groups, varied rhythmic diminutions, and registral separation. Stravinsky innovates by stratifying not just lines but entire layers and by using more radical contrasts to differentiate (and hence decontextualize) those layers. He often opposes incompatible tonal or pitch centers, scalar collections, meters, topics, and styles. In using these devices to differentiate the Ballerina and the Moor from each other, he also highlights their inability to interact with each other—each lives in a separate world, a separate virtual environment created by oppositional key, mode, theme, meter, and style (in addition to traditional oppositions of register and timbre). What they share, however, is the textural-pedal layering of movement without clear intention, a mindless repetition without the affordances that could support an interpretation of strongly willed actions or expressed emotions. Petruschka, however, is given a *leitmotif* that encapsulates his existential rift. Torn between C major and F♯ major triads, his puppetlike and humanlike aspects are shown to be ultimately irreconcilable, paradoxically fused in a torment that can be interpreted allegorically as exemplifying cognitive dissonance.

Ongoing spatial layering is complemented by a similar technique in the temporal plane that has been described as intercutting, interruption, or montage (the latter by analogy with emerging film techniques). This strategy treats formal units as disjunct successions rather than as unfolding a continuous progression. Traditionally, disjunctions function as rhetorical gestures, cadential evasions, or dramatic shifts; loaded with expressive tension, they can become thematic premises implying resolutions that are not always delivered. In Stravinsky disjunction takes on the character of intentional artifice, suggesting that textural layers without teleology may be broken off at any point, displacing the listener to attend to still other static layers.

Without closure or logical continuation, the alternation of sections or themes does not add up to a rondo in any traditional sense. Rather, Stravinsky creates a new formal rhythm in which disruptions are heard as splicings, interpolations, or truncations of thematic sections.[18] Together with stratification (a substitute for counterpoint) and textural-pedal layers (a substitute for refractive counterpoint), intercutting imposes an estrangement on any attempt to construct a virtual agential discourse through dramatic design and emotional development.

Of course, *Petruschka* has dramatic design and emotional development, since Stravinsky still employs traditional devices to achieve them. But the radical language is further developed in the *Rite*, where pitch and rhythmic dissonance are more extreme.[19] Distinctively, in the *Rite* collective agencies are vested in textural-pedal layers, and the "chosen maiden" appears trapped in an alternation of pitch-rhythmic cells that do not progress but lead by brute repetition and dynamic intensification to the climactic outcome. Regardless of his intent, Stravinsky's music can heighten our sympathetic reaction to the plight of the individual, even as it forces recognition of such harsh rituals in our collective past.[20]

Virtual Agency in a Post-tonal Virtual Environment

The problem of agential inference becomes more acute in post-tonal works. Karlheinz Stockhausen's pointillist works, such as *Kontra-Punkte*, illustrate this most dramatically. Schoenberg, however, in his early, experimentally post-tonal *Drei Klavierstücke*, op. 11, no. 1, continues to implement many of the traditional techniques by which agency may be inferred.[21]

As example 10.1 shows, an initial 014 set is treated to developing variation by means of gradual interval expansion.[22] Allen Forte's theory, presented in *The Structure of Atonal Music* (1973), cannot readily account for the thematic similarity of such expansions, since they produce increasingly dissimilar sets: 014, 015, and most radically, 026. Yet by hearing the process more traditionally— that is, characterizing the pattern as a descending third followed by a descending second—we find a single motivic type (third + second) composed of three individual tokens: m3 + m2, M3 + m2, and M3 + M2. The developing variation of a motivic type thus supports an interpretation of agential identity as evolving over time. What is new is the expressive emotional effect of these more dissonant chromatic gestures.

As Ethan Haimo (2006) clearly demonstrates, Schoenberg's gradual stylistic evolution appears not to confirm Forte's theoretical presuppositions about Schoenberg's compositional adherence to networks of set classes. Indeed, aspects of the language of late nineteenth-century chromatic music are obvious enough in these transitional works as to suggest more than one stage in the so-called emancipation of the dissonance. Emancipation from necessary resolution is found in Op. 11, no. 1, but one can still hear the expressive significance of dissonance— for example, in formations that sound like appoggiaturas even when their note of resolution is actually more dissonant (compare mm. 3 and 11). I have coined the term "negative cadence" for these phrase endings where dissonant agglomerations refuse to resolve even when their gestural deployment suggests the formal function of ending.

The ways in which Schoenberg plays with and against traditional phrase structures are often lost in an all-consuming focus on the analysis of pitch-class sets (and the sometimes counterintuitive segmentations they tempt analysts to make).[23] In Op. 11, no. 1, we hear traces of a presentation phase in the sequence of the basic idea marked in bars 1–3, but the absence of tonic prolongation marks the phrase as already developmental. By contrast, what might have constituted a continuation phase (note both developmental inversion and fragmentation of the motive in mm. 4–8) refuses to sequence, instead getting "stuck" with two repetitions varied only by temporal expansion. Thus, the rhetoric of the sentence is reversed, necessitating a ternary "return" in measure 9. Schoenberg brings the

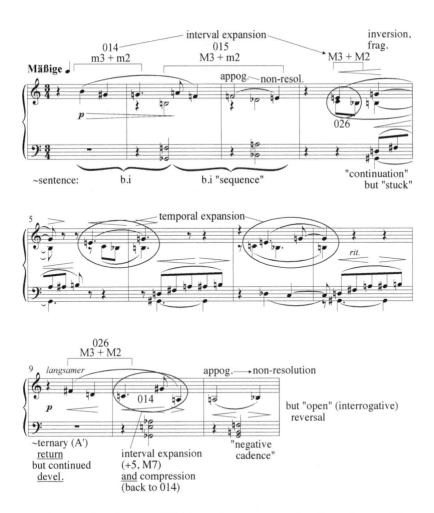

Example 10.1. Schoenberg, *Drei Klavierstücke*, op. 11, no. 1, first theme (mm. 1–11). Used by permission of Belmont Music Publishers, Los Angeles.

thematic gesture back in its expanded form (026, as first introduced in the continuation phase), but he continues to develop the motive in measure 10 by means of a literal intervallic expansion that is also a pitch-class-set compression. The "third + second" motive is here expanded to an augmented fifth (enharmonically a minor sixth) followed by a major seventh, but the set class is a compression of the previous measure's 026 to 014. The wrenching troping of two antithetical processes—intervallic expansion and set class contraction—may help account for the intensely expressive effect of this moment, which marks the climactic development of the motive in this opening theme. The implied cadence is made negative by lack of any tonal resolution of these expressive dissonances, but its implied appoggiatura (from m. 3) now moves in a rhetorically reversed direction, suggesting not only negation but interrogative openness to future developments.

Other Perspectives on Virtual Agency 277

Thus, Schoenberg deftly combines traditional and post-tonal strategies to produce an original rhetorical design and a radically unique expressive effect. Regardless of difficulties that listeners may have in assimilating such a high level of dissonance and lack of tonal grounding, the virtual environment in Op. 11, no. 1, still possesses virtual gravity. Although its platform or point of orientation is constantly shifting, we do not lose the essential opposition of up versus down in both pitch and rhythmic/metric realms. Since a humanly expressive thematic gesture is motivically treated to developing variation, and its dramatic journey is mediated within the framework of a familiar formal scheme, we can be reasonably confident in interpreting agential development through an actorial protagonist experiencing a rich inner subjectivity. It is then relatively straightforward to interpret formal distortion (of a prototypical sentence structure) and blockage (of the continuation, which becomes a static "B" section) as signifying inner frustration. The climactic motivic expansion is readily heard as a culminating expression of anguish—not that different from the climactic anguish expressed toward the end of Bach's Prelude in E♭ Minor (chap. 3) or Sinfonia in E Minor (chap. 4).

Problematized Agential Narratives

Sometimes virtual agency is left intentionally ambiguous. Such is the case with Schoenberg's monodrama, *Erwartung* (Expectancy; 1909, premiered in 1924), in which the listener is unsure whether the agency is that of the virtual protagonist or her feverish imagination. Presumably, the listener engages with this ambiguously split subject as a pathological form of subjectivity. But other aspects of agency and plot are also indeterminate, such as the identity of the dead man, whether he was her lover, whether he was killed by her, and if so, whether she remembers anything—and finally, whether he actually ever existed. These ambiguities help situate virtual subjectivity within a Freudian model, as in the repression of a severe psychic trauma. The leaking of horrific imagery provides a trace through which we can gauge the intensity, if not the exact nature, of that trauma.

By contrast, Philip Glass's opera *Galileo Galilei* (2002) recounts events in the life of the scientist in reverse order, marking a clear narrative intervention that distances the viewer/listener from the kind of cathartic subjectivity implied by many of my earlier examples.[24] In an earlier opera, *Satyagraha*[25] (1980), Glass presents Mahatma Gandhi as a displaced virtual agent in tandem with three figures who either influenced or were influenced by him: Leo Tolstoy, Rabindranath Tagore, and Martin Luther King Jr. Although presented in historical sequence, these refractions of Gandhi's own agency offer a similarly refractive counterpoint to his life. Thus, they expand the virtual subjectivity by which we are artistically led to engage with Gandhi's virtualized historical presence.

Sarah Reichardt (2008) demonstrates how Shostakovich in his Eighth String Quartet manipulates his own musical initials (DSCH, translated as D–E♭–C–B♮) as a self-referential motive. The subject implied by a personal musical signature then "conjures" quotations from Shostakovich's more programmatic works to stage his death. Here, there is sufficient evidence to consider the virtual agent as identifiable with the composer as a virtualized persona.

To what degree, however, can composers undermine a strong human tendency to anthropomorphize any actant, regardless of its nonhuman attributes? Consider the pointillist style pioneered by Anton Webern in the middle movement of Variations for Piano, op. 27 (1936) and further explored by Stockhausen in *Kontra-Punkte* (1952–53). How might these works degrade our capacity to infer (human) agency and actoriality? If we cannot hear logical connections between pitches (in the absence of linear, registral, or dynamic continuities, to say nothing of the absence of tonal hierarchies), it is harder to organize them into meaningful gestures. And without thematized gestures being treated to developing variation, we lack the basis of a continuous musical discourse in which we could infer actorial roles and an expressive trajectory based on dramatic or narrative archetypes. In fact, the most basic conditions for hearing music as movement (as *melos* flowing through and providing the temporal gestalt that is the basic of our understanding of melody as flow) are severely degraded.[26] In the absence of a live performance, where at least the continuous bodily movements of performers can substitute for that flow, we are more likely to hear individual notes as just that—points in a virtual space that lacks gravitation or magnetism or the means to generate implicative momentum. When a spatial orientation begins to dominate over a temporal one, dynamics may also shift their signification, implying not the flow of agential energy (as in the movements of willing or desiring) but rather the cueing of distance: louder pitches will sound closer and softer ones more distant in that virtual space. And unlike visual dots on the screen, which can be manipulated in patterns of motion and within archetypal schemes of interaction (whether within or among walls and containers or in alternation with other identifiable streams of dots), the pointillist musical work may offer a sensation of Brownian motion—inconsequential and untraceable—thereby degrading the affordances of intentional human movement.[27]

Remarkably, however, an emergent virtual subjectivity appears possible even in the absence of clear human agency and actoriality. Simply knowing that *Kontra-Punkte* is an intentionally composed musical work is sufficient to spark an artistic attitude of empathetic engagement in which listeners can imagine, or virtualize, an inner world that these disparate pitches might virtually inhabit. Such imaginative constructs could vary widely and would likely be more subjective than intersubjective—hence not as clearly linked to a shared musical style competency as was more obviously the case in the previous tonal music examples. Consider three possible interpretations as examples of the extremes to which an artistically oriented subjectivity might interpret a pointillistic work: (1) hearing the disjunct tones as emblematic of neurons communicating in the brain and hence as a model for the deepest interstices of neural intelligence; (2) hearing the sounds as akin to an aural kaleidoscope whose designs are appreciated like an abstract work of visual art, without any implied agency or story; or (3) hearing the pitches as representative of a precompositional formal design studied in advance that, while nearly impossible to follow aurally, provides a sense of security that the output is "significant" and can be intuited as such, even if not completely understood by the listener.

György Ligeti is another composer whose works have defied conventional agential analysis, although Eric Drott (2001, 2011) has closely considered the issue. "Micropolyphony," in which individual lines are imitated in dense registers and tight stretti, denies the aural affordance of hearing individual contrapuntal lines as agential. Instead, the strands coalesce into a sound mass that vibrates with the resonance of an overloaded refracted counterpoint. A listener is hard-pressed to distinguish any individuality in a collective texture that moves and evolves as a relatively undifferentiated sound mass. One may thus default to the sound mass in inferring virtual agency.[28] Just as melodies are emergent from individual pitches, sound masses are emergent from individual instrumental lines. Dynamic intensification, changing density, evolving (orchestral) timbre, and a Stravinskian formal play of layers (via stratification and intercutting) can then offer the basis for plausible actantial interpretation, if not plausible human agency. Once again, the propensity that humans have to agentialize the "source of the force" can enable listeners to reconstruct elementary dramas or narratives, but without a richer syntax the potential of such styles for a comparably rich subjectivity may appear limited. Having experimented with the possibilities of these radical structures, such composers often move past their exclusive use in organizing entire works. Instead, they begin to incorporate sound masses as textural or topical effects in works constructed largely on other principles.

Penderecki's four operas, from the expressionistic *Devils of Loudon* (1969) to the absurdist *Ubu Rex* (1991), afford a unique perspective on the anti-Romantic innovations of a range of significant twentieth-century operas.[29] In an article on Penderecki's operas in the context of twentieth-century opera (Hatten 1999), I examine the central trope of dramatic distancing as achieved through ritual, allegory, the absurd, and a postmodern plurality of styles. One of the central problems many modernist and postmodernist operas have faced is the potential loss of cathartic engagement with characters and drama in such distanced styles, especially when combined with Brechtian distancing effects.[30]

Examples of shattered subjectivity are legion in the twentieth century, and thus it is tempting to map that interpretation onto nineteenth-century musical works that feature extreme disjunctions, as in Susan McClary's (2000) interpretation of the first movement of Beethoven's Op. 132. I have argued for an alternative interpretation that might more plausibly exemplify a contemporaneous historical competency (Hatten 2004, 267–78). Michael Klein's (2015) Lacanian interpretations go still further, positing a radically different view of subjectivity that (as briefly noted in chap. 5) confers power on the Symbolic, in which language and culture (and by extension musical style) constrain the possibilities of human subjectivity, at least a subjectivity that is revealed as a construct incapable of achieving the Real. The hermeneutic quest for meaning is charged by attempts to explain a telling symptom, Lacan's *sinthome*, which, as Klein notes, "sounds curiously like *sent-homme*: the man (*homme*) who senses (*sent*) or who makes sense"

(2015, 118). The symptom, in this double sense, provides evidence for agency and subjectivity in a work even as it leads further than the musical work to implicate all of a culture's meanings. Klein's virtuoso interpretations in *Music and the Crises of the Modern Subject* thus invite a still broader conception of subjectivity (despite the hovering presence of the Symbolic as an interpretive Big Brother) that promises to reveal music's deepest cultural practices. It is a prospect that will have interesting consequences for the theory of agency I develop in this book.

Notes

1. For an important collection of essays devoted to this issue, see Klein and Reyland 2013.

2. See Hatten 1997 and 2006b and Hatten and Pearson 2006 for further discussion of music's cueings of temporal perspective as alternatives to language's markers for tense and aspect.

3. There is a parallel here to Ian Gerg's (2015) "virtual observing agent." Of course, any actual listener to music composed in the past will bring an actual, present-day temporal perspective to the experience.

4. For further interpretation of these movements, see Hatten 2004, 201–16, and 1994, 107–9, respectively.

5. For further discussion of the temporal implications of this passage, see Hatten 2006b, 66–68.

6. As documented extensively by Walter Frisch (1984).

7. There is a clearly marked opposition between moves to the dominant ("forward-looking, dynamic, dissonant, and non-closural") and to the subdominant ("backward-directed, static, stable, and closural" (Hatten 1994, 43). As I have further noted, "Rosen (1972, 23–27) generalizes the opposition to include any modulations to the sharp (dominant) side vs. the flat (subdominant) side as mapped by the circle of fifths for any given tonic key" (43).

8. For an outline of the varieties of temporality to be found in twentieth-century music, see Almén and Hatten 2013, 64–71.

9. See Hatten 2004, 228–29, for a more detailed discussion.

10. The interpretation of Beethoven's Op. 102, no. 1 in this section is drawn from Hatten 2004, 210–16.

11. For an early approach to intertextuality in music, see Hatten 1985. In a series of groundbreaking articles, Kevin Korsyn (1991, 1996, 2001) has explored intertextuality in wider contexts. Michael Klein's (2005) indispensable study expands the concept beyond influence, explaining the significance of later works as they affect our interpretation of earlier ones. Thus, to take my earlier example, we can also interpret Schubert's last song in *Winterreise* more profoundly because of its intertextual relationship with Debussy's "Des pas sur la neige."

12. Crumb quotes Johann Sebastian Bach's harmonization of the melody from Gottfried Heinrich Stölzel's aria "Bist du bei mir," BWV 508, as entered into the 1725 *Notebook for Anna Magdalena Bach*.

13. As I have previously summarized, "Kivy (1984, 124–42) . . . [concludes] that expressiveness may contribute to the success of musical representation, but that not all representations are expressive (although expressive representations appear to be preferred by composers)" (Hatten 1994, 242).

14. Scott Burnham further explores the "juxtaposition of human and machine at the end of the Ninth Symphony" (2009, 75) and the "subhuman" violin subject of the *Grosse Fuge*, op. 133, in which "the first violin mouths a lobotomized version of the theme, gapped, stunted, drained of volition" (83). In Burnham's examples, Beethoven is "testing the limits of subjectivity" or even "forcing . . . the issue of subjectivity by contrasting human and machine, human and subhuman, human and divine" (83).

15. For more extensive discussion of these issues, see the essays in *The Rite of Spring at 100* (Neff, Carr, and Horlacher 2017).

16. By my use of the term "estrangement" I echo the Russian Formalists' original concept of *priem ostranenie* (making strange) and its adaptation by Bertolt Brecht as the *Verfremdungseffect*, part of his innovative approach to what he called epic and didactic theater, in which the audience is prevented from closely identifying with characters or assuming a familiar worldview (see Shklovsky 1916; Brecht 1964). Brecht hoped in this way to provoke his audience to engage with deeper ideological issues. For an instructive account of Brecht's political reconstrual of the concept from its earlier theorization by Victor Shklovsky (1916), see Jameson 1972, 58.

17. The discussion of Stravinsky's techniques in this section is drawn from Robert S. Hatten, "Teaching Stravinsky from the Wennerstrom *Anthology*," *Indiana Theory Review* 33, no. 1–2 (2017): 68–75.

18. For more on this compositional process as revealed in the sketches, see Carr 2014 and Horlacher 2011. The first to theorize this process was Edward T. Cone (1962).

19. With *Histoire du soldat* (Soldier's tale; 1918) the same techniques are employed in a pitch environment that ranges from pandiatonic to heterophonic dissonance, and distortions feature a more sardonically tinged parody, as appropriate for an ironic allegory. The plot is sketched in disjunctive tableaus, and the work ends without tonal closure. But dramatic closure is nevertheless achieved: the percussion, associated with the Devil, has the last word.

20. Obvious actoriality in these works is sustained by actual bodies on stage (whether dancing or reciting), but human characteristics within the virtual actoriality are increasingly objectified and distanced. Stravinsky rings changes on these techniques throughout his neoclassical period, guiding the listener's inferences through the use of familiar musical material from earlier styles, where the reference to tonality may be implicit rather than explicit.

21. The analysis of Schoenberg's Op. 11, no. 1, in this section is drawn from Robert S. Hatten, "Reconceiving Analysis," in *International Journal of Musicology*, vol. 2, ed. Elliott Antokoletz and Michael von Albrecht (Frankfurt: Peter Lang), 237–52. Copyright 2016 by Peter Lang Verlag. Used by permission.

22. Gary Wittlich (1975, 460–68) attempts to demonstrate the systematic use of hexachordal sets as a precursor to serialism in Schoenberg's Op. 11, no. 1. Problems in his analysis can to some degree be addressed by more traditional approaches to motivic development.

23. Recall the importance for agential interpretation of a play with traditional phrase structures in the opening themes of Beethoven's Op. 10, no. 2, and Op. 22, as discussed in this book's prelude and chapter 5.

24. The examples in this paragraph are discussed in Almén and Hatten 2013, 72–73.

25. This is a Sanskrit word meaning "truth and obstinacy" and a term for Gandhi's policy of passive political resistance.

26. Arnie Cox (2016, 208–13) has also considered the issue of apparent disembodiment in works such as Stockhausen's *Studie II* that appear to lack analogues

to human movements. Judy Lochhead explains how embodied reactions to radical post-tonal music are nevertheless possible, taking as her example Rihm's *Am Horizont*, for violin, cello, and accordion. As she observes, "the sounds of *Am Horizont* have a palpable affect on my listening body, but they transport me to realms that transform the realities of my bodily existence. The sensations of edge and precipice, of falling, and of cottony softness permeate my bodily awareness in an imaginative place of musical sound. And, in the musical transport to this place, the sensations of the body are transformed—they are unconstrained by the material realities of the world" (2010, 197).

27. Psychological experiments involving mere dots flashing on a computer screen have established human perception of apparent motion from otherwise static images (a brief summary is found in Yantis 2013, 238; for a more extensive review that includes studies of point-light animation, see Blake and Shiffrar 2007). Dots that appear to move can, by their relationships with other dots, imply action and reaction and, despite the absence of other human features, can lead to implications of agency (motivation, will, and even emotion) based on archetypal dramatic schemas. Music, never a language of mere dots on the page, draws on these cognitive capacities to achieve so much more.

28. Consider Krzysztof Penderecki's early sonorism in this respect as well. The systematic oppositions underlying his timbral, textural, and formal innovations have been convincingly reconstructed by Danuta Mirka (1997).

29. *The Devils of Loudon* offers a fascinating example of the topical use of sonorism, imported to convey extreme expressionist states of madness, in this example of the "demented nun" operatic subgenre. Compare, in this sense, the topical use of electronic music in Menotti's *Juana la Loca*.

30. I explore this issue in connection with Hans Werner Henze's opera *We Come to the River* in Hatten 1990.

Postlude

A conclusion suggests completion. By offering a postlude instead, I acknowledge that the task of explaining virtual agency in music is an ongoing one. Some further thoughts may help convey the current state of that ongoing investigation. I begin by considering two complementary perspectives on agency that are foundational for understanding musical expression. Next, I explore some consequences of the theory of virtual agency for analysis and counter any possible confusion with an outdated organicism. I then summarize why listeners may find it advantageous to infer virtual agency in music. Finally, I draw on evidence from prehistorical artifacts that supports the hypothesis of an early cognitive leap to virtualizing and indirectly grounds my claims for a relatively early, emergent capacity to interpret virtual agency in music.

Virtual Agency and Expression

The theory of virtual agency is in accord with the positions of two philosophers of music on the importance of hearing expression *in* the music: (1) by imagining a persona, similar to a character in a novel, who is experiencing those emotions (Robinson 2005); and (2) by simulating actions in a "musical virtual terrain" or a scenario in a "virtual musical space" (Nussbaum 2007, 214 and 23, respectively; see also Robinson 2007).[1] Both Jenefer Robinson and Charles Nussbaum emphasize the imaginative simulation of action based on various expectations and encounters that what I call a virtual agent or actor would experience in the music. As Robinson glosses, "Nussbaum suggests . . . that we do not merely listen to the unfolding musical structure—we move through the virtual musical terrain, encountering obstacles, moving freely and smoothly through open stretches, struggling with conflicting tendencies. . . . And we experience the feelings of these action tendencies" (2013, 160). This is also close to one of two perspectives from which we may experience musical movement, as explained by Mark Johnson and Steve Larson (2003) and further elaborated as virtual agency within a virtual musical environment (Hatten 2004, 2012d).[2]

Robinson also gives due weight to the cognitive appraisal approach to musical emotion, while emphasizing that appraisal can occur unconsciously as well as consciously. She cites the assessment of Klaus Scherer (2001, 370), who notes that "many appraisal theorists, rather than limiting the term to a cortically based propositional calculus, adopt a broader view of cognition and assume that appraisal can occur, in more or less complex forms, at several levels of processing" (quoted in Robinson 2013, 157).[3] Michael Spitzer has further expanded the notion of a persona in ways that are consonant with the theory of virtual agency: as exhibiting human character and personality, intentionality, and even reflection (2013, 19). His book-in-progress on music and emotion will ground this claim for music-stylistic competencies throughout Western music history.

To these perspectives on the persona I add an encompassing framework for conceiving of the various levels at which we may interact with virtual agency in the music: from the perception of gestures as events and their interpretation as actions in a virtual environment to their merger into the behavior of a virtual agent with humanlike qualities who may take on an actorial role in a fictional drama and, ultimately, to the folding of actorial roles into a larger subjectivity as interactive streams of "feelingful thought." As virtual agents and actors are internalized into virtual subjectivity, they both simulate consciousness and stimulate further engagement with emotions and meanings as a listener negotiates the virtual with both his past experiences and his present growth.

Some Consequences of a Theory of Virtual Agency for Analysis and Interpretation

All composed notes are presumably intentional outcomes of composers' agencies, but not all composed notes are equivalent in their projection of virtual agency. Tonal styles create typical settings (in both senses: set places or environments, and the dialed-up settings of sound variables) ranging from the virtual environments of tonality and meter to the standard harmonic progressions and phrase structures (or schemata) basic to the Classical style. These settings may be unmarked agentially and hence can function as backgrounds—places and events against which more marked musical events (creative, rhetorical, etc.) can stand out as more virtually agential.

The pastoral mode would appear to be unmarked in this sense—that is, if the pastoral were simply equated with naturalness. But the pastoral mode is also marked by features that support affective meaning—pedal points, slow harmonic rhythm, and parallel thirds and sixths. Far beyond suggesting the emotional equilibrium of contentment, pastoral simplicity may imply a state of innocence that may trigger powerful emotions, such as nostalgia for the loss of that innocent state.[4] Despite these marked expressive aspects of the pastoral mode, however, it may also be understood as providing a larger unmarked environment relative to various marked (dramatic) events that may occur within. While the pastoral may serve as background in this sense, it is never neutral: it places a certain mood or emotional framework over those events that may occur within its bounds and constrains the kind of expressive trajectories that one is likely to encounter. Furthermore, it is possible to infer agency in the dynamic contours of a pastoral introduction (as noted with the Chopin Ballade in chap. 9) and to personify various aspects of Nature (as discussed in chap. 10), even when those aspects suggest "being" rather than "becoming."

Formal functions in the Classical style, when manifested in prototypical structures (e.g., sentences or periods) and forms (e.g., sonatas or sonata-rondos), may also create virtual backgrounds against which more salient events can be interpreted as actorially agential. I explore this possibility in chapter 5 with the first-movement opening themes of Beethoven's Piano Sonatas, op. 10, no. 2, and op. 22. There, we see that typical sentence openings are left behind by continuations or interpolations that suggest virtual agential freedom in their (willful) transcending of implied structures. All kinds of expansions, compressions, and interpolations may imply agential (and hence subjective) freedom, whether expressed as actions or reactions—as outward expressions or inward ruminations. As we have seen with topics, formal functions in themselves have marked features: the continuation phase of a sentence is marked by developmental strategies (fragmentation, sequence, compression, or acceleration) that already suggest agency by way of thematically unique instantiations of an unaltered prototype. Indeed, the (varied) repetition of a basic idea in a presentation phase is already strategically marked by thematization (as achieved through foregrounding and use).[5] Immediate reiteration serves to foreground by clearly defining the length of an idea. Use of an idea is built into the schema of the sentence as repetition, sequence, or statement and response.[6] Less prototypical developing variational strategies may then cut across the lines of formal functional sections without undermining them, promoting a complementary level of thematic continuity.[7] The resulting thematic discourse supports the formal/structural discourse embedded in prototypical phrase structures and forms. Like those contrapuntal lines we saw merging into a continuous *melos* (a thickened stream of musical attending that features complementary intervallic scaffolding and shared thematic content), developing variation may be understood as merging with formal structuring to create an ongoing formal discourse. These two interactive strands can be further braided into the complex cable of musical time as an ongoing experience of significant events.

The advantage of virtualizing a singular agent or self-conscious subjectivity is that all these multiple forms of structural organization can be synthesized into a coherent experience that focuses significant expressive meaning through a humanlike agency. That ultimately coherent subjectivity comprises actions, reactions, and their attendant emotions (or "feelingful thoughts") as negotiated with the situational grounding we provide through our engagement with the music.

A New Organicism?

The emphasis on interpreting music through its humanlike agencies (and further integrating musical events into coherent parts of a functioning virtual organism) may suggest to some readers a return to organicism. According to an organicist ideology, musical works that display organic unity—as analytically demonstrated by motivic connectedness and (later) by the kind of voice-leading hierarchies demonstrated by Schenker—were claimed to be superior artistically to those works based on alternative aesthetics and styles.[8] The theory of virtual agency does not entail such judgments (at least not overtly). Rather, the theory provides a framework for assessing the degree to which any given work can stage, or be interpreted as staging, various levels of virtual agency. Nor does the theory propose organic unity as an ideal. Instead, it provides a lens through which we can interpret those strategies that composers might use to create integrated agents and actors who engage in a coherent discourse or drama, which might then be interiorized in terms of a singular subjectivity.

Disruptions—deliberate ruptures and discontinuities that might prove problematic for an organicist account—are thus interpreted more positively as cueing the virtual freedom of an agent or subjectivity for which conventional structures could serve as foils. Nevertheless, a defining feature of the Classical style—and a classical principle for many Romantics and moderns—is that of compensating for such rhetorical swerves by some overarching or integrative strategy that can resolve tonal departures, reconcile thematic conflicts, or at least acknowledge in dramatic summation the incompatibility of a conflict.[9] Thus, the theory of virtual agency need not shy away from explaining coherence, since there are many alternatives to the narrow conception of organic unity that was the focus of earlier critiques. Indeed, many of those alternatives recognize innovations in styles outside the German tradition associated with nineteenth- and twentieth-century organicism.

By replacing the organic metaphor with coherent human intentionality, the theory recognizes that many composers have explored not only the (presumably organic) embodiment of energetic gestures but the often complex (yet still humanly conceived) "enmindment" of interiorizing reflections. Both organicism and structuralism (its more scientific cousin) arose from observations that mattered artistically to composers, theorists, and philosophers of music. E. T. A. Hoffmann's merging of expressive and structural insights offers an early model of the attempt to reconcile form and feeling—ultimately, to ground feeling in form and to explain the expressive significance of intentionally organized sound. I would like to proceed in that spirit, acknowledging analogues of virtual subjectivity and even actoriality in the sound masses of Krzysztof Penderecki or György Ligeti while also acknowledging that composers who consciously undermine the cognitive conditions for hearing virtual agency may be pursuing equally interesting and artistically engaging but clearly alternative means of organizing sound and meaning.

Advantages of Interpreting Virtual Agency

To summarize, why do at least some listeners find it so compelling to identify with virtual agencies that are inferred from musical events?

1. Inferring agency helps us follow the discourse of a musical work, making it coherent from the standpoint of dramatic trajectories involving agents as actors. We can allegorize gestures, topics, and themes in ways that help motivate their developing variation throughout the work. From this

perspective, agency might be viewed as a metaphor for the various musical processes whose logical relationships we are most interested in, or a heuristic for helping us remember and relate significant musical materials and processes.

2. The inference of virtual agencies helps make a musical discourse relevant to our own lives. At this level, we can identify with virtual musical agents to the extent that they
   a. simulate, and stimulate, emotional and psychological development,
   b. enact the achievement of moral or spiritual states through analogues with human life and ongoing human experience in the world, and
   c. reflect the multileveled and complex operations of thought and feeling as embraced by a larger, virtual subjectivity that we can own or imagine as our own.

3. Hearing virtual agents as fictional actors in music allows us to experience and learn from a full range of human emotions without risking our bodies (or minds) when we virtually embody ("enmind") states that might have more negative consequences were they the result of actual events in our lives. We can thus "practice" and "simulate" profound and psychically intense experiences.

4. Hearing virtual agency also has a pleasurable spinoff: it allows us danger-free access to virtual physical states (i.e., vertiginous waltzes, flying), and it offers pleasurable intellectual enjoyment (as in following and successfully understanding a complex and challenging work) as well as presenting even simpler forms of entertainment.

5. Finally, hearing virtual agency recognizes historically plausible compositional means of hearing and staging emotions and thoughts in music as virtually expressed or enacted rather than merely represented.

Hearing Virtual Agency as Emergent from Sound and Structure

A virtual conception and understanding of music thus moves us beyond sound to virtual realms of intertwined thought and feeling, enlarging our own subjectivity. My theory of virtual agency presupposes three fundamental modes of emergence.

First, music is emergent from physical sound. We can hear virtually, as Beethoven was able to do despite his encroaching deafness to actual sound. But this is not simply to say that we can mentally represent sounds and manipulate their relationships (compose, interpret, and perform) within our minds—a skill that many hearing musicians possess to a high degree. We are also able to group sounds into significant, affective gestalts and infer affective gestures with various degrees of (virtual) agential motivations, as outlined in the preceding chapters.

Second, the semiotic interpretation of music through virtual agency emerges from lower-level structural and even expressive signification (one-to-one mappings of association, correlation, representation, and even immediate forms of expression) as it triggers the fullness of our ongoing, symbolic, imaginative life (and its infinite chains of interpretants, to invoke Charles Sanders Peirce).[10] Musical meaning thus models consciousness in its emergence from lower levels of one-to-one and even many-to-many mappings, progressing to the functional coherence of perceptual and gestural meaning, and, ultimately, arriving at a coherent identity directing and evaluating those perceptions as "feelingful thoughts" experienced by a musically nuanced Self.

Third, we can participate subjectively in music's triggering of its symbolic worlds—not only by tracking the paths laid out by a musical work's own trajectories of form and syntax, drama and narrative, but by making them our own, by bringing our own experience to the intertwined merging and emergence of meaning. Thus, a deeper musical understanding surfaces from virtual subjectivity or consciousness that not only models but also stimulates individual listeners' actual subjectivities. We can exceed simple analogical mappings by means of tropological emergence (metaphor, conceptual blending) and a participatory creativity that goes beyond mere communication (at times fulfilling the intent of some composers to foster a shared, spiritual communion). In this way, listening to music's virtual subjectivity enables us to develop, and explore in our own way, music's numinous quality. This engendering of a profound, unspecified, yet powerfully significant experience is characteristic of the symbolic in its metaphysical sense—as a significance that transcends direct paraphrase or translation.

Perhaps it is this spiritual realm that Hoffmann invokes when he speaks of "infinite yearning" in the music of Beethoven ([1810] 1994, 146). We need a way to approach this semiotic reality, if only in metaphorical language. As discussed in chapter 5, Daniel Chua (1999), Mark Evan Bonds (2014), and Michael Steinberg (2004) have each offered historical and theoretical accounts of the emergence of subjectivity in music of the late eighteenth and early nineteenth centuries. However, all three of the modes of emergence I previously outlined could also be claimed for the music of Hildegard of Bingen. Her music emerged from an imagination that virtually conceived of sounds through mental representations within the learned modal frameworks of her earlier instruction, uniquely notated through dictation to her scribe. Her improvised compositions, or composed improvisations, were expressions of a spiritual joy that emerged from elements we can analyze today, miming gestures and virtual expansions of the spirit through its contours and emblematic (symbolic) motives. Hildegard's music not only modeled consciousness in its perceptual and cognitive integration as the expression of a coherent individual but moved beyond consciousness to a deeper level of subjectivity conditioned by her extraordinary spirituality. When these works were sung by the nuns in her abbey, one can imagine a communal mapping of expressive contours and a spiritual communion emerging from their communal ritual; each individual was participating in the transformative spiritual experience both virtualized in and inspired by the music. Thus, from some of the earliest Western music for which we can attribute individual creativity, the conditions for virtual subjectivity were present.[11] And virtual subjectivity may have been experienced directly, without the mediation of actant, agent, and actor as stages.[12]

The Earliest Evidence of Virtualizing by Humans

Gary Tomlinson's *A Million Years of Music: The Emergence of Human Modernity* provides strong evidence for the earliest forms of what I would consider to be human virtualizing, including what he terms the "copresent sociality" and "embodiment" (2015, 289) involved in the miming of actions, even prior to what we might want to consider as conscious intentionality (66–67).[13] Tomlinson offers evidence that these competencies were already present in early hominids, implied by the way they learned to fashion stone tools. He argues that protomusical behavior coevolved alongside protolinguistic communication by building on what I would consider the virtualization of technology—or, in Tomlinson's felicitous phrasing, "the cognitive release from proximity" (287).

This coemergence depended on the close interdependency of the following seven elements of "modernity": "language and symbolism; musicking; the hypertrophied technology nascent already in the Middle Paleolithic period; a transcendental sociality gesturing toward metaphysics; social differentiation; ritual; and institutional structuring" (Tomlinson 2015, 287). For Tomlinson, the pride of place given to *musicking* (Small 1998) comes from its preservation, to a greater extent than language, of human embodiment: "Musicking is a human activity unique in the degree to which it highlights somatic [bodily] experience while structuring it according to complex, abstract, and relatively recent outgrowths of our cognition," which, in turn, "can only be fully understood in deep historical perspective" (Tomlinson 2015, 289). It would trivialize this important insight to specify a particular time or even an era for the emergence of music as we know it, but one can see in Tomlinson's "deep historical perspective" the importance of what I call "virtualizing" as fundamental to human consciousness, including imaginative thinking in sound and the capacity to infer agency in music.

Aspiring to the Virtual

All the evidence presented in this book suggests that music's degrees of virtuality have developed and emerged beyond the immediacies of dynamic embodiment or physiological "moving with" the music's energetic shaping through time, as extensively explored by Arnie Cox (2016).[14] Listeners have moved beyond naïve subjectivity to encompass virtual actantial or human agential identities, interacting actorial roles, and the flow of agential streams into a more dynamically complex human subjectivity. That subjectivity, for which each listener contributes his or her own past experiences and present openness to future growth, is what I consider to be the ultimate goal of musical understanding.

It remains for future scholars to work out all the evidence—historical, theoretical, analytical, and interpretive—for virtual meanings in individual musical styles and compositions throughout Western music history (and to explore how these principles may be helpful for explaining non-Western musical styles). It remains for cognitive and empirical researchers to work out the mechanisms by means of which an integrative (and stylistically competent) body-mind can access various levels of aesthetically warranted meanings. I trust the multiple interpretive perspectives provided by a theory of virtual agency may help these scholars, as well as other musicians and lay listeners, in their shared goal of musical understanding. The best evidence is in the music—in its spurring of our cognitive, imaginative, and empathetic engagements at every level of our awareness.

Notes

1. Nussbaum (2007, 305n1) acknowledges my conception of a virtual environment (Hatten 2004, 103) and Eric Clarke's account of "virtual musical space" (2005, 154).

2. Some of the material from Johnson and Larson 2003 also appears in Johnson 2007, chap. 11 ("Music and the Flow of Meaning"), and Larson 2012, chap. 3 ("Something in the Way She Moves").

3. My doctoral student Bree Guerra is currently working on a dissertation demonstrating how appraisal takes place within an actively simulated and enacted virtual world of the music. This work promises to bridge approaches to virtual agency and emotional appraisal while providing analytical grounding for listeners' understanding and potential experiencing of expressed emotions in music.

4. For more on formal and expressive expectations associated with the pastoral as a mode, see Hatten 2004, 53–67.

5. For this perspective on thematization, see Hatten 1994, 111, and 2004, 123.

6. See Caplin 1998, 37–39, for distinctions among these three possible treatments of a basic idea in the presentation portion of a sentence.

7. The continuity of motivic unfolding draws on the association of motives as much or more than their hierarchy (for the distinction between association and hierarchy, see Lerdahl and Jackendoff 1983, 17, 117). The networklike structure of motives, however, complements the often tighter hierarchical structuring of formal functions as well as the looser hierarchical levels of Schenkerian voice-leading analysis. Peter Smith's concept of "dimensional counterpoint" merges motivic and voice-leading insights (roughly the approaches of Arnold Schoenberg and Heinrich Schenker) into a more coherent account of form (2005, 31–65).

8. However, as Kevin Korsyn (1993) explains, Schenker's early essay, "Der Geist der musikalischen Technik" (The spirit of musical technique; [1895] 1988), presents a decidedly anti-organicist position, "congruent with the psychological approach that he advocates in the same essay" (Korsyn 1993, 116). As Korsyn elaborates, "by prioritizing the listener's perceptions rather than the composition itself, he would have had no motivation to see pieces as autonomous, organic entities" (116). Schenker's psychological explanations (in *Harmony* [(1906) 1954], for example), are based on the principle of association and the expectation of continuation (Korsyn 1993, 117, n87) that were likely influenced by the scientific epistemology of Ernst Mach (109). Schenker's essay, then, was an attempt to reject the Romantic notion of music as "organic" or "alive" with "the unity of a mind or consciousness" (90). Only later, in *Der freie Satz* (Free composition), did Schenker return to a "cryptosubjectivity" (Korsyn 1993, 91) in which music is (itself) a subject: "We perceive our own life-impulse in the motion of the fundamental structure, a full analogy to our inner life" (Schenker [1935] 1979, 9, cited in Korsyn 1993, 91).

9. For the latter, see my analysis and interpretation of the first movement of Beethoven's String Quartet, op. 130 (Hatten 1994, 133–45).

10. Recall the invocation of "numinous symbols" at the end of my interpretation of a theme from Schubert's String Quartet in G Major in chapter 5.

11. See also the introduction and the first part of chapter 5.

12. Again, let me emphasize that I make no claims about any necessary cognitive sequence in those inferences concerning my four levels of agency in music or any necessary developmental sequence in their compositional staging.

13. Indeed, as James N. Bennett notes in an insightful review, Tomlinson argues that the inventory of discrete pitches associated with early hominid instruments "brought with [them] an abstraction, a distancing of the pitches themselves from meaning," such that "music was from the first, in this sense, *absolute*" (Tomlinson 2015, 258–59, cited in Bennett 2016, 275; emphasis in original). I would differ with Tomlinson only by substituting my concepts of "virtual" in place of "abstract," and "distilled" in place of "absolute."

14. Recall the discussion in interlude I.

References

Abbate, Carolyn. 1988. "Erik's Dream and Tannhäuser's Journey." In *Reading Opera*, edited by Arthur Groos and Roger Parker, 129–67. Princeton, NJ: Princeton University Press.

———. 1991. *Unsung Voices: Opera and Musical Narrative in the Nineteenth Century*. Princeton, NJ: Princeton University Press.

———. 2001. *In Search of Opera*. Princeton, NJ: Princeton University Press.

———. 2004. "Music—Drastic or Gnostic?" *Critical Inquiry* 30: 505–36.

Adorno, Theodor W. 1981. *In Search of Wagner*. Translated by Rodney Livingstone. London: Verso.

Agawu, V. Kofi. 1991. *Playing with Signs: A Semiotic Interpretation of Classic Music*. Princeton, NJ: Princeton University Press.

———. 2008. *Music as Discourse: Semiotic Adventures in Romantic Music*. Oxford: Oxford University Press.

Allanbrook, Wye Jamison. 1983. *Rhythmic Gesture in Mozart: Le Nozze di Figaro and Don Giovanni*. Chicago: University of Chicago Press.

———. 1992. "Two Threads through the Labyrinth: Topic and Process in the First Movements of K. 332 and K. 333." In *Convention in Eighteenth- and Nineteenth-Century Music: Essays in Honor of Leonard G. Ratner*, edited by Wye J. Allanbrook, Janet M. Levy, and William P. Mahrt, 125–71. Stuyvesant, NY: Pendragon.

———. 2014. *The Secular Commedia: Comic Mimesis in Late Eighteenth-Century Music*. Edited by Mary Ann Smart and Richard Taruskin. Berkeley: University of California Press.

Almén, Byron. 2008. *A Theory of Musical Narrative*. Bloomington: Indiana University Press.

Almén, Byron, and Robert S. Hatten. 2013. "Narrative Engagement with Twentieth-Century Music: Possibilities and Limits." In *Music and Narrative since 1900*, edited by Michael L. Klein and Nicholas Reyland, 59–85. Bloomington: Indiana University Press.

Annoni, Jean-Marie, G. Devuyst, A. Carota, L. Bruggimann, and J. Bogousslavsky. 2005. "Changes in Artistic Style after Minor Posterior Stroke." *Journal of Neurology, Neurosurgery and Psychiatry* 76 (6): 797–803.

Auerbach, Erich. 1953. *Mimesis: The Representation of Reality in Western Literature*. Princeton, NJ: Princeton University Press.

Austin, J. L. 1962. *How to Do Things with Words*. Cambridge, MA: Harvard University Press.

Auyang, Sunny Y. 2000. *Mind in Everyday Life and Cognitive Science*. Cambridge, MA: MIT Press.

Avatar. 2009. Directed by James Cameron. Century City, CA: Twentieth Century Fox.

Bach, Carl Philipp Emanuel. (1762) 1949. *Essay on the True Art of Playing Keyboard Instruments*. Translated and edited by William J. Mitchell. New York: Norton.

BaileyShea, Matthew L. 2012. "Musical Forces and Interpretation: Some Thoughts on a Measure in Mahler." *Music Theory Online* 18 (3). http://www.mtosmt.org/issues /mto.12.18.3/mto.12.18.3.baileyshea.html.

Bakhtin, M. M. (1935) 1981. *The Dialogic Imagination: Four Essays by M. M. Bakhtin.* Edited by Michael Holquist. Translated by Caryl Emerson. Austin: University of Texas Press.

Balter, Tamara. 2009. "A Theory of Irony in Music: Types of Irony in the String Quartets of Haydn and Beethoven." PhD diss., Indiana University, Bloomington.

Baragwanath, Nicholas. 2005. "Musicology and Critical Theory: The Case of Wagner, Adorno, and Horkheimer." *Music and Letters* 87 (1): 52–71.

Batteux, Charles. 1746. *Les beaux arts réduits à un même principe* [The fine arts reduced to a single principle]. Paris: Durand.

Becker, Judith. 2001. "Anthropological Perspectives on Music and Emotion." In *Music and Emotion: Theory and Research*, edited by Patrik N. Juslin and John A. Sloboda, 135–60. Oxford: Oxford University Press.

Bennett, James N. 2016. "Review: *A Million Years of Music: The Emergence of Human Modernity*, by Gary Tomlinson." *Music Theory Spectrum* 38 (2): 274–78.

Benson, Bruce Ellis. 2003. *The Improvisation of Musical Dialogue: A Phenomenology of Music.* Cambridge: Cambridge University Press.

Bent, Ian. 1994. *Music Analysis in the Nineteenth Century.* Vol. 2, *Hermeneutic Approaches.* Cambridge: Cambridge University Press.

———. 2002. "Steps to Parnassus: Contrapuntal Theory in 1725 Precursors and Successors." In *The Cambridge History of Western Music Theory*, edited by Thomas Christensen, 554–602. Cambridge: Cambridge University Press.

Bergson, Henri. (1889) 1910. *Time and Free Will: An Essay on the Immediate Data of Consciousness.* Translated by F. L. Pogson. New York: Macmillan.

Bharucha, Jamshed J. 1984. "Event Hierarchies, Tonal Hierarchies, and Assimilation." *Journal of Experimental Psychology* 113 (3): 421–25.

Blake, Randolph, and Maggie Shiffrar. 2007. "Perception of Human Motion." *Annual Review of Psychology* 58: 47–73.

Boethius. (524) 2008. *The Consolation of Philosophy.* Translated by David R. Slavitt. Cambridge, MA: Harvard University Press.

Boisjoli, Eloise. 2018. "Haydn's Aesthetics of Sensibility: Interpretations of Sentimental Figures, Topics, Mode, and Affect in the String Quartet Slow Movements." Ph.D. diss., University of Texas, Austin.

Bonds, Mark Evan. 2014. *Absolute Music: The History of an Idea.* New York: Oxford University Press.

Bourdieu, Pierre. 1977. *Outline of a Theory of Practice.* Translated by Richard Nice. Cambridge: Cambridge University Press.

Bower, Calvin M. 2002. "The Transmission of Ancient Music Theory into the Middle Ages." In *The Cambridge History of Western Music Theory*, edited by Thomas Christensen, 136–67. Cambridge: Cambridge University Press.

Bowie, Andrew. 2003. *Aesthetics and Subjectivity: From Kant to Nietzsche.* 2nd ed. Manchester: Manchester University Press.

Brecht, Bertolt. 1964. *Brecht on Theatre: The Development of an Aesthetic.* Translated and edited by John Willett. New York: Hill and Wang.

Bribitzer-Stull, Matthew. 2015. *Understanding the Leitmotif: From Wagner to Hollywood Film Music.* Cambridge: Cambridge University Press.

Brown, A. Peter. 1983. "Brahms's Third Symphony and the New German School." *Journal of Musicology* 2 (4): 434–52.

Brown, Lesley, ed. 1993. *New Shorter Oxford English Dictionary*. Oxford, UK: Clarendon.

Budd, Malcolm. 2011. "Music's Arousal of Emotions." In *The Routledge Companion to Philosophy and Music*, edited by Theodore Gracyk and Andrew Kania, 233–42. London: Routledge.

Burney, Charles. 1773. *The Present State of Music in Germany, the Netherlands and United Provinces*. London: T. Becket, J. Robson, G. Robinson.

Burnham, Scott. 1995. *Beethoven Hero*. Princeton, NJ: Princeton University Press.

———. 2005. "Landscape as Music, Landscape as Truth: Schubert and the Burden of Repetition." *19th-Century Music* 29 (1): 31–41.

———. 2009. "Intimacy and Impersonality in Late Beethoven: Contrast and the Staging of Subjectivity." In *New Paths: Aspects of Music Theory and Aesthetics in the Age of Romanticism*, edited by Darla Crispin, 69–84. Leuven, Belgium: Leuven University Press.

———. 2013. *Mozart's Grace*. Princeton, NJ: Princeton University Press.

Byrne Bodley, Lorraine. Forthcoming. *Schubert: A Musical Wayfarer*. New Haven, CT: Yale University Press.

Byros, Vasili. 2012. "Meyer's Anvil: Revisiting the Schema Concept." *Music Analysis* 31 (3): 273–346.

———. 2014. "Topics and Harmonic Schemata: A Case from Beethoven." In *The Oxford Handbook of Topic Theory*, edited by Danuta Mirka, 381–414. Oxford: Oxford University Press.

Calcagno, Mauro. 2012. *From Madrigal to Opera: Monteverdi's Staging of the Self*. Berkeley: University of California Press.

Cambini, Giuseppe Maria. (c. 1803) 1972. *Nouvelle méthode théorique et pratique pour le violon* [New theoretical and practical method for the violin]. Facsimile reprint, Geneva: Minkoff.

Caplin, William E. 1998. *Classical Form: A Theory of Formal Functions for the Instrumental Music of Haydn, Mozart, and Beethoven*. New York: Oxford University Press.

———. 2009. "What Are Formal Functions?" In *Musical Form, Forms, Formenlehre: Three Methodological Reflections*, edited by Pieter Bergé, 21–40. Leuven, Belgium: Leuven University Press.

Carlson, Licia. 2016. "Music, Intellectual Disability, and Human Flourishing." In *The Oxford Handbook of Music and Disability Studies*, edited by Blake Howe, Stephanie Jensen-Moulton, Neil Lerner, and Joseph Straus, 37–53. New York: Oxford University Press.

Carr, Maureen. 2014. *After the Rite: Stravinsky's Path to Neoclassicism (1914–1925)*. Oxford: Oxford University Press.

Chafe, Eric Thomas. 1991. *Tonal Allegory in the Vocal Music of J. S. Bach*. Berkeley: University of California Press.

Chatwin, Bruce. 1988. *The Songlines*. London: Penguin.

Christensen, Thomas. 1993. "Music Theory and Its Histories." In *Music Theory and the Exploration of the Past*, edited by Christopher Hatch and David W. Bernstein, 9–39. Chicago: University of Chicago Press.

Chua, Daniel K. L. 1999. *Absolute Music and the Construction of Meaning*. Cambridge: Cambridge University Press.

———. 2017. *Beethoven and Freedom*. Oxford: Oxford University Press.

Clarke, Eric. 2005. *Ways of Listening: An Ecological Approach to the Perception of Musical Meaning*. Oxford: Oxford University Press.

Clarke, Eric, and Nicholas Cook, eds. 2004. *Empirical Musicology: Aims, Methods, Prospects*. Oxford: Oxford University Press.

Clater, Michelle. 2009. "Interposed between God and Man: Agency in the Requiems of Berlioz and Fauré." PhD diss., Indiana University, Bloomington.

Clynes, Manfred. 1977. *Sentics: The Touch of Emotions*. New York: Anchor.

Colapietro, Vincent. 1989. *Peirce's Approach to the Self: A Semiotic Perspective on Human Subjectivity*. Albany: State University of New York Press.

Cone, Edward T. 1962. "Stravinsky: The Progress of a Method." *Perspectives of New Music* 1 (1): 18–26.

———. 1968. *Musical Form and Musical Performance*. New York: Norton.

———. 1974. *The Composer's Voice*. Berkeley: University of California Press.

Cook, Nicholas. 1999. "Analyzing Performance and Performing Analysis." In *Rethinking Music*, edited by Nicholas Cook and Mark Everist, 239–61. New York: Oxford University Press.

———. 2003. "Music as Performance." In *The Cultural Study of Music: A Critical Introduction*, edited by Martin Clayton, Trevor Herbert, and Richard Middleton, 204–14. New York: Routledge.

———. 2005. "Prompting Performance: Text, Script, and Meaning in Bryn Harrison's *être-temps*." *Music Theory Online* 11 (1). http://www.mtosmt.org/issues/mto.05.11.1 /mto.05.11.1.cook_frames.html.

———. 2007. *The Schenker Project: Culture, Race, and Music Theory in Fin-de-siècle Vienna*. Oxford: Oxford University Press.

Cope, David. 2001. *Virtual Music: Computer Synthesis of Musical Style*. Cambridge, MA: MIT Press.

Cottrell, Stephen. 2012. "Musical Performance in the Twentieth Century and Beyond: An Overview." In *The Cambridge History of Musical Performance*, edited by Colin Lawson and Robin Stowell, 725–51. Cambridge: Cambridge University Press.

Cox, Arnie. 2001. "The Mimetic Hypothesis and Embodied Musical Meaning." *Musicae Scientiae* 5 (2): 195–209.

———. 2006. "Hearing, Feeling, Grasping Gestures." In *Music and Gesture*, edited by Anthony Gritten and Elaine King, 45–60. Aldershot, UK: Ashgate.

———. 2011. "Embodying Music: Principles of the Mimetic Hypothesis." *Music Theory Online* 17 (2). http://www.mtosmt.org/issues/mto.11.17.2/mto.11.17.2.cox.html.

———. 2016. *Music and Embodied Cognition: Listening Moving, Feeling, and Thinking*. Bloomington: Indiana University Press.

Cumming, Naomi. 2000. *The Sonic Self: Musical Subjectivity and Signification*. Bloomington: Indiana University Press.

Czerny, Carl. (1839) 1970. *On the Proper Performance of All Beethoven's Works for the Piano*. Edited by Paul Badura-Skoda. Vienna: Universal Edition.

Daverio, John. 1997. *Robert Schumann: Herald of a "New Poetic Age."* New York: Oxford University Press.

Davies, Stephen. 1991. "The Ontology of Musical Works and the Authenticity of Their Performances." *Noûs* 25: 21–41.

———. 1997. "Contra the Hypothetical Persona in Music." In *Emotion and the Arts*, edited by Mette Hjort and Sue Laver, 95–109. Oxford: Oxford University Press.

Davis, Andrew. 2017. *Sonata Fragments: Romantic Narratives in Chopin, Schumann, and Brahms*. Bloomington: Indiana University Press.

Deleuze, Gilles. (1966) 1988. *Bergsonism*. Translated by Hugh Tomlinson and Barbara Habberjam. New York: Zone.

———. (1972) 1994. *Difference and Repetition*. Translated by Paul Patton. New York: Columbia University Press.

Delsarte, François. 1884. *The Art of Oratory, System of Delsarte, from the French of M. l'abbé Delaumosne, and Mme. Angelique Arnaud (Pupils of Delsarte): With an Essay on the Attributes of Reason*. 2nd ed. Translated by Frances A. Shaw. Albany, NY: E. S. Werner.

Dickensheets, Janice. 2003. "Nineteenth-Century Topical Analysis: A Lexicon of Romantic *Topoi*." *Pendragon Review* 2 (1): 5–19.

Downham, Clay. 2016. "Virtual Incarnation in Schumann's Carnaval: A Case Study of Tropologically Emergent Avatars and Romantic Irony." In *Virtual Identities: Semiotics 2015*, edited by Jamin Pelkey and Stéphanie Walsh Matthews, 11–24. Charlottesville, VA: Philosophy Documentation Center.

Dreyfus, Laurence. 1996. *Bach and the Patterns of Invention*. Cambridge, MA: Harvard University Press.

Drott, Eric. 2001. "Agency and Impersonality in the Music of Gyorgy Ligeti." PhD diss., Yale University, New Haven, CT.

———. 2011. "Lines, Masses, Micropolyphony: Ligeti's Kyrie and the 'Crisis of the Figure.'" *Perspectives of New Music* 49 (1): 4–46.

Dunkirk. 2017. Directed by Christopher Nolan. Burbank, CA: Warner Bros.

Echard, William. 2005. *Neil Young and the Poetics of Energy*. Bloomington: Indiana University Press.

———. 2017. *Psychedelic Popular Music: A History through Musical Topic Theory*. Bloomington: Indiana University Press.

Emerson, Caryl. 1989. "Back to the Future: Shostakovich's Revision of Leskov's *Lady Macbeth of Mtsensk District*." *Cambridge Opera Journal* 1 (1): 59–78.

Esposito, Joseph L. 2017. "Virtuality." *Digital Encyclopedia of Charles S. Peirce*. Accessed June 28. http://www.digitalpeirce.fee.unicamp.br/p-virtuality.htm.

Fassler, Margot. 1998. "Melodious Singing and the Freshness of Remorse." In *Voice of the Living Light: Hildegard of Bingen and Her World*, edited by Barbara Newman, 149–75. Berkeley: University of California Press.

Fay, Laurel E. 2000. *Shostakovich: A Life*. Oxford: Oxford University Press.

Floros, Constantin. 1980. *Brahms und Bruckner: Studien zur musikalischen Exegetik* [Brahms and Bruckner: Studies in musical exegetics]. Wiesbaden, Germany: Breitkopf and Härtel.

Forkel, Johann Nikolaus. [1780?] *Commentar über die 1777 gedruckte Abhandlung "Über die Theorie der Musik, insofern sie Liebhabern und Kennem nothwendig und nützlich ist," zum Gebrauch akademischer Vorlesungen entworfen von Johann Nic. Forkel* [Commentary on the treatise printed in 1777, "On the Theory of Music, insofar as it is necessary and useful to lovers and connoisseurs," for use in academic lectures designed by Johann Nic. Forkel]. Manuscript, Carl von Ossietzky State and University Library, Hamburg, Germany.

Forte, Allen. 1973. *The Structure of Atonal Music*. New Haven, CT: Yale University Press.

Foucault, Michel. 1997–1999. *Essential Works of Foucault, 1954–1984*. Edited by Paul Rabinow. 3 vols. New York: New Press.

Frisch, Walter. 1984. *Brahms and the Principle of Developing Variation*. Berkeley: University of California Press.

Frye, Northrop. 1957. *Anatomy of Criticism: Four Essays*. Princeton, NJ: Princeton University Press.

Gebuhr, Ann K. 2012. *Hildegard!* Friendswood, TX: TotalRecall.

Gerg, Ian. 2015. "The Virtual Observing Agent in Music: A Theory of Agential Perspective as Implied by Indexical Gesture." PhD diss., University of Texas, Austin.

Gilman, Richard. 1995. *Chekhov's Plays: An Opening into Eternity*. New Haven, CT: Yale University Press.

Gjerdingen, Robert O. 2007. *Music in the Galant Style*. Oxford: Oxford University Press.

Goehr, Lydia. 1992. *The Imaginary Museum of Musical Works: An Essay in the Philosophy of Music*. Oxford: Oxford University Press.

———. 2008. *Elective Affinities: Musical Essays on the History of Aesthetic Theory*. New York: Columbia University Press.

Gombrich, Ernst. 1960. *Art and Illusion: A Study in the Psychology of Pictorial Representation*. London: Phaidon.

Goodman, Nelson. 1968. *Languages of Art: An Approach to a Theory of Symbols*. Indianapolis: Bobbs-Merrill.

———. 1975. "The Status of Style." *Critical Inquiry* 1: 799–811.

———. 1978. *Ways of Worldmaking*. Indianapolis, IN: Hackett.

Gordon-Seifert, Catherine. 2011. *Music and the Language of Love: Seventeenth-Century French Airs*. Bloomington: Indiana University Press.

Grabócz, Márta. 1996. *Morphologie des oeuvres pour piano de Liszt: Influence du programme sur l'évolution des forms instrumentals* [Morphology of the piano works of Liszt: The influence of programs on the evolution of instrumental forms]. Paris: Éditions Kimé.

———. 2008. "Classical Narratology and Narrative Analysis in Music." In *A Sounding of Signs: Modalities and Moments in Music, Culture, and Philosophy*, edited by Robert S. Hatten, Pirjo Kukkonen, Richard Littlefield, Harri Veivo, and Irma Vierimaa, 19–42. Imatra: International Semiotics Institute; Semiotic Society of Finland.

———. 2009. *Musique, narrativité, signification* [Music, narrativity, signification]. Paris: L'Harmattan.

Gracyk, Theodore, and Andrew Kania, eds. 2011. *The Routledge Companion to Philosophy and Music*. London: Routledge.

Grave, Floyd. 2001. "Concerto Style in Haydn's String Quartets." *Journal of Musicology* 18: 76–97.

Graybill, Roger. 2011. "Whose Gestures? Chamber Music and the Construction of Permanent Agents." In *New Perspectives on Music and Gesture*, edited by Anthony Gritten and Elaine King, 221–41. Farnham, UK: Ashgate.

Gregory the Great. (591) 1979–1985. *Moralia in Job* [Moral reflections on the Book of Job]. Edited by Marcus Adriaen. 3 vols. Turnhout, Belgium: Brepols.

Greimas, Algirdas Julien. (1966) 1983. *Structural Semantics: An Attempt at a Method*. Translated by Daniele McDowell, Ronald Schleifer, and Alan Velie. Lincoln: University of Nebraska Press.

Grey, Thomas. 2011. "Hanslick." In *The Routledge Companion to Philosophy and Music*, edited by Theodore Gracyk and Andrew Kania, 360–70. London: Routledge.

Grimshaw, Mark, ed. 2014. *The Oxford Handbook of Virtuality*. New York: Oxford University Press.

Guck, Marion. 1994. "Analytical Fictions." *Music Theory Spectrum* 16 (2): 217–30.

Gutkind, Lee. 2012. "What Is Creative Nonfiction?" *Creative Nonfiction*. https://www
.creativenonfiction.org/online-reading/what-creative-nonfiction.

Haimo, Ethan. 2006. *Schoenberg's Transformation of Musical Language*. Cambridge:
Cambridge University Press.

Hallam, Richard S. 2009. *Virtual Selves, Real Persons: A Dialogue across Disciplines*. Cambridge: Cambridge University Press.

Hallam, Susan, Ian Cross, and Michael Thaut. 2009. *The Oxford Handbook of Music Psychology*. Oxford: Oxford University Press.

Hamburger, Käte. (1957) 1973. *The Logic of Literature*. Bloomington: Indiana University
Press.

Hanning, Barbara. 1989. "Conversation and Musical Style in the Late Eighteenth-Century
Parisian Salon." *Eighteenth-Century Studies* 22 (4): 512–28.

Hanslick, Eduard. (1854) 1986. *On the Musically Beautiful*. Indianapolis, IN: Hackett.

Hasty, Christopher. 2010. "The Image of Thought and Ideas of Music." In *Sounding the
Virtual: Gilles Deleuze and the Theory and Philosophy of Music*, edited by Brian
Hulse and Nick Nesbitt, 1–22. Farnham, UK: Ashgate.

Hatten, Robert S. 1982. "Toward a Semiotic Model of Style in Music: Epistemological and
Methodological Bases." PhD diss., Indiana University, Bloomington.

———. 1985. "The Place of Intertextuality in Music Studies." *American Journal of Semiotics* 3 (4): 69–82.

———. 1989. "Semiotic Perspectives on Issues in Music Cognition." *In Theory Only* 11 (3):
1–10.

———. 1990. "Pluralism of Theatrical Genre and Musical Style in Henze's *We Come to the
River*." *Perspectives of New Music* 28 (2): 292–311.

———. 1991. "On Narrativity in Music: Expressive Genres and Levels of Discourse in Beethoven." *Indiana Theory Review* 12: 75–98.

———. 1994. *Musical Meaning in Beethoven: Markedness, Correlation, and Interpretation*.
Bloomington: Indiana University Press.

———. 1995. "Metaphor *in* Music." In *Musical Signification: Essays in the Semiotic Theory
and Analysis of Music*, edited by Eero Tarasti, 373–91. Berlin: Mouton de Gruyter.

———. 1997. "Music and Tense." In *Semiotics around the World: Synthesis in Diversity;
Proceedings of the Fifth Congress of the International Association for Semiotic
Studies, Berkeley, 1994*, edited by Irmengard Rauch and Gerald F. Carr, 627–30.
Berlin: Mouton de Gruyter.

———. 1998. "Gestural Troping in Music and Its Consequences for Semiotic Theory." In
*Musical Signification: Between Rhetoric and Pragmatics; Proceedings of the 5th
International Congress on Musical Signification*, edited by Gino Stefani, Eero
Tarasti, and Luca Marconi, 193–99. Bologna: Cooperative Libraria Universita-
ria Editrice Bologna).

———. 1999. "Penderecki's Operas in the Context of Twentieth-Century Opera." In
*Krzysztof Penderecki's Music in the Context of 20th-Century Theatre: Stud-
ies, Essays and Materials*, edited by Teresa Malecka, 15–25. Kraków: Akademia
Muzyczna.

———. 2001. "The Expressive Role of Disjunction: A Semiotic Approach to Form and
Meaning in the Fourth and Fifth Symphonies." In *Perspectives on Anton Bruck-
ner*, edited by Crawford Howie, Paul Hawkshaw, and Timothy Jackson, 145–84.
Aldershot, UK: Ashgate.

———. 2004. *Interpreting Musical Gestures, Topics, and Tropes: Mozart, Beethoven, Schubert*. Bloomington: Indiana University Press.

———. 2006a. "A Theory of Musical Gesture and Its Application to Beethoven and Schubert." In *New Perspectives on Music and Gesture*, edited by Anthony Gritten and Elaine King, 1–23. Farnham, UK: Ashgate.

———. 2006b. "The Troping of Temporality in Music." In *Approaches to Meaning in Music*, edited by Byron Almén and Edward Pearsall, 62–75. Bloomington: Indiana University Press.

———. 2009a. "Interpreting the 'Tempest' through Topics, Gestures, and Agency." In *Beethoven's* Tempest *Sonata: Contexts of Analysis and Performance*, edited by Pieter Bergé, Jeroen D'hoe, and William E. Caplin, 163–80. Leuven, Belgium: Peeters.

———. 2009b. "Opening the Museum Window: Improvisation and Its Inscribed Values in Canonic Works by Schumann and Chopin." In *Contemplating Improvisation in Music: Art, Society, Education*, edited by Gabriel Solis and Bruno Nettl, 281–95. Chicago: University of Illinois Press.

———. 2010a. "Aesthetically Warranted Emotion and Composed Expressive Trajectories in Music." *Music Analysis* 29 (1–3): 83–101.

———. 2010b. "Musical Agency as Implied by Gesture and Emotion: Its Consequences for Listeners' Experiencing of Musical Emotion." In *Semiotics 2009: "The Semiotics of Time,"* edited by Karen Haworth, Jason Hogue, and Leonard Sbrocchi, 162–69. New York: Legas.

———. 2010c. "Performance and Analysis—or *Synthesis*: Theorizing Gesture, Topics, and Tropes in Chopin's F-Minor Ballade." *Indiana Theory Review* 28: 45–66.

———. 2012a. "Constructions of Musical Agency and Musical Narrative." Paper presented at the First International Meeting on Narratology and the Arts, Institut Hongrois de Paris.

———. 2012b. "Enlarging the Musical Discourse: Mozart's Piano Quartet in G Minor, K. 478." In *Mozart's Chamber Music with Keyboard*, edited by Martin Harlow, 182–97. Cambridge: Cambridge University Press.

———. 2012c. "Interpreting the Grotesque in Music." In *Semiotics 2011: The Semiotics of Worldviews*, edited by Karen A. Haworth, Jason Hogue, and Leonard G. Sbrocchi, 419–26. New York: Legas.

———. 2012d. "Musical Forces and Agential Energies: An Expansion of Steve Larson's Model." *Music Theory Online* 18 (3). http://mtosmt.org/issues/mto.12.18.3/mto.12.18.3.hatten.php.

———. 2012e. "On Metaphor and Syntactic Troping in Music." In *Music Semiotics: A Network of Significations: In Honour and Memory of Raymond Monelle*, edited by Esti Sheinberg, 87–103. Aldershot, UK: Ashgate.

———. 2013. "Narrative Agency in Music: Its Consequences for Shostakovich's Opera Based on Leskov's *Lady Macbeth of Mtsensk*." Paper presented at Semiotic Society of America, Dayton, Ohio, October 24 and 25.

———. 2014a. "Performing Expressive Closure in Structurally Open Contexts: Chopin's Prelude in A Minor and the Last Two Dances of Schumann's *Davidsbündlertänze*." *Music Theory Online* 20 (4). http://www.mtosmt.org/issues/mto.14.20.4/mto.14.20.4.hatten.html.

———. 2014b. "The Troping of Topics in Mozart's Instrumental Works." In *The Oxford Handbook of Topic Theory*, edited by Danuta Mirka, 514–38. Oxford: Oxford University Press.

———. 2015a. "Commentary: 'Up' within 'Down' (Response to Jonathan Still, 'How Down Is a Downbeat? Feeling Meter and Gravity in Music and Dance')." *Empirical Musicology Review* 10 (2): 138–39.

———. 2015b. "Melodic Forces and Agential Energies: An Integrative Approach to the Analysis and Expressive Interpretation of Tonal Melodies." In *Music, Analysis, Experience: New Perspectives in Musical Semiotics*, edited by Constantino Maeder and Mark Reybrouck, 315–30. Leuven, Belgium: Leuven University Press.

———. 2016a. "Reconceiving Analysis." In *International Journal of Musicology*, vol. 2, edited by Elliott Antokoletz and Michael von Albrecht, 237–52. Frankfurt: Peter Lang.

———. 2016b. "Schubert's Alchemy: Transformative Surfaces, Transfiguring Depths." In *Schubert's Late Music: History, Theory, Style*, edited by Lorraine Byrne Bodley and Julian Horton, 91–110. Cambridge: Cambridge University Press.

———. 2017a. "Review, Edward Klorman, *Mozart's Music of Friends: Social Interplay in the Chamber Works* (Cambridge: Cambridge University Press, 2016)." *Music Theory Spectrum* 39 (2): 261–65.

———. 2017b. "Teaching Stravinsky from the Wennerstrom *Anthology*." *Indiana Theory Review* 33 (1–2): 68–75.

———. 2017c. "Staging Subjectivity as Spiritual Freedom: Beethoven's 'Emergent' Themes." In *Utopian Visions and Visionary Art: Beethoven's Empire of the Mind'—Revisited*, edited by William Kinderman, 75–88. Vienna: Der Apfel.

Hatten, Robert S., and Charls Pearson. 2006. "Aspect in Music." In *Music and the Arts*, edited by Eero Tarasti, 83–91. Imatra: Finnish Network University of Semiotics and International Semiotics Institute; Helsinki: Semiotic Society of Finland.

Hénault, Anne. 1979. *Les enjeux de la sémiotique* [Issues in semiotics]. Paris: Presses universitaires de France.

Hepokoski, James, and Warren Darcy. 2006. *Elements of Sonata Theory: Norms, Types, and Deformations in the Late Eighteenth-Century Sonata*. Oxford: Oxford University Press.

Hoeckner, Berthold. 2002. *Programming the Absolute: Nineteenth-Century German Music and the Hermeneutics of the Moment*. Princeton, NJ: Princeton University Press.

Hoffmann, E. T. A. (1810) 1994. "Review: Beethoven's Symphony No. 5 in C Minor." In *Music Analysis in the Nineteenth Century*, vol. 2, *Hermeneutic Approaches*, edited by Ian Bent, translated by Martin Clarke, 145–60. Cambridge: Cambridge University Press.

———. (1816) 1972. "The Sandman." In *Tales of E. T. A. Hoffmann*, edited by Leonard J. Kent and Elizabeth C. Knight, 93–125. Chicago: University of Chicago Press.

Hoppin, Richard. 1978. *Medieval Music*. New York: Norton.

Horlacher, Gretchen. 2011. *Building Blocks: Repetition and Continuity in the Music of Stravinsky*. New York: Oxford University Press.

Howe, Blake. 2016. "Music and the Agents of Obsession." *Music Theory Spectrum* 38 (2): 218–40.

Howe, Blake, Stephanie Jensen-Moulton, Neil Lerner, and Joseph Straus, eds. 2016. *The Oxford Handbook of Music and Disability Studies*. New York: Oxford University Press.

Humboldt, Wilhelm von. (1836) 1999. *On Language: The Diversity of Human Language-Construction and Its Influence on the Mental Development of the Human Species*. Edited by Michael Losonsky. Translated by Peter Heath. New York: Cambridge University Press.

Huron, David. 2006. *Sweet Anticipation: Music and the Psychology of Expectation*. Cambridge, MA: MIT Press.

Hyland, Anne. 2016. "In Search of Liberated Time, or Schubert's Quartet in G Major, D887: Once More between Sonata and Variation." *Music Theory Spectrum* 38 (1): 85–108.

Ito, John Paul. Forthcoming. *Focal Impulse Theory: Musical Expression, Meter, and the Body.* Bloomington: Indiana University Press.

Jacques-Dalcroze, Émile. 1939. "Eugène Ysaÿe: Quelques notes et souvenirs" [Eugène Ysaÿe: Some notes and reminiscences]. *Revue Musicale* 1939: 188.

James, William. (1902) 1958. *The Varieties of Religious Experience: A Study in Human Nature.* New York: New American Library.

Jameson, Fredric. 1972. *The Prison-House of Language: A Critical Account of Structuralism and Russian Formalism.* Princeton, NJ: Princeton University Press.

Jander, Owen. 1983. "Romantic Form and Content in the Slow Movement of Beethoven's Violin Concerto." *Musical Quarterly* 69 (2): 159–79.

———. 1985. "Beethoven's 'Orpheus in Hades': The 'Andante con moto' of the Fourth Piano Concerto." *19th-Century Music* 8 (3): 195–212.

Jerold, Beverly. 2003. "Fontenelle's Famous Question and Performance Standards of the Day." *College Music Symposium* 43: 150–60.

Johnson, Mark. 2007. *The Meaning of the Body: Aesthetics of Human Understanding.* Chicago: University of Chicago Press.

Johnson, Mark, and Steve Larson. 2003. "'Something in the Way She Moves': Metaphors of Musical Motion." *Metaphor and Symbol* 18 (2): 63–84.

Johnston, Blair. 2014. "*Salome*'s Grotesque Climax and Its Implications." *Music Theory Spectrum* 36 (1): 34–57.

Jones, Evan. 2003. "Dynamics and Dissonance: The Implied Harmonic Theory of J. J. Quantz." Paper presented at Music Theory Midwest, Indiana University, Bloomington, May 17.

Karl, Gregory, and Jenefer Robinson. 1997. "Shostakovich's Tenth Symphony and the Musical Expression of Cognitively Complex Emotions." In *Music and Meaning*, edited by Jenefer Robinson, 154–78. Ithaca, NY: Cornell University Press.

Kendon, Adam. 1981. "Introduction: Current Issues in the Study of Nonverbal Communication." In *Nonverbal Communication, Interaction, and Gesture: Selections from Semiotica*, edited by Adam Kendon, 1–53. The Hague: Mouton.

———. 2004. *Gesture: Visible Action as Utterance.* Cambridge: Cambridge University Press.

Kielian-Gilbert, Marianne. 2010. "Music and the Difference in Becoming." In *Sounding the Virtual: Gilles Deleuze and the Theory and Philosophy of Music*, edited by Brian Hulse and Nick Nesbitt, 199–225. Farnham, UK: Ashgate.

Kinderman, William. 2006. *Mozart's Piano Music.* New York: Oxford University Press.

———. 2013. *Wagner's "Parsifal."* Oxford: Oxford University Press.

Kivy, Peter. 1980. *The Corded Shell: Reflections on Musical Expression.* Princeton, NJ: Princeton University Press.

———. 1984. *Sound and Semblance: Reflections on Musical Representation.* Princeton, NJ: Princeton University Press.

———. 2009. *Antithetical Arts: On the Ancient Quarrel between Literature and Music.* Oxford, UK: Clarendon.

Klein, Michael L. 2004. "Chopin's Fourth Ballade as Musical Narrative." *Music Theory Spectrum* 26: 23–55.

———. 2005. *Intertextuality in Western Art Music.* Bloomington: Indiana University Press.

———. 2015. *Music and the Crises of the Modern Subject.* Bloomington: Indiana University Press.

Klein, Michael L., and Nicholas Reyland, eds. 2013. *Music and Narrative since 1900.* Bloomington: Indiana University Press.

Kleist, Heinrich von. (1810) 1978. "St. Cecilia or the Power of Music (a Legend)." In *The Marquise of O—and Other Stories,* translated by David Luke and Nigel Reeves, 217–30. London: Penguin.

Klorman, Edward. 2013. "Multiple Agency in Mozart's Chamber Music." PhD diss., City University of New York.

———. 2016. *Mozart and the Music of Friends: Social Interplay in the Chamber Works.* Cambridge: Cambridge University Press.

Knowles, Mark. 2009. *The Wicked Waltz and Other Scandalous Dances: Outrage at Couple Dancing in the 19th and Early 20th Centuries.* Jefferson, NC: McFarland.

Kockelman, Paul. 2013. *Agent, Person, Subject, Self: A Theory of Ontology, Interaction, and Infrastructure.* Oxford: Oxford University Press.

Koestler, Arthur. 1969. "Beyond Atomism and Holism: The Concept of the Holon." In *Beyond Reductionism,* edited by Arthur Koestler and J. R. Smythies, 192–232. London: Hutchinson.

Korsyn, Kevin. 1991. "Towards a New Poetics of Musical Influence." *Music Analysis* 10 (1–2): 3–72.

———. 1993. "Schenker's Organicism Reexamined." *Intégral* 7: 82–118.

———. 1996. "Directional Tonality and Intertextuality: Brahms's Quintet op. 88 and Chopin's Ballade op. 38." In *The Second Practice of Nineteenth-Century Tonality,* edited by William Kinderman and Harald Krebs, 45–83. Lincoln: University of Nebraska Press.

———. 2001. "Beyond Privileged Contexts: Intertextuality, Influence, and Dialogue." In *Rethinking Music,* edited by Nicholas Cook and Mark Everist, 55–72. Oxford: Oxford University Press.

Kramer, Lawrence. 1990. *Music as Cultural Practice: 1800–1900.* Berkeley: University of California Press.

———. 1995. *Classical Music and Postmodern Knowledge.* Berkeley: University of California Press.

———. 1998. *Franz Schubert: Sexuality, Subjectivity, Song.* Cambridge: Cambridge University Press.

———. 2002. *Musical Meaning: Toward a Critical History.* Berkeley: University of California Press.

Krebs, Harald. 1999. *Fantasy Pieces: Metrical Dissonance in the Music of Robert Schumann.* New York: Oxford University Press.

Kurth, Ernst. (1913) 1973. *Die Voraussetzungen der theoretischen Harmonik und der tonalen Darstellungssysteme* [The presuppositions of theoretical harmony and tonal schemas]. Munich: Katzbichler.

———. 1931. *Musikpsychologie* [Music psychology]. Berlin: Hesse.

Lakoff, George. 1987. *Women, Fire, and Dangerous Things: What Categories Reveal about the Mind.* Chicago: University of Chicago Press.

Lakoff, George, and Mark Johnson. 1980. *Metaphors We Live By.* Chicago: University of Chicago Press.

———. 1999. *Philosophy in the Flesh: The Embodied Mind and Its Challenge to Western Thought.* New York: HarperCollins.

Larson, Steve. 1994. "Musical Forces, Step Collections, Tonal Pitch Space, and Melodic Expectation." In *Proceedings of the Third International Conference on Music Perception and Cognition*, 227–29. Liège, Belgium: European Society for the Cognitive Sciences of Music.

———. 2012. *Musical Forces: Motion, Metaphor, and Meaning in Music*. Bloomington: Indiana University Press.

Lavacek, Justin. 2011. "Contrapuntal Confrontation and Expressive Signification in the Motets of Machaut." PhD diss., Indiana University, Bloomington.

LeDoux, Joseph. 1996. *The Emotional Brain: The Mysterious Underpinnings of Emotional Life*. New York: Simon and Schuster.

Leech-Wilkinson, Daniel. 2009. "Recordings and Histories of Performance Style." In *The Cambridge Companion to Recorded Music*, edited by Nicholas Cook, Eric Clarke, Daniel Leech-Wilkinson, and John Rink, 246–62. Cambridge: Cambridge University Press.

———. 2013. "The Emotional Power of Musical Performance." In *The Emotional Power of Music: Multidisciplinary Perspectives on Musical Arousal, Expression, and Social Control*, edited by Tom Cochrane, Bernardino Fantini, and Klaus R. Scherer, 41–54. Oxford: Oxford University Press.

Le Guin, Elisabeth. 2006. *Boccherini's Body: An Essay in Carnal Musicology*. Berkeley: University of California Press.

Lenneberg, Hans. 1958. "Johann Mattheson on Affect and Rhetoric in Music (I)." *Journal of Music Theory* 2 (1): 47–84.

Leppert, Richard. 2007. "Music and the Body: Dance Power, Submission." In *Sound Judgment: Selected Essays*, 205–43. Aldershot, UK: Ashgate.

Lerdahl, Fred, and Ray Jackendoff. 1983. *A Generative Theory of Tonal Music*. Cambridge, MA: MIT Press.

Lerer, Seth. 2008. "Introduction." In *Boethius: The Consolation of Philosophy*, translated by David R. Slavitt, xi–xxii. Cambridge, MA: Harvard University Press.

Lerner, Neil, and Joseph N. Straus, eds. 2006. *Sounding Off: Theorizing Disability in Music*. New York: Routledge.

Leskov, Nikolai. (1865) 2003. *Lady Macbeth of Mtsensk: A Sketch*. Translated by Robert Chandler. London: Hesperus.

Levin, Robert. 2003. "Mozart's Solo Keyboard Music." In *18th-Century Keyboard Music*, edited by Robert L. Marshall, 308–49. New York: Routledge.

Levinson, Jerrold. 1990. *Music, Art, and Metaphysics: Essays in Philosophical Aesthetics*. Ithaca, NY: Cornell University Press.

———. 1996. "Musical Expressiveness." In *The Pleasures of Aesthetics*, 90–125. Ithaca, NY: Cornell University Press.

———. 2006. "Musical Expressiveness as Hearability-as-Expression." In *Contemporary Debates in Aesthetics and the Philosophy of Art*, edited by Matthew Kieran, 192–204. Oxford, UK: Blackwell.

Lidov, David. 2005. "Mind and Body in Music." In *Is Language a Music? Writings on Musical Form and Signification*, 145–64. Bloomington: Indiana University Press.

Liszka, James Jakób. 1989. *The Semiotic of Myth: A Critical Study of the Symbol*. Bloomington: Indiana University Press.

Littlefield, Richard C. 1996. "The Silence of the Frames." *Music Theory Online* 2 (1). http://www.mtosmt.org/issues/mto.96.2.1/mto.96.2.1.littlefield.html.

Litzmann, Berthold, ed. 1971. *Letters of Clara Schumann and Johannes Brahms, 1853–1896*. Vol. 2. New York: Vienna House.

Lochhead, Judy. 2010. "Logic of Edge: Wolfgang Rihm's *Am Horizont*." In *Sounding the Virtual: Gilles Deleuze and the Theory and Philosophy of Music*, edited by Brian Hulse and Nick Nesbitt, 181–97. Farnham, UK: Ashgate.

Longyear, Rey. 1970. "Beethoven and Romantic Irony." In *The Creative World of Beethoven*, edited by Paul Henry Lang, 145–62. New York: Norton.

Lowe, Melanie. 2007. *Pleasure and Meaning in the Classical Symphony*. Bloomington: Indiana University Press.

Lowinsky, Edward. 1956. "On Mozart's Rhythm." *Musical Quarterly* 42 (2): 162–86.

Mansfield, Nick. 2000. *Subjectivity: Theories of the Self from Freud to Haraway*. New York: New York University Press.

Marenbon, John. 2013. "Anicius Manlius Severinus Boethius." In *The Stanford Encyclopedia of Philosophy*, Summer 2013 ed., edited by Edward N. Zalta. http://plato.stanford.edu/archives/sum2013/entries/boethius/.

Margulis, Elizabeth Hellmuth. 2014. *On Repeat: How Music Plays the Mind*. New York: Oxford University Press.

Mathiesen, Thomas J. 1999. *Apollo's Lyre: Greek Music and Music Theory in Antiquity and the Middle Ages*. Lincoln: University of Nebraska Press.

Mattheson, Johann. (1739) 1954. *Der vollkommene Capellmeister* [The complete music-master of the chapel]. Kassel, Germany: Bärenreiter.

Maus, Fred. 1989. "Agency in Instrumental Music and Song." *College Music Symposium* 29: 31–43.

———. 1997. "Music as Drama." In *Music and Meaning*, edited by Jenefer Robinson, 105–30. Ithaca, NY: Cornell University Press.

McClary, Susan. 1986. "A Musical Dialectic from the Enlightenment: Mozart's Piano Concerto in G Major, K 453, Movement 2." *Cultural Critique* 4: 129–69.

———. 1987. "The Blasphemy of Talking Politics during a Bach Year." In *Music and Society: The Politics of Composition, Performance, and Reception*, edited by Susan McClary and Richard Leppert, 13–62. Cambridge: Cambridge University Press.

———. 2000. *Conventional Wisdom: The Content of Musical Form*. Berkeley: University of California Press.

———. 2004. *Modal Subjectivities: Self-Fashioning in the Italian Madrigal*. Berkeley: University of California Press.

———. 2012. *Desire and Pleasure in Seventeenth-Century Music*. Berkeley: University of California Press.

McClelland, Clive. 2014. "*Ombra* and *Tempesta*." In *The Oxford Handbook of Topic Theory*, edited by Danuta Mirka, 279–300. Oxford: Oxford University Press.

McDonald, Matthew. 2014. *Breaking Time's Arrow: Experiment and Expression in the Music of Charles Ives*. Bloomington: Indiana University Press.

McKee, Eric. 2012. *Decorum of the Minuet, Delirium of the Waltz: A Study of Dance-Music Relations in 3/4 Time*. Bloomington: Indiana University Press.

———. 2014. "Ballroom Dances of the Late Eighteenth Century." In *The Oxford Handbook of Topic Theory*, edited by Danuta Mirka, 164–93. Oxford: Oxford University Press.

Mead, Andrew. 1999. "Bodily Hearing: Physiological Metaphors and Musical Understanding." *Journal of Music Theory* 43: 1–19.

Meyer, Leonard B. 1956. *Emotion and Meaning in Music*. Chicago: University of Chicago Press.

———. 1973. *Explaining Music: Essays and Explorations*. Berkeley: University of California Press.

———. 1989. *Style and Music.* Philadelphia: University of Pennsylvania Press.

Millán-Zaibert, Elizabeth. 2007. *Friedrich Schlegel and the Emergence of Romantic Philosophy.* Albany: State University of New York Press.

Miller, George A. 1956. "The Magical Number Seven, Plus or Minus Two: Some Limits on Our Capacity for Processing Information." *Psychological Review* 63: 81–97.

Mirka, Danuta. 1997. "The Sonoristic Structuralism of Krzysztof Penderecki." PhD diss., University of Helsinki; Music Academy in Katowice, Poland.

———. 2014. "Introduction." In *The Oxford Handbook of Topic Theory*, edited by Danuta Mirka, 1–57. Oxford: Oxford University Press.

Momigny, Jérôme-Joseph de. 1805. *Cours complet d'harmonie et de composition, d'après une théorie nouvelle et générale de la musique* [Complete course in harmony and composition, according to a new and general theory of music]. Vol. 2. Paris: Momigny.

Monahan, Seth. 2013. "Action and Agency Revisited." *Journal of Music Theory* 57 (2): 321–71.

Monelle, Raymond. 1992. *Linguistics and Semiotics in Music.* Chur, Switzerland: Harwood Academic.

———. 2000. *The Sense of Music: Semiotic Essays.* Princeton, NJ: Princeton University Press.

Moreno, Jairo. 2004. *Musical Representations, Subjects, and Objects: The Construction of Musical Thought in Zarlino, Descartes, Rameau, and Weber.* Bloomington: Indiana University Press.

Mori, Masashiro. (1970) 2012. "The Uncanny Valley." Translated by K. F. MacDorman and N. Kageki. *IEEE Robotics and Automation Magazine* 19 (2): 98–100.

Mott, Joel. 2018. "A New Theory of Symphonism: Agency and Linearity in Prokofiev's War Symphonies." PhD diss., University of Texas, Austin.

Mozart, Wolfgang Amadeus. 1960. *Sonatas and Fantasies for the Piano.* Edited by Nathan Broder. Bryn Mawr, PA: Theodore Presser.

Muxfeldt, Kristina. 2012. *Vanishing Sensibilities: Schubert, Beethoven, Schumann.* Oxford: Oxford University Press.

Narmour, Eugene. 1977. *Beyond Schenkerism: The Need for Alternatives in Music Analysis.* Chicago: University of Chicago Press.

Neal, Lana. 2015. *The Earliest Instrument: Ritual Power and Fertility Magic of the Flute in Upper Paleolithic Culture.* Hillsdale, NY: Pendragon.

Neff, Severine, Maureen Carr, and Gretchen Horlacher, eds. 2017. The Rite of Spring *at 100.* Bloomington: Indiana University Press.

Newcomb, Anthony. 1997. "Action and Agency in Mahler's Ninth Symphony, Second Movement." In *Music and Meaning*, edited by Jenefer Robinson, 131–53. Ithaca, NY: Cornell University Press.

Newman, Barbara. 1985. *Hildegard of Bingen: Visions and Validato.* Cambridge: Cambridge University Press.

Newman, Ernest. (1927) 1970. *The Unconscious Beethoven.* New York: Knopf.

Nussbaum, Charles. 2007. *The Musical Representation: Meaning, Ontology, and Emotion.* Cambridge, MA: MIT Press.

Nussbaum, Martha C. 1986. *The Fragility of Goodness: Luck and Ethics in Greek Tragedy and Philosophy.* Cambridge: Cambridge University Press.

———. 2001. *Upheavals of Thought: The Intelligence of Emotions.* Cambridge: Cambridge University Press.

Oatley, Keith, and Mitra Gholamain. 1997. "Emotions and Identification: Connections between Readers and Fiction." In *Emotion and the Arts*, edited by Mette Hjort and Sue Laver, 263–81. Oxford: Oxford University Press.

Palfy, Cora. 2015. "Musical Agency as Intersubjective Phenomenon," PhD diss., Northwestern University, Evanston, IL.

Parker, Mara. 2002. *The String Quartet, 1750–1797: Four Types of Musical Conversation.* Burlington, VT: Ashgate.

Pearson, Keith Ansell. 2005. "The Reality of the Virtual: Bergson and Deleuze." *MLN* 120 (5): 1112–27.

Peirce, Charles S. 1902. "Virtual." In *Dictionary of Philosophy and Psychology*, vol. 2, edited by James Mark Baldwin, 763–64. London: Macmillan.

Peretz, Isabelle, and Robert J. Zatorre, eds. 2003. *The Cognitive Neuroscience of Music.* Oxford: Oxford University Press.

Peterson, Ellsworth. 2017. "Elgar's Noble Englishness." Lecture at the Georgetown Festival of the Arts XIII, Palace Theater, Georgetown, TX, May 27.

Peterson, John. 2014. "Intentional Actions: A Theory of Musical Agency." PhD diss., Florida State University, Tallahassee.

Pierce, Alexandra. 2007. *Deepening Musical Performance through Movement: The Theory and Practice of Embodied Interpretation.* Bloomington: Indiana University Press.

Plantinga, Leon. 1967. *Schumann as Critic.* New Haven, CT: Yale University Press.

Propp, Vladimir. (1928) 1968. *Morphology of the Folktale.* 2nd ed. Translated by Laurence Scott. Austin: University of Texas Press.

Quantz, Johann Joachim. (1752) 1966. *Essay of a Method for Playing the Transverse Flute.* Translated by Edward R. Reilly. New York: Schirmer.

Randel, Don Michael, ed. 1986. *The New Harvard Dictionary of Music.* Cambridge, MA: Belknap Press of Harvard University Press.

Ratner, Leonard. 1980. *Classic Music: Expression, Form, and Style.* New York: Schirmer.

Reichardt, Jasia. 1978. *Robots: Fact, Fiction, and Prediction.* London: Penguin.

Reichardt, Sarah. 2008. *Composing the Modern Subject: Four String Quartets by Dmitri Shostakovich.* Aldershot, UK: Ashgate.

Ridley, Aaron. 1995. *Music, Value and the Passions.* Ithaca, NY: Cornell University Press.

———. 2007. "*Persona* Sometimes *Grata*: On the Appreciation of Expressive Music." In *Philosophers on Music: Experience, Meaning, and Work*, edited by Kathleen Stock, 130–46. Oxford: Oxford University Press.

Riegl, Aloïs. 1893. *Stilfragen, Grundlegungen zu einer Geschichte der Ornamentik* [Problems of style: Foundations for a history or ornament]. Berlin: Georg Siemens.

Riley, Matthew. 2004. *Musical Listening in the German Enlightenment: Attention, Wonder and Astonishment.* Burlington, VT: Ashgate.

Rings, Stephen. 2012. "The Learned Self: Artifice in Brahms's Late Intermezzi." In *Expressive Intersections in Brahms: Essays in Analysis and Meaning*, edited by Heather Platt and Peter H. Smith, 19–50. Bloomington: Indiana University Press.

Rink, John. 1999. "Translating Musical Meaning: The Nineteenth-Century Performer as Narrator." In *Rethinking Music*, edited by Nicholas Cook and Mark Everist, 217–38. New York: Oxford University Press.

Robertson, Anne Walters. 2007. *Guillaume de Machaut and Reims: Context and Meaning in His Musical Works.* Cambridge: Cambridge University Press.

Robinson, Jenefer. 2005. *Deeper than Reason: Emotion and Its Role in Literature, Music, and Art.* Oxford, UK: Clarendon.

———. 2007. "Expression and Expressiveness in Art." *Postgraduate Journal of Aesthetics* 4 (2): 19–41.

———. 2011. "Expression Theories." In *The Routledge Companion to Philosophy and Music*, edited by Theodore Gracyk and Andrew Kania, 201–11. London: Routledge.

———. 2013. "Three Theories of Emotion—Three Routes for Musical Arousal." In *The Emotional Power of Music: Multidisciplinary Perspectives on Musical Arousal, Expression, and Social Control*, edited by Tom Cocharane, Bernardino Fantini, and Klaus R. Scherer, 155–68. Oxford: Oxford University Press.

Robinson, Jenefer, and Robert S. Hatten. 2012. "Emotions in Music." *Music Theory Spectrum* 34 (2): 71–106.

Rodgers, Stephen. 2009. *Form, Program, and Metaphor in the Music of Berlioz*. Cambridge: Cambridge University Press.

Rosen, Charles. 1972. *The Classical Style: Haydn, Mozart, Beethoven*. New York: Norton.

———. 1995. *The Romantic Generation*. Cambridge, MA: Harvard University Press.

Rosenwein, Barbara H. 2006. *Emotional Communities in the Early Middle Ages*. Ithaca, NY: Cornell University Press.

———. 2016. *Generations of Feeling: A History of Emotions, 600–1700*. Cambridge: Cambridge University Press.

Rothfarb, Lee. 1988. *Ernst Kurth as Theorist and Analyst*. Philadelphia: University of Pennsylvania Press.

———. 2002. "Energetics." In *The Cambridge History of Western Music Theory*, edited by Thomas Christensen, 927–55. Cambridge: Cambridge University Press.

———. 2005. "August Halm on Body and Spirit in Music." *19th-Century Music* 29 (2): 121–41.

Rothstein, William. 1989. *Phrase Rhythm in Tonal Music*. New York: Schirmer.

———. 1995. "Analysis and the Act of Performance." In *The Practice of Performance: Studies in Musical Interpretation*, edited by John Rink, 217–40. Cambridge: Cambridge University Press.

Rousseau, Jean-Jacques. 1768. *Dictionnaire de musique* [Dictionary of music]. Paris: Chez la veuve Duchesne.

Ruby Sparks. 2012. Directed by Jonathan Dayton and Valerie Faris. Century City, CA: Fox Searchlight.

Rumph, Stephen. 2012. *Mozart and Enlightenment Semiotics*. Berkeley: University of California Press.

Rupprecht, Philip. 2013. "Agency Effects in the Instrumental Drama of Musgrave and Birtwistle." In *Music and Narrative since 1900*, edited by Michael L. Klein and Nicholas Reyland, 189–215. Bloomington: Indiana University Press.

Sacks, Oliver. 1992. *Migraine*. Berkeley: University of California Press.

Schenker, Heinrich. (1895) 1988. "The Spirit of Musical Technique." Translated by William A Pastille. *Theoria* 3: 86–104.

———. (1906) 1954. *Harmony*. Edited by Oswald Jonas. Translated by Elisabeth Mann Borgese. Chicago: University of Chicago Press.

———. (c. 1911) 2000. *The Art of Performance*. Edited by Heribert Esser. Translated by Irene Schreier Scott. Oxford: Oxford University Press.

———. (1921–24) 2005. *Tonwille: Pamphlets/Quarterly Publication in Witness of the Immutable Laws of Music*, edited by William Drabkin. 2 vols. Oxford: Oxford University Press.

———. 1930. "Beethovens Dritte Sinfonie zum erstenmal in ihrem wahren Inhalt dargestellt" [Beethoven's Third Symphony presented for the first time in its true content]. In *Das Meisterwerk in der Musik, Jahrbuch III* [The masterwork in music, yearbook III], 10–68. Munich: Drei Masken.

———. (1935) 1979. *Free Composition (Der freie Satz).* Translated by Ernst Oster. New York: Longman.

Scherer, Klaus R. 2001. "The Nature and Study of Appraisal: A Review of the Issues." In *Appraisal Processes in Emotion: Theory, Methods, Research*, edited by Klaus R. Scherer, Angela Schorr, and Tom Johnstone, 369–91. Oxford: Oxford University Press.

———. 2004. "Which Emotions Can Be Induced by Music? What Are the Underlying Mechanisms? And How Can We Measure Them?" *Journal of New Music Research* 33 (3): 239–51.

Schmalfeldt, Janet. 1985. "On the Relation of Analysis to Performance: Beethoven's Bagatelles op. 126, nos. 2 and 5." *Journal of Music Theory* 29: 1–31.

———. 1995. "Form as the Process of Becoming: The Beethoven-Hegelian Tradition and the Tempest Sonata." In *Beethoven Forum 4*, edited by Christopher Reynolds, Lewis Lockwood, and James Webster, 37–71. Lincoln: University of Nebraska Press.

———. 2011. *In the Process of Becoming: Analytic and Philosophical Perspectives on Form in Early Nineteenth-Century Music.* New York: Oxford University Press.

Schmitter, Amy M. 2006. "17th and 18th Century Theories of Emotions." In *The Stanford Encyclopedia of Philosophy*, Winter 2016 ed., edited by Edward N. Zalta. https://plato.stanford.edu/archives/win2016/entries/emotions-17th18th/.

Schoenberg, Arnold. (1947) 1975. "Brahms the Progressive." In *Style and Idea*, edited by Leonard Stein, translated by Leo Black, 398–441. Berkeley: University of California Press.

———. (1934, 1936) 2006. *The Musical Idea and the Logic, Technique, and Art of Its Presentation*, edited and translated by Patricia Carpenter and Severine Neff. Bloomington: Indiana University Press.

Schwarz, David. 1997. *Listening Subjects: Music, Psychoanalysis, Culture.* Durham, NC: Duke University Press.

Scruton, Roger. 1997. *The Aesthetics of Music.* Oxford: Oxford University Press.

Searle, John. 1969. *Speech Acts.* Cambridge: Cambridge University Press.

The Shawshank Redemption. 1994. Directed by Frank Darabont. Los Angeles, CA: Castle Rock.

Sheinberg, Esti. 2000. *Irony, Satire, Parody and the Grotesque in the Music of Shostakovich: A Theory of Musical Incongruities.* Aldershot, UK: Ashgate.

Shields, Rob. 2003. *The Virtual.* London: Routledge.

Shklovsky, Viktor. (1916) 1990. "Art as Device." In *Theory of Prose*, translated by Benjamin Sher, 1–14. Normal, IL: Dalkey Archive Press.

Shostakovich, Dimitri. 1932. "Tragediya—satira" [Tragedy—satire]. *Sovetskoye iskusstvo* [Soviet art], October 16.

———. 1934. "Moyo ponimaniye 'Ledi Makbet'" [My understanding of "Lady Macbeth"]. In *Ledi Makbet Mtsenskogo uyezda: Opera D. D. Shostakovicha* [*Lady Macbeth of Mtsensk*: Opera of D. D. Shostakovich]. Leningrad: Gosudarstvennïy Akademicheskiy Malïy Opernïy Teatr.

Singer, Charles Joseph. (1928) 1958. "The Visions of Hildegard of Bingen." In *From Magic to Science: Essays on the Scientific Twilight*, 199–239. New York: Dover.

Skagestad, Peter. 2017. "Peirce, Virtuality, and Semiotic." *Paideia Project Online.* Accessed June 28. https://www.bu.edu/wcp/Papers/Cogn/CognSkag.htm.

Sloboda, John. 1999. "Musical Performance and Emotion: Issues and Developments." In *Music, Mind, and Science,* edited by Suk Won Yi, 220–38. Seoul: Western Music Research Institute.

Small, Christopher. 1998. *Musicking: The Meanings of Performing and Listening.* Middletown, CT: Wesleyan University Press.

Smith, Barbara H. 1969. *Poetic Closure, or Why Poems End.* Chicago: University of Chicago Press.

Smith, Peter H. 2005. *Expressive Forms in Brahms's Instrumental Music: Structure and Meaning in His "Werther" Quartet.* Bloomington: Indiana University Press.

Spitzer, Michael. 2004. *Metaphor and Musical Thought.* Chicago: University of Chicago Press.

———. 2006. *Music as Philosophy: Adorno and Beethoven's Late Style.* Bloomington: Indiana University Press.

———. 2013. "Sad Flowers: Analyzing Affective Trajectory in Schubert's 'Trockne Blumen.'" In *The Emotional Power of Music: Multidisciplinary Perspectives on Musical Arousal, Expression, and Social Control,* edited by Tom Cochrane, Bernardino Fantini, and Klaus R. Scherer, 7–21. Oxford: Oxford University Press.

Steinberg, Michael P. 2004. *Listening to Reason: Culture, Subjectivity, and Nineteenth-Century Music.* Princeton, NJ: Princeton University Press.

Straus, Joseph N. 2011. *Extraordinary Measures: Disability in Music.* Oxford: Oxford University Press.

Sutcliffe, W. Dean. 2003a. "Haydn, Mozart and Their Contemporaries." In *The Cambridge Companion to the String Quartet,* edited by Robin Stowell, 185–209. Cambridge: Cambridge University Press.

———. 2003b. "The Keyboard Music." In *The Cambridge Companion to Mozart,* edited by Simon P. Keefe, 59–77. Cambridge University Press.

———. 2013. "The Shapes of Sociability in the Instrumental Music of the Later Eighteenth Century." *Journal of the Royal Musical Association* 138 (1): 1–45.

Suurpää, Lauri. 2014. *Death in Winterreise: Musico-Poetic Associations in Schubert's Song Cycle.* Bloomington: Indiana University Press.

Syer, Katherine R. 2009. "From Page to Stage: Wagner as *Regisseur.*" In *Richard Wagner and His World,* edited by Thomas S. Grey, 3–22. Princeton, NJ: Princeton University Press.

———. 2014. *Wagner's Visions: Poetry, Politics, and the Psyche in the Operas through Die Walküre.* Rochester, NY: University of Rochester Press.

Tan, Daphne. 2013. "Ernst Kurth at the Boundary of Music Theory and Psychology." PhD diss., Eastman School of Music, Rochester.

Tarasti, Eero. 1978. *Myth and Music: A Semiotic Approach to the Aesthetics of Myth in Music, Especially That of Wagner, Sibelius, and Stravinsky.* Helsinki: Suomen Musiikkitieteellinen Seura.

———. 1994. *A Theory of Musical Semiotics.* Bloomington: Indiana University Press.

———. 2012. *Semiotics of Classical Music: How Mozart, Brahms and Wagner Talk to Us.* Berlin: De Gruyter.

Taruskin, Richard. 1997. *Defining Russia Musically: Historical and Hermeneutical Essays.* Princeton, NJ: Princeton University Press.

———. 2005. *The Oxford History of Western Music.* Vol. 4, *The Early Twentieth Century.* New York: Oxford University Press.

Temperley, Nicholas. 2009. "Preluding at the Piano." In *Musical Improvisation: Art, Education, and Society*, edited by Gabriel Solis and Bruno Nettl, 323–41. Urbana: University of Illinois Press.

Thompson, Trina. 2018. "The Rhetoric of Suggestion in Debussy's Melodies: Thematicity, Temporality, and Agency." PhD diss., Indiana University, Bloomington.

Thorau, Christian. 2003. *Semantisierte Sinnlichkeit: Studien zu Rezeption und Zeichenstruktur der Leitmotivtechnik Richard Wagners* [Semanticizing the sensuous: Studies in the reception and sign structure of Richard Wagner's leitmotif technique]. Stuttgart: Franz Steiner Verlag.

Thumpston, Rebecca. 2015. "Agency in Twentieth-Century British Cello Music." PhD diss., Keele University, Staffordshire, UK.

Tomlinson, Gary. 1999. *Metaphysical Song: An Essay on Opera*. Princeton, NJ: Princeton University Press.

———. 2015. *A Million Years of Music: The Emergence of Human Modernity*. Cambridge, MA: MIT Press.

Treitler, Leo. 1980. "History, Criticism, and Beethoven's Ninth Symphony." *19th-Century Music* 3 (3): 193–210.

———. 1982. "To Worship That Celestial Sound: Motives for Analysis." *Journal of Musicology* 1 (2): 153–70.

Trivedi, Saam. 2011. "Resemblance Theories." In *The Routledge Companion to Philosophy and Music*, edited by Theodore Gracyk and Andrew Kania, 223–32. London: Routledge.

Tull, James Robert. 1976. "B. V. Asaf'ev's Musical Form as a Process: Translation and Commentary." PhD diss., Ohio State University, Columbus.

Tunbridge, Laura. 2011. "Deserted Chambers of the Mind (Schumann Memories)." In *Rethinking Schumann*, edited by Roe-Min Kok and Laura Tunbridge, 395–410. Oxford: Oxford University Press.

Uno Everett, Yayoi. 2009. "Signification of Parody and the Grotesque in György Ligeti's *Le Grand Macabre*." *Music Theory Spectrum* 31 (1): 26–56.

Vermazen, Bruce. 1986. "Expression as Expression." *Pacific Philosophical Quarterly* 67: 196–224.

Walton, Kendall. 1990. *Mimesis as Make-Believe: On the Foundations of the Representational Arts*. Cambridge, MA: Harvard University Press.

Wheelock, Gretchen. 2003. "The 'Rhetorical Pause' and Metaphors of Conversation in Haydn's Quartets." In *Haydn und das Streichquartett*, vol. 2, edited by Georg Feder and Walter Reicher, 67–88. Tutzing, Germany: Hans Schneider.

Whittall, Arnold. 2013. "Optional Extra? Contextualizing Narrative in the Critical Interpretation of Post-tonal Composition." In *Music and Narrative since 1900*, edited by Michael L. Klein and Nicholas Reyland, 86–100. Bloomington: Indiana University Press.

Wilde, Oscar. (1891) 1968. "The Critic as Artist." In the *Norton Anthology of English Literature*, rev. ed., vol. 2, edited by M. H. Abrams, 1393–1402. New York: Norton.

Wittgenstein, Ludwig. (1933–35) 1960. *The Blue and Brown Books*. New York: Harper and Row.

Wittlich, Gary. 1975. "Sets and Ordering Procedures in Twentieth-Century Music." In *Aspects of Twentieth-Century Music*, edited by Gary Wittlich, 388–476. Englewood Cliffs, NJ: Prentice-Hall.

Wollheim, Richard. 1968. *Art and Its Objects*. New York: Harper and Row.

Wu, Chia-Yi. 2010. "Schubert's String Quartet No. 15 in G Major, D 887: Opera without Words." Paper presented at the American Musicological Society annual conference, Indianapolis, Indiana, November.

Yantis, Stephen. 2013. *Sensation and Perception*. London: Palgrave Macmillan.

Yearsley, David. 2002. *Bach and the Meanings of Counterpoint*. Cambridge: Cambridge University Press.

Zbikowski, Lawrence M. 2002. *Conceptualizing Music: Cognitive Structure, Theory, and Analysis*. Chicago: University of Chicago Press.

———. 2008. "Dance Topoi, Sonic Analogs and Musical Grammar: Communicating with Music in the Eighteenth Century." In *Communication in Eighteenth-Century Music*, edited by Danuta Mirka and Kofi Agawu, 283–309. Cambridge: Cambridge University Press.

———. 2012. "Music, Dance, and Meaning in the Early Nineteenth Century." *Journal of Musicological Research* 31 (2–3): 147–65.

———. 2017. *Foundations of Musical Grammar*. Oxford: Oxford University Press.

Index of Names and Works

Fassler, Margot, 145
Fauré, Gabriel, 38; "Clair de lune," 121–122, 123–126, *124*, *125*; Requiem in D Minor, op. 48, 38
Fay, Laurel, 208
Ficino, Marsilio, 6
Floros, Constantin, 205, 217n9
Fontenelle, Bernard Le Bovier de, 67, 147
Forkel, Johann Nikolaus, 130n38
Forte, Allen, 276
Foucault, Michel, 150, 174n30, 174n33
Frisch, Walter, 192, 281n6
Frye, Northrop, 127n6, 210, 262
Fux, Johann Joseph, 129n29

Gabrieli, Andrea and Giovanni, 146, 257n1
Gandhi, Mahatma, 282n25
Gebuhr, Ann K., 145, 173n16
Gerg, Ian, x, 10, 205, 207, 216, 281n3
Gershwin, George, 33; *Porgy and Bess*, 273
Gilman, Richard, 133
Gjerdingen, Robert O., 138, 200n20, 261
Glass, Philip: *Galileo Galilei*, 278; *Satyagraha*, 278
Gluck, Christoph Willibald: *Iphigénie en Tauride*, 200n28; *Orfeo ed Euridice*, 273
Goehr, Lydia, 195
Goethe, Johann Wolfgang von, 68, 130n38, 147
Gombrich, Ernst, 85
Goodman, Nelson, 134–135, 185
Gordon-Seifert, Catherine, 145
Grabócz, Márta, 12, 23, 215
Grave, Floyd, 82n21
Graybill, Roger, 10, 68
Gregory the Great (Pope Saint Gregory I), 170n2
Greimas, Algirdas Julien, 10, 37–38, 86, 191, 215
Grey, Thomas, 127
Guck, Marion, 10, 46n8, 126n1
Guerra, Bree, x, 291n3
Gutkind, Lee, 46n9

Haeckel, Ernst, 197n7
Haimo, Ethan, 276
Hallam, Richard S., 72
Halm, August, 80–81n12
Hamburger, Käte, 217n5
Hanning, Barbara, 81n15
Hanslick, Eduard, 18, 19, 28n7, 127n5, 195, 273
Hasty, Christopher, 12n1
Hatten, Robert S.: composed fermata for Haydn, Piano Sonata in Ab Major, Hob. XVI/46 (C. Landon 31), ii, 231–232, *232*; composed improvisatory elaboration of return for Mozart, Piano Sonata in A Minor, K. 310, ii, 233–234, *234*; "Wordless Carol," 59–61, *60*, 68n17
Haydn, Franz Joseph, 146–147; Piano Sonata in C Minor, Hob. XVI/20 (C. Landon 33), ii, 106, *107*; Piano Sonata in Ab Major, Hob. XVI/46 (C. Landon 31), ii, 232; Piano Sonata in Eb Major, Hob. XVI/49 (C. Landon 59), 156; String Quartet in Bb Major, op. 50, no. 1, 175n39; Symphony No. 92 in G Major (*Oxford*), 269
Heine, Heinrich, 159, 272
Hénault, Anne, 216
Henze, Hans Werner: *We Come to the River*, 283n30
Hepokoski, James, 100, 200n19, 258n10
Hildegard of Bingen, 144–145, 169, 289; *Ordo virtutum*, 6; 172n13
Hoeckner, Berthold, 173n24
Hoffmann, E. T. A., 272, 287, 289
Hoffmann, Josef, 220
Homer, 142
Honneger, Arthur: *Pacific 251*, 272
Hoppin, Richard, 145–146
Horlacher, Gretchen, 282n15, 282n18
Howe, Blake, 200n28
Humboldt, Wilhelm von, 150–151, 174n37
Huron, David, 77, 200n25, 259n18
Hyland, Anne, 176n50

Ito, John Paul, 64n15

Jackendoff, Ray, 291n7
Jacques-Dalcroze, Émile, 258n8
James, William, 185
Jander, Owen, 242n10
Jerold, Beverly, 80n10
Johnson, Mark, 137–138, 138n5, 284
Johnston, Blair, 218n15
Jones, Evan, 198n9
Joseffy, Rafael, 229

Kagel, Mauricio, 45, 271
Kant, Immanuel, 6, 174n29
Karl, Gregory, 10
Kendon, Adam, 46n1
Kielian-Gilbert, Marianne, 28n12
Kinderman, William, 200n23, 272
Kirnberger, Johann Philipp, 129n29
Kivy, Peter, 10, 23, 25, 195, 272, 281n13
Klein, Michael, x, 150, 174n29, 174n34, 258n11, 258n14, 280–281, 281n1
Kleist, Heinrich von, 199n17

Paganini, Niccolò, 146
Palestrina, Giovanni Pierluigi da, 129n29
Palfy, Cora, 10, 29n16, 201n30
Parker, Mara, 81n15
Pearson, Keith Ansell, 12n1
Peirce, Charles S., 1, 10, 152, 289
Penderecki, Krzysztof, 282n28, 287; *Devils of Loudon*, 280, 282n29; *Ubu Rex*, 280
Penner, Nina, x
Peretz, Isabelle, 265
Peterson, Ellsworth, 200n27
Peterson, John, 10, 63n0
Petrarch, Francesco, 143, 172n7
Pierce, Alexandra, 64n14, 220
Plantinga, Leon, 177n59
Plato, 140, 184, 199n13
Plutarch, 143
Poliziano, 142
Porphyry, 171n3
Pressler, Menahem, 221
Propp, Vladimir, 86

Quantz, Johann Joachim, 184, 198n9
Quintilianus, Aristides, 99

Randel, Don Michael, 101
Ratner, Leonard, 272
Reichardt, Sarah, 278
Richter, Jean Paul, 90, 203, 231
Ridley, Aaron, 10, 25, 129n26, 191, 194
Riegl, Aloïs, 81n19
Rihm, Wolfgang: *Am Horizont*, 283n26; *Jakob Lenz*, 271
Riley, Matthew, 130n38
Rings, Stephen, 117–118, 131n43
Rink, John, 10, 242n12
Robertson, Anne Walters, 145
Robinson, Jenefer, 10, 11, 13n10, 25, 69, 82n22, 25, 83n32, 185, 191, 194, 197n4, 215, 284–285
Rochberg, George, 271
Rodgers, Stephen, 127n12
Rorem, Ned, 207
Rosen, Charles, 9, 35, 116, 146, 258nn13–14, 252
Rosenwein, Barbara, 170n2
Rothfarb, Lee, 63n3, 80–81n12, 200n26
Rothstein, William, 100, 175n40, 175n43, 241n5
Rousseau, Jean-Jacques, 176n57
Rubinstein, Artur, 220, 241n4
Ruby Sparks, 3–4
Rumph, Stephen, 175n46
Rupprecht, Philip, 44–45

Sacks, Oliver, 144
Schenker, Heinrich, 21, 47, 49, 69, 81–82n19, 138n2, 155, 175n44, 220, 223, 286, 291n8
Scherer, Klaus R., 199n15, 284–285
Schering, Arnold, 200n26
Schlegel, Friedrich, 148, 172n10
Schmalfeldt, Janet, 175n39, 217n3, 241n7
Schmitter, Amy M., 82n27
Schnabel, Artur, 205
Schnebel, Dieter, 45
Schoenberg, Arnold: 21, 62, 91–92, 96–97, 190, 192, 198n7; *Drei Klavierstücke*, op. 11, no. 1, 46n4, 59, 131n44, 276–278, *277*; *Erwartung*, op. 17, 278; *Sechs Kleine Klavierstücke*, op. 19, no. 4, 213–214, *214*; *Verklärte Nacht*, 130n36
Schubert, Franz: 7; *Fierrabras*, D. 796, 165, 168; Piano Sonata in A Minor, D. 784, i, 95–96, 259n16; Piano Sonata in A Major, D. 959, iv, 203; Piano Sonata in B♭ Major, D. 960, i, 211–213, *212*; *Schwanengesang*, D. 957/13, "Der Doppelgänger," 272; String Quartet in G Major, D. 887, i, 164–169, *165*, *167*; *Winterreise*, D. 911, 36, 169, 269–270
Schumann, Clara, 120
Schumann, Robert: 10, *Carnaval*, op. 9, 87–90, 271: "Chiarina," 89–90, *89*; "Chopin," 87, *88*; "Coquette," 89; "Eusebius," 87, *88*; "Florestan," 87–89, *88*; *Davidsbundlertänze*, op. 6: no. 11, 204, 268; no. 18, 229–231, *230*; "Erlkönig," D. 328, 159; *Dichterliebe*, op. 48: no. 10, "Hör' ich das Liedchen klingen," 163; no. 12, "Am leuchtenden Sommermorgen," 159–163, *160–162*, 176n48, 195, 273; *Fantasy*, op. 17, i, 156, 204, 268; *Phantasiestücke*, op. 12, no. 6, "Fabel," 204
Schwarz, David, 174n36
Scruton, Roger, 13n8, 152
Schopenhauer, Arthur, 6, 21
Scruton, Roger, 13n8
Searle, John, 27n2
Seneca, 142
Serkin, Rudolph, 220, 241n4
Shafer, R. Murray: *Adieu, Robert Schumann*, 271
Shakespeare, 144
Shawshank Redemption, The, 39
Sheinberg, Esti, 218n15
Shields, Rob, 12n1
Shklovksy, Viktor, 282n16
Shostakovich, Dimitri, 274; *Lady Macbeth of the Mtsensk District*, op. 29, 28f11, 207–210, 218n16; String Quartet No. 8 in C Minor, op. 110, 278–279
Singer, Charles Joseph, 144

Sloboda, John, 198n8
Small, Christopher, 174n32, 290
Smith, Barbara H., 50, 64n6
Smith, Peter H., 291n7
Smithson, Harriet, 90
Socrates, 139
Spitzer, Michael, x, 13n7, 82n27, 130n38, 173n25, 285
Steinberg, Michael P., 148, 173nn27–28, 289
Stockhausen, Karlheinz, 45; *Kontra-Punkte*, 276, 279; *Studie II*, 220
Straus, Joseph N., 174n32
Strauss, Richard: *Salome*, 208, 218n15
Stravinsky, Igor, 274–276; *Histoire du soldat* (Soldier's Tale), 282n19; *Petruschka*, 274, 275; *Le sacre du printemps* (*The Rite of Spring*), 274, 275
Sutcliffe, W. Dean, 29n17, 68, 81n15, 97, 238
Suurpää, Lauri, 177n60
Syer, Katherine, 273

Tan, Daphne, 63n3
Tarasti, Eero, 10, 12, 23, 37–38, 69, 191, 215, 218n21
Taruskin, Richard, 198n7, 208, 217n14, 274
Tchaikovsky, Pyotr, 128n14
Temperley, Nicholas, 242n17
Thompson, Trina, 131n47
Thorau, Christian, 128n13
Thumpston, Rebecca, 63n0
Tomlinson, Gary, 6, 82n23, 173n24, 290
Treitler, Leo, 242n11
Trivedi, Saam, 13n10
Tunbridge, Laura, 271
Turci-Escobar, John, x

Uno Everett, Yayoi, 218n15

Varèse, Edgard, 13n2
Verdi, Giuseppe: *Il forza del destino*, 223
Verlaine, Paul, 121–123
Vermazen, Bruce, 191
Virgil, 142

Wagner, Richard, 92; *Der fliegende Holländer* (*The Flying Dutchman*), 273; leitmotifs (from *Der Ring des Nibelungen*), 91; *Lohengrin*, 272; *Parsifal*, 269; *Tannhäuser*, 178; *Tristan und Isolde*, 207, 269
Walton, Kendall, 46n8, 126n1, 184
Weber, Gottfried, 6
Webern, Anton: Variations for Piano, op. 27, ii, 279
Wheelock, Gretchen, 81n15
Whittall, Arnold, 213–214
Wilde, Oscar, 178, 194
Wilder, Thornton, 207
Wittlich, Gary, 282n22
Wollheim, Richard, 152
Wu, Chia-Yi, 165

Xenakis, Iannis, 13n2

Yearsley, David, 13n5, 129n30
Ysaÿe, Eugène, 258n8

Zarlino, Gioseffo, 6
Zatorre, Robert J., 265
Zbikowski, Lawrence M., 10, 26, 67, 190
Zimmer, Hans, 201n29
Zorn, John: *Spillane*, 271

Index of Concepts

abnegation, 141, 171n4, 265. *See also* resignation

absolute music, 6, 148, 173n24; non-programmatic, 27n4

abstracting. *See* distilling

actant: 18–20, 31; combining into single virtual agent, 69; tendency to anthropomorphize, 279; as virtual, 19

action, 2, 10, 19, 31

actor, actoriality, 2, 8, 12, 146; as characters in a novel (E. Hanslick), 127n5; as distilled from musical actions, 86; as distinct virtual-fictional characters, 159; as personified motives (H. Schenker), 81–82n19; as protagonist vs. external agency, 92; retrospective interpretation as, 247; roles vs. characters, 79, 86; as various voices in dialogue within overarching virtual consciousness, 159

actual agents. *See* agent, composer, listener, performer

affect, affective meaning, 15, 17, 18, 20, 62–63; global (as virtual environment), 61. *See also* emotion

affordance: as degraded for movement or agency, 279–280, of prior emotional experience, 185; of semiotic systems (culture, language, gesture, artistic style), 150–151

agency: 10, 31–35; agent vs. patient, 37–38; ascribable to institutions (Foucault), 150, 174n33; ascribable to language (Lacan), 150; in chamber music (R. Graybill, E. Klorman), 10; four level of musical agency (S. Monahan), 10, 27n3, 174n34; indeterminacy of (F. Maus), 21, 26, 191; internal vs. external, 37; objectively vs. subjectively interpreted, 33, 34; in relation to emotion and gesture, 35–40, 37; temporary vs. permanent (E. T. Cone), 21. *See also* virtual agency

agent: actual vs. virtual, 2, 5, 7, 8, 26, 29f17, 31, 34; instrumental, 45; primary vs. secondary (M. Clater), 38. *See also* virtual agent

agentially motivated counterpoint, 101–115; anomalies as enacting Enlightenment subjectivity, 113–114, 114; defense

of "presentist" theory for, 129n29; as subjectivity-staging, 158. *See also* counterpoint, refractive counterpoint

allegory, allegorizing: 3, 23, 51, 140, 141, 144, 146, 226, 231, 246, 287; of cognitive dissonance, 275; from allegorical to actual, 142; in fiction (M. Kielian-Gilbert), 28f12; meanings of counterpoint, 129n30; of responses to death, 168; of past, 124

alter ego, 87

amelioration: 181; of tragic, 166, 167

analog vs. discrete, 3, 62, 292n13

analogy, analogue: 8, 53, 102, 287; of 2–3 suspension and repulsion, 54, 64n13; of chamber music and conversation (Goethe), 68, 81n17; for human actions (L. Zbikowski), 10; of thought and emotion, 154

analytical fictions (M. Guck), 10

animistic agency (F. Maus), 10

apotheosis, 254, 255, 259n15

arrival $^6_4$, 84, 162, 200n23; definition of, 127n3; elevational $^6_4$, 211; arrival $^6_3$, 203; arrival $^5_3$, 192

background, backgrounding, 98. *See also* foregrounding

Bildung. *See* emotion: as development

canon, 146 (*See also* chace)

cartoons, 4

catharsis, 141, 184, 199n13, 208, 280

chace, 146

chamber music, 146–147

closure, 64n6

codification (of stylistic meanings), 25

cognition, 6, 7, 12, 27n5, 35, 68, 80n11, 136, 137, 138n5, 258n9, 261–265, 283n27, 291; chunking (as event bundles), 190, 201n31; on complexities of music cognition, 262–265; levels of attending, 261, 263; problem of cognitive sequence, 265; problems for empirical testing and conceptualization of listener processes, 261–262; and style competency, 184 competency: complexity for agency, 247; historical style, 11. *See also* style

composer, 8; as narratizing agent, 12; stylistically competent, 9; virtualized, 87

concerto, 146; allegory of individual and society, 146; virtuosity of actual performer/composer, 146

consciousness (in music): role in constructing integrated self, 72; as virtual subjectivity, 23, 26, 100, 158, 169, 271

continuity, 62; across discontinuity, 237; discursive actorial, 102; lack of, degrading agential inference, 279, of musical discourse, 17; as ongoing *melos*, 23; temporal (melodic), 21; of texture, 64n19; of virtual agent, 12, 20, 21, 94; of voice leading across rhetorical shift, as integrative, 155

convention (stylistic), 67. *See also* style

counterpoint: allegorical meanings of (D. Yearsley), 129n30; history of, 101–102; shaping expressive climax, 106; strategies for creating *melos* and merging into singular actor/subjectivity, 114–115; structural intervallic scaffolding, 104–107, *105, 107*. *See also* agentially motivated counterpoint, refractive counterpoint

cross-modal generalization, 18. *See also* intermodality

cultural practice (L. Kramer), 13n6

dance, 145–146

dance types. *See* topics

developing variation (A. Schoenberg): continuous motivic unfolding, 192; of counterpoint and derivation of countersubject and derived second subject, 103, *104*; with generative texture, 116; gestural, 16, 21; melody-and-accompaniment textures, 106–113; merging with formal structuring, 286; as part of "dimensional counterpoint" (P. Smith), 291n7; of a rhetorical gesture, 131n42; of a sequence, 106; thematic, 91–92, 96–97, 100, 115, 130n40, 269, 276; vs. developing of variation, 118

dialectical themes, 22, 95, *96*

dialogical: actorial response, 182; agents, 39, *40*, 78, 83n30, 223; concerto, 173n19; gestures, 15–16, 17, 27n1, 95; as interaction among virtual agents, 22; motives, 120, 192, 193; musical voices, 68; opposition of topic, 92, 93, *93*; piano quartet, 238; responsorial psalms, 173n18; trains of thought and feeling, 23

dialogue: inner (self-awareness), 140; pedagogical (Plato, Boethius), 140

diegesis, 204, 227

digital, 33. *See also* analog

disability, 174n32

discourse (musical), 12, 13n11, 99; as continuous consciousness of (virtual) subject, 169; as gestural (D. Lidov), 128–129n24; reconstruction of, 261; rupture in, as interiorizing moment of reflection, 120, 119; as spiritual, 145; as thematized gestural discourse, 17

discourse about music, 11; direct vs. indirect, 162–163

distancing, 274–276; as heightening sympathy, 276

distilling (vs. abstracting): of actorial roles, 86; of emotion, 187; for gesture, 81n18; of virtual embodiment without recourse to actual agency, 68–69; of virtual subjectivity without literal embodiment, 133. *See also* "enmindment"

doubling (chordal), 167–168

dramatic irony, 191–192

dramatic trajectory: 2, 22, 38, 87–88, *88*, 95, 245; as composed expressive trajectory, 179–180; of existential emotional struggle, 141; as series of tableaux, 87, 89

dynamics: as implying virtual spatial or temporal distance, 237, 279

embodiment, embodying: 2, 6, 8, 11, 12; apparent disembodiment, 279–280, 282–283n26; dis-embodiment prior to (virtual) re-embodiment, 65–70, 80n6; heuristic process, 186; *Korperlichkeit* (A. Halm), 80–81n12; matrix of degrees of embodiment, identification, and mode of inference, 44–45, *45*; as transcending physical embodiment, 79; as transformative inference for virtual agency: 20–22; via modalities, 37–38; virtual, 65–70; virtual re-embodiment cues, 69–70; virtualizing gap, 67

emergence, emergent: definition of, 151; emotion, 187; of empathy, 170n2; of figure as thematic, 110; of meaning through troping, 152; of modern subject, 148; of musical discourse in Hildegard, 173n16; of self beyond embodied limits, 72; of semiotic inferences, 1; of style conventions, 73; of subjectivity, 6, 148; of themes, 152–158; 268–269; of thematic discourse, 16; three fundamental modes of, 288–290; of virtual agency, 11; vs. reductionism, 151 emotion, 4–5, 11, 12, 23, 69; aesthetically warranted, 9, 24, 73, 76, 178–194, 197fn2; appraisal, 197; appraisal of virtual agential, 23; critique of arousal theory, 195–197; as compassion for agential repression of tragic, 191; defined, 179; development (as *Bildung*), 26, 97; development (as dramatic trajectory leading to virtual subjectivity), 73, 158; development (as negotiated by virtual agent), 97; effects of thematic returns, 268; emotional education (J. Robinson), 25; ennobling without embodying, 195; as evidence for embodiment, 73–79, *74–76*; expectation response systems (D. Huron), 200n25; "feelingful thought," 24, 26, 28n13, 163; as enrapturing insight, 182; experienced but not aesthetically warranted, 171n5, 178, 179, 182; growth through suffering, 250; inferred from formal distortion, 278; inferred from movement, 35; intensifying via dissonance, dynamics, 184; intensifying via shifts, 77; mixed, 168; moral and philosophical, 141, 154; moral and sensual, 143; moral to spiritualized, 183; motivations for, 179, 184; music-historical evidence for, 13n7, 82–83n27; 170n2; once-removed, 194–195; refining interpretation of basic, 73; response as clue to structure, 78; situated by listener, 180; subjective personalizing of expressed, 178; tragic trajectory of, 77. *See also* emergence, engagement, epiphany

empathy, 3, *37*, 38, 79, 136, 170n2, 196, 205, 208, 273; as *Einfühlung*, 200n26. *See also* engagement, identification, sympathy

energy: energetics, 20; as continuous, *32*, energetic trace, 19, 20; expenditure of, 31; as force, 32; kinetic, 69; producer or receiver of, 32; source of, 32, *33*; transmission of, 32; vs. higher style conventions, 134

engagement (by interpreter/listener), 2–5, 24–25, 136–137, 169–170, 178, 195–197; as congruent (or not) with expressed emotion, 187; deepened for distanced or estranged agent, 274; degrees of (four scenarios), 43–45; historical precedents for, 66, 170n1; as identification with protagonist, 159; levels of, 37–38, *37*; "mystical susceptibility" (W. James), 185; once-removed, 194; prehistorical evidence, 170n1; as response, 193–194; sharing with others, 25; varied emotional responses, 193–194. *See also* empathy, identification, sympathy

"enmindment," 12, 70–72, 81n18, 133, 134

epiphany (emotional), 154, 156, 254, *255*; cathartic, 231

estampie, 145

estrangement, 274–275, 282n16

evaluation: as leading to higher-level emotions, 39

evolutionary: adaptation, 34, coadaption, 262–263; reflexes bypassing conscious will, 71, 82n22

expression, expressive, 6, 9; fallacy, 185; genre, 95; as intransitive, 13n8, (and hence emergent), 152; meaning, 8, 194; as unique token of familiar type(s), 152; vs. coexperiencing virtual emotion, 38; vs. "expressive of" (Kivy), 23; vs. representation, 271, 281n13; by virtual agent, 271. *See also* emotion

fear circuit (J. LeDoux), 82n22

fiction, fictionality: creative nonfiction, 42, 46n9; demands of (contracts), 41–42; entailments of (imperatives), 41; fictional in relation to virtual agents, 2–5, 39–42, *42*; fictional world, 4–5; make-believe (K. Walton), 46n8, 184; as story in virtual world, 22; vs. fantasy, 42

fictionalizing, 2, 84–90, *88–90*; as transformative inference for virtual agency: 22–23

film, 3–5; montage effects in music, 275

focal impulse (J. Ito), 64n15

forces: musical (S. Larson), 10, 20, 21, 47–63, *56*, 136; agential interventions, 55–56, *57*; agential intensification, 57, *57*; hierarchical effects of harmony and voice leading on, 49–50, *48*. *See also* agential energy, friction, gravity, inertia, magnetism, momentum

foregrounding; as didactic, 221; of harmony, 164, 235; of instrument, 236; mediated, 116; of melody, 116, 120, 122, 246; of motive, 62; of musical gesture, 15, 16; of narrative agency, 209; of pedal point, 223; in performance, 198n10, 235; by repetition, 286; of texture, 70

formalism, 19

framing. *See* narrative

freedom: free will, 139–140; of imagination, 140; melodic, 49; outward vs. inward expression of, 286; as semiotic fact, 151; subjective, as staged through emergent themes, 100, 151–158, *153*, *157*, 175n39, 175n44; via counterpoint, 115; via harmonic unpredictability, 162; virtual, 139. *See also* virtual subjectivity

friction (musical), 51–53, *53*, *56*; interpreted as agential conflict, 53, *53*, *56* gender, 10; feminist interpretation of Hildegard, 172n15; gender-coding, 89, 90; inversion of, 127n8

genre, 70; *Romanze*, 176n57. *See also* expressive genre, mode

gestalt: perception, 18; temporal gestalt, 19, 190. *See also* gesture (musical)

gesture (human): facial, 5; unwitting, 46n1; performers' degrees of visible gesturing, 220

gesture (musical), 4–5, 20, 33; articulatory, 164; definition of (R. Hatten), 21, 61, 185, 261; functional coherence, 61; imagistic and temporal gestalts, 261; immediate/energetic vs. stylistically coded, 38; integrated, 182; kinetic energy of, 69; and motive, 190; prototypical, 261; in relation to emotion and agency, 35–40, *37*; as synthesis of features, 38; theories of (D. Lidov), 10, 81n18; (N. Cumming), 10; (R. Hatten), 15–17, (A. Pierce), 220.

gravity (S. Larson), 20, 47–48, 56; in atonal context, 59, 278; shifting tonal platform of, 49

grotesque, 209, 210, 218n15

growth: as emotional, psychological, spiritual development of virtual agent, 20

Grundgestalt (A. Schoenberg), 96–97; derivations of as implying agential growth, 97

gymel, 101

hermeneutic, 148, 264; via *sinthome* (symptom) (Lacan), 280–281

heteroglossia (M. M. Bakhtin), 171n6

holarchy (form of hierarchy), 187, 199n18

humor (musical), 95; as narrative agential, 95

iconic, 91

idée fixe, 90

identity: establishing agential, 86–87; sustaining (persevering), 69, 87; of virtual agent, 20.

identification: as coexperiencing, 38, 136; as negotiated, 24; as projection of one's own subjectivity, 169; as recognition of, 22; recognition vs. identification with, 22, 38

ideological interpretation of agential portrayal, 274

implication (L. B. Meyer): denial of: as cueing agency, 61; as cueing emotion, 77; of phrase structure, as freely willed escape, 155. *See also* momentum

improvisation: 44, 46n2; of cadenza, 231–233, *232*, cadenza-like elaboration, 78

indexical, 91

individual, individuality: of virtual agent, 19, 20; as singular, 37

inertia (S. Larson), 47, *48*, 49–50; for atonal context, 59; vs. (agentially initiated) momentum, 49–51

inference, 1–2, 27n5; coadapted from real to virtual world, 45; transformative inferences for virtual agency, 18–26

integration: of agents/actors into single virtual subjectivity, 37; of form/genre, 165; melodic, 154; into *melos*, 106–113, *108–109*, *110–111*; motivic, 252, *252*; motivic and textural, 110, *111*; psychic, 155; supporting actorial and narrative agency, 252

intention, intentional: 33; music expressive design, 18; as musical inference, 20; vs. intentional fallacy, 34–35

interiorizing, 117, 159, 169, 182, 246, 269; global vs. local, 193; as transformative inference for virtual agency, 23–24, 133; via diminutions, 249

intermodality, 79n3, 91. *See also* cross-modal generalization

intersubjective, 2, 29n16, 77; codification of shared meaning, 25

intertextuality, 9, 128n14, 142, 145, 165, 176n54, 211, 264, 265, 269, 281n11; and meta-agency, 271

intonation (of speech as analogous to music), 17, 69

intonatione, 244, 257n1

"irreducible significance of the surface" (R. Hatten), 184

irony, 126, 270; dramatic, 191–192; as narrative archetype, 210–211, *211*, 212, 213. *See also* Romantic irony

leitmotif, 91, 128n13, 128n14; melody as, 124

level of discourse. *See* shift in level of discourse

linkage technique (H. Schenker), 120

liquidation (A. Schoenberg), 246; performance of, 247

listener, listening: 18, 169–170, 171; actualizing emotional states, existential meaning, 158; advantages of auralizing/audiating as virtual listening, 241n6; bringing shared experience (personally situating), 154, 257; coexperiencing (with performer), 78–79; coexperiencing (with virtual agent), *37*, 38, 39; critically evaluating, 176n47; enhancement as personalized further development of, 25; entrained for epic Romantic works, 254n5; habitus of, 199n12; hearing virtual agency as emergent, 288–289;

identification with order or transgression, 211, *211*; initial stance of, 183; interactive participation, 2; interpreting virtual agency, 287–288; listening subject (J. Moreno), 6; multiple interpretations, 213–214; range of emotional responses, 186, 187; stylistically competent, 8, 38; three scenarios of interpretive engagement, 263–265, 266n1. *See also* empathy, engagement, identification, sympathy

magnetism (S. Larson), 47, *48*, 53–54, 64n10; for atonal context, 59; vs. pull (BaileyShea), 64n8. *See also* repulsion
markedness: expressively marked opposition, 73, 281n7; marked gestures, 180–182; marked timbre, 273; strategic growth of, 82n26; theory of, 9, 198n8; unmarked harmonic progression, 245; unmarked theme, 191; unmarked vs. marked pastoral mode, 285
melody, 21, 98; displaced from singing voice (foregrounded but unsung), 121–126; as prismatic refraction of texture, 117; refraction into counterpoint, 116; as splayed unfolding or arpeggiation, 116, *117*, 120, *121*; strategies of integration or merger with harmony and counterpoint, 115–126; voice part as refractive of foregrounded melody in piano, 126
melos, 12, 80n5, 98–126, 131n45, 158, 243n20, 246, 249, 252, 286; definition of, 21, 99–100; historical uses of term, 99; as "musical melisma" (A. Ridley), 129n26; relationship to synthesis (E. T. Cone), 127n4; textural enrichment of, 117. *See also* melody, refractive counterpoint
metaphor, 126, 134–135; as creative, 138; as conceptual, 80n7, 137–138; conceptual metaphor vs. expressive schemata, 138; metaphorical exemplification as expression (N. Goodman), 134–135; for motion and force in music (E. Kurth), 63n3; physiological for bodily hearing (A. Mead), 10; as troping, 137–138
meter, 191; hypermeter, 258n7; hypermetric displacement, 156, *157*, 258n7; metric reorientation of rhythm, 57–58, *58*; as virtual (gravitational) environment, 20, 57–58, 62
metonymy, 87, 89, 91
mimetic hypothesis (A. Cox), 68, 79nn1–2, 136, 137; moving with and moving beyond, 290; vs. moving *against* the music, 136
mirror neurons, 66

mode (for music): comic, 84; lyric, dramatic, narrative, or epic, 70, 84; lyric within dramatic, 165; pastoral, 84; tragic to heroic, 252. *See also* pastoral mode
modalities (A. J. Greimas): 37–38; for music (E. Tarasti), 37–38, 69
momentum (musical), 47, 50–51, 55; agential, 55; attenuation of, 51, *52*; implicative, 51, *56*
motivation, 5, 8, 265; biographical, 90, 165; expressive, 131n43, 184; of movement, 5; of movement through time, 19; psychological, 168
multiple agency (E. Klorman), 29n17, 68, 243n22
musical grammar (L. Zbikowski), 26
musical meaning. *See* emotion, expression
musicking (C. Small), 174n32, 290
myth, 210, 274

narrative, narrativity, 10, 23, 216; archetypes (N. Frye), 23, 127n6, 210, 226; epic preterite, 204, 217n5; framing, 204, 217n6, 246, 267–268; narrative vs. drama, 202, 205; problematized agential narratives, 278–281; reverse order of events, 278; theory of for music (Almén), 85–86, 210–215; without a narrator, 210, 216n1. *See also* shift in level of discourse, temporality. *See also* narrative agency
narrative agency, narrator, 11, 12, 202–216, 246; composer as, 207–210; cued by parody, 208, 209; intervention via recitative, 225; narrative protagonist, 126; orchestra as Greek chorus, 208; performer as, 229, 231, 233; self-narratizing virtual agent, 205–207; staging of (in the work), 207; without clear virtual human agent, 246. *See also* narrative, protagonist
negative cadence, 35, 46n4, 276

objective vs. (inter)subjective, 45
obligatory register (H. Schenker, *obligate Lage*), 155
obsession, 90; 200n28; with death/fate, 164, 166, 168, tragic, 226
organicism, 286–287; coherence/integration vs. organic unity, 287; compensating for disruption, 287; Schenker's anti-organicist position, 291n8; substituting coherent human intentionality for, 287
oxymoron, 126

parenthetical insertion, 24, 120, 227; performance of, 247–248
pastoral mode, 84, 285

performance, performer, 8, 186; as actual agent contributing to composition (cadenza, elaborated return), 231–235, *232*, *234*; as actualizing virtual agency, 42, 219, 223, 233, 248; choosing a performative stance (from self-projecting to self-effacing), 239–241; degrees of embodiment by, 220–21; didactic, 221; drastic vs. gnostic (C. Abbate), 222; "expressive inflation" (D. Leech-Wilkinson), 241n4; as guiding listener interpretation, 220; heuristic approach to, 220; as instrumental agent, 45; as narrator (J. Rink), 10, 242n12; performance and analysis, 222–227; performance practice, 222; performing virtual narrativity via multiple expressive closures, 227–231; as shaman-like, 241n3; simultaneous roles, 240; as surrogate, 241n2

performative, 27n2. *See also* speech act

performative agency, 11, 12, 27n2, 78; as embodied subjective interiority, 235; of emerging oppositional agencies, 236–238, *237*; gestures, 241n2; less ornamented to promote *melos*, 235, *236*, 242n19, 243n20; more extravagant elaboration, 233, *234*; multiple options in interpreting rhetorical gesture, 227; as narrative agency, 227–231; of the performer, 220

persona, 10–11, 13n10, 28n6, 129–130n31, 191, 198n11, 206, 217nn10–11, 284–285; compositional persona as controlling agent, 127n7; as mask in *Carnaval*, op. 9, 87–90, *88–89*; critique of, 25; E. T. Cone's theory, 10, 25; vs. "work persona" (S. Monahan) and "composer's voice" (E. T. Cone), 133

personification, 35, 246, 271–272; of death, 168; of mechanical, 272; as ventriloquistically envoiced flowers, 159

perspective: as viewpoint of virtual agent/protagonist, 22, 37

phrase vs. phase, 175n40

plenitude: thematic and textural, 110, 130n41, 164, 233, 254; of stretto, 238

poetic criticism, 168, 177n59

popular music, 9; gesture and topics in, 13n9

preservation (perseverance, persistence) of virtual agential identity, 20, 21, 37, 87, 89, 96

presuppositions for theory of virtual agency, 6–9

protagonist, 5, 22, 78, 92, 95, 103, 168; *Doppelgänger*, 272–273; as narrator, 159, 247; vs. antagonist, 215

psychoanalytical interpretation, 272–273; as repression, 96, 191, 278

quotation, 88–89, *88*, 271, 281n12

reaching over (H. Schenker), 130n37, 130n39

recitative chord, 24, 40, 203, 204, 225

recognition (by listener of virtual agent), 38. *See also* engagement

recognition (Aristotelian, dramatic), 4, 36, 84, 113, 163, 218n17, 227, 228

reflectivity. *See* self-reflectivity

reflexivity. *See* self-reflexivity

refractive counterpoint, 21, 103, *104*, 113, *114*, 232, 252; in galant style, 106; as inner voice, 249; as stretto, 103, 107, 238, *239*

repetition, 80n4

representation of emotion. *See* expression

repulsion, 54–55, *55*, *56*

resignation, 172n9: as positive acceptance, 158

resonance, 164–165, *165*

reverberation, 163; (A. Pierce), 64n14; absorption of energy, 250, 258n13; bell-like, 231, 255; as echoes, 237–238, *239*, 255, *256*

reversal: dramatic (Aristotelian), 84; of event sequence, 278; as interrogative, 277, *277*; of major to minor, 166; of melodic direction, 105, 106, 187; of sentence rhetoric, 276; of theme (tragic), 255; of voice leading, 164, 166; "willful," 95

rhetorical: break, 15–16, 158; breakthrough, 192; cueing external agency, 182; cueing higher level of discourse, 205; as enhancing reflection, 26; gesture, 15–16, 17, 23, 27n1, 92, 151, 155, 182, 187, 189, 192, 205, 226; harmonic shift, 158, 164; operatic, 165; shift as intensification, 77; silence, 154, 158; as thematized, 16

rhythm. *See* meter

Romantic irony (in music), 94, 242n14; as narrative-agential, 203; as self-critical, 172n10; as self-reflectivity, 23. *See also* irony

rubato, 246, 258n8

sacred and secular, 6, 145

secondary parameters (L. Meyer), 135–136; thematized as primary, 136; raw contour of melody as, 136

self: as construct (virtual), 72, healthy capacities of, 149–150; as integrated body-mind, 70–73; as integrated in listener, 26; Peirce's concept of, 10; as virtual subjectivity, 23

self-reflectivity, 23, 120, 141, 145, 155, 156, 182, 202, 225, 237, 238, 247, 257; as agency, 238; as memory, 231; as mystical, 164; as profoundly contemplative, 165; and self-reflexivity, 5, 141, 171n6; via fermata, 225, 246

sensibility, 170, 173n23
shift in level of discourse, 11, 23, 203–205, 228, 229
sigh figure. *See* topics: *pianto*
simulation, 1, 4, 5, 19, 284; of agency, 148; of complex interiorities, 143; of performance, 123, and stimulation, 285, 287
sociability (D. Sutcliffe), 29n17, 68, 97, 147
sonata, 147; sonata form, 165, 190, 223, 233, 248, 250, 254, 258nn10–11; medial caesura, 164
speech act, 27n2; for music, 17, 27n2
spiritualization, 24; spiritual release, 152
spontaneous gesture, 15, 27n1
Steigerung (intensification), 106, 130n38, 238
stratification, 275
style: competency, 9, 135, 184, 261; definition of, 8, 9, 199n12; lack of competency in virtualizing, 67; and strategy, as warranted, 2, 73
style type: bichord, 231; descent in thirds, 134; "stoic-heroic," 95; 5–6 sequence (E. Narmour), 130n36
subjectivity, 173–174nn25–29; actual (personal), 8; complex/multi-dimensional, 163, 182; of composer via musical initials and self-quotation, 278–279; compositional staging of, 9, 150, 151, 154; with conflicting virtual narrators, 229; crises of, 149–151; deeper, existentially tragic, 159; "dialogic subjectivity" (M. Calcagno), 172n7; dissociated, 269; distancing/estrangement, 274; documentary historical literary evidence for, 139–144; dream state, 273; emergent, 239, 289; enlarged by orchestra in opera, 273; flourishing, 174n32; historical musical evidence for, 144–147, 172n8; historical philosophical and aesthetic evidence for, 147–149; human, 12; incorporating multiple actorial roles, 163; integration of virtual and actual, 26; interiorized, 117, 133, 134; as interpreted by performer, 219; internal staging of, through form, 147; Lacanian, 280–281; mechanical, 272, 282n14; with multiple emotions yet integrative, 141; musical: (S. McClary, L. Kramer), 7; negotiation of personal and virtual, 137; overwhelmed, 271; pathological, 278; Peircean account (N. Cumming), 28n6; profound inner life, 183; psychically integrated, 155; psychically disintegrated, 257; psychically split, 159, 163; robust, 149–150, 174nn32–33; shortcuts to engagement with virtual, 137, 289–290;

spiritualized (distilled) vs. embodied, 133; staged as freedom, 152, *153*, 156, *157*; summary of syntheses of, 169; supersubjective, 227; tragic, 91, 95; as unable to escape, 169; virtual, 2, 5, 8, 103, 133. *See also* interiorizing, narrative agent, self, self-reflectivity, temporality
sublimation (internalizing virtual actors as ideas), 23
symbol, 91, 164; of interiority, 168; mythic, 169; numinous vs. signified(s), 9, 168
sympathy, 38, 136, 203, 218n16; as distanced, 206; lack of, 274; positive and negative, 136. *See also* empathy, engagement
synecdoche, 215. *See also* metonymy
synthesis: of gesture/emotion/agency, 39; of gesture and voice leading (N. Cumming), 129–130n31; of multiple forms of musical structuring into coherent subjectivity, 137, 286; of passionately embodied thoughts, 140; of subjectivity, 169; of texture and topic, 102; tropological, 137, 138; vs. embodiment, 134; *See also* gesture

temporality, 262, 267–269, 272; in Schubert, 176n50; extratemporality of cadenza, 233; narrative shift, 216n2; parenthetical interiorizing, 120, *119*; 247–248; past vs. future perspectives, 268–269; spatial vs. temporal orientation, 279; thematic return as reminiscence, 268. *See also* narrative, narrativity
texture, 21, 116, 117, 163; continuity of, 16, 64n19; developing variation, 106–113; dialogue, 238; marked changes of, 16, 78; radical shift of, 154, 156; stretto as culmination, 238
thematic: gesture, 15–17, 27n1; discourse, 16
thematic transformation, 166
token (of a type), 9, 152, 174n38, 276
tonality. *See* virtual environment
"tonally moving forms" (E. Hanslick), 19
topics: aria, 76, 172n11, 233; barcarolle, 248; bardic, 204; chorale/hymn, 17, 70, 95, 194, 211; cueing narrative, 204; dance types, 173n17; Empfindsamkeit, 76; fanfare figure, 16, 90, 95, 226, 268; fantasia, 249, 254; French overture, 76; funereal cortège, 226, 228; funeral march, 95; galant (trio sonata), 102; georgic pastoral, 157; horn fifths, 35; historical transformation via dances, 80n9; lament bass, 91; *Ländler*, 70, 92; learned style, 92, 109, 239, 268, 270; lullaby, 60, 258n11; men's choir, 204; minuet, 92; *ombra*, 94, 226;

MUSICAL REPRESENTATIONS, SUBJECTS, AND OBJECTS:
THE CONSTRUCTION OF MUSICAL THOUGHT IN ZARLINO,
DESCARTES, RAMEAU, AND WEBER
Jairo Moreno

THE RITE OF SPRING AT 100
Severine Neff, Maureen Carr, and Gretchen Horlacher

MEANING AND INTERPRETATION OF MUSIC IN CINEMA
David Neumeyer

DEEPENING MUSICAL PERFORMANCE THROUGH MOVEMENT:
THE THEORY AND PRACTICE OF EMBODIED INTERPRETATION
Alexandra Pierce

ALLUSION AS NARRATIVE PREMISE IN BRAHMS'S
INSTRUMENTAL MUSIC
Jacquelyn E. C. Sholes

EXPRESSIVE INTERSECTIONS IN BRAHMS:
ESSAYS IN ANALYSIS AND MEANING
Heather Platt and Peter H. Smith

EXPRESSIVE FORMS IN BRAHMS'S INSTRUMENTAL MUSIC:
STRUCTURE AND MEANING IN HIS *WERTHER* QUARTET
Peter H. Smith

MUSIC AS PHILOSOPHY: ADORNO AND BEETHOVEN'S LATE STYLE
Michael Spitzer

DEATH IN *WINTERREISE*: MUSICO-POETIC ASSOCIATIONS IN
SCHUBERT'S SONG CYCLE
Lauri Suurpää

MUSIC AND WONDER AT THE MEDICI COURT: THE 1589
INTERLUDES FOR *LA PELLEGRINA*
Nina Treadwell

REFLECTIONS ON MUSICAL MEANING AND ITS REPRESENTATIONS
Leo Treitler

DEBUSSY'S LATE STYLE
Marianne Wheeldon

ROBERT S. HATTEN is Marlene and Morton Meyerson Professor in Music at the University of Texas at Austin and President of the Society for Music Theory. He is author of *Musical Meaning in Beethoven: Markedness, Correlation, and Interpretation* (IUP) and *Interpreting Musical Gestures, Topics, and Tropes: Mozart, Beethoven, Schubert* (IUP).

CPSIA information can be obtained
at www.ICGtesting.com
Printed in the USA
BVHW04s0832110918
527164BV00009B/133/P